Civility in the Digital Age

How Companies and People Can Triumph over Haters, Trolls, Bullies, and Other Jerks

ANDREA WECKERLE

800 East 96th Street,
Indianapolis, Indiana 46240 USA

Civility in the Digital Age: How Companies and People Can Triumph over Haters, Trolls, Bullies, and Other Jerks

ISBN-13: 978-0-7897-5024-2
ISBN-10: 0-7897-5024-4

Library of Congress Cataloging-in-Publication Data is on file.

Printed in the United States of America

First Printing: February 2013

Trademarks

All terms mentioned in this book that are known to be trademarks or service marks have been appropriately capitalized. Que Publishing cannot attest to the accuracy of this information. Use of a term in this book should not be regarded as affecting the validity of any trademark or service mark.

Warning and Disclaimer

Every effort has been made to make this book as complete and as accurate as possible, but no warranty or fitness is implied. The information provided is on an "as is" basis. The authors and the publisher shall have neither liability nor responsibility to any person or entity with respect to any loss or damages arising from the information contained in this book.

Bulk Sales

Que Publishing offers excellent discounts on this book when ordered in quantity for bulk purchases or special sales. For more information, please contact

U.S. Corporate and Government Sales
1-800-382-3419
corpsales@pearsontechgroup.com

For sales outside of the U.S., please contact

International Sales
international@pearson.com

Associate Publisher
Greg Wiegand

Sr. Acquisitions Editor
Katherine Bull

Development Editor
Karen E. Klein

Managing Editor
Kristy Hart

Project Editor
Andy Beaster

Copy Editor
Apostrophe Editing Services

Indexer
Lisa Stumpf

Proofreader
Dan Knott

Technical Editor
Kami Watson Huyse

Publishing Coordinator
Romny French

Book Designer
Anne Jones

Compositor
Nonie Ratcliff

Graphics
Tammy Graham

Que Biz-Tech Editorial Board
Michael Brito
Jason Falls
Rebecca Lieb
Simon Salt
Peter Shankman

CONTENTS AT A GLANCE

TABLE OF CONTENTS

Foreword

In today's hyper-connected world, maintaining and sustaining a civil online culture is incredibly important because it serves as the ethical foundation for the best the Internet has to offer today and in the future.

Unfortunately, it's easy to hear stories of horrible online abuse and throw up our hands in despair thinking that nothing can be done.

That's a big mistake. Of course there is difficulty in balancing the demands of freedom of expression and prevention of abuse. This challenge exists at both the level of private website rules and at the level of legislation. Still, a civil online culture is achievable, with the right mindset, willingness, and tools.

We live in an era where billions of people are already online, and billions more are coming online. Citizens can communicate with each other, share knowledge, debate issues, and become better human beings in the process. Citizens can also engage in horrible abuse, idiotic commentary, and the spread of falsehoods. We have a choice about how to behave ourselves, but we also have a choice about what kinds of systems and social norms we create. That's why we can and must choose wisely.

I hardly need to tell you about the incredible success of Wikipedia. Today, nearly 500 million people per month access the website in hundreds of languages. Academic studies of the quality of Wikipedia show that it is comparable to the quality of traditional encyclopedias—with notable strengths and some equally notable weaknesses. It is common for people to assume that this came about automatically through the "magic" of "crowdsourcing" but that wasn't the case.

Wikipedia became a success in no small part through the fundamental social rules that are the bedrock principles of its community. Entire books could be written about how and why Wikipedia works (and, of course, how and why it sometimes doesn't work as well as I would want!). But let me single out just two of the most important principles that have helped Wikipedia to thrive.

First, we have a policy of neutrality, which our neutrality policy defines as "representing fairly, proportionately, and as far as possible without bias, all significant views that have been published by reliable sources." Essentially the concept here is that in any controversy, Wikipedia itself should not take a stand, but should instead describe thoughtfully to the reader what the controversy is.

This is a fundamental principle of human respect: I am not telling you what to think nor am I telling you what position to take on a controversial issue; I'm giving you the facts you need to begin to make up your own mind.

Neutrality at Wikipedia is always a goal. We do not kid ourselves that we have always achieved it. Achieving as much neutrality as we can is a long, hard process of discussion and debate, and it is only possible to make progress towards it when we do so in a collegial and respectful atmosphere.

This brings me to a second important principle of Wikipedia: No personal attacks. Without this rule, the discussion and debate at Wikipedia would be like that at so many thousands of other web forums and newspapers: hateful vitriol spewed by people who have no interest in working together to seek the truth.

Implementing a rule against personal attacks is tricky and complex. The process of getting to and implementing those rules is a very messy and human thing, even if it is done well. People are people, and sometimes they lose their cool or don't phrase a comment in an elegant, well understood way. The majority of the time, an apology is made and everyone moves on. If Wikipedia implemented a draconian police state where every little rough remark resulted in a lifetime ban, we'd end up excessively restraining an interesting and important debate.

But even though drawing the appropriate line online is tricky and complex, it must never be an excuse not to set parameters or to allow all manner of ongoing harassment, insults, and abuse. To abdicate moral responsibility in the face of bullies is to hand society over to the most vicious among us. We can be both understanding about the human propensity to outbursts, while at the same time insisting on norms requiring apology and a generally good behavioral track record over time by the organizations and the individuals representing them.

All of us understand this intuitively from our interactions with other people offline. If a friend insults you and then gives a genuine apology, you find a way to move past it. But if someone is obnoxious and abusive, people quite rightly stop inviting them to social occasions. This is not rocket science, and moving the problem online doesn't change human nature.

We can look across the Internet landscape and find examples of thousands of communities with either better and worse track records of protecting their community members from obnoxious people. There are a lot of cautionary tales out there, and a lot of lessons to be learned.

Andrea Weckerle's book is a valuable and important starting point for us to read and thoughtfully consider. A survivor of online abuse herself, and a person who embodies the qualities of thoughtfulness and forgivingness that exemplify some of the best human traits, she brings to the issue a wit and wisdom that we should all heed. I'm sure you're going to find *Civility in the Digital Age* incredibly useful both professionally and personally!

—**Jimmy Wales**, Founder of Wikipedia

About the Author

Andrea Weckerle, an attorney, founded and leads CiviliNation, a nonprofit dedicated to reducing online hostility and character assassination. She previously worked at the Legal Management Services division of a global professional services firm, helping to design, develop, and implement comprehensive alternative dispute resolution systems for Fortune® 500 firms. She also underwent extensive mediation training, earning certificates in Commercial Mediation and Conflict Resolution Processes. Her work has been featured in *The Wall Street Journal*, CNN.com, *NY Daily News*, and *Advertising Age*. In addition to a JD, she holds an MA in Public Relations/Conflict Analysis and Resolution.

Dedication

To Grayson and Maddox, with love and admiration

Acknowledgments

I would like to thank the magnificent team at Que Publishing for their assistance and support throughout the development, writing, editing, and designing of the book.

I want to give a special thank you to my editor, Katherine Bull, for her unwavering enthusiasm for the book. Her guidance and support were invaluable through the whole process.

I also want to thank Andy Beaster, my production editor; Anne Jones, who designed my cover; and San Dee Phillips, my copy editor—you helped bring the book to life.

I am grateful to Kami Watson Huyse for her technical insights and ongoing championing of this book. She believed in *Civility in the Digital Age* long before a single word was written and continues to be a driving force in helping spread its ideas.

I am thankful to the people who have shared with me their personal stories of being the targets of online attacks and defamation. Some have gone public, whereas others have chosen to remain private, but in every case, they've inspired me with their courage and resilience.

Finally, I want to express sincere thanks to all the anti-cyberbullying advocates, conflict resolution professionals, and civility champions who devote every day working to make the online world become a more positive and embracing environment.

We Want to Hear from You!

As the reader of this book, *you* are our most important critic and commentator. We value your opinion and want to know what we're doing right, what we could do better, what areas you'd like to see us publish in, and any other words of wisdom you're willing to pass our way.

We welcome your comments. You can email or write to let us know what you did or didn't like about this book—as well as what we can do to make our books better.

Please note that we cannot help you with technical problems related to the topic of this book.

When you write, please be sure to include this book's title and author as well as your name and email address. We will carefully review your comments and share them with the author and editors who worked on the book.

Email: feedback@quepublishing.com

Mail: Que Publishing
           ATTN: Reader Feedback
           800 East 96th Street
           Indianapolis, IN 46240 USA

Reader Services

Visit our website and register this book at quepublishing.com/register for convenient access to any updates, downloads, or errata that might be available for this book.

1

Who Gives a Darn About Conflict?

If It Happened to Them, It Can Happen to You

As an outspoken critic of social oppression and inequality, feminist pop culture media critic Anita Sarkeesian[1] has had her share of detractors, but it was her Kickstarter video project that caused the proverbial s**t to hit the fan. In May 2012, Sarkeesian launched her project "Tropes Vs. Women in Video Games" on the fundraising platform to raise money for the creation of a video series examining the most common stereotypes of female characters in video games, stereotypes such as *Damsel in Distress*, *The Fighting F#@k Toy*, *The Sexy Sidekick*, and *The Sexy Villainess*.[2] Despite its positive purpose, her project rubbed some people the wrong way, and Sarkeesian found herself the target of the most vicious online attacks imaginable.

Her harassers tried to hack into her email and social media accounts and post her address and telephone number online,[3] putting her safety at risk. Her Wikipedia page was vandalized to read "[she] is an entitled [n-word]" and "holds the world record for maximum amount of toys in the posterior."[4] Numerous vile and hateful technologically manipulated images of her were also posted online, including two rape drawings featuring her likeness and a photograph of her face with a cartoon-drawn penis ejaculating over it.[5] Her YouTube video asking viewers to support her Kickstarter project received more than 4,000 comments, among them ones like tri-AceFanboy's "I want to put my d**k into you"[6] and Blutteufel's "Typical feminazi ignorance and [unwarranted] self-importance. Get back to the kitchen and hurry up with the f**king sandwich, c**t."[7] Even an interactive *Beat Up Anita Sarkeesian* game was created, complete with bruises and welts appearing on her face when the screen was clicked.[8]

You may think that Anita Sarkeesian's story is unique, but in terms of severity, unfortunately it's not. Just ask Sue Scheff, who became the target of an online smear campaign that started when one person went after her for work related to her organization, Parents' Universal Resource Experts, which helps families with at-risk teens.[9] As Scheff describes it, this individual "had others join them as part of a 'gang mentality' approach...in a systematic attempt to emotionally destroy me, my organization, my career, my family and anything else that meant something to me. My life was being ruined one keystroke at a time."[10] Scheff ultimately sued her attacker and in 2006 won the largest defamation jury award in American legal history, $11.3M.

Michael Roberts, too, understands how easily the Internet can be used as a weapon against someone. Shortly after Roberts filed for divorce in 2004, his ex-wife began an aggressive Internet smear campaign against him, his business, and individuals who tried to lend him any kind of support. The attacks against his reputation and his business crippled his company and forced him to sell it for considerably less than it was worth.[11] According to Roberts, these attacks continued until July 2011, when his ex-wife was arrested on charges of first-degree murder in the death of Dustin Wehde. She is now in prison serving a life sentence without the possibility of parole.

Today Roberts admits, "Had I not gone through this fiery trial, I would've been like so many other people and considered the issue of online attacks and character assassination a mere trifle not worthy of serious attention. I would probably have also dismissed the victims who issue anguished cries for help as thin-skinned weaklings, as seems to be the reaction by most people who have not experienced this tragedy firsthand and simply refuse to see what is happening online."[12] As a result of his ordeal, Roberts founded Rexxfield, a company that helps and supports individuals who've been the victims of online lies, defamation, and privacy invasion. It offers assistance in retracting or hiding deceptive materials from the public domain and restoring victims' good name and reputation.[13]

Janice Duffy, Ph.D., is another victim who knows that online attacks can have life-altering consequences.[14] As part of an online support group that posted about scam artists taking advantage of vulnerable people, she registered on what she thought was a legitimate complaint site. However, Duffy says that unbeknown to her at the time, the website directly passed on the identities of people who wrote complaints to the businesses and individuals that they were concerned about. As a result, she was cyberbullied and also received threatening phone calls. Duffy claims that Google searches for her name reveal terms such as "ripoff," "fraud," "scams," "she hacked my computer," and "she stalked me on the computer," annihilating her reputation and forcing her out of her profession.

Years later she is still fighting to clear her name. Duffy explains the harm online attacks can have: "One is being the target of actual attacks, which can blindside you. The other is having to endure the hit to your self-confidence and sense of safety, both which can take a long time to rebuild.... It is difficult for many to believe that actions that do not entail physical proximity can have such a devastating effect on victims."[15]

How This Book Will Help You

Hopefully you'll never be on the receiving end of attacks like those suffered by Anita Sarkeesian, Sue Scheff, Michael Robert, and Janice Duffy. However, this book will help you in your daily interactions online as you deal with challenging situations and people and the inevitable conflicts that arise.

Civility in the Digital Age is a practical guide to help you deal with difficult people online, keep your cool, solve problems, and effectively communicate your point of view. It will give you the knowledge and skills necessary to navigate and successfully participate in a frequently uncertain and volatile online environment, discover skills to recognize the different types of conflict and conflict protagonists, heading them off when possible, and managing them when not. Simply put, this book can help you take control by proactively dealing with the inevitable conflict inherent in online exchanges.

It All Began on August 6, 1991

The world changed with the birth of the World Wide Web on August 6, 1991.

Businesses wanting to remain competitive flocked online and Internet-only companies mushroomed, setting off the dotcom frenzy. A few years later, Web 2.0 witnessed the advent of blogs and Really Simple Syndication (RSS), empowering everyone with an Internet connection to become a publisher with no barrier to entry. Social networking sites made it even easier for people to meet online and share common interests, and millions of people joined MySpace, LinkedIn, Flickr, Facebook, YouTube, Bebo, Twitter, Pinterest, and others since their creation in the last 10 years.

Now there is talk that Web 3.0 is upon us, an era reflected by the *symantic web*, a term coined by World Wide Web inventor Sir Timothy Berners-Lee to describe a web navigated not only by traditional keyword searches, but also by the context added by friends and others online, for example through Facebook's Like button and the Google+ button that help people find information they are interested in.

At the same time, insidious elements have also taken hold online—the crippling insults and mockery of people, the widespread use of snark weakly justified as innocent humor, and the destruction of business reputations and individuals through shockingly easy and anonymous means.

With commerce and society having become inextricably intertwined with the Web, remaining offline no longer is an option, whereas protecting one's emotional well-being and reputation against vicious attacks has become increasingly difficult.

Every Single Day People and Businesses Take a Hit on the Internet

According to the Internet World Stats, as of December 2011 there were more than 2 billion Internet users around the world,[16] representing more than 30% of the world's population. To get an idea of what 2 billion looks like, see Figure 1.1 There are 340 undecillion (340 trillion trillion trillion) unique IP addresses in the world, a number that continues to grow.[17]

Figure 1.1 *The box above contains 1,000 dots, each representing one individual. It would take 2 million boxes like this one to reflect the 2 billion people who are on the Internet*

The Pew Internet and American Life Project reported that 72% of all Americans use search engines,[18] and 65% of adult Internet users use a social networking site like Facebook or LinkedIn,[19] whereas 82% of all American adults ages 18 and older say they use the Internet or email at least occasionally, with 67% of all adults doing so on an average day.[20] Among American seniors, 53% of American adults age 65 and older use the Internet or email, with 70% using the Internet on an average day.[21]

With such a large number of people active online, it's no surprise that online clashes, misunderstandings, reputational harm, and public relations disasters are commonplace.

The bottom line is that what happens online matters—a lot. Whether via emails between employees of a company or between executives and their business clients, or whether via discussions on social networking sites or online forums, online communication has become the norm for how people interact with each other in the modern world. More and more people talk about you and your organization— and they also have the ability to find out what others say about you, both the good and the bad, often without being able to tell the difference between truth and lies.

Now look at three business scenarios. In Scenario #1, a customer service representative at the world's largest communications holding company logs onto her private Twitter account and admits, "I'd rather get a root canal then go to work. Anyone have a root canal? Please tell me it's worse than talking to idiots all day long."[22] She also gets in a public fight with the reporter of a leading technology website about a piece he wrote on her employer, saying, "This entire article is garbage" and "this is bulls**t."[23]

Scenario #2 involves a customer of a global technology products retailer who takes his mobile phone in to be serviced, forgetting to log out of his phone's Facebook app. Shortly after leaving the store, his Facebook status falsely says, "I am gay, I'm coming out."[24] The company responds to media inquiries, but a year after the incident, the customer still hasn't received a formal apology from the retailer.

Scenario #3 involves one of the employees of a nightclub located in a major U.S. city who has a hate-filled meltdown on her personal Facebook page, using the N-word to describe the club's African-American patrons and saying, "Wow so insane how one race of people can be so f**king incompetent and disgusting" and "They really are apes and must not be fully developed."[25] This incident gets picked up in major media outlets.[26]

All three scenarios actually happened and are among many examples of businesses taking reputational hits because of others' actions. When it comes to the reputational assassination of individuals, there is no shortage either. From fabricated allegations of fraud on consumer complaint sites, false accusations of sexually transmitted diseases on dating sites, vindictive claims about promiscuity on gossip sites, and insinuations about mental illness in newspaper comment sections, online smears are rampant. These attacks sometimes escalate to the point of death threats against individuals and their families.[27] Social networking sites have become a favorite playground for online attacks; Calestous Juma, a Harvard University professor and editor of the peer-reviewed *International Journal of Technology and Globalisation*, was quite gracious when he commented on the vast number of insults one can find on Twitter (see Figure 1.2): "Some people produce so many insults on Twitter you would think they are a weaver-bird colony at dawn."[28] This doesn't even include the modern-day phenomenon of online stalking, of which one in five Americans claim to be the victim.[29]

Figure 1.2   *Calestous Juma's tweet of May 16, 2012*

The Negative Effects of Unresolved Conflict

The negative effects of unresolved online hostility, attacks, and reputational harm are daunting. On the business side this conflict can include lower employee morale, reduction in work quality, lower productivity, absenteeism, loss of employee loyalty, employee retaliation, higher employee turnover, costs associated with recruitment and training of new employees, loss of customers and clients, reputational damage (sometimes irreparable and permanent), a lowering of company valuation, and legal problems.

On the personal side, ongoing or unresolved conflict can result in stress, anxiety, and depression, diminished work productivity, job loss, social isolation, reputational damage so severe that individuals become virtually unemployable, retributional violence, and feelings of suicide. In the online world, children and teenagers taking their own lives as a result of being bullied has become so frequent that it's sparked the creation of the new term *bullycide*.

Unique Aspects of Online Communications

The unique aspects of online communication exacerbate these problems. Before going further, what is online communication? For the purposes of this book, it is any communication that takes place through technology-assisted (mediated) means, such as email, instant messaging, text messaging, conversations on online forums or social networking sites, comment sections on websites and newspapers, videos, and related media. Information can be disseminated instantaneously, globally, 24 hours a day every day of the year. But unlike in face-to-face interactions or conversations over the phone (where you can observe and respond to the reactions of those you communicate with and thus often create an emotional connection even if only for a short time), the online environment's frequent absence of paralinguistic, namely nonverbal, cues make it easy to objectify others. This in turn makes it easier to vilify an opponent or perceived enemy.

Anonymity and Pseudonymity

Online anonymity and pseudonymity amplify this problem. When people don't need to appear online as their true selves, it becomes easier to take on false personas or act in ways that they would never even dream of doing if they were held accountable via their real identities. Of course there are legitimate reasons for why anonymity must continue to be a viable option for people online:

- Whistleblower cases
- Politically repressive environments
- Situations in which someone's health history would cause them to be discriminated against
- If an individual is harassed or stalked and their physical safety is at risk

But hiding behind anonymity to mistreat, abuse, or defame someone is cowardly. Even when done against a company or business, it's risky and can backfire, as Whole Foods CEO John Mackey found out. For almost 8 years, Mackey posted about his company on Yahoo! bulletin boards under the pseudonym "Rahodeb," both writing flattering things about Whole Foods and blasting its then-competitor Wild Oats Markets[30] with statements like "[management] clearly doesn't know what it is doing" and "[the company] has no value and no future."[31] When the online shenanigans were revealed, Whole Foods tried to minimize the damage by saying the statements were the personal posts of Mackey and not those of the company. Mackey, meanwhile, admitted he "posted on Yahoo! under a pseudonym because I had fun doing it" and that "sometimes I simply played 'devil's advocate' for the sheer fun of arguing."[32]

Not knowing who is behind online statements or actions doesn't just make it difficult to respond effectively. In some cases it also makes it impossible to take defensive action to clear one's name and reputation.

The Legal System's Weaknesses

The legal system poses other problems. Due to both their lack of uniformity and inherent limitations, national and international laws offer incomplete and weak protection or recourse for individuals or entities against online reputational smears, cyberbullying, privacy violations, and online defamation. Although the Internet is cross-jurisdictional, laws are geographically based, and what makes something impermissible in one area isn't so in another. Germany, for example, "expressly limits the protection of free speech when necessary to protect 'personal honor,'" according to Ronald Krotoszynski, Jr., Professor of Law at Washington and Lee University School of Law,[33] whereas Japan "provides for civil and criminal liability for truthful statements that damage or injure reputation."[34] Meanwhile, "the United States approach, which protects demonstrably false speech in order to give a free press adequate breathing room, very much represents a minority approach."[35]

When It's Online, It's Permanent

In addition, when something has been placed online, it's virtually impossible to completely remove it and all of its traces from the Internet. You would hope that negative and false information is buried deep in the search engine indexes or even removed from the originating site, but that doesn't ensure that someone some-where hasn't already directly passed along the information or taken screenshots, or that the Wayback Machine (which is an Internet archive database that saves websites and web pages) hasn't archived something in perpetuity that you would rather not have be available and findable.[36] Sometimes even those trying to cor-rect a mistake online are intentionally thwarted. Politiwoops,[37] taking its inspira-tion from Dutch counterpart Politwoops.nl, is a Sunlight Foundation-produced website that runs a live list of tweets that U.S. politicians have published and then deleted. It lists the politician's name, political affiliation, the exact tweet, and the time between when the tweet was posted and then deleted. (Examples range from 8 seconds, 1 minute, 10 hours, and 1 day.) Viewing itself as a public service, the site says, "Sure, we all tweet things we don't mean to share, but now politicians have no way to hide them.[38]

Three Scenarios Revisited

Take a moment to revisit the three previous business scenarios. The customer ser-vice representative in Scenario #1, Rachael Pracht,[39] had a history of venting online about her work environment, at one point keeping an active blog where she posted a series[40] called "Confessions in a Call Center."[41] It can be assumed that shortly after her outburst was covered on TechCrunch, Ms. Pracht was no longer employed at the company. But what about AT&T, the company in question? How did its reputation fair with existing and prospective customers? The writer of a tech blog wrote, "Her general tweets, curse-filled as they are, act as distasteful representations of AT&T customer service rep[s] as a whole. And her blog solidifies her negative opinions of customers and reflects horribly on AT&T."[42] Is this fair? Should AT&T be held accountable for its employee's unauthorized behavior? Does the fact that Ms. Pracht was a customer service representative hold her to a higher standard? Should AT&T have been previously aware of Ms. Pracht's outspokenness by having a program in place that monitors its employees' public social media activities?

In Scenario #2, technology products retailer Best Buy fired the employee, but a year after the event took place, it still hadn't yet apologized to Rich Dewberry whose phone was accessed without his permission, instead issuing a statement that "If an employee violates privacy and/or data protection policies, they may be subject to disciplinary action up to, and including, dismissal and/or legal action if applicable."[43] Do you think that Best Buy firing the employee made up for the employee's misdeeds, or should it have apologized to Mr. Dewberry as well? Would your view of Best Buy change if you knew that the company had won international think tank Ethisphere® Institute's "2012 World's Most Ethical Companies" designation?[44] Although Ethisphere's award factors favorably for Best Buy's reputation, would you start to wonder if Best Buy has business ethics problems if you knew that company CEO Brian Dunn resigned his position in Spring 2012 after the start of a corporate probe into his "personal conduct"?[45]

In Scenario #3, do you think the firing of the employee by the Proof nightclub owner was enough to erase the association between former employee Jessica Harr's statements and the negative mark on the club's reputation? Would it make a difference if you knew that Proof's manager left a comment on Ms. Harr's Facebook page, saying "This is in violation of your social media contract, please remove it ASAP?"[46] What if you knew that the club didn't make a formal announcement of this incident on its website?

In many cases, there are no easy answers.

Where should you draw the line between someone's professional and personal lives? Can an organization's social media policy place limitations around an individual's behavior outside of work? How transparent should a company be about how it manages employee misdeeds? What is the appropriate response time to react to online disputes?

All this together underscores the importance of learning how to successfully navigate today's exciting yet also frequently uncertain online environment. More than ever before, it's vital to have the skills necessary to accurately assess different types of conflicts, head them off when possible, and effectively manage them when it's not.

What Is Conflict and How Can Conflict Management and Resolution Help?

Conflict sometimes gets a bad rap, but that's actually unfair because conflict isn't inherently bad. In reality, *conflict* is simply a disagreement or dispute between two or more parties in which they feel threatened in some way about an issue that's important to them. The issue can be a particular interest, need, or value. Some experts make a distinction between disputes, which are short-term disagreements, and conflicts, which are longer-term, more deeply rooted issues,[47] but here the terms are used interchangeably.

The parties having a conflict can be individuals, groups of people, an organization or business, or government entities and nation states, among others. This book focuses on online conflicts involving individuals and groups, understanding that the conflicts can, of course, migrate offline as well.

An important point to keep in mind is that conflict is unavoidable. It is absolutely impossible to eliminate all conflict, and conflict is a normal part of being human.

The challenge isn't the existence of conflict, but rather unresolved conflict that's risen to the level in which it negatively interferes with or affects something believed important by one or more of the parties involved.

Conflict actually provides a wonderful opportunity to challenge incorrect assumptions, acknowledge problems and bring them to the surface, develop creative solutions, and ultimately resolve problems between individuals or groups—if done right. In other words, conflict is simply a sign that something needs to be resolved. Ultimately a business's or individual's reaction to conflict, namely whether it's regarded as an opportunity or an aggravation, helps determine how successfully the conflict is dealt with. And that's where conflict management and conflict resolution come in.

Conflict management is the process to effectively deal with and handle ongoing or intractable disputes without violence that, for one reason or another, cannot be fully resolved. *Conflict resolution*, meanwhile, is the process to address the underlying and deep-rooted causes of conflict to find applicable solutions to these disputes without the use of violence.

Effectively using conflict management and resolution skills can

- Help increase workplace productivity
- Improve relationships between staff and management
- Reduce employee turnover and recruitment and training costs
- Strengthen business interactions between companies and their customers

- Help minimize legal problems and reduce legal fees
- Lessen personal stress, anxiety, and depression

Foundational Concepts in Conflict Management and Resolution

Because disputes and conflicts occur as a result of feeling threatened about an interest, need, or value that's important to one or more of the parties, you must understand each of these concepts.

But first review the famous story about the orange. Once upon a time there were two children fighting over an orange, with each insisting they should get the entire piece of fruit. The children's mother, finally exasperated by the ongoing bickering, took a kitchen knife and divided the orange, handing one half to each now miserable child. But unfortunately this didn't solve the problem. The girl grumbled that she didn't have enough orange slices for the fruit salad she was making, whereas the boy grumbled that he didn't have enough peel from which to grate zest for the cookies he was baking. There are several variations to this story, but you get the point. The children were so focused on what they wanted that they didn't explore why they each wanted it, and as a result they both lost out.

Positions

Based on that story, you can probably figure out what a position is. A *position* is the particular stance that someone takes with regard to an issue or situation. For example, "I want the entire orange." This is a *want*. An *interest*, meanwhile, is the reason or the "why" someone wants or doesn't want something. For example, "I want the orange because I want to make a fruit salad or bake cookies."

Needs

Needs, meanwhile, are a little bit more complex. Needs are usually talked about in connection with psychologist Abraham Maslow's Hierarchy of Needs Theory and Basic Human Needs Theory best known through the work of John W. Burton and other leaders in the conflict analysis and resolution field.

Maslow's theory basically states that humans are driven to satisfy a select group of needs, moving from those most necessary for survival to higher ones.[48] Commonly represented in pyramid form (see Figure 1.3), Maslow's needs are, from most basic to more complex:

- Physical needs such as water, food, shelter, and rest
- Safety needs, both physical and psychological

- Love needs such as feelings of belongingness, affection, friendship, and love
- Esteem needs such as self-respect and self-esteem, achievement, esteem of others, and recognition
- Self-actualization needs, which vary from one person to another but can include things such as an accurate perception of reality, autonomy, feelings of appreciation for life, independence from the opinions of others, and other things

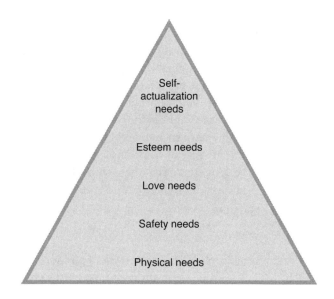

Figure 1.3   *Maslow's Hierarchy of Needs theory*

Meanwhile, as shown in Figure 1.4, Burton's theory[49] focuses on the universal basic human needs of identity, recognition, security, and personal development[50] which, in his view, do not have a predetermined hierarchical order but are pursued in a nonlinear fashion depending on the needs felt most urgently by individuals or groups of people at a particular time. Furthermore, he states that deep-rooted social conflict is the result of unsatisfied basic human needs, which is particularly interesting to consider in the rough-and-tumble online environment.

Values

Values are personal and moral principles and beliefs about something that guides individuals' and groups' thoughts and behaviors. Values help people decide whether something is desirable or right versus unacceptable or wrong, and which standards to apply in making that determination. Values are deeply held beliefs that cannot be forcibly changed from the outside but instead require an internal shift from within if they are to be modified.

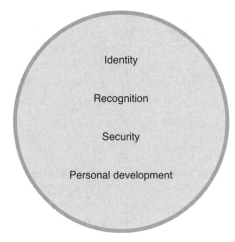

Identity

Recognition

Security

Personal development

Figure 1.4   *Burton's Basic Human Needs theory*

Identifying values is important in conflict management because disputes about values are particularly polarizing and are unlikely to be won on their own merits. This doesn't mean that a dispute is unresolvable, however. For example, if people are opposed to abortion because they believe embryos are full-fledged human beings as of the moment of conception, and that termination of pregnancy is therefore murder, there is no middle ground or room for debate. A discussion between anti-abortion and pro-choice individuals about the ethics of abortion is therefore not useful. However, if the discussion is reframed to focus on the emotional and financial burden placed on women and families due to unwanted pregnancies, the two people are much more likely to come to a mutually agreeable solution, such as talking about adoption as a viable option, without having to change their personal values about abortion.

Different Types of Conflict Management and Resolution

There are several different types of conflict management approaches, each with its own unique strengths. Depending on the kind of online conflict you find yourself in or have to deal with, you'll chose the type of approach, or combination of approaches, that can best be tailored for the online environment and that stand the greatest chance to help you move toward resolution.

The traditionally recognized conflict management approaches are negotiation, facilitation, mediation, and arbitration. Chapter 8, "Into the Trenches: Conflict Resolution Skills and Strategies," will delve deeper into specific conflict resolution skills and strategies, such as how to effectively use language to neutralize situations, when to use open versus closed questions to move toward resolution, and if, when, and how to reach out to online critics and attackers and engage directly with them. All these approaches will be discussed and then revisited in a later chapter when talking about how they can be used, sometimes in modified form, to resolve your unique online conflict.

Negotiation

Negotiation is a foundational process to resolve disputes and is used in many of the other approaches. Simply stated, negotiation is when two or more individuals or parties communicate about and ultimately try to come to an agreement on an issue they are at odds on. It is a process where people share their wants, needs, or interests with each other and then attempt to reach a mutually agreed-upon solution or outcome.[51] The benefit of negotiation is that it can be done informally, often requiring no special tools except a willingness to come to the table and negotiate openly and honestly. However, a drawback is that, in general, individuals or groups must be willing to negotiate and can't be forced to do so. (There are exceptions such as in legal proceedings, but generally negotiation is viewed as a voluntary process.) In addition, if the parties are unequal in strength, one of them may actively attempt to pressure the other, or one side may simply feel pressured, to come to an agreement even if they are not yet ready to do so or if the terms of the proposed agreement are unfavorable to them.

Facilitation

Facilitation is a process in which a person helps guide the communication between different parties. The facilitator ensures that the interaction goes smoothly, for example by ensuring the parties follow the agreed-upon agenda, by enforcing the group's rules of conduct, by structuring the environment in such a way that everyone has an opportunity to be heard, by helping the parties clarify what they want, by openly writing down the content of what was communicated so all can see and refer to it, and by helping move the parties toward their stated goal. The facilitator focuses exclusively on the process and does not try to influence the content of what is communicated.

The benefit of facilitation is that people participating in the process generally get to collaboratively identify the goals they are seeking and the process and behavioral rules they want to follow, thus they feel they have a large degree of control and stake in the matter. Another benefit is that anyone can serve as a facilitator. A drawback to facilitation, however, is that a biased or non-neutral facilitator can sabotage the process by trying to interject his views. Additionally, facilitation only works if the parties allow the facilitator to do his job and don't try to control the process. Furthermore, a facilitated session may be inappropriate in situations in which there is power inequality between the participants.

Mediation

Mediation is a voluntary process in which a neutral third person assists the parties to a dispute in communicating about and potentially negotiating a mutually agreed-upon resolution to their conflict. Mediators are trained individuals who understand the issues at stake, help the parties establish and agree upon procedural ground rules for the mediation, document any points of agreement between the parties, and memorialize any settlement they may reach.

The benefits of mediation include the parties' ability to control the process, the parties' opportunity to interact directly with one another, the fact that the process can be quicker and less expensive than litigation, the ability to maintain confidentiality about the information shared and the statements made (unlike in a legal setting, where proceedings are a matter of public record), and that parties are not required to reach agreement unless they voluntarily want to do so. A drawback to mediation is that the skill of the mediator in managing the process and having knowledge about the substantive matter of the dispute is enormously important, that any agreement reached by the parties is not binding unless recognized by a court, and the possibility that in some cases, the presence of attorneys attending a mediation alongside their clients to protect their legal rights might still be necessary, thus increasing the costs of mediation. In addition, some situations are not suitable for mediation, such as those in which one or more of the parties are determined to hurt or exact revenge on the other, where one or more of the parties in not forthcoming and honest about critical information, in situations where one party has been victimized by the other, and in criminal cases.

Arbitration

The next conflict management approach discussed is arbitration. *Arbitration* is the process in which a partial third person or a panel determines the outcome of a dispute. In some situations the arbitrator's decision is advisory, whereas in other situations it is binding and has the same force as a court-rendered decision. The benefits of arbitration are that a dispute can be resolved outside the traditional legal system, which cuts down on time and costs and that arbitrators are not held to the same strict legal parameters regarding discovery, evidence, and procedural rules as are the courts and can thus both consider information that might be impermissible in a court of law and reach decisions that are not as black-and-white as a litigated case would be. Furthermore, in nonbinding arbitrations the disputing parties can see the strengths and weaknesses of their case and what a court might look at if they decide to pursue their conflict through traditional legal channels. Additionally, some parties like the fact that arbitration decisions are not automatically a part of the public record. The drawbacks are that while it is less expensive than litigation, the arbitration process can be financially untenable by some parties; attorneys must often be hired to represent the parties in an arbitration hearing; binding arbitration decisions are not appealable; and depending on the specifics of a dispute, arbitrators might not be as financially generous as juries in particular matters.

Civil Litigation

Adding *civil litigation* to the list of conflict management methods is a bit controversial because litigation might be considered a rather aggressive approach to problem solving. However, particularly in the online environment, sometimes it is a necessary approach for attack victims to take, which is the reason it is covered here. Civil litigation is the process to take a legal dispute between two or more parties before a court and have a judge or jury determine the outcome of the case. The benefits of litigation include the definitive resolution of a case (although this should not be confused with the parties' ability, in many situations, to appeal a decision if certain factors are met); the creation of a legal precedent; that a public record is maintained of the outcome of the case, which is important to some litigants; and the ability for a party to pursue injunctive relief (asking the court to require the other party to do or refrain from doing something); among other things. The drawbacks to litigation include that it is usually a costly process; it takes a long time compared to other methods of dispute resolution; the relationship between the parties is usually severely strained and often irreparable after one is designated the "winner" and the other the "loser"; and that the law alone often can't make right an ethical or social wrong. At this point an important difference between civil and criminal law should be noted. In *criminal law*, the case isn't filed by a private person or entity, but instead by the state or federal government that is represented by the prosecutor, with the goal of punishing the defendant for wrongdoing. Chapter 9, "Legal Aspects of Online Disputes and Conflicts," further discusses the relevance of this.

See Table 1.1 for a comparison between the level of control that the parties have, the degree of formality, the cost, and the level of adversity between negotiation, facilitation, mediation, arbitration, and litigation.

Table 1.1   Comparison of Conflict Management Approaches

Process	Control	Formality	Cost	Adversarial
Negotiation	High	Low	Low	Variable
Facilitation	High	Low	Low	Variable
Mediation	High	Medium	Medium	Variable
Arbitration	Low	High	High	High
Litigation	Low	High	High	High

Three Foundational Skills Necessary in Conflict Management and Resolution

Several skills are foundational to effective conflict management, especially for online conflict.

Foremost is learning how to listen. Most people think that they already know how to listen—after all, they've been doing it all their lives—but in reality, active listening is something that few people do correctly. Among other things, it involves:

- Giving the other person your full attention (listening to them while multitasking doesn't count!)
- Refraining from interrupting or cutting them off before they are done talking
- Asking open-ended and clarifying questions
- Accurately paraphrasing and reflecting the information back to ensure that what you think you heard is actually what the person was trying to express
- Suspending judgment until you have all the necessary information on which to base an informed decision

Paraphrasing helps people avoid the tendency to mentally prepare rebuttal statements or counter arguments before they've heard all the relevant information, because it requires them to concentrate on the present and what is in front of them at that moment. This can also help diffuse the emotionality of a situation because communication problems often involve people feeling they've not been given the opportunity to express their feelings and speak their minds.

Some people have a problem with the idea of paraphrasing and reflecting back because they fear it somehow suggests that they are agreeing with the other person's statements or viewpoints. However, nothing could be further from the truth. Paraphrasing is simply a tool to make sure you heard and understood correctly what was said and does not require that you agree with the communication. Simply acknowledging that you've accurately *heard* what the other person said is sometimes enough to minimize a dispute.

In text-only communication, active listening is harder to do well than in live, face-to-face situations. The absence of cues offered by body language, facial expressions, and vocal intonations leaves lots of room for misinterpretation about both intent and content. For example, if you've just emailed your friend about a high-paying speaking engagement you received and he sends back a message that simply says, "Congratulations, I guess you're in the big times now," does this mean he is sincerely happy for you but perhaps pressed for time and therefore didn't write a longer message, or that he's passive-aggressive and therefore not honest about feeling jealous about your success? It's impossible to tell by the words alone. Of course, even when tone isn't directly an issue, written text carries all sorts of other inherent risks, one of them being typos that can make an important, and in some cases, tragic difference, as in an English case that ended in murder. Neil Brook of Salford in northern England was sending his friend Josef Witkowski several text messages, one of which contained the word "mutter," which is a local term for a person who behaves in an antisocial or vulgar manner. Unfortunately Brook's predictive text function[52] changed it to "nutter" instead, which is slang for deranged. Witkowski took offense at this and headed to Brook's apartment with a knife, stabbing Brook 104 times.[53] (Fortunately most people don't react to an autocorrect error in the same extreme, horrific, and psychologically imbalanced way as Witkowski did.)

Another important skill is learning how to focus on the problem without attacking the person or business. When emotions are high and a lot is at stake, it's easy to become so blinded that inflicting as much pain as possible becomes the primary goal. However, taking such an approach means that you've lost control of yourself and are letting your baser emotions dictate the course of action, instead of taking a well-thought-out, rational approach based on likely longer-term benefits. Key to this is effective emotional management, particularly knowing how to manage one's own frustration and anger and keeping them in check. You'll learn how to do this in Chapter 6, "The 101 of Anger Management."

The third skill, related to the second one mentioned, is not falling prey to ad hominem fallacies. *Ad hominem fallacies* ("ad hominem" comes from the Latin meaning "directed toward the person") are logical fallacies that involve focusing on a characteristic, statement, belief, or action of a person as a means to weaken or negate what the person said or did. For example, "Dr. Jane Goodall talks about fostering compassion in humans, but what does she know? She works with chimpanzees," or "I know Jim Smith acted like a jerk online, but he's given a lot of money to charity, so I'm sure he acted that way by accident" or "Sheryl Sandberg has tens of thousands of Twitter followers, so she *MUST* know what she's talking about." There are numerous other types of fallacies that come into play online as well, such as *appeal to emotion* (for example, "You know Senator Smith isn't looking out for you, he's a Democrat/Republican"), *appeal to authority* (for example, "George Foreman was a great boxer, so I know his fat-reducing frying pan must be a good product"), or *straw man fallacy* in which an individual's position is intentionally misrepresented to weaken it (for example, one person says, "We need to hold people accountable for their defamatory statements online" and his opponent argues, "You say accountability, but what you really want is to take away people's freedom of speech").

What This Book Covers

This chapter discussed the negative effects of unresolved conflict, explained the unique aspects of conflicts in online environments, and provided foundational concepts in conflict resolution.

Chapter 2, "Why Your Online Reputation and Privacy Matter," talks about why your online reputation and privacy matter, how to create a positive online footprint for yourself and your organization, and how to measure and monitor these reputations.

Chapter 3, "The Different Types of Conflicts and Which Ones Matter Most," explains the different types of individuals or groups that clash online and the different types of conflict issues that you are most likely to come across.

Chapter 4, "Who Are the Troublemakers?" analyzes the most common types of difficult personalities you'll encounter online and what strategies work best with each of them.

Chapter 5, "What's Your Conflict Style?" addresses the different personal conflict resolution styles, helps you identify which one applies to you, and discusses the benefits and drawbacks of each of the styles.

Chapter 6, "The 101 of Anger Management," explains why anger management is a foundational skill necessary for conflict management online, what anger is and how it differs from seemingly similar emotions, the real reasons people get angry, and how to express anger online in a productive and safe manner.

Chapter 7, "Digital Literacy in a Hyperconnected World," covers the basics of digital literacy, specifically the framework for analyzing and evaluating online information for accuracy, bias, and authorship, and explains why digital literacy plays a key role in effective conflict management.

Chapter 8, "Into the Trenches: Conflict Resolution Skills and Strategies," gets into the nitty-gritty of conflict analysis and resolution, covering details such as the different strategic approaches to managing online conflicts, the importance to effectively handle others' hostility and frustration, the successful use of neutral versus inflammatory language, and the different approaches to deal with single occurrence versus repeat occurrence conflicts.

Chapter 9, "Legal Aspects of Online Disputes and Conflicts," covers the basic legal concepts that you should know to safely participate in the online environment, discusses individuals' rights and responsibilities, and talks about how to draft and implement robust corporate social media policies that both recognize the need for clear rules of behavior and simultaneously support the First Amendment protections individuals enjoy.

And finally, Chapter 10, "30-Day Plan for Better Conflict Management Online," draws on the information and skills covered in this book and translates them into a 30-day plan of action that includes concrete steps and accompanying checklists.

Endnotes

1. Feminist Frequency blog. Link: http://www.feministfrequency.com/about/

2. Anita Sarkeesian's Kickstarter campaign "Tropes Vs. Women in Video Games." Link: http://www.kickstarter.com/projects/566429325/tropes-vs-women-in-video-games

3. Anita Sarkeesian, "Image Based Harassment and Visual Misogny," Feminist Frequency, July 1, 2012. Link: http://www.feministfrequency.com/2012/07/image-based-harassment-and-visual-misogyny/

4. Screenshot of Anita Sarkeesian's Wikipedia page of June 6, 2012 posted on Feminist Frequency blog. Link: http://feministfrequency.com/archive/wikipedia_harassment1.png

5. Anita Sarkeesian, "Image Based Harassment and Visual Misogny," Feminist Frequency, July 1, 2012. Link: http://www.feministfrequency.com/2012/07/image-based-harassment-and-visual-misogyny/

6. FeministFrequency's YouTube Channel's "Support My Kickstarter Project - Tropes vs. Women in Video." Link: http://www.youtube.com/all_comments?v=l8I0Wy58adM&page=6

7. FeministFrequency's YouTube Channel's "Support My Kickstarter Project - Tropes vs. Women in Video." Link: http://www.youtube.com/all_comments?v=l8I0Wy58adM&page=6

8. Helen Lewis," This is what online harassment looks like," New Statesman," July 6, 2012. Link: http://www.newstatesman.com/blogs/internet/2012/07/what-online-harassment-looks

9. Andrea Weckerle, "Former Cyberbullying Victim Turned Antibullying Advocate Sue Scheff Talks About What Needs To Change Online," CiviliNation, February 14, 2012. Link:http://www.civilination.org/blog/cyberbullying-victim-turned-antibullying-advocate-sue-scheff-talks-about-what-needs-to-change-online/

10. Andrea Weckerle, "Former Cyberbullying Victim Turned Antibullying Advocate Sue Scheff Talks About What Needs To Change Online," CiviliNation, February 14, 2012. Link: http://www.civilination.org/blog/cyberbullying-victim-turned-antibullying-advocate-sue-scheff-talks-about-what-needs-to-change-online/

11. Andrea Weckerle, "Rexxfield Founder Michael Roberts Shares His Personal Story of Defamation and Explains How His Company Helps Other Victims Regain Their Good Name," CiviliNation, April 10, 2012. Link: http://www.civilination.org/blog/rexxfield-founder-michael-roberts-shares-his-personal-story-of-defamation-and-explains-how-his-company-helps-other-victims-regain-their-good-name/

12. Andrea Weckerle, "Rexxfield Founder Michael Roberts Shares His Personal Story of Defamation and Explains How His Company Helps Other Victims Regain Their Good Name," CiviliNation, April 10, 2012. Link: http://www.civilination.org/blog/rexxfield-founder-michael-roberts-shares-his-personal-story-of-defamation-and-explains-how-his-company-helps-other-victims-regain-their-good-name/

13. Rexxfield. Link: http://www.rexxfield.com/

14. Andrea Weckerle, "Defamation Victim Janice Duffy, Ph.D. Says that Online Complaint Sites Can Ruin People's Lives," CiviliNation, May 10, 2012. Link: http://www.civilination.org/blog/defamation-victim-janice-duffy-phd-says-online-complaint-sites-can-ruin-peoples-lives/

15. Andrea Weckerle, "Defamation Victim Janice Duffy, Ph.D. Says that Online Complaint Sites Can Ruin People's Lives," CiviliNation, May 10, 2012. Link: http://www.civilination.org/blog/defamation-victim-janice-duffy-phd-says-online-complaint-sites-can-ruin-peoples-lives/

16. World Internet Usage and Population Statistics, Internet World Stats, December 31, 2011. Link: http://www.internetworldstats.com/stats.htm

17. David Goldman, "The Internet now has 340 trillion trillion trillion addresses," CNNMoney, June 6, 2012. Link: http://money.cnn.com/2012/06/06/technology/ipv6/index.htm

18. Kristen Purcell, "Search and email still top the list of the most popular online activities," Pew Internet & American Life Project, August 9, 2011. Link: http://www.pewinternet.org/Reports/2011/Search-and-email.aspx

19. Mary Madden and Kathryn Zickuhr, "65% of online adults use social networking sites," Pew Internet & American Life Project, August 26, 2011. Link: http://www.pewinternet.org/Reports/2011/Social-Networking-Sites.aspx

20. Mary Madden and Kathryn Zickuhr, "Older adults and internet use," Pew Internet & American Life Project, June 6, 2012. Link: http://www.pewinternet.org/Reports/2012/Older-adults-and-internet-use.aspx

21. Mary Madden and Kathryn Zickuhr, "Older adults and internet use," Pew Internet & American Life Project, June 6, 2012. Link: http://www.pewinternet.org/Reports/2012/Older-adults-and-internet-use.aspx

22. MG Siegler, "AT&T Customer Service Rep Tells Us How She Really Feels: 'This Is Bullsh*t,'" TechCrunch.com, January 13, 2011. Link: http://techcrunch.com/2011/01/13/att-rep-verizon-iphone/

23. MG Siegler, "AT&T Customer Service Rep Tells Us How She Really Feels: 'This Is Bullsh*t,'" TechCrunch.com, January 13, 2011. Link: http://techcrunch.com/2011/01/13/att-rep-verizon-iphone/

24. Susanna Kim, "Best Buy Employee Wrongly 'Outed' Denver Man," ABC News, May 3, 2012. Link: http://abcnews.go.com/blogs/business/2012/05/best-buy-employee-wrongly-outed-denver-man/

25. "Proof Bartender's Racist Rant Put On Blast," 312 Diving Diva, March 29, 2012. Link: http://312diningdiva.blogspot.com/2012/03/proof-bartenders-racist-rant-put-on.html

26. Maudlyne Ihejirika, "Rush Street club fires bartender over racist Facebook rant," Chicago Sun-Times, April 5, 2012. Link: http://www.suntimes.com/news/metro/11713679-418/rush-street-club-fires-bartender-over-racist-facebook-rant.html

27. Sam Biddle, "This Is What Happens When Anonymous Tried to Destroy You," Gizmodo, June 1, 2012. Link: http://gizmodo.com/5914671/this-is-what-happens-when-anonymous-tries-to-destroy-you/

28. Calestous Juma, personal Twitter account @Calestous, May 16, 2012 at 6:11 p.m. Link: https://twitter.com/Calestous/status/202899182003032066

29. Matt Brownell, "1 in 5 Americans Report Being Stalked Online," MainStreet, January 24, 2012. Link: http://www.mainstreet.com/article/smart-spending/technology/1-5-americans-report-being-stalked-online

30. Brad Stone and Matt Richtel, "The Hand That Controls the Sock Puppet Could get Slapped," *The New York Times*, July 16, 2007. Link: http://www.nytimes.com/2007/07/16/technology/16blog.html?_r=1

31. The Associated Press, "Whole Foods CEO's anonymous online life," MSNBC, July 12, 2007. Link: http://www.msnbc.msn.com/id/19718742/ns/business-us_business/t/whole-foods-ceos-anonymous-online-life

32. Peter Kaplan, "John Mackey panned Wild Oats on Web," Reuters, July 12, 2007. Link: http://www.reuters.com/article/2007/07/12/us-wholefoods-ftc-idUSN1133440820070712

33. Ronald Krotoszynski, Jr., Defamation in the Digital Age: Some Comparative Observations on the Difficulty of Reconciling Free Speech and Reputation in the Emerging Global Village, 62 WASH. & LEE. L.REV. 339 (2004) at 349.

34. Ibid at 348.

35. Ibid at 350.

36. The Wayback Machine is a project of the 501(c)(3) non-profit Internet Archive. Link: http://archive.org/web/web.php

37. Politiwoops. Link: http://politwoops.sunlightfoundation.com/

38. Politiwoops Homepage. Link: http://politwoops.sunlightfoundation.com

39. Rachael Pracht https://plus.google.com/101866976681938831577/about

40. http://rachaelchesnutt.tumblr.com/ and http://rachaelchesnutt.tumblr.com/tagged/ Confessions_in_a_Call_Center (Both links are now defunct.)

41. Knowlton Thomas, "Rachael Chesnutt's Guide on How to Get Fired Through Social Media," Techvibes, January 13, 2011. Link: http://www.techvibes.com/blog/ rachael-chesnutts-guide-on-how-to-get-fired-through-social-media-2011-01-13

42. Knowlton Thomas, "Rachael Chesnutt's Guide on How to Get Fired Through Social Media," Techvibes, January 13, 2011. Link: http://www.techvibes.com/blog/ rachael-chesnutts-guide-on-how-to-get-fired-through-social-media-2011-01-13

43. Susanna Kim, "Best Buy Employee Wrongly 'Outed' Denver Man," ABC News, May 3, 2012. Link: http://abcnews.go.com/blogs/business/2012/05/best-buy-employee-wrongly-outed-denver-man/

44. Ethisphere, "2012 World's Most Ethical Companies." Link: http://www.ethisphere.com/ wme/

45. Miguel Bustillo, "Best Buy CEO Quits in Probe," *The Wall Street Journal*, April 10, 2012. Link: http://online.wsj.com/article/SB1000142405270230381540457733555179480 8074.html

46. "Bartender Fired Over Racist Facebook Post," NBCChicago.com, April 3, 2012. Link: http://www.nbcchicago.com/the-scene/events/proof-Bartender-Fired-Over-Racist-Facebook-Post-145965315.html

47. John Burton, *Conflict: Resolution and Prevention* (New York: St. Martin's Press, 1990).

48. Abraham H. Maslow, "A Theory of Human Motivation," Psychological Review 50, 370–96 (1943). Link: http://psychclassics.yorku.ca/Maslow/motivation.htm

49. John W. Burton, *Conflict: Human Needs Theory* (Palgrave Macmillan, 1990).

50. Richard E. Rubenstein, "Basic Human Needs: The Next Step In Theory Development," The International Journal of Peace Studies, Spring 2001, Volume 6, Number 1. Link: http://www.gmu.edu/programs/icar/ijps/vol6_1/Rubenstein.htm

51. Christopher W. Moore, "Negotiation" Air University, Air Force Negotiation Center of Excellence. Link: http://www.au.af.mil/au/awc/awcgate/army/usace/negotiation.htm

52. According to Wikipedia, predictive text can "allow for an entire *word* to be input by single keypress. Predictive text makes efficient use of fewer device keys to input writing into a text message, an e-mail, an address book, a calendar and the like." Link: http:// en.wikipedia.org/wiki/Predictive_text

53. "Predictive text error leads UK man to fatally stab friend," news.com.au, February 11, 2011. Link: http://www.news.com.au/world/predictive-text-error-leads-uk-man-to-fatally-stab-friend/story-e6frfkyi-1226004174826

2

Why Your Online Reputation and Privacy Matter

More and More, Everything You Do Is Public and Subject to Public Scrutiny

On June 19, 2002, American citizen Hasan Elahi,[1] an artist and professor, returned from an overseas trip and entered the United States through the Detroit airport. Unlike the standard procedure in which citizens show their passports to U.S. immigration agents and are then passed through, the agent in this case instructed Elahi to follow him into the Immigration and Naturalization Service's airport office where he was interrogated about his trip and specifically where he had been on September 12, 2001, the day after the terrorist suicide attacks against the United States. A few weeks later, Elahi was instructed to show up for a meeting with the FBI, where he was interrogated in more depth about his recent trip, whether he had any information about acts that might be harmful to the United States, if he had ever met anyone from Al Qaeda, Islamic Jihad, Hamas, or Hezbollah, and if he had any explosives in his personal storage unit. This questioning went on for 6 months and culminated in a series of polygraph tests, after which Elahi was cleared.[2]

Fearing that once flagged his name might again mistakenly show up on a terrorist watch list, he contacted the FBI before taking his next international trip and was told to call the FBI agent with his flight information to ensure everything went smoothly. It did and as a result Elahi decided to call before every trip and let the bureau know his itinerary. But he went one step further and started sending the FBI long emails that included photographs of his activities, even turning his phone into a tracking device. Ultimately he decided to document nearly every hour of his life, creating a combination of performance art and a stay-out-of-jail card through his website.[3]

You might think that Elahi's is a rare situation, and for being wrongly placed on the terrorist watch list you are probably right. You might also think, except for extraordinary reasons, no one would ever consider documenting his life in real time the way he does. On this point, however, you would be wrong. As Elahi aptly notes, "You're all doing it. This is something we are all doing on a daily basis, whether we're aware of it or not."[4] Every time you take a photo and post it on Facebook, and every time you send a status update to your social networks or text a message to a friend, you're leaving a digital trail that documents your life.

Sharing and Oversharing

There are the self-identified lifecasters, inspired by Justin Kan who in 2007 launched the Internet reality show named Justin.tv that featured 24-hour live streaming of his life via a camera attached to a cap he wore on his head.[5] (Today Justin.tv is a venture capital-backed live video web portal with tens of millions of users a month.)[6]

There are the parents who post sonogram images of their unborn children online, thus creating a digital footprint for their offspring even before they officially enter the world, who continue the day-by-day, month-by-month chronicling of their children's lives before they are old enough to make informed decisions about what information they want about themselves online.

And there are the massive number of people who provide so many details about their lives and daily activities that it's like handing would-be stalkers a personal dossier. They disclose their home addresses and phone numbers online; post their own and their children's birthdays on Facebook; conduct regular check-ins via geolocation apps such as foursquare; share real-time public photos via Instagram; tweet when they are leaving town for business or vacation while sharing the exact airline and flight they are taking; upload photos with embedded geotags which enable viewers to discover where the image was taken; and talk in detail about serious illnesses and diseases they have.

Of course don't forget the unintended oversharing that occurs because users of social networking sites don't understand that they need to adjust their privacy settings. Facebook, for example, enables you to select who you want to share your status updates with, whether that's all your friends, friends except people who are acquaintances, only yourself, or whether you want what you post to become public and be shared with the entire world. You also need to remember to regularly moni-tor social networking sites to make sure their settings haven't been updated in such a way that your information is exposed to people you don't want to share it with.

Even some bloggers are amazed that what they post online can be viewed by every-one in the world, believing that because they aren't famous and write their blogs just for a small audience of family and friends, no one else would read them.

People are also unaware that some of their online actions can have unintended consequences, such as seemingly endorsing products that perhaps would best be left unmentioned. That's what happened to Nick Bergus when he posted a link from his Facebook page to an Amazon.com product he found amusing, a 55-gallon barrel of personal lubricant, along with the comment, "For Valentine's Day. And every day. For the rest of your life."[7] Shortly afterward, Bergus's friends started see-ing his post, which you can see in Figure 2.1, among official ads on Facebook pages because Facebook's algorithm had transformed his post, without his direct consent, into an advertisement for the online retailer.[8]

Figure 2.1   *Screenshot of Nick Bergus's sponsored story on Facebook*

Perhaps people should just accept that privacy is dying and make peace with the new world order of things. That seems like the opinion of Sun Microsystems's co-founder Scott McNealy who in 1999 said, "You have zero privacy anyway" and then suggested people should "Get over it."[9] Facebook founder Mark Zuckerberg explains it this way, "People have really gotten comfortable not only sharing more information and different kinds, but more openly and with more people. That social norm is just something that has evolved over time."[10]

But you should care and here's why: Your online privacy—the combination of what you and others share about you online and what you manage to keep off the Web—and reputation are inextricably intertwined. As you'll see in the next section, your digital footprint is used by others in decision making that impacts virtually every aspect of your life, including what college you can attend, whether you'll be hired for that coveted job, what health insurance coverage you'll receive, what your line of credit will be, and your dating potential and desirability as a mate.

Businesses's online reputations of course matter as well. As noted in global public relations firm Weber Shandwick's report "The Company Behind the Brand: In Reputation We Trust - CEO Spotlight" and reflected in Figure 2.2, 60% of a company's market value is attributed to its reputation, whereas 49% of a company's reputation is attributed to the CEO's reputation.[11] According to Micho Spring, Weber Shandwick's global corporate practice chair, "In an increasingly seamless world, more consumers are exposed and attuned to corporate actions than ever before. CEOs can't assume that what they say and their teams do are going unnoticed by the public."[12]

Total Executives

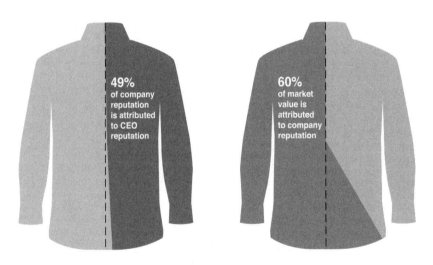

Figure 2.2   *Screenshot from Weber Shandwick, "The Company Behind the Brand: In Reputation We Trust - CEO Spotlight"*

Your Digital Footprint Matters, Whether You Want It to or Not

What is the first thing most people do when they want to find out more about a particular individual or organization? They enter the name into a major search engine such as Google, Bing, or Yahoo to see what shows up on the first page. If they like what they see—nothing negative or questionable posted by you or others—that's great. But if not...well, welcome to the digital age where anything you've ever done in your life, and everything anyone has ever said about you, can be discovered and used against you and your business, and often is.

What if you're not even active online and have decided, for whatever reason, not to participate in any social networks, join any forum discussions, or leave online comments on newspaper articles? It's likely that even then an online footprint about you exists based on what's available through public records, which at a minimum consist of your name, age, your past or current spouse, adult family members, a history of where you've lived and your current home address. More likely other information can be quickly and easily found about you through people search sites such as PeopleFinders, sites such as Classmates that provides access to more than a 100,000 yearbooks dating back to the 1920s,[13] as well as formerly print-only digitized letters to the editor, online tax records, or real estate records and court records.

How Online Information About You Affects Your Reputation and Life

Now look at some of the ways the information found about you online directly affects one of the most important times in your life, namely getting a job, whether it's your first or tenth one. Aside from having to compete against other qualified candidates and trying to favorably stand out in a market that, these days, with few exceptions, is strongly stacked in favor of employers, you need to ensure that your online footprint is favorable, or at least neutral and doesn't contain some unexpected surprises. Human resource professionals and hiring managers are increasingly performing background checks on candidates, which, as in previous times, include checking professional references and ensuring criminal and financial records are clean. Today, however, it's also standard to check out candidates' online activities and what others have posted about them. According to a recent CareerBuilder survey, 37% of all companies check social networks and social media not only to see if candidates present themselves professionally, but also to "look for reasons not to hire the candidates."[14] Among reasons given by hiring managers for why candidates didn't get the job include posting provocative or inappropriate information, evidence of drinking or drug use, bad-mouthing of previous employers, and discriminatory remarks about race, gender and religion.[15]

It's easy to conduct a name search for the person on major search engines to get links to their Twitter, Facebook, and LinkedIn accounts, many of which are set so that contents are public. And as long as hiring rejections are not made based on a protected class such as gender, ethnicity, race, religion, and other protected categories, potential employers in the United States can turn down candidates for any number of reasons, including no particular reason at all.

HR departments may also simply decide to outsource background checks, hiring companies such as Social Intelligence to do the work. Social Intelligence is a social media screening and research solutions company that provides its clients with information about prospects' online behavior and reputation from the past 7 years via its "proprietary technology [that] searches millions of [publicly available] websites, including the most well-known social networking websites."[16] The company searches for things such as racist statements or activities, excessive and illegal drug use, potentially violent tendencies, and sexually explicit images.[17] (A copy of an actual report can be seen via a link in the end notes.[18])

Some prospective employers have even gone so far as to demand the passwords to candidates' and employees' social networking sites, an act so outrageous that in March 2012, Maryland became the first U.S. state that banned employers from "requesting or requiring that an employee or applicant disclose any user name, password, or other means for accessing a personal account or service through specified electronic communications devices," including taking related disciplinary action against the person.[19] (It should be noted that the specifics of the situation that led to this are delicate because the employer in question happened to actually be the state of Maryland, or more specifically, the Maryland Division of Corrections,[20] which requested the Facebook login information from a corrections officer who was up for recertification).

Nevertheless, in an environment in which people are often cavalier and careless about their privacy settings and even more so about what they say and do online, no doubt employers will continue to have enough direct sources of information to use when making hiring decisions.

Online Information About You Affects Your Education, Too

The importance of having a positive digital footprint starts before attending a college or university. In a 2012 Infographic,[21] Kaplan Test Prep revealed that 20% of admissions officers have Googled prospective students and 22% have looked them up on Facebook, with 12% saying they have found information that has negatively impacted an applicant.[22]

When in college, the online reputation clock keeps ticking, something that not enough college students appear to be taking to heart. Taylor Jennings, who on his Twitter profile explains that he graduated from Bethel High School and is attending Southern Methodist University for a Criminal Justice degree,[23] (in other words, provides enough information that someone can determine his real identity), may not have put his best foot forward when he tweeted that "Some people probably think I'm an asshole. but I'm Just [sic]honest and I'm going to do what iiiiii want. Not why you want."[24]

Ross Kressel, meanwhile, found out that sometimes even information on profiles set to private have a way of becoming public. Kressel, who in 2011 was the student body president at College of Charleston in South Carolina, tweeted a few questionable messages via his private and now defunct @CofCPolitico account, including statements like "just saw big tits freshman, who is now a sophomore."[25] Screenshots of these tweets were made public, and the story was covered locally in the United States and internationally in the U.K.[26] Kressel, who subsequently faced an impeachment attempt, released a public statement saying that "My actions in this case were unprofessional, inappropriate and misguided and I sincerely do apologize and have begun work towards [sic]repairing the damage from my actions" but also argued that "I believe that the letter from Treasurer Rozansky asking for my impeachment is an inappropriate course of action and only distracts from the great work I look forward to doing as your Student Body President."[27]

For individuals who go to graduate school, what they post online continues to be a determining factor in admissions. Kaplan Test Prep said that 27% of business school admissions officers have Googled prospective students, and 24% have looked them up on Facebook, with 14% saying they have found information that has negatively impacted an applicant. For law schools, which have stringent admissions requirements, the percentages are the highest: 41% of law school admissions officers have Googled prospective students, and 37% have looked them up on Facebook, with 32% saying they have found information that has negatively impacted an applicant.[28]

Online Information About You Impacts Your Career Success

When you're in the workforce, maintaining a positive image is obviously still important. Unless he wants to know the way she really feels about him, let's hope that Ghislane Nunez's boss doesn't check out her Twitter profile. Nunez, who, according to her Facebook profile, is from Sao Paulo, Brazil and now lives in New York City, tweeted "I hate my fu**ing boss. He completely f**ed up my social life. DAMN YOU A**HOLE. I got something coming for u!!!!!!!"[29] And Melissa Petro, who has two master's degrees and 3 years' experience teaching art at an elementary school in New York City, learned the hard way that one's past can come back to haunt you when she was forced to resign her teaching position as a result of the fallout from having publicly written about her short stint as a sex worker.[30]

Whether the impressions made from these individuals' statements are accurate, either way it might give prospective, current, and future employers pause.

Of course even members of professions where you would think individuals should know better make these mistakes. Winnebago County, Illinois assistant public defender Kristine Ann Peshek lost her job[31] after calling a judge "Judge Clueless" and posting information about her clients on her personal yet public blog. The clients were easily recognizable via their first name, a derivative thereof, or their jail identification number.[32] Meanwhile, rather than be fired, Indiana state trooper Chris Pestow resigned after an investigation began into the appropriateness of what he was posting on his personal Facebook page. Pestow had boasted about his alcohol drinking and posted a photo of another police officer pointing a gun to his head.[33] No doubt these actions by members of law enforcement and the bar didn't score any public relations points for their respective professions.

Online Information Affects More Than You Think

But what's posted online doesn't just affect your ability to find and maintain a job, it can also affect how financial institutions determine your credit score,[34] which influences what kind of financing you can get for major purchases such as car loans, what mortgage rate you'll qualify for, and what credit card interest rate you receive. Lenddo, for example, which describes itself as "the world's first online platform that helps the emerging middle class use their social connections to build their creditworthiness and access local financial services," uses a client's social network to determine creditworthiness.[35] Meanwhile, Germany's largest credit agency, SCHUFA, has plans to use social networks Facebook, Xing, LinkedIn, and Twitter, as well as Google Street View and personal search engine Yasni for its project SCHUFALab@HPI that would determine an individual's creditworthiness.[36]

Whether you receive health insurance benefits can also be affected by what's found online. Canadian Nathalie Blanchard was denied continuation of her employer-sponsored benefits for a diagnosis of major depression after online photos of her on vacation were found by her health insurance provider on Facebook. Even more mysterious is how insurer Manulife found these pictures because Blanchard claims her Facebook profile was set to private and could be seen only by those to whom she directly gave access.[37] Perhaps someone who had legitimate access to her profile shared the photos with the insurer.

What about company secrets? TechCrunch founder and CrunchFund partner Michael Arrington blogged about an incident involving a high-ranking company executive who discussed "extremely sensitive corporate information" on his phone in an airplane before takeoff, enabling Arrington to figure out the name of the company and the identity of the company's COO who was allegedly being fired.[38] So much for confidentiality.

Maintaining a positive impression is highly critical for the military as well. But with such easy access to technology and the ability to upload everything instantaneously, shocking examples of some military members' misconduct become international incidents that threaten the reputation of the United States, as was the case when a video appearing to show U.S. marines desecrating the corpses of Taliban fighters went viral.[39]

Reputational Hits from the Outside

Of course it's not just a question of refraining from posting potentially damaging information online; it's also an issue of making sure others don't do so about you. Sometimes reputational hits come from the inside. An individual at Chrysler's social media agency New Media Strategies tweeted via the auto company's @ChryslerAutos' account "I find it ironic that Detroit is known as the #motorcity and yet no one here knows how to fu**ing drive."[40] Supplemental insurance provider Aflac fired comedian Gilbert Gottfried,[41] who had served as the company's "duck" voice for more than a decade, after he tweeted a series of distasteful jokes about the 2011 tsunami and earthquake in Japan, among them, "I was talking to my Japanese real estate agent. I said 'is there a school in this area.' She said, 'not now, but just wait" and "I fu**ed d a girl in japan [sic]. She screamed, 'I felt the earth move and I'm getting wet.' " [42]

But nothing beats a company's own executives who go ballistic online, which was the case in the Twitter postings between Li Guoqing, the CEO of Chinese Amazon DangDang, and someone who was posing as a Morgan Stanley banker. Upset about what he perceived to be undervaluing DangDang shares by Morgan Stanley for the U.S. IPO,[43] Li published a song about Morgan Stanley he made up, which contained such lines as "Don't f**k with me. I'm really pissed off.... And let me fu** all of you up after this drama is over."[44]

Reputational Hits from the Inside

Meanwhile, more commonly the hits come from the outside. For example, although online consumer rating and review sites such as Yelp, Epinions.com, Top Consumer Reviews, and others in theory can help consumers make informed decisions by enabling them to see what people have said about a particular company, service, or product, they are frequently misused. Often disgruntled individuals use them to "get even" with businesses they feel have slighted or wronged them is some way—and sometimes go overboard out of spite and revenge. They also seek out sites that specifically exist to enable people to vent, for example ComplaintsBoard, Complaints.com, iRipoff.com, and Pissed Consumer. Even craigslist contains a "rants and raves" section (which may only be accessed by people over 18 years old and older because it includes explicit and sexual content) that posts critical content. Many of the complaint sites earn online advertising revenue, and thus have a strong financial interest in having people visit the site to unleash their fury. For those who can't be bothered to do the dirty work, there are entrepreneurial types who offer to "write up to three negative reviews for you with three different pro-files against your competition for $10."[45] There are also sites where personal reputations are easily tarnished, such as DontdateHimGirl.com or ThePayback.com, which people use with the intent to harm and exact revenge against others.

Although there is nothing illegal about posting a negative review that is factually correct, when consumers go out of their way to leave nasty comments, and the feedback is heavily laced with expletives, vague accusations of wrongdoing, and non-specific statements that the business or individual was "terrible" or "sucked," there is a strong likelihood that the person is simply looking for an opportunity to inflict damage. Even when the review is not negative, the value of such sites is questionable due to the common practice of posting inflated reviews. A Dallas-based Internet marketing and online reputation management firm "found that 57% of the reviews for a sampling of businesses in the Google Places directory appeared to be fabricated."[46]

There is an additional reason why your digital footprint matters. In the post-September 11, 2001 world, the U.S. Department of Homeland Security's National Operations Center (NOC) carefully monitors news stories, media reports, and social media postings for information that may be relevant to national security and safety interests. The list of terms used by the NOC to monitor social media sites, featured in the 2011 Department of Homeland Security National Operations Center Media's Monitoring Capability Desktop Reference Binder that was obtained through a Freedom of Information Act lawsuit by the Electronic Privacy Information Center,[47] includes words also used for non-nefarious discussions or commentary:

> attack, law enforcement, prevention, threat, national security, epidemic, toxic, United Nations, Federal Bureau of Investigations, Central Intelligence Agency, infection, flu, evacuation, World Health Organization, airport, communications, infrastructure, transportation security, service disruption, drug, gang, violence, terrorism, target, emergency, storm, flood, lightening, forest fire, cyber security, denial of service, malware, virus, spammer, phishing, hacker, and social media.[48]

How unfortunate it would be to receive unwanted attention due to innocent use of these terms.

Hopefully by now you agree that your digital footprint is critical to your business and personal success and understand the seriousness of what can happen if something goes awry. But how do you correctly assess what your online reputation looks like? What are some ways you can build a positive and strong reputation? And how can you continue to track and monitor your digital reputation? That's what you'll examine next.

Measuring Your Existing Digital Footprint

To take inventory of your existing online presence, you need to examine the sites and the profiles you've created about yourself, the ones created about you by others, and the sentiment of the various sites or discussions taking place about you, as well as their accuracy, weight, and importance.

Start by making a list of all the websites you've created and any other sites that carry your name. Most likely this includes your business URL and your various social media properties. Say your business sells refurbished computers and your website is called Refurbishedtek.com. (This name is fabricated.) Your Facebook profile might therefore be https://www.facebook.com/Refurbishtek, and on Twitter you might be known as https://twitter.com/refurbishtek. Make a list of all the social media sites you use (popular ones include Facebook, Twitter, Instagram, and Pinterest). Next, make a list of all the discussion boards and forums you participate in. (If you are a business, you may use your business name, but more likely a designated person will be posting and commenting on your business's behalf, identifying themselves as speaking on behalf of the organization.) Add to these any shopping sites such as Amazon.com or eBay, music sites such as Pandora or Last.fm, and other sites you might frequent.

After you complete the list of sites you know you participate in and are active on, start making a comprehensive list of all the places you're possibly mentioned online. The first thing to do is to put your business's name into search engines and see what comes up. While most people only check the first one or two pages on search engines (and assuming you end up finding something bad about you online, this can be a good thing), make the effort to look at the first 10 pages. Don't assume that what is listed as the top items on one search engine will be identical on all of them, which is why at a minimum you need to see what comes up on Google, Yahoo!, and Bing, and ideally also blekko and DuckDuckGo. And depending on whether there is a connection to your business or other relevant reason, check other country-specific ones as well such as Yandex, which is the leading search engine in Russia.

Make sure to remember to check the images and videos featured on search engines Google, Yahoo!, and Bing. It's also wise to check image-specific search engine Imagery,[49] photo-sharing sites Flickr and Photobucket, and websites such as Ask.com.[50] For videos, check out YouTube, Metacafe, Vimeo, Dailymotion, Viddler, Revver, and blip.tv.

In addition to checking the main social networking sites, naturally you also need to make a list of the discussion boards and forums that cover your particular industry. A good place to start is Big Boards,[51] which currently has more than 2,000 message boards in its database covering such diverse categories as computers, business, games and art, entertainment, health, science, and sports. Boardtracker[52] is a useful tool that enables you to search forums organized by category. (The basic functions are free, with advanced ones available with the paid plan.) You can also enter a search term such as "list of [industry or topic term] forums" into your favorite search engine to see which specific forums come up.

When conducting online searches, make sure to do so both while logged into and out of any Google products such as Gmail, Google calendar, or YouTube. You'll likely notice a considerable difference in the search results and can comprehensively see what others searching online find.

Consumer Review and Complaint Sites

You must look at consumer review sites as well. General ones include membership-based Angie's List, which covers more than 550 home repair and health care categories, and Epinions, a service of Shopping.com Inc., which covers a diverse range of products and services related to computers and the Internet, business and technology, electronics, gifts, and media. A must-check is online retailer Amazon.com, perhaps still best known for its book offerings, but also a leader in the sales of electronics and computers, digital games and software, movies, music, and a variety of other personal use and home products, which features a 5-star customer review system. The Better Business Bureau, which accredits businesses and enables consumers to register complaints, should be included into the mix. Industry-specific sites include Yelp, which covers restaurants and eating establishments, and TripAdvisor, which focuses on the travel industry and features reviews of hotels, resorts holiday rentals, and vacation packages. Vitals is an information source about doctors that enables consumers to post comments about physicians. Teacher review sites include RateMyteachers.com and RateMyProfessor.com.

Finally, don't skip online complaint sites. As mentioned previously, these can often reveal particularly important, albeit unpleasant, and hard-hitting criticism of which some may be defamatory, so this is a critical step to measure your digital footprint and online reputation. A non-exhaustive list includes Complaints Board, Pissed Consumer, iRipoff.com, and Ripoff Report, and specialized ones such as Unhappy Franchisee or Bitterwaitress.com. To find other industry- or job-specific complaint sites, you can enter the search term and then add a word such as "sucks" at the end, for example "engineerssuck.com," to see if something comes up.

The same process previously described applies when you check online for your organization's key employees or your own name. However, there are a few additional places you need to look. Make sure to enter the individual's name in people search directories and data aggregation sites such as:

- Spokeo at http://www.spokeo.com/
- PeopleFinders at http://www.peoplefinders.com/
- RapLeaf.com at http://www.rapleaf.com/
- Intelius http://www.intelius.com/
- US Search at http://www.ussearch.com
- iSearch at http://www.isearch.com/
- Pipl at http://pipl.com

Include in your search GovRecordsAccess (http://www.govrecordsaccess.com), which provides a list of all public records maintained by government agencies such as marriage and divorce records, warrant and arrest records, criminal records, and court records. From a purely practical position, the less demographic and similarly personal information about you online, the smaller the chance of someone using something against you, trying to impersonate you online, or physically locating and harassing or stalking you.

Local and Hyperlocal Sites

You also need to check local sites such as the comments sections of your hometown or regional newspaper for your name to see if someone may have written about you. Don't forget "hyper local" sites that focus on particular areas, communities, or neighborhoods. Despite their size, some of them have an impressive number of readers and also feature discussion forums that increase the possibility of you or your business being mentioned. West Seattle Blog, for example, has more than 1 million page views a month.[53]

Of particular importance are city-based sites such as Patch or Topix.com. Patch is "a community-specific news and information platform dedicated to providing comprehensive and trusted local coverage for individual towns and communities,"[54] whereas Topix.com describes itself as "the leading news community on the Web, connecting people to the information and discussions that matter to them in every U.S. town and city. A Top 10 online newspaper destination (comScore, June 2011), the site links news from 67,000 sources to 450,000 news topics."[55] Unfortunately, Topix has a history of serving as a fertile ground for gossip, venting, and online attacks against individuals, many of them by anonymous sources, so it is imperative for everyone to see if they've been on the receiving end of such actions.

You've now taken an inventory of where you're present online and where you are discussed. Now what? Well, now you need to measure the sentiment of what's said.

Sentiment Analysis

Sentiment analysis is the examining, measuring, and analyzing of feelings, opinions, and attitudes toward something or someone as presented online via text, video, and other means of communication. These communications can fall into three broad categories: positive, neutral, or negative. You likely want a predominantly positive sentiment, but there are instances in which a neutral one might be good as well, for example in situations in which your business has just come out of a public relations crisis and you've been hammered online or in the media. In cases like that, neutral sentiments seem like a breath of fresh air.

Communications can be further broken down by more specific groupings of emotions, for example excited, happy, and content on the positive end, and frustrated, sad, annoyed, or angry on the negative end. Certain words, phrases, or statements can be identified as having a positive meaning (love), a neutral one (indifference), a negative one (hate), reflecting a particular emotion such as frustration (the app doesn't work!), or anger (I just wasted an hour waiting to talk to the service tech!). By looking at these meanings, you get more nuanced insights into what is said about you. In addition, the intensity of the feelings communicated is also significant. It can alert you to individuals you may tap into as brand ambassadors (assuming they like your product or service), or those you need to keep a closer eye on (assuming they dislike your business).

Understanding the exact meaning of words is important, especially in the online realm in which unique terminology exists, where slang is rampant, and where using terms specific to particular situations or environments is part of the culture. Take the word "sick." As historically used, it refers either to the medical definition of being physically or mentally ill in some way, or it refers to the popular meaning of something being distressing, disturbing, or disgusting. However, the word "sick" is also increasingly used to reflect a positive meaning, with something called sick actually meaning it is cool, neat, or great.

Context is also critical and must be taken into consideration when measuring sentiment. For example, people admitting they were "sad" and cried while watching the newest drama in the movie theaters might be good, whereas saying they were "sad" that the comedy club routine wasn't funny would not be. Similarly, a negative statement about something relatively benign, for example a customer's insulting remark about your CEO's haircut, is considerably less concerning than criticism about your company's new cell phone design.

Your overall sentiment score on its own may offer a limited amount of information (unless you try to measure an increase or decrease over time), whereas benchmarking it against the percentage rating for your direct competitors or the entire industry gives it greater meaning.

The specific source making the statement about you or your business must also be carefully examined. For example, if the individual in question doesn't have a lot of online influence or the criticism comes from a lightly trafficked site, that's better than criticism coming from a powerful and heavily read website. And generally speaking, a one-time complaint by someone about your business is less damaging than being pounded by an individual who is a regular and motivated critic. However, if the person is angry about a particular issue and highly motivated to make as big a ruckus as possible, his complaint or criticism may become amplified and be picked up by others to the point where it snowballs into a much larger problem for you.

Another issue that can be extremely important to your online reputation and the management of online disputes is accuracy, namely the degree to which the statements about you and your business are correct and true. Again, depending on the content and context, you need to decide how much time and energy you want to focus on correcting any inaccuracies about yourself, your key executives, or your business. If someone states that you were married more than once and you're 20 years into your first marriage, perhaps that's not worth spending valuable time and effort on to set the record straight (even if it is a bit uncomfortable), whereas if someone claims that they heard you were unfaithful to your spouse or that your company's earnings are lower than you reported, that could have serious reputational, social, and legal repercussions. Determine the damage the false information might cause if it is heard and passed on by someone with a grudge against you or someone with a competitive interest, and make that a factor you look at when considering whether to go about trying to make corrections.

Depending on your business's unique requirements, you may decide to design and build your own sentiment analysis system and customize the data mining, sentiment classification, summarization elements, and visualization tools to your specific needs. However, perhaps you'd rather use the tools and services already on the market. Here are two to look at:

- **Clarabridge:** Sentiment and text analysis software that turns text-based content into quantitative and easily consumed reports, available at http://www.socialmention.com/.

- **Serendio:** A service that provides sentiment mining and analysis from social media and enterprise data sources, available at http://www.serendio.com/.

Also make sure to check out Gnip, available at http://gnip.com, which is a leading provider of raw social media data used by eight of the largest social media monitoring firms.

Many online and social media monitoring tools already have sentiment analysis tools built in, such as some of those mentioned in the "Measuring Your Existing Digital Footprint" section.

When measuring sentiment, remember that the accuracy of any automated tool won't be 100% percent. Humor or sarcasm, for example, are hard to measure without knowing the greater context, and an 80–85% accuracy rate is considered good. It's therefore wise to not rely exclusively on tools or services and instead also have an actual person review the findings, at a minimum giving greater attention to select statements that might have a negative bearing on your online reputation.

Creating a Strong Online Reputation

Okay, you've measured your existing digital footprint and the online sentiment of your name, brand, product names, and business and that of your key and high-profile executives. The next step is actively working to create a positive and strong online reputation, which hopefully you've already started doing. The key thing to remember is that YOU should be the one to build and control your online reputation, not someone else.

An important distinction needs to be made for businesses or people who have unique names and those who don't. If you are one of the thousands of Bob Smiths or Jane Smiths living today, carving out a unique online footprint will be more challenging (are you Bob Smith the computer programmer or Bob Smith the scientist?), but also reflect its own unique set of benefits. For example, negative information about you online stands a greater chance of getting buried among all information found about Bob or Jane Smith, but someone looking for you online may easily mistake you with the information found about another individual with the same name who has done something questionable or even dicey. Having a unique name reduces the likelihood of identity confusion, but also makes any questionable or negative information you posted or that someone has posted about you online much easier to find, and correspondingly harder to bury later. It's a trade-off.

In terms of your online identity, most likely your business already has a website and main URL reflecting its name. This can serve as the main source of information about you online.

As an individual you need to do the same—buy your domain name and set up a website or blog that you control and update, which can serve as the go-to destination for news, photos, contact information, and so forth about you. If you have a common name or share the name of a famous person, think about adding your middle initial or nickname to your personal URL.

Using the name Refurbishtek.com as in the previous example, make sure you purchase related domain names such as Refurbishtek.net, Refurbishtek.info, and Refurbishtek.biz to ensure someone doesn't try to misrepresent or hijack your identity. If they are available, buy the domains for variations or common misspellings of your name as well, such as Refurbishteck, Refurbishtec, or Refurbishtech, and direct searches for these URLs to your main website.

Adding subdomains is an easy way to extend your online footprint. A subdomain is a domain that is part of a larger and main website that contains special and unique content separate from the main site. Using the previous example, a subdomain might be support.Refurbishedtech.com or products.Refurbishedtech.com

Don't forget to buy domains that critics and haters might use to smear you. These can include [yourbusinessname]sucks.com (for example, Refurbishedteksucks.com) and all variations thereof (for example, Refurbishedteksucks.net) and Fake [yourbusinessname].com and its variations (for example, FakeRefurbishedtek.net). You may also want to buy the domain that contains the word "Facts," namely [yourbusinessname]facts.com (for example Refurbishedtekfacts.com) because this is increasingly used by critics and opponents and appears to be particularly popular in the political arena to counter the information candidates or sitting politicians share about themselves.

The same rules apply to you individually; purchase the major domain endings for your names, including those that represent any common nicknames you might have, as well as the domain for your last name if it is especially unique or famous (for example, if your name is Lisa Zavoriaer, buy Zavoriaer.com). Although you cannot purchase all possible domain name iterations someone might use to attack you, scooping up the main ones is a proactive step you can take to protect your name.

In addition to having a website or blog, also set up accounts on major social networking sites such as Facebook, Twitter, LinkedIn, Google+, MySpace, Flickr, YouTube, Bebo, Pinterest, and any others that are popular and of particular interest to your business or industry. Also consider joining websites such as question-and-answer aggregation site Quora or social information network Diigo. Carefully chose a username—make it something unique and identifying, preferably your or your business's full name—and consistently use it for all the sites you register with. This can give you greater name recognition and make it harder for someone else to try to impersonate you. After you choose your username, create a brief profile on all these sites, linking back to your website or blog. You do not need to be active on these sites (although the more you are, the greater the likelihood that the site with your name will rank prominently on the major search engines). Instead, the purpose is to lay claim to your online identity, which is a crucial step to manage your online reputation.

Another important benefit to having a presence on several sites is that this enables you to cross-link from one to the other, strengthening your ranking on search engines. For example, say you have a Google+ account. On the profile section of Google+, you can post the links to profiles you have on other sites, as well as links to your website or blog.

> *The ultimate goal is to be the one who owns the top properties that rank high in the search engines, whether directly through your own domains or via profiles on important social networking sites.*

If you're a business, consider getting listed in online directories, both the ones found on the major search engines and those relevant to your company and industry. Some possibilities include Ask.com, Yellowpages.com, Whitepages, Switchboard, CitySearch, Local.com, ThinkLocal, Mapquest, and BizJournals.com.

Another way to strengthen your online presence is by using contextual ads on news or other websites relevant to you or your business. It works this way: You sign up with a contextual advertising network (the overwhelming leader in the space is Google with its Google Adwords,[56] but Media.net[57] is hoping to make a bid for top spot), which then places display ads of your company on relevant websites or news stories. Here is a quick example: Say you are a provider of electronic educational games for children. The top parenting magazines are running holiday stories about the best toys parents can give their kids as gifts. You've signed up with an advertising network, and *Winning Parents* magazine, a client of the ad network, is running an article called "Want Your Kids to Have Fun and Get Smarter This Holiday Season? Here's a List of the Toys That Education Experts Recommend and Why." Links to your company website or products appear within the online article in contextually relevant locations, perhaps within the word "educational" or "game."

In times of crisis, such as when your business is attacked online, you can also buy online advertisements that appear next to more prominent organic searches that might be negative.

The Importance of Trust and Goodwill

Aside from some of the infrastructure and technical approaches, there are several additional practical and immensely important things you can do to strengthen your online reputation. One involves trust, the other goodwill.

Trust is built by doing what you say you will do, acting fairly toward others, being consistent, and apologizing and making things right when you mess up. Welcoming sincere and constructive feedback—and reacting as graciously as possible to harsh and perhaps unelegantly expressed criticism—also can go a long way.

That's how NMTW Community Credit Union[58] might have better handled a complaint by customer Chris Brogan, a *New York Times* bestselling author, entrepreneur, and marketing and social media expert with a Twitter following of more than 200,000. After having his account closed due to a brief negative balance, Brogan sent a message to the credit union's published email address, asking whether it wanted to lose a 20-year member instead of working with him to rectify the situation. When he didn't receive a reply, he left a comment on the credit union's Facebook page, which you can see in Figure 2.3: "You lost a 20-year member today. I emailed your info@ email address to forward the reason why to your president. Wishing you better in the future."[59] The next morning his comment received the following reply: "NMTW takes pride in its member service and we strive to add value to everyone's day. We regret that in your situation we were unable to assist you any further at the time of your branch visit. NMTW would like to thank you for bringing this to our attention and in doing so will prevent similar events in the future," to which Brogan commented in part, "Awesome auto response." Brogan was apparently angry enough about what he perceived to be a mishandling of his situation that he wrote an entire blog post dedicated to this issue on his influential website Chrisbrogan.com, "How Not to Manage a Brand's Social Presence," in which he took the credit union to task for mishandling his complaint and outlined several steps it could have taken to remedy the problem, among them taking the argument offline, apologizing for the experience, and reaching out to him to learn more,[60] which was retweeted several hundred times.

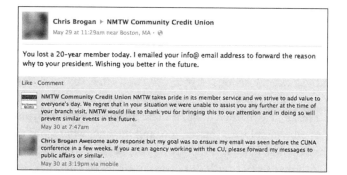

Figure 2.3   *Screenshot of NMTW's Facebook Page*

An example of taking ownership of your mistakes can be illustrated by a recent situation involving actor, director, and comedian Jason Alexander of sitcom *Seinfeld* fame. Alexander appeared on *The Late Show with Craig Ferguson* and made misguided jokes about the sport cricket (ones which he'd previously made in another country and which had apparently been well received), describing it as a "gay game...there's a lot of people wearing white...everybody breaks for tea in the middle...and then you just kinda run back-and-forth without any rhyme or reason."[61] He went on to explain that the reason he knew it was a "gay game" is because of the pitch which, "if you saw it in slow motion..." [and then proceeded to imitate the negative effeminate stereotype of a gay man], adding that "it's not like a manly baseball pitch, it's a queer British gay pitch." Alexander was quickly taken to task by the GLBT community and by many members of the public. Roughly a week later, he released a long, contrite statement on The Gay & Lesbian Alliance Against Defamation website,[62] which he also linked to from his Twitter account,[63] taking full responsibility for his words and apologizing for playing into negative and hurtful stereotypes. Although not all the feedback he received was positive, overwhelmingly the responses to his apology were along the lines of "Now THAT's how you apologize for something...Good job, Jason Alexander. I hope to be that gracious admitting my mistakes"[64], which you can see in Figure 2.4, and "As apologies go, this is pretty hard to fault."[65]

Figure 2.4   *Matthew Southworth's Tweet of June 4, 2012*

If you are a business, the actions of your CEO and other key executives are immensely important. As you saw earlier, having even one of them make an online mistake isn't just a personal screw-up, it's one that affects the company as well. But the actions of other employees matter, too, and the ones whose jobs require them to deal with the public (such as PR professionals) and customers (such as technical support or customer service representatives) must also ensure they deal with people honestly, openly, quickly, and fairly. Trust doesn't happen overnight, and it's not something you can simply demand people give you. Trust is *earned*, and when it is broken, all attempts must be made to *re-earn* it, which is a time-consuming, difficult endeavor with no guarantee of success.

Goodwill, meanwhile, is created by being generous with your time and knowledge, and by enthusiastically and authentically engaging with others on a regular and ongoing basis.

Although you'll likely invest much of your time and resources in managing your own online properties, participating in conversations elsewhere, such as one of the thousands of interest-based Facebook groups, shows that one of your goals is to sincerely give back to the community via contributions that don't carry a direct monetary payoff. Facebook has Pages and Groups connected by geography (the Washington, D.C., page is managed by Destination DC, the official Convention and Tourism Corporation for Washington, D.C., and has more than 290,000 likes[66]), by company (Apple Inc. has more than 6 million likes[67]), and industry (the Everyday Health, a provider of online health information, resources, tools, and news, has more than 250,000 likes[68]), among others.

Sharing some of your personality (as long as it doesn't involve oversharing or posting something highly controversial that would alienate your audience) brings an element of humanity to the picture that positively resonates with people. You can do this whether you are an individual or a business because even the latter is composed of individuals with their own unique interests and stories to tell. Think of how the Virgin Group benefits from founder Richard Branson's adventurous and colorful personality, which he shares via Twitter (Branson's Twitter account says, "Screw Business as Usual"[69]) and other communication tools.

Creating a network of online supporters, fans, and allies is also important. Publicly saying, "Thank You" to people who are fans of your service or products, and regularly acknowledging that your success is based upon their continued interest in your products or services, goes a long way to create goodwill. Then, if and when something bad happens online—and it likely will—the only questions are whether it is the result of outside forces or your own mistake or wrongdoing, and how damaging it is—these supporters and allies could make the difference between recovering relatively quickly or being torn to shreds without the ability to rehabilitate your reputation, business, or life.

Having built up goodwill with individuals and groups will increase your chances that they will come to your aid when the chips are down. How this can play out can often be seen on Facebook, where many company brands, nonprofits, and celebrities are active and have public profiles. A recent example illustrating the power of devoted supporters involved American actor and director Selena Gomez. Gomez is best known for her leading role on the Disney Channel television series "Wizards of Waverly Place" and for having been in a relationship with international pop star Justin Bieber. During one of their dates, Bieber allegedly got in a scuffle with a paparazzo who was blocking his car, preventing the two stars from leaving. The paparazzo filed a police report, and questions about Bieber's possible arrest were all over the gossip sites. Although a few days later a law enforcement source stated, "The photographer had no visible injuries and he didn't require any further medical attention when he went to the emergency room. The injuries that the photographer claims to have are rather unremarkable,"[70] the entire unpleasant incident nevertheless left the celebrities shaken. The day of the event Gomez wrote on her Facebook page, "THANKS [sic] YOU SO MUCH to my fans for always protecting me and being there for me. I can't thank you guys enough. I'm sorry I had to rush out. Love you guys."[71] Within just a few days her status update had been shared 498 times on Facebook, had received 4,734 comments (the vast majority of which were supportive along the lines of "We love you too Selena, we're always here to support you forever!" and "you are very much wellcome [sic] we will always be there for you") and had 30,412 likes. Imagine having this number of supporters come to your aid when you most need help!

If You Make a Mistake, Own It

If reputation problems occur through the business's or a key executive's wrong-doing or mistake, you need to immediately spring into action to try to minimize damage and reputation loss. Later parts of the book discuss specific conflict resolution skills and strategies, but for now keep in mind the following points: React quickly, take responsibility, be authentic, be forthcoming, and be honest. Figure 2.5 will help you easily remember what to do. Also, quickly squelch any false rumors and be open about perhaps not yet knowing all the facts or having all the answers to a problem or situation. In the online environment, in which information gets passed along at lightning speed, where rumors are rampant, and where critics and competitors are eager to take advantage of any weaknesses they see, you must keep the lines of communication open between you and your stakeholders, the public, and any others who have an interest in your success. Deciding if and under which circumstances to communicate with critics is another important consideration. Sometimes by reaching out to them directly, whether they are formal groups or simply passionate and vocal individuals, and offering to tell your side of the story, you can succeed in dialing down the criticism and attacks, and perhaps even turn them into future allies on issues of mutual interest.

Step 1:   React quickly
Step 2:   Take responsibility
Step 3:   Be Forthcoming

Remember: Always be authentic and honest

Figure 2.5 *What to Do if You Make a Mistake*

Monitoring Your Online Reputation

After you measure your existing digital footprint and make sure you have in place all the steps necessary to create a strong online reputation, the next step is to monitor your online reputation. In reality, whether or not you've previously had an online presence, you should have been regularly and consistently monitoring your name or your business's name online.

This monitoring should include, as mentioned earlier in the section on measuring your digital footprint, conducing ongoing checks for your name and any relevant variations, looking through the image search capabilities of the major search engines and checking video sites, and checking the comments on blogs, discussion boards, forums, and social networking sites and others.

When conducting searches on the main search engines, look for your business's name, those of key employees, and your own name, as well as additional terms that might reveal weaknesses and vulnerabilities, such as "[your company name] + complaints," "[your company name] + lies," "[your company name] + hate," or "[your company name] + reviews."

One of the easiest things you should do is set up a free Google Alerts[72] account, which you can see in Figure 2.6, which is a service whereby you receive email updates of the latest relevant Google results based on your queries. You select the search query and the result type ("everything," "news," "blogs," "video," "discussions," or "books"—the author recommends choosing "everything"), the frequency ("as-it-happens," "once a day," or "once a week"—the author recommends choosing at a minimum "once a day"), and how many alerts you want to receive ("only the best results" or "all results"—the author recommends "all results" unless you find that you receive a lot of inapplicable ones). Google Alerts, as the name indicates, provides results for only the Google search engine and not others.

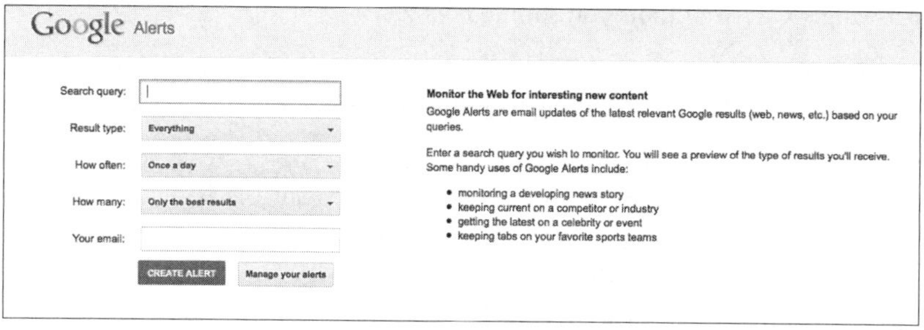

Figure 2.6   *Screenshot of Google Alerts dialog box*

As mentioned earlier, it's wise to regularly look at the consumer review and complaint sites to see if you or your business are mentioned. TheSqueakyWheel.com, for example, has a Browse Complaints feature that enables you to search for different types of complaints (categories include All Types of Complaints, Bait and Switch complaints, Broken Promises complaints, Poor Quality complaints, Poor Service complaints, Price Unfairly Changed complaints, Rude Employee complaints, or Other complaints) within Canada, Mexico, South Africa, and the United States. Because disgruntled individuals sometimes post on more than one site as a way to try to negatively affect a company's or individual's reputation, keep your eyes open to see if any new complaint sites have been launched in addition to the ones previously mentioned. Also remember that contents of these sites can be easily shared with others. TheSqueakyWheel.com has a Facebook "share" button that, in theory at least, enables anyone reading a complaint to share it with Facebook's 800 million users. Also check out sites that focus on particular professions (examples include RateMyProfessors.com or RateMDs.com) or industries (such as the contractor review Kudzu.com, which enables people to both find and post reviews on everything from general contractors to cleaners, electricians, and movers) if they are relevant to you.

Using Monitoring Tools

If you are simply monitoring your personal online presence, there is a good likelihood you can do it by regularly checking the major search engines, signing up for Google Alerts, and keeping on top of what's said about you on the leading social networking sites. But if you are well known in your online community or in your field, are influential, are for some reason considered controversial, or are a public figure, even a lesser well-known one, you should consider using one of the numerous online monitoring tools available today. These tools vary from easy-to-use and free ones, to enterprise-level tools that require a considerable monthly investment. Following are a list of tools you should consider:

- **Social Mention:** A free, real-time social media and analysis platform, available at http://www.socialmention.com/.

- **Mention:** A free monitoring tool that enables you to create alerts for your name, company, brand, or industry, available at https://en.mention.net/ (a greater number of tracked mentions are available with one of the four professional plans).

- **CustomScoop:** A customizable news and social media monitoring tool available at http://www.cAustomscoop.com/ (available at five different price levels).

- **Trackur:** An online reputation and social media monitoring tool available at http://www.trackur.com (available at four different price levels).

- **Radian6 Social Media Monitoring:** A comprehensive, enterprise-level social media monitoring and engagement platform available at http://www.radian6.com/ (available at four different price levels).

- **Attensity:** A provider of social analytics and engagement solutions available at http://www.attensity.com.

- **Simplify360:** A social media management platform available at http://simplify360.com/.

- **Visible Technologies:** A social media monitoring, analytics, and services platform for enterprises available at http://www.visibletechnologies.com.

- **HootSuite:** A free social media dashboard for Twitter with simple analytics available at http://hootsuite.com/dashboard (advanced analytics available with paid membership).

- **Followerwonk:** A free tool that enables you to search, compare, analyze and track Twitter followers, available at http://followerwonk.com/.

If none of these monitoring tools work for you, there is a robust list of more than 300 tools, along with descriptions, which Nathan Gilliat maintains at http://socialmediaanalysis.com/.

Occasionally you might need outside help and can turn to professional reputation management services firms. There are several to choose from, each with their strengths and competencies. Reputation.com is a leader in the field and definitely worth checking out. (The prices for basic services are available on the company's website, with the cost for customized services available upon request.) Others to look at and compare include Reputation Changer (http://www.reputationchanger.com, pricing available upon request) and Reputation Hawk (http://www.reputationhawk.com, pricing available upon request). For those interested in a do-it-yourself and free service specializing in assisting individuals, look at BrandYourself (http://brandyourself.com/), which takes the position that "people should be able to control their own online reputation, without spending thousands on an online reputation company."[73] (BrandYourself co-founder Pete Kistler personally understands the serious harm that negative and false online information can have on individuals. According to his company bio, in 2008 he had "an online identity crisis" after discovering that he was being mistaken for a drug dealer with the same name. This experience, and the hope of helping others avoid some of his anguish, led him to create BrandYourself.[74])

For companies, reputation monitoring is something that should be at the top of all employees' lists. The organization's communications team, often composed of public relations and marketing professionals, as well as social media experts, naturally is at the frontlines when it comes to seeing and reacting to critical online issues and is therefore most commonly tasked with monitoring and responding. However, given the importance of online reputation management, everyone in the executive suite, as well as division or department leaders, must take an active interest. In addition, although not traditionally a responsibility of the legal team, in today's global online environment with its constant risk of irreparably damaging online attacks, and the associated possibility of having to take appropriate legal action, legal counsel should be a part of the designated "reputation management" team.

Endnotes

1. Biography of Hasan M. Elahi. Associate Professor of Art at University of Maryland. Link: http://www.art.umd.edu/faculty/helahi/

2. Hasan M. Elahi, "You Want to Track Me? Here You Go, F.B.I.," *The New York Times*, October 29, 2011. Link: http://www.nytimes.com/2011/10/30/opinion/sunday/giving-the-fbi-what-it-wants.html?_r=1

3. Hasan M. Elahi's websites are Tracking Transience and Tracking Transience v2.0. Links: http://trackingtransience.net/ and http://www.elahi.umd.edu/track/

4. Hasan Elani, "FBI, here I am!" TEDGlobal 2011, July 2011. Link: http://www.ted.com/talks/hasan_elahi.html

5. Jessica Guynn, "It's Justin, Live! All Day, All Night!" *San Francisco Chronicle*, March 30, 2007. Link: http://www.sfgate.com/cgi-bin/article.cgi?f=/c/a/2007/03/30/MNG8OOUQI81.DTL&ao=all

6. Christopher Steiner, "The Disruptor in The Valley," *Forbes*, October 20, 2010. Link: http://www.forbes.com/forbes/2010/1108/best-small-companies-10-y-combinator-paul-graham-disruptor.html

7. Somini Sengupta, "On Facebook, 'Likes' Become Ads," May 31, 2012, *The New York Times*. Link: http://www.nytimes.com/2012/06/01/technology/so-much-for-sharing-his-like.html

8. Nick Bergus, "How I became Amazon's pitchman for a 55-gallon drum of personal lubricant on Facebook," Nick Bergus, February 23, 2012. Link: http://nbergus.com/2012/02/how-i-became-amazons-pitchman-for-a-55-gallon-drum-of-personal-lubricant-on-facebook/

9. Polly Sprenger, "Sun on Privacy: 'Get Over It'" *Wired*, January 26, 1999. Link: http://www.wired.com/politics/law/news/1999/01/17538

10. Marshall Kirkpatrick, "Facebook's Zuckerberg Says The Age of Privacy Is Over," RedWriteWeb, January 9, 2010. Link: http://www.readwriteweb.com/archives/facebooks_zuckerberg_says_the_age_of_privacy_is_ov.php

11. Weber Shandwick, "The Company behind the Brand: In Reputation We Trust - CEO Spotlight," May 2, 2012.

12. "CEO Reputation Greatly Impacts Consumer Images of Companies, Weber Shandwick Survey Finds," May 2, 2012. Link: http://www.webershandwick.com/Default.aspx/AboutUs/PressReleases/2012/CEOReputationGreatlyImpactsConsumerImagesof CompaniesWeberShandwickSurveyFinds

13. Classmates.com claims it provides access to "more than 100,000 high school yearbooks" in the United States dating back to the 1920s. Link: http://www.classmates.com/about/

14. Ryan Hunt, "Hiring managers share why they screen with social media, and explain what they're looking for in candidates' profiles," PRNewswire, April 18, 2012. Link: http://www.prnewswire.com/news-releases/thirty-seven-percent-of-companies-use-social-networks-to-research-potential-job-candidates-according-to-new-careerbuilder-survey-147885445.html

15. CareerBuilder Infographic, "Employers are Scoping Out Job Candidates on Social Media - But What Are They Finding?" 2012. Link: http://www.careerbuilder.com/JobPoster/Resources/page.aspx?pagever=2012SocialMedia&template=none &sc_cmp2=JP_Infographic_2012SocialMedia

16. Frequently Asked Questions, Social Intelligence. Link: http://www.socialintel.com/faqs/

17. Social Intelligence Hiring, Social Intelligence. Link: http://www.socialintel.com/social-media-employment-screening/process/

18. Matt Hohan, "I Flunked My Social Media Background Check. Will You?" Gizmodo, July 7, 2011, Gizmodo. Link: http://gizmodo.com/5818774/this-is-a-social-media-background-check

19. Emil Protalinski, "Maryland first to ban employers asking for your Facebook password," ZDNet, April 11, 2012. Link: http://www.zdnet.com/blog/facebook/maryland-first-to-ban-employers-asking-for-your-facebook-password/11674?tag=content;siu-container

20. Meredith Curtis, "Want A Job? Password, Please!" Blog of Rights, ACLU, February 18, 2012. Link: http://www.aclu.org/blog/technology-and-liberty/want-job-password-please

21. "Kaplan Test Prep Infographic Illustrates the Use of Social Media and Google in the Law School, Business School and College Admissions Processes" Kaplan Test Prep, March 19, 2012 via BusinessWire. Link: http://www.businesswire.com/news/home/20120319005926/en/Kaplan-Test-Prep-Infographic-Illustrates-Social-Media

22. "Checking Applicants' Digital Trails: A Growing Trend in Admissions," Kaplan Test Prep, March 19, 2012. Link: http://www.kaptest.com/oneoff/socialmediainfographic.jhtml

23. Taylor Jennings, Twitter profile accessed on May 20, 2012. Link: http://twitter.com/#!/TaylorJennings_

24. Taylor Jennings, 12:00 a.m. May 20, 2012 tweet. Link: http://twitter.com/#!/TaylorJennings_/status/204074065722486784

25. Paul Bentley, "Just like his heroes in Washington: Student leader in text scandal after tweeting about freshman's breasts," MailOnline, September 12, 2011. Link: http://www.dailymail.co.uk/news/article-2036538/Student-leader-faces-impeachment-tweeting-freshman-s-breasts.html

26. Paul Bentley, "Just like his heroes in Washington: Student leader in text scandal after tweeting about freshman's breasts," MailOnline, September 12, 2011. Link: http://www.dailymail.co.uk/news/article-2036538/Student-leader-faces-impeachment-tweeting-freshman-s-breasts.html

27. Brad Wood, "Impeachment to proceed, Kressel faces removal from office," CisternYard.com, September 8, 2011. Link: http://site.cisternyard.com/2011/09/08/impeachment-to-proceed-kressel-faces-removal-from-office/

28. "Checking Applicants' Digital Trails: A Growing Trend in Admissions," Kaplan Test Prep, March 19, 2012. Link: http://www.kaptest.com/oneoff/socialmediainfographic.jhtml

29. Viva_La_Ghissy (Twitter name of GhisLane Nunez), 4:56 p.m. May 19, 2012 tweet. Link: http://twitter.com/#!/GhislaneN/status/203967415581802497

30. Melissa Petro, "The 'Hooker Teacher' tells all," Salon, May 4, 2011. Link: http://www.salon.com/2011/05/05/hooker_teacher_what_i_was_thinking/

31. John Schwartz, "A Legal Battle: Attitude vs. Rules of the Bar," *The New York Times*, September 12, 2009. Link: http://www.nytimes.com/2009/09/13/us/13lawyers.html?_r=1&hp

32. Complaint, Before The Hearing Board of the Illinois Attorney Registration And Disciplinary Commission, In the Matter of: KRISTINE ANN PESHEK, Attorney-Respondent, No. 6201779, FILED - August 25, 2009. Link: https://www.iardc.org/09CH0089CM.html

33. Bob Segall, "Trooper resigns after Facebook controversy," 13 WTHR Indiana, June 18, 2009. Link: http://www.wthr.com/story/10552361/trooper-resigns-after-facebook-controversy

34. Adrianne Jeffries, "As Banks Start Nosing Around Facebook and Twitter, the Wrong Friends Might Just Sink Your Credit," Betabeat, December 13, 2011. Link: http://betabeat.com/2011/12/13/as-banks-start-nosing-around-facebook-and-twitter-the-wrong-friends-might-just-sink-your-credit/?show=all

35. "What is Lendoo?" Lendoo. Link: https://www.lenddo.com/pages/what_is_lenddo

36. "Surfing for Details: German Agency to Mine Facebook to Access Creditworthiness," Spiegel Online, June 7, 2012. Link: http://www.spiegel.de/international/germany/german-credit-agency-plans-to-analyze-individual-facebook-pages-a-837539.html

37. "Depressed woman loses benefits over Facebook photos," CBC News, November 21, 2009. Link: http://www.cbc.ca/news/canada/montreal/story/2009/11/19/quebec-facebook-sick-leave-benefits.html

38. Michael Arrington, "This Daniel Guy Is definitely Getting Fired," Uncrunched, February 26, 2012. Link: http://uncrunched.com/2012/02/26/this-daniel-guy-is-definitely-getting-fired/

39. Corey Flintoff, "Viral Images, The Military's recurring Nightmare," NPR, January 12, 2012. Link: http://www.npr.org/2012/01/12/145117940/viral-images-the-militarys-recurring-nightmare

40. Sarah Kessler, "Chrysler's Twitter Account Accidently Drops the F-Bomb [UPDATED]" Mashable, March 9, 2011. Link: http://mashable.com/2011/03/09/chrysler-drops-the-f-bomb-on-twitter/

41. Mark Cina, "Gilbert Gottfried Fired as Aflak Duck After Japan Tweets," *The Hollywood Reporter*, March 14, 2011. Link: http://www.hollywoodreporter.com/news/gilbert-gottfried-fired-as-aflac-167382

42. Matt Stopera, "The 10 Worst Gilbert Gottfried Tsunami Jokes," BuzzFeed, March 14, 2011. Link: http://www.buzzfeed.com/mjs538/the-10-worst-gilbert-gottfried-tsunami-jokes

43. "Morgan Stanley Undervalued Dangdang's U.S. IPO, Chinese Company's CEO Says," Bloomberg News, January 17, 2011. Link: http://www.bloomberg.com/news/2011-01-17/li-tweet-says-morgan-stanley-undervalued-dangdang-in-272-million-u-s-ipo.html

44. Gus Lubin, "CEO Of Chinese Amazon Flips Out In Twitter Fight With Alleged Morgan Stanley Banker," Business Insider, January 18, 2011. Link: http://www.businessinsider.com/dangdang-li-guoqing-morgan-stanley-sina-2011-1?op=1

45. "I will write up to 3 negative reviews for you with 3 different profiles against your competition for $10" tenrr.com. Link: http://www.tenrr.com/Advertising/904/write-up-to-3-negative-reviews-for-you-with-3-different-profiles-against-your-competition via "Tweet Revenge: Consumers Wage Cyber War on Companies" *The Fiscal Times*, November 3, 2011. Link: http://www.thefiscaltimes.com/Articles/2011/11/03/Tweet-Revenge-Consumers-Wage-Cyber-War-on-Companies.aspx#page1

46. "Fake Positive Online Consumer Reviews Taint Review Sites' Credibility" New Release by Dalfort Media via PRLog, April 16, 2012. Link: http://prlog.org/11850695

47. "EPIC Obtains New Documents on DHS Media Monitoring, Urges Congress to Suspend Program," epic.org, February 23, 2012. Link: http://epic.org/2012/02/epic-obtains-new-documents-on-.htm

48. Analyst's Desktop Binder, Department of Homeland Security National Operations Center Media Monitoring Capability Desktop Reference Binder 2011.

49. Imagery. Link: http://elzr.com/imagery/about

50. Ask.com. Link: http://www.ask.com/pictureslanding

51. Big Boards. Link: http://www.big-boards.com/

52. Boardtracker. Link: www.boardtracker.com/

53. Alex Salkever, "In 2012: Local Loyalty Flameout, 2nd Wave of Hyperlocal News Sites, Street Fight," January 6, 2012. Link: http://streetfightmag.com/2012/01/06/ alexs-three-predictions-for-2012/

54. Patch, "What is Patch?" Link: http://www.patch.com/about

55. Topix, "About Topix." Link: http://www.topix.com/topix/about

56. Google Adwords. Link: www.adwords.google.com/

57. media.net. Link: http://media.net/about-us.php

58. NMTW Community Credit Union website. Link: https://www.nmtw.org/

59. NMTW Community Credit Union's Facebook page, comment by Chris Brogan on May 29, 2012 at 1:29 p.m. Link: https://www.facebook.com/NMTWCCU/ posts/10150858101758386

60. Chris Brogan, "How Not to Manage a Brand's Social Presence," Chrisbrogan.com, June 4, 2012. Link: http://www.chrisbrogan.com/how-not-to-manage-a-brands-social-presence

61. The Late Show with Craig Ferguson, May 25, 2012. Link: http://www.youtube.com/ watch?v=Nb1WzhD3NTU

62. Matt Kane, "Actor Jason Alexander Apologizes For Jokes Made on CBS' The Late Late Show," gladd.com, June 2, 2012. Link: http://www.glaad.org/blog/actor-jason-alexander-apologizes-jokes-made-cbs-late-late-show

63. Jason Alexander's @IJasonAlexander's Twitter account, tweet dated June 3, 2012 at 12:06 a.m. Link: https://twitter.com/IJasonAlexander/status/209148978707705856

64. Tweet by Matthew Southworth @mattsouthworth on June 4, 2012 at 12:37 a.m. Link: https://twitter.com/mattsouthworth/status/209730651392458752

65. Tweet by Shaun Usher @LettersOfNote on June 4, 2012 at 2:07 a.m. Link: https:// twitter.com/LettersOfNote/status/209572038455730177

66. Washington, D.C. Facebook page. Link: https://www.facebook.com/washingtondc

67. Apple Inc. Facebook page. Link: https://www.facebook.com/pages/Apple-Inc/ 137947732957611

68. Everyday Health Facebook page. Link: https://www.facebook.com/everydayhealth

69. Richard Brandon's Twitter account. Link: http://twitter.com/richardbranson

70. Christopher Rogers, "Justin Bieber Paparazzo Assault Accuser Left With 'No Visible Injuries,'" Hollywood Life by Bonnie Fuller, May 31, 2012. Link: http://www. hollywoodlife.com/2012/05/31/justin-bieber-photographer-fight-new-evidence/

71. Selena Gomez's Facebook page, 3:30 p.m. May 27, 2012. Link: https://www.facebook. com/Selena/posts/10150864063665975

72. Google Alerts. Link: http://www.google.com/alerts

73. "About Us," BrandYourself.com. Link: http://brandyourself.com/info/about

74. Pete Kistler's BrandYourself profile. Link: http://petekistler.brandyourself.com/

3

The Different Types of Conflicts You'll Encounter Online

Whether You're a Global Giant or a Private Individual, You Can't Escape Online Conflict

Imagine you're fast food giant McDonald's and are launching a new feel-good campaign to let consumers know about the company's commitment to quality ingredients.[1] Part of this campaign involves using promoted tweets with two separate hashtags, #MeetTheFarmers and #McDStories. At first things go as planned, but then, suddenly, they turn terribly wrong. Twitter users decide to use #McDStories to vent their dislike of your products, and you find yourself in a Twitter storm wondering how to regain control. Your hashtags have been turned into "bashtags."[2]

The criticism and attacks against the Fortune 500 company ranged from people who said they had direct experience with how bad things were behind the scenes at McDonald's ("Dude, I used to work for McDonald's. The #McDStories I could tell would raise your hair"[3]), those who said they got sick from the food ("Ate McD all week long. Then got a stoMAC-disease! #McDStories"[4]) and those, like the one in Figure 3.1, who criticized the company for contributing to animal cruelty (McDonald's = McCruelty. Try Veg!"[5]). Other tweets, such as the one in Figure 3.2, expressed their dislike by being as disgusting as possible. ("I haven't been to McDonalds in years because I'd rather eat my own diarrhea."[6])

May
@Alice_2112
Follow
McDonald's = McCruelty. Try Veg!
#McDStories
Reply Retweet Favorite
9:41 PM - 23 Jan 12 via web · Embed this Tweet

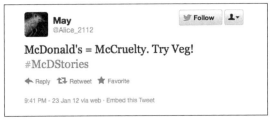

Figure 3.1 *Alice_2112's tweet of January 23, 2012*

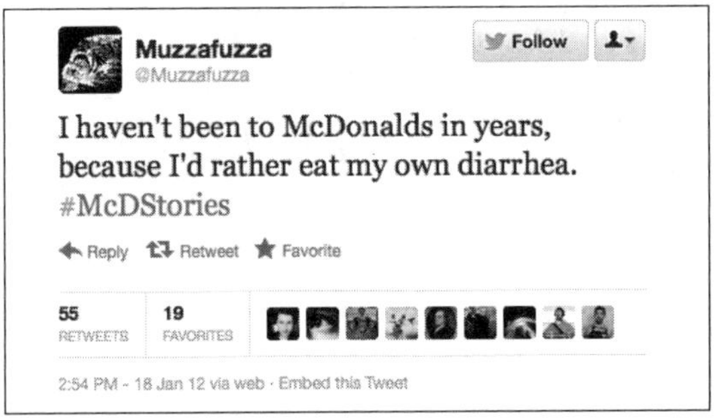

Muzzafuzza
@Muzzafuzza
Follow
I haven't been to McDonalds in years, because I'd rather eat my own diarrhea.
#McDStories
Reply Retweet Favorite
55 RETWEETS
19 FAVORITES
2:54 PM - 18 Jan 12 via web · Embed this Tweet

Figure 3.2 *Muzzafuzza's tweet of January 18, 2012*

Elizabeth Rizo was at the top of the world. She'd recently been crowned Ms. Planet Beach International 2010, winning the model search contest of the world's largest automated spa franchise, when her life unraveled. After topless digital photos taken during a private photo shoot years earlier surfaced on gossip website TheDirty.com, she lost her $100,000 modeling contract and feared her career would never recover.[7] Appearing together on "The Dr. Phil Show," Rizo pleaded with TheDirty.com creator Nik Richie, whose real name is Hooman Karamian, to remove the images, but Richie bluntly admitted that "when someone Googles Liz, I want them to come to my site."[8] He also made it clear he doesn't take responsibility for the comments left on his site, remarking that his readers can post whatever they want, nice or not.[9]

Examples of these comments include statements like "This bitch is stupid as hell. She deserves all the cards that have been dealt to her. She took naked pictures...they got out.... Get over yourself you stupid slut.... YOU ARE NOT SPECIAL. This shit happens daily. I hope you never make another dollar in your life from model/acting/pretending to be famous. DIE."[10] and "She's all fake hair, fake tan, and stuffed push up bra and hard tennis ball boobs. Without that she would be a dog. Now she's just a wannabe. Just picture her without it. Nothing special."[11]

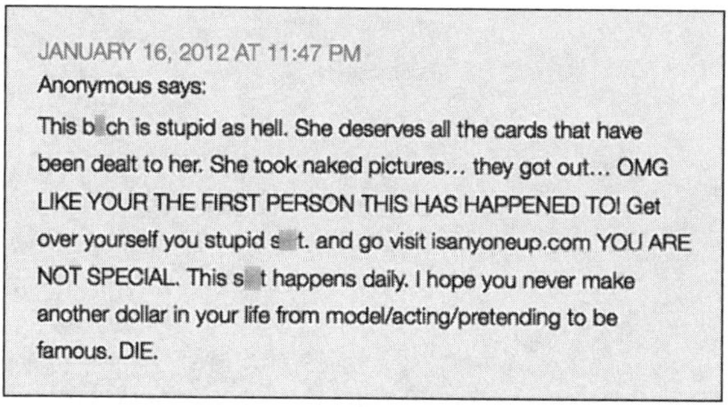

> JANUARY 16, 2012 AT 11:47 PM
>
> Anonymous says:
>
> This b■ch is stupid as hell. She deserves all the cards that have
> been dealt to her. She took naked pictures… they got out… OMG
> LIKE YOUR THE FIRST PERSON THIS HAS HAPPENED TO! Get
> over yourself you stupid s■t. and go visit isanyoneup.com YOU ARE
> NOT SPECIAL. This s■t happens daily. I hope you never make
> another dollar in your life from model/acting/pretending to be
> famous. DIE.

Figure 3.3 *Anonymous Comment on TheDirty.com of January 16, 2012*

How Many Different Types of Online Conflicts Are There?

As discussed in previous chapters, there's no shortage of online conflicts. In fact, because the number of people who are active online is increasing, the likelihood that the total number of conflicts will continue to rise is high. But what types of conflicts are there? And who are they between? That's what you'll look at now.

As you can see in Figure 3.4, there are numerous permutations the parties to an online dispute can take, but many of these different groupings can overlap. For example, one-on-one conflict can take place in a private setting and involve people who know each other, or can take place in a public online environment between people who don't know each other. Similarly, conflict can take place publicly between several people who already know each other, or can take place privately between people who don't have a preexisting relationship and don't know each other.

One-on-One Conflict

Probably the most common type of online conflict is one-on-one. Because of their interpersonal nature, the emotions associated with them can become intense. Furthermore, with the focus just on two people, there is a strong likelihood of falling into the trap of overly personalizing the dispute. If the dispute becomes public, this increases the hope of the two parties to save face — who wants to look bad in front of the world? Within this category there are several variations.

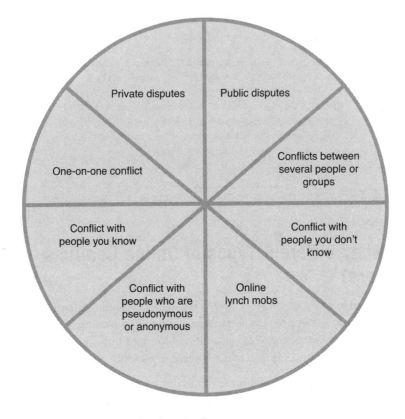

Figure 3.4 *Permutations of Online Conflicts*

One-on-One Conflict Between Individuals with a Prior Relationship

One variation of one-on-one conflicts involves individuals who have a prior existing relationship that may be personal, professional, or a combination of both. An example of this type of conflict is an extreme case involving a 2012 double murder in Tennessee. Billie Jean Hayworth and her fiancé Billy Payne Jr. had experienced problems with Jenelle Potter and her family in the past, even going so far as filing a criminal complaint against Potter. But it was Hayworth's decision to "defriend" Potter on Facebook (in other words, remove Potter from her list of friends and contacts on Facebook) that set tragedy into motion. The act so enraged Potter's father and boyfriend that they went to Hayworth's home, shot her and her fiancé Billy Payne Jr., slashed Payne's throat, and left their infant son an orphan.[12] The two killers have now been charged with first-degree murder. Although it's obvious that the Potters had serious anger management issues that manifested in violent and criminal ways, the public snub, which took place on the most popular social networking site in history, was a key factor in the rage-filled outburst that claimed two lives. This sad case emphasizes that what happens online doesn't occur in a vacuum and instead can have frightening real-world consequences.

A second disturbing example of one-on-one conflict resulted in arson and involved then Navy Fire Controlman 2nd Class Petty Officer Russell Tavares and John G. Anderson. The two men got into an online dispute that started on a picture-sharing website in which both actively participated in using pseudonyms.[13] The men insulted each other online, whereupon Anderson posted a digitally altered photo of Tavares standing under a "Revenge of the Nerds" sign looking like a skinny boy in high-water pants holding a gun and a laptop. Outraged, Tavares searched for and found Anderson's real name and address online. He proceeded to drive the 1,300 miles from his post in Virginia to Anderson's home in Texas, all the while posting online photos of the state welcome signs he passed on his way there. When he arrived, he lit fire to Anderson's trailer, causing extensive damage and injuring Anderson. Tavares is now in jail serving a 7-year sentence. Anderson, who claims he continued to be harassed online after the attack, later said, "I didn't think anybody was stupid enough to try to kill anybody over an Internet fight."[14] This case shows that it's important to remember that mocking and aggressive online behavior can easily morph into serious, no-holds-barred strife.

A third example illustrating this type of one-on-one conflict involved two men who were active in an online chat room about Islam, where their interaction resulted in one of them insulting the other online.[15] Paul Gibbons accused John Jones of spreading rumors about him and, seeking to vindicate his name, used information he found online to locate Jones's home address. He then drove 70 miles to his opponent's house to confront and attack him with a pickax handle. Jones received injuries to his hands, head and neck, but survived. His partner and children had been at home at the time of the attack.

Fortunately the incidences of online disagreements culminating in physical attacks are relatively infrequent when compared to those resulting in reputational harm and psychological devastation, but they do show what can happen when emotions get out of control and people decide to transfer their web-based conflicts to the "real" world.

One-on-One Conflict Between Individuals Who Are Known to Each Other

Another variation of one-on-one disputes involves people who are known to each other but don't have a prior relationship. One such public example involved the daughter of former General Motor's CEO Fritz Henderson. Henderson left GM in December 2009 amid concerns by the company's board that not enough progress had been made in stabilizing GM's financial situation after the U.S. government's bailout of the automaker. Shortly after Henderson's separation was announced in the media, the automotive industry gossip blog Jalopnik reported that Henderson's daughter Sarah allegedly posted a message on GM's public Facebook page with these choice words about GM's new CEO Ed Whitacre:

> "HE F**KING GOT ASKED TO STEP DOWN ALL OF YOU F**KING IDIOTS. IM FRITZ'S F**KING DAUGHTER, AND HE DID NOT F**KING RESIGN. WHITACRE IS A SELFISH PIECE OF SHIFT [sic][S**T], WHO CARES ABOUT HIMSELF AND NOT THE F**KING COMPANY. HAVE FUN WITH GM, I HOPE TO NEVER BUY FROM THIS GOD FORESAKEN COMPANY EVERY AGAIN [sic]. F**K ALL OF YOU."[16]

The post was subsequently removed (by whom exactly is unknown, and how long it actually remained on GM's Facebook page is unclear), [17] but it ended up being there sufficiently long enough to draw what surely must have been negative and unwanted attention to the Henderson family.

An additional example of an online dispute between two people who know each other but don't have a prior relationship concerned a New York University student who was applying for a Wall Street summer analyst position. As is common, he shared his resume and cover letter with interviewers.[18] Unfortunately the cover letter, which was written in an overly confident style, was forwarded by a Bank of America Merrill Lynch director to his entire team. It apparently wasn't enough for this handful of people to privately make fun of the student. Instead, the letter and resume were passed along to more than a dozen other investment banking and accounting firms.

Eventually they were seen by employees at Goldman Sachs, Morgan Stanley, Nomura, Citi, Deutsche Bank, PricewaterhouseCoopers, KPMG, Wells Fargo, Keefe, Bruyette & Woods, Perella Weinberg Partners, and Barclays Capital.

Ultimately the story made it online, and the individual was mocked by numerous readers, with no opportunity for the student to pull back his material and cease the mocking. On Yahoo!, one of the media outlets where the story appeared, there were more than 8,000 comments, many of them along the lines of, "The letter writer is a nut job. He deserves to have his letter passed around and laughed at"[19] and, "He sounds like an arrogant prick."[20] Interestingly, however, some of the comments identified the reputational hits the investment banks might take. One person noted that "What a monumental bunch of jerks these 'interviewers' are. To pass on something like this to everyone they know for the sake of ridicule is beyond wrong. Those who are in the banking and investment business have no ethics anyway so this kind of treatment of an applicant should come as no surprise."[21] Someone else wrote, "So...basically poor college kid tries hard to apply for a job, and these rich corporate a-holes not only make fun of him, but pass it along to others, so they can laugh at the kid...these are the people running our banks?"[22]

One-on-One Conflict Between Individuals with Only a Superficial Prior Relationship

A third variation of one-on-one conflict exists where the individuals are not close other than in the most cursory or superficial sense, perhaps simply as Twitter "followers" or Facebook "friends." Friends by this definition aren't actually friends, but simply people connected on Facebook via one of the social networking site's name designations.

An example of this involved WUSA veteran TV reporter Andrea McCarren, who reported about a Washington D.C. liquor store that sold alcohol to underage drinkers.[23] Her story resulted in email and Facebook attacks against her by parents and students who were livid over her exposé of illegal drinking. It also led to Facebook attacks against her children by their classmates. McCarren's response was to transfer coverage of the story to her colleague and stay off-air for a week. As noted by Mike Cavender, executive director of the Radio Television Digital News Association, what makes this incident stand out is the aggressiveness with which the television viewers expressed themselves toward a local TV journalist.[24]

Another example is one that involves matters of the heart that should have remained private. It concerned a dating situation in which a young man named Dave, who used the Match.com dating service, created a spreadsheet he'd made to keep track of women he was interested in. He shared it with a young lady named Arielle who topped his list.[25] In a move that said just as much about her willingness to mock people who make a mistake as about the man's tendency toward being overly analytical about his romantic life, the 26-year-old woman subsequently shared the spreadsheet with several of her friends. The story went viral and made the rounds on online gossip and news sites. When contacted for a response, Dave said, "my comments [about the women on the spreadsheet] aren't malicious or mean. This was an honest attempt to stay organized," adding that sending the information was "an extraordinarily dumb decision" and that the day the story broke was "the worst day of his life."[26]

Conflicts Between Several People or Groups

Probably the second most common type of online conflict is between several people or groups. In terms of potential volatility, there's an important distinction between a dispute involving two individuals and a dispute between several people.

The latter can careen out of control much quicker. The false courage of those emboldened by the strength of numbers is a leading factor in these types of disputes, as is the infrequent demand for, or often complete absence of, accountability required of the online transgressors for their online attacks. And as with the one-on-one conflict category, here, too, there are several variations.

Conflicts Between Several People or Groups Who Share a Common Identity

One variation involves conflicts between people who share a common group or community identity. Recurring incidences of this take place in the political arena and are especially prevalent in the United States among conservative Republicans and liberal Democrats. Two recent examples involving Andrew Breitbart illustrate this point. Breitbart, a conservative writer and publisher who was a polarizing figure both revered and despised for his no-holds-barred criticism of Democrats, sent several distasteful tweets shortly after the death of Senator Edward Kennedy was announced. Among them were the statements that "Kennedy was a special pile of human excrement"[27] and "he was a f@#$er. a big ass motherf@#$er."[28] When Breitbart died in the Spring 2012, his detractors returned the favor, tweeting messages such as "Andrew Breitbart died? Is it wrong that I'm happier about that than when they got bin Laden and Saddam?" and "I wonder if the state of Douchery will lower its flags at half-mast?"[29] In the online arena, the adage that "two wrongs don't make a right" is often changed to "two wrongs mean you keep on fighting."

Conflicts Between Several People or Groups Who Don't Share a Common Identity

Another variation of conflicts between several individuals or groups involves situations between people who don't share a common group or community identity but are nevertheless embroiled in a dispute with a second group. An example of this includes the online attacks against women by misogynists who don't know each other and don't have any formal or organized connection beyond simply sharing a hatred for women. Statements sent to women via email or on Twitter include, "I've got a good way for you to lose weight, I could cut your limbs off one by one and make you eat them,"[30] "[women] deserve to die at the rusty scissors of a backstreet abortionist"[31] and variations thereof. Online misogyny is a tremendously serious and widespread problem but something that many women, and even men, are afraid to tackle for fear they will become the target of attacks for having the courage to speak out.

Conflicts Between an Individual and Several Community Members

A further variation of this type of online conflict involves disputes between one person and several members of a community, often someone who is an instigator or intentional antagonist. An example of this is reflected by the actions of Nimrod Severn, real name Darren Burton, who is notorious for leaving offensive and ugly messages on tribute and memorial sites, such as the hateful "rot in piss" he posted on murdered university student Anuj Bidve's memorial Facebook page.[32] Burton is a well-known troll, and we'll discuss the demented psychology and behavior of online trolls in detail in the next chapter.

Conflicts Between Community Members and Site Representatives

A third variation of conflict between several individuals or groups involves disputes between one or more community members and a site moderator, community manager, or site owner.

Common examples of this include individuals who act out because they disagree with the way community managers manage the site, disagree with one or more community rules, or want to dominate the conversation. Other times disputes occur because people feel singled out for their views, or want to disrupt the activities of the group for purposes of amusement and sport. The next chapter covers this type of behavior.

The first issue, disagreeing with a community manager, was at the heart of the problem facing one of the online communities managed by Short-Media. What happened in the 8-plus-year-old community concerned a new member who felt that the volunteer moderators were overstepping their bounds. As described by Short-Media's Brian Ambrozy, "He began firing off long, well-written explanations of what he felt was wrong with the way the site was run, all under the guise of being concerned for the health of the community. He then began mentioning 'backroom' discussions with other unhappy members (off-channel: either they were discussing things on another medium or via the private messaging system), making it seem as if a tide of popular opinion was rising against the site. His consistent and deliberate arguments made it seem as if he [were] speaking for a whole group of community members—despite no actual evidence that this was the case."[33] After careful investigation, the site's community manager discovered that the individual in question was a troublemaker who was dragging the community culture down, and he was banned from the site.

Conflict with People Who Are Pseudonymous or Anonymous

Notoriously difficult types of online conflict to deal with involve those in which the protagonists are anonymous or pseudonymous. Trying to fight an unknown opponent is extremely difficult, and that's perhaps the main reason why those who seek to inflict maximum harm choose to remain hidden when attacking others online.

One man whose life was turned upside down due to cowardly anonymous attacks was Gene Cooley, a man who lived and worked in Blairsville, a small town in Georgia with less than 1,000 residents. After his fiancée was murdered, rumors accusing him of drug use, perversion, and involvement in her death began anonymously circulating on Topix,[34] a news and forum aggregator focused on small towns and communities. As a result of these online lies, Cooley lost his job and became suicidal. Two years after the attacks began, he was finally able to get Topix to provide the IP address of his attacker and subsequently discovered she was Sybil Denise Ballew, a woman who harbored a grudge against him from when they worked together a decade earlier. Cooley sued Ballew in court for defamation and won $404,000, of which $250,000 was for punitive damages.

Pseudonymous and anonymous attackers don't just go after innocent victims, however. They are indiscriminate and occasionally target people who themselves have colorful pasts. Such was the case with Jennifer Emick, owner of Asherah Research Group, who around 2008 was active in the anti-Scientology group Project Chanology[35] which was composed of members of the loosely organized "hacktivist" group Anonymous. When Anonymous's actions broadened and become more aggressive and anti-establishment, Emick distanced herself from the group. Instead, she created a business based on collecting information about Anonymous and selling it to members of law enforcement, as well as detractors of the group. Not surprisingly, this put her on the group's target list.[36]

Herself no shrinking violet (see her Twitter account @asherahresearch where she tweets comments like "Anonymous is a bunch of non-contributing, self-involved, spoiled brats. Nobody cares what Anonymous thinks"[37]), she and her family have been under ongoing attack from unknown individuals who make filthy statements against her, such as @JokerSec1's tweet "@AsherahResearch C**T C**T C**T C**T C**T C**T C**T C**T C**T C**T C**T C**T C**T C**T C**T C**T C**T C**T C**T C**T C**T C**T C**T C**T,"[38] and threaten her children.

Mocking and attacking with impunity is exactly what anonymous posters bank on. That's what the users of PSUacb.com, Pennsylvania State University's version of campus gossip website College ACB, the Anonymous Confessions Board, were expecting when they went online and left colorful comments and insults about fellow students. Normally that would be the end of the story because the victims would have no real ability to defend themselves against such shadow figures. But in a twist of fate, the creator of the site revealed that PSUacb.com had always been intended as a lesson in anti-cyberbullying and that therefore the full names and university email usernames of the registered users were being posted online as a lesson to those who have nefarious intentions.[39] Nevertheless, the site owner showed sympathy for the users and made a final update to the site, saying, "I have removed the names of the people who posted.... I'm not cruel enough to embarrass someone in front of the whole country for something stupid they did in college, especially when everyone at Penn State (or at least 7,846 people) has already realized you suck."[40]

Online Lynch Mobs

Another particularly difficult situation to deal with is attacks made by online lynch mobs. With a ferocity amplified through sheer numbers, the individuals taking part in these mobs operate on a foundation of raw emotion in which anger and hostility dominate and rationality is put on hold. The danger of online lynch mobs is based in part on the deindividuation that happens when people group together in anger or hostility. *Deindividuation* is a psychological term that means loosening of or losing one's self-awareness in groups, and the corresponding reduction or elimination of a sense of personal responsibility for one's actions that also takes place. Historically, the excuse that "I was just following the crowd" or "Everyone was doing it" is frequently heard as justification for why people participated in immoral, illegal, and otherwise horrific acts.

Quite frequently the mobs are made up of individuals who use pseudonyms or hide behind anonymity while intentionally rousing public hostility and rage. The speed and aggression with which these mobs focus on their targets often leaves the victims of such attacks not knowing what hit them or how to try to deflect the onslaught.

That's what happened to Bimbo's Cantina patron Andrew Meyer, who not only didn't tip bartender Victoria Liss, but allegedly also left a note on the receipt stating, "you could stand to [lose] a few pounds." Liss, angered by both actions, vented on her Facebook page and posted a picture of Meyer. As a result, Meyer's own Facebook page was identified, and he received hundreds of vicious online comments and emails. The media, including online gossip sites, picked up the story. However, the problem, and a large one at that, was that the photo Liss posted was of a different and innocent Meyer. Realizing her mistake, Liss wrote an apology on her Facebook page:[41] "I need glasses, I put up the picture of the wrong guy. I'm a douche for that. SO SORRY. Blinded by rage."[42] But by then it was too late and the damage had been done. As attorney Jack Marshall noted on his Ethics Alarm blog, "Web shaming should be reserved for the dangerous, corrupt, dishonest and criminal, and not leveled at the rude, thoughtless, or socially inept. The internet is powerful, and siccing thousands of bored web surfers on some jerk because of a moment's bad judgment is irresponsible and an abuse of that power."[43]

The danger of online lynch mobs also lies in their frequent absence of truth-seeking behavior and the negative repercussions that can result. The killing of unarmed teenager Trayvon Martin by George Zimmerman gripped the United States in early 2012, with racial relations, civil rights, and the perceived unequal application of the law at the forefront of the discussions taking place in news stories, on the streets, and in living rooms around the country. Passions ran high, calls for justice and retribution were nonstop, and Zimmerman went into hiding amid death threats. Against this backdrop, movie director and filmmaker Spike Lee, with a Twitter following of more than 200,000 at the time, retweeted what he believed was the address where Zimmerman was staying. Unfortunately the address, first shared online by Marcus D. Higgins, was wrong.[44] Instead, the location was that of elderly couple Elaine and David McClain, whose son's name was William George Zimmerman but who was not the killer and no longer lived there. As a result of the threats they received for allegedly harboring the defendant Zimmerman, the McClains fled their home and escaped to a local hotel for their safety. As noted in Figure 3.5, Lee posted an apology on Twitter ("I Deeply Apologize To The McClain Family For Retweeting Their Address. It Was A Mistake. Please Leave The McClain's In Peace.Justice In Court")[45] and, according to the McClain's attorney, agreed to "compensate them for their loss and for the disruption into their lives."[46]

Figure 3.5   *Spike Lee's tweet of March 28, 2012*

Particularly disturbing kinds of online lynch mobs are called *human flesh searches*, which combine the online and physical worlds. People first identify and then hunt down and in some way punish perceived violators or transgressors of ethical or social norms or expectations. That's what happened to advertising executive Wang Fei, whose wife Jiang Yan committed suicide after learning about his affair with a female co-worker. After Yan's death, her sister posted her private diary, which outlined her anguish and plans to kill herself, which a reader then reposted on a popular Chinese bulletin board.[47] Rage about Yan's death and mistreatment angered the readers, who located Fei and his girlfriend Dong Fang and caused them to be fired from their positions at the international advertising agency Saatchi and Saatchi. Fei was still in hiding 2 years after his wife's death.

Private Versus Public Disputes

An important distinction needs to be made between private and public disputes. For purposes of discussion, private disputes are defined as those whose distribution is limited in some way or whose means of communication is via private or semi-private channels. Back and forth communication between two people via email or social networking sites' message function would fall in this category, whereas tweets sent back and forth between two people on their public streams would not.

By keeping things private, or at least limited in terms of dissemination, the parties can try to resolve their differences in a discreet and hopefully respectful manner that maintains confidences. The goal isn't to intentionally publicize the communication to gain some advantage in the court of public opinion or to use public humiliation for revenge or punishment. Instead, the purpose is usually to manage the dispute between the parties in as much a civil, effective, and expedient a manner as possible. However, the private versus public distinction is in some ways an artificial one because technology makes it incredibly easy to forward, copy, scan, and otherwise share previously private communication with others.

The story of Ryan Tate, CEO of Christian-based firm Tate Publishing & Enterprises, is a case in point. An anonymous employee sent an internal email addressed to fellow colleagues about the company's plans to outsource work to the Philippines, an action that apparently didn't sit well with Tate, who demanded that the unnamed person identify himself. In a secret recording of a company meeting, subsequently shared with the media, Tate threatened to fire 25 employees because the culprit didn't come forward: "Good people are going to lose their jobs—it's not fair. It's not right, but that's the reality of the situation. Jesus himself is the perfect mix of mercy, grace, and justice. I have probably failed you in that I have been a little too lenient and a little too on the side of mercy and grace and not on the side of justice."[48]

The story, along with the actual recording, was covered by national and international media alike, with the statement putting into question Tate's and his company's reputation: "Jesus may Save, but apparently he can't do much about job retention" said ABC News, [49] and the *Christian Post* wrote, "Those familiar with Tate Publishing are astonished at the recording, which directly contradicts the Christian mission of the company. Tate regularly attends church with his family, but after the rant and directly attacking his employees, some are wondering how the two figures can be the same person."[50] The United Kingdom's *Daily Mail* commented, "Secretly recorded by an irate employee, Tate began his meeting with a group prayer before tearing into his staff calling them 'morons' and 'idiots,' whilst he himself takes the Lord's name in vain within the first two minutes of his speech."[51]

In summer 2012, leaked emails were a problem for Brett McGurk, ambassadorial nominee to Iraq under President Obama and former national security staffer for President George W. Bush, and former *Wall Street Journal* reporter Gina Chon. In 2008, McGurk was serving as chief negotiator during the 2008 U.S.-Iraq security agreement talks, and Chon covered them for the newspaper.[52] McGurk and Chon sent each other personal and steamy emails from their respective @state.gov and @wsj.com addresses.[53] Complicating the matter was that both McGurk and Chon were married to others at the time; although they later divorced their respective spouses and got married. Aside from the questionable use of government and business email addresses for romantic purposes, the emails raised concerns because of insinuations by McGurk that he would give Chon access to confidential information if their relationship progressed.[54] It's not clear whether that was simply flirtatious and playful banter not to be taken seriously within the context of their exchange. After the emails were leaked, Chon resigned from *The Wall Street Journal* under Code of Conduct violations for having shared unpublished news articles with McGurk and for not having disclosed her personal relationship to her editor at the time.[55] The time lag between McGurk's and Chon's email exchanges and when the emails were leaked—just in time for McGurk's confirmation hearings by the Foreign Relations Committee—were convenient and suggest that the leaks were intentionally made by someone who wanted to throw a wrench in McGrath's confirmation. The bottom line: If something is memorialized electronically, it can and most likely will be shared and made public for personal, professional, or political gain.

Conflict Issue Categories

In addition to the different parties to a dispute, you also need to consider different types of conflict issues, such as content-, personality-, power-, and identity-based ones. Each of these have their own unique triggers and drivers that you need to know about to successfully identify and manage them if they come your way.

Content-Based Conflicts

Content-based conflicts involve differences between people's goals, beliefs, or values. They concern how individuals try to achieve or fulfill them, and how they regard, interpret, and react to the differences they may have about them with others. These types of conflicts deal with the *substance* of the dispute, although, the form of expression and the personalities involved naturally also come into play.

Perhaps one of the most polarizing issues of recent memory concerns global warming. There is no mistaking the animosity between those who believe in human-caused climate change and those who believe it is pro-environmental propaganda intended to harm the fossil fuel industry. In a CNN Opinion piece, climate scientist Michael Mann describes the online smears launched against him by antiscience forces: "Imagine you are sitting in your office simply doing your job and a nasty e-mail pops into your inbox accusing you of being a fraud. You go online and find that some bloggers have written virulent posts about you."[56] The witch hunt against him included ongoing attempts by global warming skeptic Virginia Attorney General Ken Cuccinelli II to gain access to Mann's grant applications and emails to prove Mann had committed scientific fraud, which after a 2-year battle culminated in the Virginia Supreme Court's rejection of Cuccinelli II's request.[57] Mann was exonerated of any wrongdoing by a series of investigations and inquiries, among them by the prestigious National Science Foundation, which stated, "No direct evidence has been presented that indicates the subject fabricated the raw data he used for his research or falsified his results."[58] Mann later wrote a book about his and other climate scientists' ordeal called *The Hockey Stick and the Climate Wars: Dispatches From the Front Lines*, which was published in early 2012.[59] However, none of this has changed the online war between climate change proponents and climate change deniers, which remains as virulent as ever.

Another current example of a content-based conflict that caused people to draw online "lines in the sand," usually along politically liberal versus conservative lines, concerned the Occupy Wall Street movement. Occupy Wall Street (OWS), a protest that was initiated by the Canadian activist group Adbusters and which began in New York City September 17, 2011,[60] concerned the economic inequality between the richest 1% of the American population and rest of the nation's citizenry. It spread to numerous other cities in the United States and also to other countries via its sister movement Take the Square.[61] OWS has become a veritable online powerhouse, with its main website OccupyWallStreet.org; Occupy.net, which provides a list of local assemblies; and OccupiedStories.com, which offers eye-witness accounts. Meanwhile, OccupyStreams.org posts livestreams from all locations, and Twitter is used to share messages via the hashtags #OWS, #occupy, and #occupywallstreet.

Although it became a force that even the mainstream media finally started taking seriously, OWS continues to have its detractors and vocal opponents who believe the movement's supporters are a bunch of lazy, anticapitalist losers. Lawyer-turned blogger and conservative *Washington Post* columnist Jennifer Rubin wrote, "Unlike the OWS crowd, Americans don't want an even larger government picking winners and losers (or, more precisely, trying to prevent losers). Unlike the OWS crowd, Americans don't expect the government to wipe out their debts or guarantee them cradle-to-grave benefits."[62] And in response to an online article about two New York City small business owners who countered the OWS protests with signs reading "Get a Job" and "Occupy a Desk," one reader commented, "These [OWS] guys don't want jobs—they've been brainwashed into believing that the government should support them, pay for their education, pay for their healthcare, and then pay for their retirement. Why would you want to work if you don't have to?"[63]

Personality-Based Conflicts

Personality-based conflicts are extremely common online and involve clashes between two or more people whose characteristics or behaviors differ and result in them rubbing each other the wrong way. These types of conflicts can also occur unilaterally, with one person taking issue with another and then harping on them online. Issues of bias, respect, recognition, and dominance frequently come into play.

Real estate mogul and billionaire Donald Trump isn't known for subtlety, and his feud with talk show host and comedienne Rosie O'Donnell, herself opinionated and outspoken, is no exception. The bad blood between them goes back several years, with O'Donnell's Wikipedia entry[64] hinting that it might stem from O'Donnell's 2006 criticism of Trump's involvement with the Miss USA pageant and his decision to allow then winner Tara Conner to keep her crown if she entered rehab for alcohol misuse. O'Donnell is quoted as saying on her television show, "The View," that Trump "Left the first wife, had an affair. Left the second wife, had an affair. Had kids both times—but he's the moral compass for 20 year olds in America!"[65] Trump publicly responded by criticizing her appearance and behavior, saying, "Take a look at her. She's a slob. She talks like a truck driver."[66] The conflict between them was reignited in early 2012 when Trump expressed pride in his prediction that her talk show on the OWN network would be canceled[67] and when he included O'Donnell in an online attack against singer and actress Cher's criticism of U.S. presidential hopeful Mitt Romney on Twitter, where he fired back with "@Cher attacked @MittRomney. She is an average talent who is out of touch with reality. Like @RosieO'Donnell, a total loser!"[68] O'Donnell responded with "he returns—like a raging herpes rash...."[69]

An example of a more unilateral conflict involves Paula Deen. For many years, American cooking show host and television personality Deen was known for her extremely calorie-rich and fat-laden dishes, such as deep fried butter balls and Krispy Kreme bread pudding cheesecake. Although fans often heralded her for her down-home style comfort foods, more health conscious individuals were understandably appalled. Even before her public revelation in early 2012 that she has diabetes, which she later admitted she was diagnosed with 3 years earlier, she became the target of "The Travel Channel's" "No Reservations" TV host Anthony Bourdain who called her "the worst, most dangerous person to America"[70] due to her cooking and took issue with her "for having her brand be 'excess without guilt' when she knew 'in a very personal way what this could and might very well lead to' [ill health]."[71] Bourdain commented on Deen's contract with Novo Nordisk to promote its antidiabetes drug by tweeting, "Thinking of getting into the leg-breaking business, so I can profitably sell crutches later."[72]

As a celebrity, she's also been targeted online with the @FakePaulaDeen Twitter account, whose tagline states, as you can see in Figure 3.6, "I've never met a stick of butter I didn't love"[73] and which publishes statements such as "Y'all, I'm partnering with @KrispyKreme to bring you Paula's Insulin Glazed Donuts! Everyone please form a single file (but very wide) line!"[74] and "Y'all, I'm not just the butt of the joke. My butt *is* the joke."[75] The Twitter account @PaulaDeenVagina, whose tagline is "Add a heaping helping of butter on your coochie Y'ALLL,"[76] is also perhaps one of the vilest parody accounts online.[77] It's posted statements such as "Diabetes is transmitted by unprotected anal butter insertion. Use protection or you'll end up like me [78] and "Insert a blow torch in my p**sy and turn it on full blast to burn my flesh like the fat and succulent pig that I am."[79] Disappointingly, this account has more than 8,000 followers, making you wonder who in their right mind would find such tweets amusing or even marginally acceptable.

Figure 3.6 *Screenshot of fake Paula Deen's Twitter profile*

Power-Based Conflicts

Power-based conflicts, as the name implies, concern issues of power between two or more people or groups. They often include struggles of dominance, hierarchy, influence, autonomy, decision-making ability, and resources. Power can be established in several different ways. One way is expertise via one's knowledge or skill (for example, Tim Berners-Lee and Robert Cailliau for creating the World Wide Web), and another is referent power via someone being respected, admired, or liked (for example, international soccer star and Spaniard Cristiano Ronaldo). There is also legitimacy via one's position (for example, the U.S. Supreme Court Justices) and power-based on the ability to reward or punish (for example, an employee's boss who can promote or fire his subordinate).

One area in which power conflicts are frequently manifested online is in the political realm. Politics are the ultimate power game, and nowhere more so than online where politicians battle it out for citizens' hearts, minds, and votes. Often viewed as a zero-sum game, politics are fueled by controversy, and political websites are no exception. On the conservative side, RedState.org published articles stating, "In order to become President, Barack Obama had to swear to preserve, protect, and defend the Constitution.... Has he forgotten about the separation of executive, judicial, and legislative branches found in our founding document? Our founders gave us a system of checks and balances so that one person could never seize more power than was provided in the Constitution. President Obama's actions demonstrate that he thinks he's above the law."[80] Meanwhile, on the liberal side, Daily Kos posts articles saying, "Republicans wouldn't be Republicans if all they did was lie about the success of Democratic policies. No, they also like to simultaneous with their lies take credit for the popular parts.... Claim a law failed, while taking credit for its successes. Rinse and repeat. That's the Republican way."[81]

Politics have also become a popular participant sport in which there's no shortage of individuals eager to silence their opponents while clamoring to express their own opinions, no matter how divisive, ugly, or removed from the truth they may be. Sample tweets include, as you can see in Figure 3.7, Country Princess's "I know it's not classy to hate on others, but that's the nicest feeling I can have toward liberals. #sorrynotsorry,"[82] and Trash Socialism's "Why are they all so stupid? Well because they are all liberals. It's a global Satanic jihad hugging cult."[83] Rocket Grunt Casi wrote, "Friendly reminder that i am open [sic] the opinions of others, but not if your opinion makes zero sense (shoutout to conservatives) (you suck),"[84] whereas Andybud said, "It's not so much that I've become way liberal as it is that conservatives have become so goddamned stupid."[85]

Figure 3.7   *Country Princess's tweet of July 9, 2012*

Identity-Based Conflicts

Fortunately there are organizations that try to sift through the attack rhetoric. The University of Pennsylvania's Annenberg Public Policy Center created FactCheck.org, a nonpartisan, nonprofit project that analyzes the factual accuracy of what's said by American political players.[86] And the National Institute for Civil Discourse, chaired by former presidents George H.W. Bush and Bill Clinton, seeks to "encourage civic leaders to embrace vigorous debate in a way that allows for diverse perspectives to be shared, for complex issues to be discussed thoughtfully, and for challenging topics to be explored without resorting to invective and personal attacks."[87]

Identity-based conflicts can be challenging to manage and overcome, and are among the most vicious. They are disputes that, at the most fundamental level, involve separating people into different categories or teams, a "me" or "us" versus "you" or "them" mentality. This can happen both intragroup, meaning within the same group, or intergroup, meaning between groups. Identity involves anything that people use and rely on to create a sense of who they are. This includes things such as gender, ethnicity, race, nationality, religion, language, age, profession, and any other differentiators. Because identity lies at the core of how people see themselves, perceived or actual threats to it are often taken hard, and people react intensely and emotionally.

A particularly volatile example of online conflict involves people who self-identify as people of faith, regardless of religion or denomination, and people who self-identify as atheists. There are countless incidences of attacks by one side against the other, reflecting not just differences of philosophy—religionists regarding atheists as immoral and atheists viewing religionists as irrational—but also expressions of unsheathed hatred cloaked in threats of violence. Statements against atheists include ones such as "Shoot 'em. At least we know where they're going, waste of oxygen"[88] and "Nail the atheists together make a cross out of them."[89] Atheists aren't shy about expressing themselves either, sharing statements such as "What's worse religious bigotry or racism? Practicing either is a manifestation of colossal stupidity"[90] and "Religion is like a penis. It's perfectly fine if you share it with others that also enjoy it, but please: Don't wave it around in public. | Don't hit people over the head with it. | Don't brag about how big it is. |And don't shove it down the throats of young children."[91] The aggressive individuals within the religious and atheist groups aren't representative of everyone in their camp, but it's unfortunately a fact that they are some of the most vocal online and therefore tend to amplify and entrench each side's position. Online fights between people of different religions are equally intense—the historical dispute between Christians and Muslims is perhaps the best known—with each claiming moral superiority over the other and a right way to worship and engage with their deity.

Perhaps fewer issues run deeper than how to raise one's children, and the protracted and deep-rooted identity-based conflict between working-outside-the home mothers (generally known as "working" mothers) and working-inside-the-home mothers (typically called "stay-at-home" mothers) is reflective of this.

Believed to have been escalated with the publishing of Felice N. Schwartz's 1989 article "Management Women and the New Facts of Life" in *Harvard Business Review*[92] and the 1990 *Newsweek* article "Mommy Vs. Mommy,"[93] the battle between mothers is often framed in moralistic terms like "selfish" and "career-driven" versus "lazy," "privileged," and "dependent" thrown around with abandon to prove the superiority of one side over the other. Today's economy has further complicated matters, with many families requiring two salaries simply to make ends meet, and many single women, who might have otherwise elected to be the full-time caretakers and remain at home while their children are young, having to work outside the home.

Online the attacks by each side are often ruthless. One woman wryly commented, "Does anyone remember the good old days when only your mother and/or your mother-in-law would criticize how you raised your kids?"[94] Fortunately there are women like mother and writer Elizabeth Flora Ross who created The Mom Pledge,[95] an online community of "women standing up, speaking out, and coming together to end cyberbullying among moms, fostering respect, understanding and acceptance."[96]

Why These Online Conflicts Matter

Because of the online environment's fluid nature, what starts out as one type of dispute or conflict between a defined set of individuals or groups of people can easily and quickly morph into another. Online lynch mobs can occur without warning at a moment's notice, transposing what appeared to be a clearly delineated dispute into an uncontrollable, free-for-all online brawl. And if any of the conflicts involve pseudonymous or anonymous individuals, the situation can become complicated because the opponents are unknown and therefore harder or even impossible to combat.

Any time communication takes place online, it can be and, especially in conflict situations, often is shared with others, which risks it becoming pubic. A simple click of the Send button or an easily made screenshot can catapult what was a private exchange onto the Web and into the public arena. Even when shared just between one or two select people, after a message, email, or image is passed on, like the children's *Telephone* game of yesteryear, it can snowball into the entertainment of the day. That's why constant vigilance and having strong oversight over the conflict is so critical.

Endnotes

1. Tiffany Hsu, "McDonald's to focus on quality ingredients in ad campaign," *Los Angeles Times*, December 15, 2011. Link: http://latimesblogs.latimes.com/money_co/2011/12/mcdonalds-quality-ingredients-ad-campaign.html

2. The term "bashtag" is believed to have been coined by *Forbes* staff writer Kashmir Hill in her January 24, 2012 article "#McDStories: When A Hashtag Becomes A Bashtag" at http://www.forbes.com/sites/kashmirhill/2012/01/24/mcdstories-when-a-hashtag-becomes-a-bashtag/. Link: http://www.theatlantic.com/technology/archive/2012/01/neologism-watch-from-hashtag-to-bashtag/251924/

3. Alex Roth's @alexroth3 Twitter account, tweet dated January 24, 2012 at 12:10 p.m. Link: https://twitter.com/alexroth3/status/161873590881497088

4. Edo de Roo's @edoderoo Twitter account, tweeted January 25, 2012 at 1:55 a.m. Link: https://twitter.com/edoderoo/status/162081203866968064

5. May @Alice_2112's Twitter account, tweet dated January 23, 2012 at 9:41 p.m. Link: https://twitter.com/Alice_2112/status/161654771500060673

6. L Muzzafuzza's @Muzzafuzza's Twitter account, tweeted January 18, 2012 at 2:54 p.m. Link: https://twitter.com/Muzzafuzza/status/159740460842225664

7. Brian Heap, "Fighting cyber slander," KWCH 12 Eyewitness News, October 28, 2010. Link: http://www.kwch.com/news/factfinder12/kwch-kwch-news-bh-cyber-slander-102810,0,2335292.htmlstory

8. "Tarnished Tiaras: Beauty Queens Gone Bad," Dr.Phil.com, January 2012. Link: http://drphil.com/slideshows/slideshow/6680/?id=6680&slide=0&showID=1767&preview=&versionID=

9. "Tarnished Tiaras: Beauty Queens Gone Bad," Dr.Phil.com, January 2012. Link: http://drphil.com/slideshows/slideshow/6680/?id=6680&slide=0&showID=1767&preview=&versionID=

10. Comment by Anonymous on "Nik Richie From TheDirty.com On Dr. Phil," TheDirty.com, January 16, 2012 at 11:47 p.m. Link: http://thedirty.com/2012/01/nik-richie-from-thedirty-com-on-dr-phil/

11. Comment by Let's be honest on "I Agree With You Completely," TheDirty.com, January 24, 2012 at 10:00 a.m. Link: http://thedirty.com/2012/01/i-agree-with-you-completely/

12. Facebook 'Defriendng' Led to Double Murder, Say Police," ABC News, February 10, 2012. Link: http://abcnews.go.com/blogs/technology/2012/02/facebook-defriending-led-to-double-murder-say-police/

13. Angela K. Brown, "'Nerd' taunt drove Navy man to arson," Associated Press, July 26, 2007. Link: http://www.msnbc.msn.com/id/19980505/ns/technology_and_science-internet/t/nerd-taunt-drove-navy-man-arson/

14. Angela K. Brown, "'Nerd' taunt drove Navy man to arson," Associated Press, July 26, 2007. Link: http://www.msnbc.msn.com/id/19980505/ns/technology_and_science-internet/t/nerd-taunt-drove-navy-man-arson/

15. "Internet user admits 'web-rage,'" BBC News, October 17, 2006. Link: http://news.bbc.co.uk/2/hi/uk_news/england/london/6059726.stm

16. Ray Wert, "Daughter Of Resigned GM CEO Attacks New GM CEO On Facebook," Jalopnik, December 1, 2009. Link: http://jalopnik.com/5416549/daughter-of-resigned-gm-ceo-attacks-new-gm-ceo-on-facebook

17. "Did GM CEO Fritz Henderson's Daughter, Sarah Henderson, Rant On Facebook?" *Huffington Post*, March 18, 2010, updated May 25, 2011. Link: http://www.huffingtonpost.com/2009/12/01/did-gm-ceo-fritz-henderso_n_376229.html

18. Eric Platt, "How a Tenacious Summer Analyst Applicant Got Laughed at by Goldman, Morgan and Everyone Else on Wall Street," Yahoo! Finance, February 9, 2012. Link: http://finance.yahoo.com/news/tenacious-summer-analyst-applicant-got-laughed-at-by-everyone-else-on-wall-street.html

19. Comment left by "Daniel" on Eric Platt, "How a Tenacious Summer Analyst Applicant Got Laughed at by Goldman, Morgan and Everyone Else on Wall Street," Yahoo! Finance, February 9, 2012. Link: http://finance.yahoo.com/news/tenacious-summer-analyst-applicant-got-laughed-at-by-everyone-else-on-wall-street.html?bcmt=1328816572485-12738537-1b3d-4bcc-969d-28ec25eff19f#ugccmt-container-b

20. Comment left by "Val Rojas" on Eric Platt, "How a Tenacious Summer Analyst Applicant Got Laughed at by Goldman, Morgan and Everyone Else on Wall Street," Yahoo! Finance, February 9, 2012. Link: http://finance.yahoo.com/news/tenacious-summer-analyst-applicant-got-laughed-at-by-everyone-else-on-wall-street.html?bcmt=1328821421680-ccc38b8e-e784-4747-acbf-cc8ee6eda7ff#ugccmt-container-b

21. Comment left by "NoNotMe" on Eric Platt, "How a Tenacious Summer Analyst Applicant Got Laughed at by Goldman, Morgan and Everyone Else on Wall Street," Yahoo! Finance, February 9, 2012. Link: http://finance.yahoo.com/news/tenacious-summer-analyst-applicant-got-laughed-at-by-everyone-else-on-wall-street.html?bcmt=1328816294563-4c718920-d430-48bc-a1da-eb5e295eff03#ugccmt-container-b

22. Comment left by "Angie" on Eric Platt, "How a Tenacious Summer Analyst Applicant Got Laughed at by Goldman, Morgan and Everyone Else on Wall Street," Yahoo! Finance, February 9, 2012. Link: inance.yahoo.com/news/tenacious-summer-analyst-applicant-got-laughed-at-by-everyone-else-on-wall-street.html?bcmt=1328819692802-21c5f526-10ed-43e4-b92a-627153cebb8e#ugccmt-container-b

23. Paul Farhi, "WUSA reporter Andrea McCarren balks after backlash over teen drinking stories," *The Washington Post*, February 14, 2012. Link: http://www.washingtonpost.com/lifestyle/style/wusa-reporter-balks-after-backlash-over-teen-drinking-stories/2012/02/14/gIQAmE3tER_story.html

24. Paul Farhi, "WUSA reporter Andrea McCarren balks after backlash over teen drinking stories," The *Washington Post*, February 14, 2012. Link: http://www.washingtonpost.com/lifestyle/style/wusa-reporter-balks-after-backlash-over-teen-drinking-stories/2012/02/14/gIQAmE3tER_story.html

25. Bess Levin, "Financial Services Employee's Excel Spreadsheet Of Dating Prospects Allows for 18 Year-Olds, Has No Room for 'Jappy' Girls," Dealbreaker, April 16, 2012. Link: http://dealbreaker.com/2012/04/financial-services-employees-excel-spreadsheet-of-dating-prospects-allows-for-18-year-olds-has-no-room-for-jappy-girls/

26. Katie J.M. Baker, "Creepy Finance Guy With Spreadsheet of Match.com 'Prospects' Says He Was Just Trying to Be Organized," Jezebel, April 17, 2012. Link: http://jezebel.com/5902718/creepy-finance-guy-with-spreadsheet-of-matchcom-prospects-says-he-was-just-trying-to-be-organized

27. Tweet by Andrew Breitbart @AndrewBreitbart on August 26, 2009 at 1:57 a.m. Link: https://twitter.com/andrewbreitbart/status/3553169520

28. Tweet by Andrew Breitbart @AndrewBreitbart on August 26, 2009 at 1:02 a.m. Link: https://twitter.com/andrewbreitbart/status/3552660988

29. Billy Hallowell, "'Burn in Hell!': Shocking Tweets Celebrate Andrew Breitbart's Death," The Blaze, March 1, 2012. Link: http://www.theblaze.com/stories/burn-in-hell-shocking-tweets-celebrate-andrew-breitbarts-death-on-twitter/

30. Helen Lewis-Hasteley, Zoe Williams, Bella Mackie and Catherine Redfern, The Guardian, November 7, 2011. Link: http://www.guardian.co.uk/commentisfree/2011/nov/07/abusive-sexist-comments-online

31. Helen Lewis, "'You should have your tongue ripped out': the reality of sexist abuse online," New Statesman, November 3, 2011. Link: http://www.newstatesman.com/blogs/helen-lewis-hasteley/2011/11/comments-rape-abuse-women

32. "Panorama confronts an internet troll," Panorama, BBC, February 6, 2012. Link: http://news.bbc.co.uk/panorama/hi/front_page/newsid_9693000/9693594.stm

33. Brian Ambrozy, "On dealing with bad apples," Short-Media, February 9, 2012. Link: http://short-media.com/community/on-dealing-with-bad-apples

34. Eamon McNiff, "Innocent Man's Life Destroyed by Anonymous Topix Poster," ABC News, March 21, 2012. Link: http://abcnews.go.com/Technology/topix-innocent-mans-life-destroyed-anonymous-online-poster/story?id=15963310#.T9bIgr9ZBVS

35. According to Wikipedia, Project Chanology is an anti-Scientology group comprised of members of the Anonymous group. Link: http://en.wikipedia.org/wiki/Project_Chanology

36. Sam Biddle, "This Is What Happens When Anonymous Tries to Destroy You," Gozmodo, June 1, 2012. Link: http://gizmodo.com/5914671/this-is-what-happens-when-anonymous-tries-to-destroy-you

37. Jennifer Emick's Twitter account @AsherahResearch, June 12, 2012 at 1:51 a.m. Link: https://twitter.com/AsherahResearch/status/212437022453927936

38. Joker Sec's Twitter account @JokerSec1, Aprl 10, 2012 at 11:35 p.m. Link: https://twitter.com/JokerSec1/status/189934735538130944

39. Nick DeSantis, "Creator of 'Anonymous' Gossip Site Names Names," The Chronicle of Higher Education, May 9, 2012. Link: http://chronicle.com/blogs/wiredcampus/ creator-of-penn-state-campus-gossip-site-unmasks-student-posters/36301

40. PSUacb.com home page. Link: http://psuacb.com/

41. At the time of this writing, Liss's Facebook page was unavailable.

42. Vanessa Ho, "Bartender who shamed wrong man apologizes - again," Seattle's Big Blog, October 12, 2011. Link: http://blog.seattlepi.com/thebigblog/2011/10/12/bartender- who-shamed-wrong-man-apologizes-%E2%80%93-again/

43. Jack Marshall, "A Tip For Victoria Liss—In Fact, Two: Read the Golden Rule, and Don't Use The Internet For Revenge," Ethics Alarm, October 13, 2011. Link: http://ethicsalarms.com/2011/10/13/a-tip-for-victoria-liss-in-fact-two-read-the-golden- rule-and-dont-use-the-internet-for-revenge/

44. "@d_pardee @SpikeLee GOD BLESS YOU O KNOW YOU HATE ME BUT I DON'T HAVE YOU I DID APOLOGY FOR RETWEET THE WRONG ADDRESS," Marcus D. Higgins @MACCAPONE account, March 28, 2012 at 12:35 p.m. Link: https://twitter.com/maccapone/status/185057484929642497

45. Tweet by Spike Lee @SpikeLee on March 28, 2012 at 5:50 p.m.. Link: https://twitter. com/SpikeLee/status/185177177652862977

46. Video statement by Matt Morgan, attorney for Elaine and David McClain, "Sanford Couple in Fear After Spike Lee Tweet," Associated Press, March 29, 2012. Link: http:// www.youtube.com/watch?v=rbplOUsw9Gs

47. Tom Downey, "China's Cyberposse," The New York Times, March 3, 2010. Link: http://www.nytimes.com/2010/03/07/magazine/07Human-t.html?_r=1

48. Briana Bailey, "Trouble at Tate: Publishing company fires 25 as outsourcing rumors fly," The Journal Record, May 31, 2012. Link: http://journalrecord.com/2012/05/31/ trouble-at-tate-publishing-company-fires-25-as-outsourcing-rumors-fly-general-news/

49. Abby Ellin, "Oklahoma Publisher Prays With, Fires 25 Workers," ABC News, June 8, 2012. Link: http://abcnews.go.com/Business/oklahoma-company-fires-25-employees- amid-outsourcing-rumors/story?id=16520756#.T9kSz79ZBVR

50. Sami K. Martin, "Tate Publishing President Prays With Employees Before Berating and Firing 25 (AUDIO)," The Christian Post, June 8, 2012. Link: http://www.christianpost. com/news/tate-publishing-president-prays-with-employees-before-berating-and-firing- 25-audio-76329/

51. "Christian CEO prays with, insults and then fires 25 of his employees over leaked email...but takes the Lords name in vain within the first two minutes of his speech," Daily Mail, June 8, 2012. Link: http://www.dailymail.co.uk/news/article-2156488/ Christian-CEO-prays-insults-fires-25-employees-leaked-email--takes-Lords-vain- minutes-speech.html#ixzz1xiSDWm3X

52. Dana Hughes, "Iraq Ambassador Nomination Jeopardized by Racy Emails to Journalist," ABC News, June 8, 2012. Link: http://abcnews.go.com/blogs/politics/2012/06/iraq-ambassador-nomination-jeopardized-by-racy-email-with-journalist/

53. Screenshots of emails between Brett McGurk and Gina Cho were uploaded to Flickr on June 4, 2012. Link: http://www.flickr.com/photos/80005642@N02/

54. Dana Hughes, "Iraq Ambassador Nomination Jeopardized by Racy Emails to Journalist," ABC News, June 8, 2012. Link: http://abcnews.go.com/blogs/politics/2012/06/iraq-ambassador-nomination-jeopardized-by-racy-email-with-journalist/

55. Naftali Bendavid, "Reporter Resigns After Code-of-Conduct Violation," *The Wall Street Journal*, June 12, 2012. Link: http://online.wsj.com/article/SB10001424052702303444204577462892487299020.html

56. Michael Mann, "Climate scientists and campaign smears," CNN, March 28, 2012. Link: http://www.cnn.com/2012/03/28/opinion/mann-climate-change-email-attacks/index.html

57. Anita Kuman, "Va. Supreme Court: U-Va. doesn't have to give Cuccinelli global-warming documents," *The Washington Post*, March 2, 2012. Link: http://www.washingtonpost.com/local/dc-politics/va-supreme-court-rejects-cuccinellis-bid-for-u-va-documents/2012/03/02/gIQAmo8inR_story.html

58. Douglas Fischer, "Federal Investigators Clear Climate Scientist, Again," Scientific American, August 23, 2011. Link: http://www.scientificamerican.com/article.cfm?id=federal-investigators-clear-climate-scientist-michael-mann

59. Michael Mann, "The Hockey Stick" and the "Climate Wars: Dispatches from the Front Lines," Columbia University Press (March 6, 2012).

60. Occupy Wall Street page on Adbuster's website. Link: http://www.adbusters.org/campaigns/occupywallstreet

61. Take the Square website. Link: http://takethesquare.net/about-us/

62. Jennifer Rubin, "Americans blame government more than Wall Street," *The Washington Post*, October 18, 2011. Link: http://www.washingtonpost.com/blogs/right-turn/post/americans-blame-government-more-than-wall-street/2011/03/29/gIQAKRLTuL_blog.html

63. Comment by Someone'sGottaSayIt at 9:37 a.m. on December 8, 2011 on "Anti-OWS Protesters To Hold 'Occupy A Desk American Job Fest' At Zuccotti Park...," Weasel Zippers. Link: http://weaselzippers.us/2011/12/08/anti-ows-protesters-to-hold-occupy-a-desk-american-job-fest-at-zuccotti-park/#comment-414953

64. Rosie O'Donnell's Wikipedia entry, retrieved June 24, 2012. Link: http://en.wikipedia.org/wiki/Rosie_O%27Donnell

65. "Trump, O'Donnell trade blows," *Herald Sun*, December 23, 2006. Link: http://www.heraldsun.com.au/news/more-news/trump-odonnell-trade-blows/story-e6frf7lf-1111112731304

66. "Trump, O'Donnell trade blows," Herald Sun, December 23, 2006. Link: http://www.heraldsun.com.au/news/more-news/trump-odonnell-trade-blows/story-e6frf7lf-1111112731304

67. Peter Gicas, "Donald Trump Continues Feud With Rosie O'Donnell, Calls Her a 'Bully,'" E Online, April 17, 2012. Link: http://www.eonline.com/news/donald_trump_continues_feud_with_rosie/309347

68. Donald Trump's @realDonaldTrump's Twitter account. Link: https://twitter.com/realdonaldtrump/status/200603697435246592

69. Rosie O'Donnell's @Rosie Twitter account. Link: https://twitter.com/rosie/status/200606044194480128

70. Michael Blaustein, "Is Paula Deen public enemy #1" New York Post, August 17, 2011. Link: http://www.nypost.com/p/entertainment/tv/is_paula_public_enemy_no_TICgLB51UzsmiViRm2qaOP

71. Nicole Eggenberger, "Anthony Bourdain: Paula Dean is 'Greedy,'" US Weekly, April 9, 2012. Link: http://www.usmagazine.com/celebrity-news/news/anthony-bourdain-paula-deen-is-greedy-201294

72. Sheila Marikar, "Anthony Bordain Says Paula Dean is 'Good at Playing the Victim,'" ABCNews, April 5, 2012. Link: http://abcnews.go.com/blogs/entertainment/2012/04/anthony-bourdain-says-paula-deen-is-good-at-playing-the-victim/

73. Fake Paula Deen's @FakePaulaDeen's Twitter account. Link: https://twitter.com/FakePaulaDeen

74. Fake Paula Deen's @FakePaulaDeen's Twitter account. Link: https://twitter.com/FakePaulaDeen/status/161833248773767168

75. Fake Paula Deen's @FakePaulaDeen's Twitter account. Link: https://twitter.com/FakePaulaDeen/status/172704789988261888

76. Paula Deen's vagina @PaulaDeenVagina's Twitter account. Link: https://twitter.com/PaulaDeenVagina

77. It is the author's belief that the anonymous holder of this parody account has serious mental health and anger management issues, and is in need of clinical treatment.

78. Paula Deen's vagina @PaulaDeenVagina's Twitter account. Link: https://twitter.com/PaulaDeenVagina/status/158338138794758145

79. Paula Deen's vagina @PaulaDeenVagina's Twitter account. Link: https://twitter.com/PaulaDeenVagina/status/210487126381441026

80. Rep. Michele Bachman, "Obama's Blatant Disregard for the Constitution is Appalling," Red State, June 20, 2012. Link: http://www.redstate.com/rep_michele_bachmann/2012/06/20/obama%E2%80%99s-blatant-disregard-for-the-constitution-is-appalling/

81. Laura Clawson, "Republicans to attack Obama for saving millions of jobs," Daily Kos, July 9, 2012. Link: http://www.dailykos.com/story/2012/07/09/1104470/-Republicans-to-attack-Obama-for-saving-millions-of-jobs

82. Country Princess's @cntry_princesss' Twitter account. Link: https://twitter.com/cntry_princesss/status/222418461404577792

83. Trash Socialism's @PrawgStomper' Twitter account. Link: https://twitter.com/PrawgStomper/status/221591176606777344

84. Rocket Grunt Casi's @cashOoO's Twitter account. Link: https://twitter.com/cash0o0/status/221087084012781570

85. Andybud @andybud_o's Twitter account. Link: https://twitter.com/andybud_o/status/221422419607433218

86. FactCheck.org About page. Link: http://factcheck.org/about/

87. "Frequently Asked Questions," National Institute for Civil Discourse. Link: http://nicd.arizona.edu/faq-page

88. William Hamby, "Loving Christians respond to American Atheists' WTC case," Examiner.com, July 29, 2011. Link: http://www.examiner.com/article/loving-christians-respond-to-american-atheists-wtc-case

89. K. Mason, "Death Threats, Calls to Violence and Suppression of Minorities Intact," PracticalDoubt.com, July 28, 2011. Link: http://practicaldoubt.com/2011/07/28/calls-to-violence/

90. Comment by Aayee at 11:38 a.m. on October 3, 2011 on "4 Idiots Who Show Up Whenever Religion Is Discussed Online," Cracked.com, October 1, 2011. Link: http://www.cracked.com/article_19474_4-idiots-who-show-up-wherever-religion-discussed-online.html

91. Comment by Kalmback at 11:31 p.m. on October 2, 2011 on "4 Idiots Who Show Up Whenever Religion Is Discussed Online," Cracked.com, October 1, 2011. Link: http://www.cracked.com/article_19474_4-idiots-who-show-up-wherever-religion-discussed-online.html

92. Felice N. Schwartz, "Management Women and the New Facts of Life," *Harvard Business Review*, January 1989. Link: http://hbr.org/1989/01/management-women-and-the-new-facts-of-life/ar/1

93. "Mommy Vs. Mommy," *Newsweek* Magazine, June 3, 1990, reprinted in The Daily Beast. Link: http://www.thedailybeast.com/newsweek/1990/06/03/mommy-vs-mommy.html

94. Comment by Clarissa Darling on May 11, 2012 at 6:44 p.m. on "It's Time To End The Mommy Wars," Jill Smokler, HuffingtonPost.com on May 11, 2012. Link: http://www.huffingtonpost.com/social/Clarissa_Darling/mommy-wars-time-magazine_b_1509438_153954237.html

95. The Mom Pledge Blog. Link: http://www.themompledgeblog.com/

96. The Mom Pledge's Facebook page bio. Link: https://www.facebook.com/TheMomPledge

4

Who Are the Troublemakers?

A Pathetic Loser and Coward

Danny Brown, an award-winning blogger, marketer, and VP of Partner Strategy at Jugnoo, Inc., was having a leisurely Saturday with his wife and children. They went furniture shopping and afterward enjoyed a dinner out. But upon his return, Brown was inundated with emails and Facebook alerts about the most recent posts on his Facebook page and private messages he'd sent to friends. The information ranged from inferences that Jugnoo was having problems and that he was interested in finding other employment, to accusations that his wife had an affair with a colleague at the company and that they were getting divorced. The problem was that Brown hadn't written any of this. His Facebook account had been hacked.

The incident left Brown fuming (see Figure 4.1). "I'm big and ugly enough to come after and say what you want about me when you want to try and damage me personally and professionally. But going after my family and using them to get my friends to open up on their emotions, too? That just makes you a pathetic loser and coward...."[1] Brown's recommendations for dealing with situations like this? "Don't take stuff like this lying down—fight back and work with the network or platform in question to make sure they don't get away with it, where possible."[2] He contacted both the police and Facebook[3] and vowed to take legal action[4] against the perpetrator. Sadly, Brown believes the attack wasn't random and also has suspicions about the imposter's real identity.[5]

What makes Brown's story interesting is that he's an Internet veteran and well versed in social media and networking safety. Even so, this didn't protect him when the perpetrator bypassed his security settings on Facebook. As Brown notes, "As this weekend has shown to me, we're all at risk from idiots wanting our private information, or assholes trying to damage our reputation. Don't make it easy for them.... So if someone who is very active in this space can be caught out, it shows the dangers for all of us."[6]

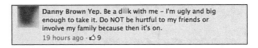

Figure 4.1   *Comment by Danny Brown on his Facebook page, July 14, 2012*

Troublemakers Come in All Sorts of Shapes and Sizes

Online troublemakers come in a wide variety of types, as the word cloud in Figure 4.2 shows. There are *trolls*, who attack others online for fun and sport, and *sockpuppets*, who assume fake identities with the intention of misleading others. There are *cyberbullies*, who misuse technology to tease and bully others, and *harassers* and *defamers* who up the ante with their frequently illegal attacks. There are a host of difficult people online who range from the power-hungry and the aggressive who leave victims in their wake, to those whose cluelessness creates all sorts of problems online. And there are dangerous people like online stalkers who become so obsessed that their victims often fear for their and their families' safety and lives.

The big question you need to ask here is what kind of people would do this? What motivates them? What makes them tick?

Anatomy of a Troll

If you grew up hearing fairy tales or mythological stories, the famous Norwegian tale "Three Billy Goats Gruff" may be familiar to you. In the story, three goats want to cross the bridge over the river to get to fresh green grass on the other side. But before they can do so, they encounter a troll who threatens to kill and eat them. Through quick thinking and cunning, the goats trick the troll, who eventually is thrown off the bridge, never to be seen again. As the story illustrates, trolls are nasty creatures, pretty much always up to no good, and ugly to boot.

Figure 4.2 *Word Cloud made with ABCya! Word Clouds for Kids*

Like their mythological counterparts, Internet trolls are also dreadful. Unfortunately, they are quite real. Internet trolls are attention-seekers whose sole goal is to wreak havoc online for the purpose of fun and pleasure. Moreover, they thrive on the perceived weakness, naiveté, and emotional reactions of their victims.

They delight in insulting, shocking, upsetting, and provoking others. They do this in a variety of ways. They write attacking and inflammatory content. They bring irrelevant and extraneous information to online exchanges to throw discussions off course. They post offensive and shocking images, often doctored to serve their purposes. No topic is off limits for them, and the more controversial, the better because outrageous actions are more likely to elicit strong responses from those targeted. According to Derek Wood, a board certified psychiatric nurse who also holds a Master's degree in psychology, trolls "often see their own self-worth in relation to how much reaction they can provoke."[7]

Trolls favor operating in full view on public message boards, forums, and comment sections of articles. After all, only if someone sees their destructive handiwork is it worth their effort. Entire posts provide pointers on how to be a successful troll. "The Subtle Art of Trolling" offers the following suggestion:

> Outwardly you need to appear sincere, but at the same time you have to tell your *real* audience that this is blatant flamebait. Your skill is shown in the easy way that you manipulate large areas of the Usenet community into making public fools of themselves.[8] [Note: Usenet is an early online communication system that's still in use.]

Although trolls are interested in going for lulz, which is shorthand for obtaining laughter at someone's expense,[9] they're not interested in having to be accountable for their actions. That's why the overwhelming majority of the time they are anonymous online or use pseudonyms. This makes it easy for them to avoid responsibility.

There are many different kinds of trolls. Wood breaks them into the following groups:[10]

- **Spamming troll:** Posts to many newsgroups with the same verbatim post
- **Kooks:** A regular member of a forum who habitually drops comments that have no basis on the topic or even in reality
- **Flamer:** Does not contribute to the group except by making inflammatory comments
- **Hit-and-runner:** Stops in, make [sic] one or two posts, and move [sic] on
- **Psycho trolls:** Has a psychological need to feel good by making others feel bad

Netlingo, meanwhile, classifies them into other categories:[11]

- **Playtime Trolls:** an individual plays a simple, short game. Such trolls are relatively easy to spot because their attack or provocation is fairly blatant, and the persona is faily two-dimensional.
- **Tactical Trolls:** This is where the troller takes the game more seriously, creates a credible persona to gain confidence of others, and provokes strife in a subtle and invidious way.
- **Strategic Trolls:** A serious form of game, involving the production of an overall strategy that can take months or years to develop. It can also involve a number of people acting together to invade a list.
- **Domination Trolls:** This is where the trollers' strategy extends to the creation and running of apparently bona-fide mailing lists.

Sometimes trolls act alone. John Lindsey is the creator of DontEvenReply.com, a website where he publishes email replies he sends to people posting classified ads. In his own words, his aim is "to mess with them, confuse them, and/or piss them off,"[12] and he succeeds in doing so on a regular basis. Here's an example:[13] The original ad stated, "hi there i am a 22 year old female babysitter looking for a job. i am available pretty much all the time so if you need someone to look after your kid, let me know!" Here's his reply, written under the fake name Timmy Tucker:

"Hey, I saw your ad about babysitting and am very interested. My grandmother is in the hospital and is probably going to die. She is never awake when I am there, and the doctors say she is only awake for about 5 minutes every couple of days. The problem is, I need her to sign a re-drafted will I wrote so I can get all of her stuff when she dies. Right now she has all of her money going to my bitch sister and her family. I don't have the time to sit there and watch her all day because I have better things to do. I need you to sit at the hospital and watch her in case she wakes up, and then make her sign the will. I will pay you $10 an hour for this job. Thanks, Tim." Timmy received the brief reply, "no thanks that is sick! show some sympathy you prick!" and the conversation escalates to more money being offered in exchange for turning off the grandmother's life support. The exasperated young woman finally responds with a "F**K OFF."[14]

Other times trolls band together to inflict pain. Such was the case after 7th grader Mitchell Henderson committed suicide in 2006. After the boy's death was mentioned on MyDeathSpace.com, a website that archives the profiles of deceased MySpace and Facebook users, members of the /b/ board on 4chan.org took note.[15] 4chan.org is well known for harboring "the rude, raunchy underbelly of the Internet,"[16] so the fact that trolls zeroed in on Henderson's death wasn't surprising in itself. But the torment they inflicted on the boy's parents was over the top. Mark Henderson, Mitchell's father, says that for a year and a half, he and his wife received calls at their home saying things like, "Hi, this is Mitchell, I'm at the cemetery" and "Hi, I'm Mitchell's ghost, the front door is locked. Can you come down and let me in?"[17] Bridget Agar suffered similar anguish when trolls sent up a fake Facebook page within 24 hours after her son Jordan died in a moped accident a day after his 16th birthday. Agar was sent a message from the site that said, "Mum, I'm not really dead. I'm sat [sic] at the computer, I just ran away" and also invited her to a birthday party for her son.[18]

Regardless of their preferred method of operation, as Figure 4.3 reminds us, it's important to remember one thing: Do Not Feed The Trolls.

Figure 4.3   *Always remember, Do Not Feed The Trolls! Photo by Patrick Africanus in the public domain via Wikimedia Common*

How to Deal with Trolls

Trolls delight in getting a reaction and will keep attacking a target as long as it gets them the outcome they want, which is recognition by their fellow trolls and an emotionally laden response by their victims. The reactions trolls receive empower them more and give them extra motivation to continue.

Keep in mind that trying to reason with trolls won't work either. Any attempt to approach them rationally will be a waste of time and will most likely backfire as well. Trolls will mock your reasonable request to consider additional viewpoints, to look at information objectively, and to stop personal attacks against you, your family, or your employer and use it as further ammunition down the road.

So what will work? "Do not feed the trolls" or DNFTT is the single most important thing to remember when dealing with trolls. Do not engage them in any way! The DNFTT approach entails two parts, ignoring them and disempowering them.

Ignoring trolls is easier said than done. After all, when someone says something that's ludicrous and not based in reality, or when they come after you, your natural inclination is to want to set them straight and defend yourself or your company. But this counterintuitive step is what you need to take if you want to get rid of a troll. Don't engage them in conversation, whether publicly or behind the scenes. And, if possible, don't let them see that they've gotten to you either because that will simply give them added credibility among their peers and encourage them to stick with you as a good victim.

Disempowering them involves having their comments removed or having them entirely blocked from participating on a particular site. If a discussion forum has a moderator, you can report the troll's actions to him. Make sure to do so in a fair and constructive way, detailing the examples of what's occurred, preferably pointing out that the troll isn't adding any value to the conversation and is undermining the discussion's continuation or group's cohesiveness.

But be careful. Trolls may be quiet for a while and then reengage, once again going after you, your business, or your website.

Dealing with Sockpuppets

Once upon a time, sockpuppets were made out of old socks adorned with a pair of buttons as eyes and decorated with additional features such as a nose and hair. Although the sockpuppets of yesteryear still exist, as the parents of young children can attest to, Internet sockpuppets are hardly innocent and happy playthings.

Today, sockpuppets are better known as the false identities used by individuals online. The reason for using a sockpuppet is to be intentionally deceptive, whether for purposes of entertainment, to undermine or attack an opponent, or to gain social, political, or business advantage. Unlike pseudonyms, which are the names that people use to represent themselves online, sockpuppets claim to be the real identities of people.

Wikipedia, the fifth largest website in the world and therefore undeniably influential, is sometimes the victim of sockpuppets. The site has an entire article that discusses sockpuppetry in relation to the online encyclopedia. The site defines sockpuppetry as "the use of multiple Wikipedia user accounts for an improper purpose such as attempts to deceive or mislead other editors, disrupt discussions, distort consensus, avoid sanctions, or otherwise violate community standards and policies."[19] Sockpuppetry can take on many forms on Wikipedia:[20]

- Creating new accounts to avoid detection
- Using another person's account
- Logging out to make problematic edits as an IP address
- Reviving old unused accounts and presenting them as different users
- Persuading friends or acquaintances to create accounts for the purpose of supporting one side of a dispute

However, it's not just Wikipedia that's subject to misuse and deceit through sockpuppets. Unfortunately, it's a widespread phenomenon, as a 28-year-old Bloomington, Minnesota high school teacher found out after being impersonated on Facebook. A fake account was set up under the instructor's name, and former and current students were sent questionable messages such as "Happy birthday, you have my permission to get intoxicated."[21] A few years earlier, in 2006, U.S. Congressman Charles F. Bass's (R-NH) policy director Tad Furtado posted damaging messages under the names "IndyHM" and "IndiNH" against rivals on political websites. As these sockpuppets, Furtado claimed to support Bass's democratic opponent but expressed uncertainly about his chances of winning the next election,[22] thus trying to create doubt in the minds of other readers about the wisdom of supporting the candidate.

In 2012, fast-food Chick-fil-A's president Dan Cathy publicly stated that the company supports the biblical definition of the family unit. Some, such as the president of the Family Research Council, agreed with its position: "Chick-fil-A is a bible-based, Christian-based business...and I commend them for what they are doing."[23] Others, such as the Jim Henson Company, which supports gay marriage and which provided Muppet toys for the Chick-fil-A kids meals, announced on its Facebook page that it had "notified Chick-Fil-A that we do not wish to partner with them on any future endeavors."[24] Shortly thereafter, Chick-Fil-A began a product recall due to a "possible safety issue," claiming that it was "a decision completely separate from the Jim Henson Company's Facebook announcement."[25] Critics considered the timing of these two events too convenient and Chick-Fil-A's action disingenuous. They were especially suspicious when two Facebook accounts popped up that appeared to solely focus on defending Chick-Fil-A.[26] One of the accounts, operating under the name Abby Farle, was labeled as a fake after the Avatar image was identified as a stock photo,[27] feeding into critics' suspicion that the fast-food company was operating unethically. However, it's possible that the sockpuppet was the creation of an overexuberant fan; Chick-Fil-A vehemently denied it was behind the creation[28] and wrote on its Facebook page that "There is a lot of misinformation out there. The latest is we have neen [sic] accused of impersonating a teenager with a fake Facebook profile. We want you to know we would never do anything like that and this claim is 100% false."[29]

Meanwhile, Scott Adams, the creator of the long-running comic strip Dilbert, created a sockpuppet to come to his own aid after writing some things that readers took issue with. First, Adams wrote a controversial blog post about gender inequality that concluded with "I realize I might take some heat for lumping women, children and the mentally handicapped in the same group. So I want to be perfectly clear. I'm not saying women are similar to either group. I'm saying that a man's best strategy for dealing with each group is disturbingly similar. If he's smart, he takes the path of least resistance most of the time, which involves considering the emotional realities of other people."[30] (Note that Adams later deleted the post, but that it was republished by others elsewhere.[31]) A few weeks later he wrote a thought-provoking *Wall Street Journal* article on "How to Get a Real Education"[32] that some readers criticized. Adams isn't the only person online to later regret having written and posted something, but most people either silently weather the storm, have friends come to their aid, ask a spokesperson to release a statement on their behalf, or directly explain their actions. Adams chose a different route, pretending to be a fan named PlannedChaos[33] who actively defended the artist on message boards such as MetaFilter [34] and Reddit.[35] When his real identity was later revealed, Adams unapologetically stated, "I am Scott Adams"[36] and "I'm sorry I peed in your cesspool. For what it's worth, the smart people were on to me after the first post. That made it funnier."[37]

At times the intentions behind using a sockpuppet are not outright self-serving or evil, but the end result still hurts innocent people. "Amina Abdallan Araf," a lesbian Syrian-American, launched the blog "A Gay Girl in Damascus"[38] in February 2011 to draw attention to political issues in the Middle East and the crackdown on protesters during the Arab Spring. In June, a post written by her cousin "Rania Ismail" said, "Amina was seized by three men in their early 20s. According to the witness (who does not want her identity known), the men were armed.... The men are assumed to be members of one of the security services or the Baath Party militia. Amina's present location is unknown and it is unclear if she is in a jail or being held elsewhere in Damascus."[39] Her kidnapping became an international event. A Facebook page in support of Araf was set up, readers were encouraged to contact the Syrian Consulate in Washington D.C., and the U.S. State Department began an investigation into her disappearance.[40]

After photos of Araf were discovered to have been impermissibly taken from the Facebook page of Jelena Lecic, a woman living in London,[41] the hoax was soon revealed.[42] Araf was in reality Tom MacMaster, a married American and Middle East activist studying at Edinburgh University.[43] MacMaster explained that he wrote the "kidnapping" post to explain Araf's absence from the blog while he and his wife were on vacation in Istanbul.[44] After his identity was discovered, MacMaster posted an apology on the "A Gay Girl in Damascus" blog: "While the narrative voice may have been fictional, the facts on this blog are true and not misleading as to the situation on the ground. I do not believe that I have harmed anyone—I feel that I have created an important voice for issues that I feel strongly about."[45] Nevertheless supporters of "Amina" were angry and felt that that the plight of legitimate bloggers, as well as gays and lesbians in the Arab world, was compromised.

How to Identify a Sockpuppet

The first thing you should do is figure out whether people are sockpuppets. Sometimes simply knowing they are fake is sufficient for you to decide to ban them from a community or block their access to a website.

Sometimes it's extremely easy. If the person uses a stock photo or an image of someone else, chances are good that the account is a fake, as mentioned in the previous "A Gay Girl in Damascus" and the Chick-fil-A examples. Next, see if there are any topics that the person talks about on a regular basis, subjects that set him off, or people she either attacks or defends. That can help identify the topics the sockpuppet is tasked to represent. It can also help narrow the possibility of backgrounds that the person comes from. For example, if someone criticizes a pro-gun position, it's unlikely that they're a member of the NRA.

Is the same or a similar comment posted on different threads by different usernames? This is a strong indication that it's the same sockpuppet. Or is there a pattern of the same members within a community always agreeing with each other? This may suggest that a single person is behind several sockpuppet aliases, and that he is having an online conversation with himself to support a particular position or point he wants to make.

Do an online search to see where else the sockpuppet is active. Is there a common thread of interest? Are there overlapping connections and friends? Often other people know the true identity of the person behind the sockpuppet, and seeing the social connections between the puppet and others is a big clue.

Determining the gender of the person is also helpful to narrow down identity. Does the writer use more pronouns, suggesting she is a woman? Or does the writer use more determiners (for example, "a," "the," "that," "these") and numbers and quantifiers such as "more" and "some"), suggesting he is a man?[46]

Are the individuals well-versed in a certain subject that requires specialized knowledge? If they seem to know about medicine, that may indicate that they are a laboratory technician, emergency medical technician, nurse, doctor. If they have legal expertise, then they may be a legal assistant or an attorney. The same, of course, applies to any other work that requires specific knowledge and expertise that most members of the public would not have.

Narrowing down geography can be done by seeing what time of day the person posts online. Is it the same time every weekday? This might indicate that they have a set schedule that revolves around work hours. Or it might help determine what time zone they write from. Does the person mention any geographical markers? How about weather patterns or events?

Analyze and track their word choices, phrasings, grammatical tendencies, and spellings to see if they match that of another person active in the community or forum. For example, some American English spellings are "catalog" and "criticize," whereas "catalogue" and "criticise" are British English. In the United States, someone is called an "ass," whereas in the United Kingdom, the more common term is "arse." An American "guy" is an English "bloke," whereas "soccer" is "football." This may point to a similar background, or perhaps even the same identity, between the sockpuppet and someone else in the group.

Of course, if you are a community moderator or otherwise have access to a website's infrastructure, looking at people's IP addresses is extremely useful in determining whether someone is a sockpuppet. The IP address can help you figure out where the person is located, whether multiple accounts are being accessed from the same IP address (this on its own isn't proof that it is the same person but can provide a useful hint), and whether accounts from the same IP address share different usernames but the same or a similar password.

Dealing with Difficult People

The largest number of online troublemakers fall within the "difficult people" category. Difficult people are those who make your online experience unpleasant or problematic in one way or another. Often arguing for the sake of arguing is what keeps them going. These people can range from those who act thoughtlessly, stupidly, or obnoxiously, to the intentionally mean, overtly aggressive, and power-hungry who want to put you in your place.

When James Holmes opened fire in an Aurora, Colorado movie theater at 12:38 a.m. on July 20, 2012, he injured 58 people and murdered 12, among them a 6-year-old girl, and caused unspeakable pain for their families. In the wake of mass shootings like the 1999 Columbine, Colorado massacre by Eric Harris and Dylan Klebold that killed 12 people; the 2007 Virginia Tech murders by Cho Seung-Hui that took 32 lives; the 2011 Tuscon, Arizona attack by Jared Loughner that killed 6 people and seriously injured U.S. Representative Gabrielle Giffords; and the 2012 Oak Creek, Wisconsin Sikh temple shooting by Michael Page that killed 6 people and injured 4, the debate about private gun ownership and American gun laws has been a frequently occurring one. What made Holmes's actions relevant to the debate about guns, personal safety, and self-defense wasn't just the extent of the carnage, but also the proximity of his actions to people's everyday lives. Holmes planned and committed the mass murder in a location, a movie theater, which made everyone feel like they could have been a potential target.

The same day of the shooting, the media and social networks lit up with heated and angry discussions about the need for stricter gun laws, on the one hand, and the inability to have prevented the murders even with stricter background checks and gun laws, on the other hand. (Holmes had no prior criminal record or visible mental health issues that would have precluded him, under current law, from purchasing the .40 Smith & Wesson Glock handgun, the 12-gauge Remington Model 870 shotgun, or the Smith & Wesson AR-15 semi-automatic rifle with a 100-round drum magazine that he used to execute his victims).

Hours after reports first surfaced about the killings, the National Rifle Association committed a highly embarrassing error. The powerful lobbying organization's official Twitter account posted a message that said, "Good morning, shooters. Happy Friday! Weekend plans?" The offensive Tweet was subsequently removed and spokesman Andrew Arulanandam said, "A single individual, unaware of events in Colorado, tweeted a comment that is being completely taken out of context."[47]

The NRA wasn't the only entity that acted carelessly that day. CelebBoutique, a U.K. online retailer with "a vision of bringing everyone celebrity style at highstreet prices," merrily tweeted "#Aurora is trending, clearly about our Kim K inspired #Aurora dress;)" early afternoon of July 20, as seen in Figure 4.4. The message immediately received a widespread negative response, and CelebBoutique realized that #Aurora was trending due to a mass shooting in the United States and not events on its website. The company issued an apology on its website saying, "We were extremely careless and sloppy in not checking the details of the trending article and wrongly assumed that it related to something entirely different."[48]

Figure 4.4   *CelebBoutique's Tweet on July 20, 2012 (since removed from CelebBoutique's Twitter stream)*

As the hours and days went by and the public was still reeling from the tragedy, the arguments between the pro-gun and anti-gun camps became more insulting. Laura R. Charron tweeted, "#LiberalBumperStickers Only drug dealers should have guns!"[49] Cutter Mills said, "if GUNS killed people, then SPOONS have made the majority of the united states FAT! #OutlawSpoons!"[50] SnoopRoc24, disagreeing with an opponent's position, responded with "guns don't kill people it's the idiot pulling the trigger but don't worry if a guy pulls a gun on you I won't use mine to save you."[51] Meanwhile, Andy Reed wrote, "You members of the @nra really are intellectually stunted troglodytes with an inferiority complex,"[52] and author Salman Rushdie went for the absurd with "Msg to gun fans (M.Python), part 3: Go and boil your bottoms, you sons of silly persons! Now go away or I shall taunt you a second time."[53] Comedian Wanda Sykes tried a bit of humor with "Sumthin's wrong, this mentally ill man was able to buy guns and explosives, and I get carded just for a box of ClaritinD. #needasinuslobby."[54]

What not enough people were doing, however, was having a serious conversation with people from all sides of the issue to find common ground. Dr. Joel Dvoskin is a clinical psychologist who conducted a community mental health forum in Tucson after the 2011 Arizona shooting. Although noting that he felt it would be better if there were not 300 million guns on U.S. streets, he also said it's unrealistic to believe the country would be disarmed. "Instead of having an absurd conversation about whether or not to withhold guns from citizens, we should be having a conversation about living safely among 300 million guns."[55] But having this discussion requires a different approach than we've historically seen, certainly online.

The New York Times bestselling horror novelist Scott Sigler had enough of the online fighting the afternoon after the shootings, as show in Figure 4.5. He wrote, "Watching people use the Aurora tragedy to promote their various political beliefs is sickening. It's not about you."[56]

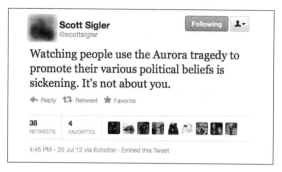

Figure 4.5 *Scott Sigler's Tweet on July 20, 2012*

On a much smaller scale than the Aurora killings, but nevertheless disturbing in its own right, is what happened to a Minnesota teenager. On December 30, 2011, Minnesota high school student and gifted ice hockey player Jack Jablonski became paralyzed due to an injury suffered in a hockey game.[57] Despite the severity of his injuries and the challenges he is facing, his positive outlook on life and spirit were immediately noticeable. Jablonski tweeted messages like "The road to success is always under construction, or reconstruction #optimism"[58] and showed a sense of humor when he described how his electric wheelchair lost power, "#thatawkwardmoment when ur mom turns off ur chair in the middle of the street in the rain w/ every1 is watchin & then ur chair losses power."[59] As an inspiration to many and now known worldwide, it was surprising that anyone would want to attack the boy. But unfortunately someone did, for weeks on end. The hateful tweets included "#4 words 1.Can. Still Walk. #jabs #he wishes" and "the olympics are coming, gonna watch all the track events and laugh because #jabs cant [sic] do anything in them."[60] The public response was strong, with statements like "To the kids posting tweets making fun of Jack Jablonski #WaychYourF**kinBack [sic]"[61] and "Heard horrible tale of Twitter bully making fun of Jack Jablonski. So pissed."[62] But it was Jabonski who reacted beautifully and addressed one of his attackers directly with a public refusal to engage in an online hate-fest, as seen in Figure 4.6: "@jabsjokes not gonna play this game buddy."[63]

Here's another example, this time from the world of entertainment, which is explained in greater detail because it's illustrative of the different ways in which people can be careless online, act without completely thinking through all of the possible consequences, and allow their tempers to get out of control. American nerdcore hip hop rapper Christopher Ward, who goes by the stage name mc chris (all lowercase), performed in Philadelphia in July 2012. Richie Branson was the opening act. As music goes, everyone has their own tastes and one person's favorite is another person's headache. In this case, a concertgoer named Mike Taylor didn't appreciate Branson's music and tweeted, "Dear ncrd rapper opening for

Powerglove/mc chris. You're not good enough to pander to me. Better luck next time."[64] That tweet set off a series of events which continued to reverberate days later.

Figure 4.6 *Jack Jablonski's Tweet on July 17, 2012*

On his blog, Branson described what happened: "The crowd in Philly were totally being good to me. Well...except one person in the audience. Apparently, he took to twitter to criticize my performance. No biggie to me, although I don't see why he just didn't go grab a drink from the bar or something during my set if he wasn't feeling it.... During my set, acting as a friend, MC Chris asked the man to leave the building for talking about me. Given that this is my first tour, Chris is working extremely hard to make sure that each show isn't a nervous experience for me...so when he saw that tweet, emotions ran high and he acted in my defense."[65]

mc chris's decision to evict Taylor from the concert quickly spread online after Taylor complained about his experience on Reddit. "I realize my tweet is snarky, but I'm a smartass and I can understand a guy being mad and protective of his opener. However, publicly kicking out a long-time paying fan because they tweeted a negative response about the opener of your show? Are you serious? I realize what I said was petty, but how immature is it to publicly humiliate someone for something tweeted to just my hundred (which are mostly bots) or so followers? Am I not allowed to have a negative opinion?...mc chris definitely came off as a dick...."[66]

Taylor apologized to Branson on Twitter for any negative fallout he might receive from the situation,[67] yet clearly saw himself as the victim and mc chris as the villain of the situation, and made sure people knew it. mc chris repeatedly apologized. As seen in Figure 4.7, he also posted a YouTube video titled, "I'm sorry,"[68] and sent numerous Tweets from his Twitter account.[69] Nevertheless, the story was picked up by MTV, E-online, *Forbes*, *Huffington Post*, and numerous blogs.

Figure 4.7   *Screenshot of mc chris's "I'm sorry" YouTube video*

Branson, the performer who attracted the original criticism, was unfortunately targeted as a result of the backlash. In addition, he was repeatedly called the N-word, prompting him to write about it on his blog[70] and on Facebook, where he asked people to refrain from using such ugly language.

Taylor, meanwhile, gave several interviews, changed his twitter profile to read, "One-day internet celebrity due to getting kicked out of a concert because of a tweet,"[71] and admitted enjoying the attention placed upon him.[72] He also took a final jab at mc chris[73] by linking to an article that mentioned how heavy metal band Iron Maiden positively dealt with a disruptive concertgoer.[74]

So what would have been a better way to have dealt with this situation? To start with, while Taylor certainly had the right to express his dislike of the opening act, he nevertheless could have chosen not to insult Branson publicly on Twitter while stating his preference. His dislike of Branson's performance could have been expressed more productively instead of in a snide and demeaning way. Even though at the time when he wrote it he had only a few hundred followers on the social networking site, everything on the Internet is visible and amplified. He must have known that his Tweet would be seen by someone, as it clearly was by mc chris. For his part, mc chris could have chosen to ignore Taylor's insult and continue on with the show, thus saving himself the grief of having the situation escalate publicly online, having others who claimed they'd attended his shows share their own stories of examples of his unrestrained and unfriendly behavior, and having to go into emergency reputation repair mode. Branson, meanwhile, is the one who came out looking the best.

Dealing with Online Defamers

Online defamers are those who make a false and unprivileged statement of fact about an individual that's harmful to the person's reputation. Defamation, which is a legal term and has a specific meaning under the law, includes libel, which is defamation that's in writing, or slander, which is defamation that's spoken. To be defamatory, the statement must have been made due to negligence or with actual malice, and must be more than simply an opinion. Proving harm to one's reputation is not as simple as it might sound. However, it can include things such as showing that a person either lost a client or didn't land a new account because of the false claims someone made about them.

A defense against defamation is that the statement is true. In other words, even if a statement is harmful to someone's reputation, because it is true means that a defamation action will likely fail. For example, posting online that a woman is old and ugly and therefore won't make as many sales as her younger and more attractive counterpart is an opinion that, although perhaps untrue and even injurious to the woman's reputation, isn't illegal. However, posting online that this same women is embezzling funds from her employer is harmful to her reputation and, if proven false, actionable in a court of law.

Fighting online defamation can be complicated. Often those posting attacking and defamatory statements are made anonymously, so one of the issues is trying to pinpoint the true identity of an anonymous author or commenter. According to attorney Colette Vogele, co-founder of Without My Consent, a nonprofit organization that assists victims of online harassment, it can cost a minimum of $10,000 in legal fees to issue a subpeona to an online company to get them to reveal someone's IP address so that the person behind a statement can be identified.[75] Furthermore, because defamers often claim they are protected under First Amendment Freedom of Speech grounds, it makes innocent victims appear as though they are opposed to freedom of speech, when actually they are opposed to lies and injury.

Carla Franklin, a former model and Columbia Business School graduate, decided to pursue legal action to reveal the identities of "JoeBloom08," "JimmyJean008," and "greyspector09" who called her a "whore" and posted other nasty and untrue statements about her on YouTube.[76] It took her months to get search engine Google to remove the content and reveal information linking her attacker to the posts in question.[77] Three years later her case still isn't fully resolved.[78]

If they know the person's identity, victims of defamation can try to contact the attacker privately and ask him to please stop saying and writing things that are hurtful and injurious. Sometimes this approach works, especially if the attacker isn't a mean-spirited individual and instead made the statement more due to negligence than to malice. The victim can also try to contact the website where the statement is posted and politely request that it be removed, along with the indexing of that page so that it won't appear in online searches for the person's name. As shown in Figure 4.8, Google receives requests to remove items from the search engine every year. However, in most cases the request will fall on deaf ears. Websites aggressively compete for readers, and anything that increases their readership, even if it's hurtful or injurious to someone, is seen as a means to an end.

▲ Product	Court Orders	Executive, Police, etc.	Items Requested To Be Removed
🖼 Web Search	92	7	777
Copyright	2	–	12
Defamation	46	1	659
Privacy and Security	36	4	67
Impersonation	1	2	3
Other	7	–	36

Figure 4.8 *Google Transparency Report for the United States between July–December 2011 showing the number of requests made for the removal of defamatory items*

Getting an attorney involved may be necessary. Climate scientist Michael Mann, whom we mentioned in Chapter 3, took a direct route against those he believed defamed him. When National Review Online published the article "Football and Hockey" by Mark Steyn[79] which stated, "Michael Mann was the man behind the fraudulent climate-change 'hockey-stick' graph," Mann fought back publicly. A few days later, as shown in Figure 4.9, Mann's lawyer sent a letter to Scott Budd, the executive publisher of *The National Review*: "The purpose of this letter is to put you on formal notice of the defamatory content of a recent article that was published on your website, National Review Online, regarding my client Michael Mann, and to demand a retraction and apology. We also demand that the publication be removed immediately....The article makes the false allegation that Dr. Mann has engaged in academic fraud, an allegation which, of course, is defamatory per se."[80]

Figure 4.9 *Letter from Michael Mann's attorney to The National Review*

Furthermore, an important thing to keep in mind is that winning a defamation suit works only for statements made in the past. These suits don't prevent an individual or online gossip site, which gets its revenue from advertisements dependent on large readerships, from continuing to attack someone in the future and make their life miserable for entertainment and money. Victims of such attacks therefore need to think long and hard whether they are up to the challenge of pursuing their legal rights, and what it will cost them emotionally and financially.

Cyberbullies, Cyberharassers, and Cyberstalkers

Unfortunately there are no uniform definitions for cyberbullying, cyberharassment, and cyberstalking. However, cyberbullies and cyberharassers generally refer to people who use technology to purposefully and repeatedly hurt others. Cyberbullying is most commonly thought of in connection with children and teenagers, but, as this book shows, it's something that frequently happens to adults as well. Many U.S. states have enacted anti-cyberbullying laws to protect children and teenagers, whereas laws that specifically protect adults from the same harms aren't as prevalent. Instead, the law tends to rely on existing antiharassment or antistalking statutes, many of which don't specifically address or sufficiently protect against Internet-based attacks that don't include actual threats of physical harm.

Cyberstalking, meanwhile, is generally defined as using electronic means to harass, frighten, and stalk a victim. Targets can feel very unsettled and frightened not only for their own safety, but their family's safety as well. Cyberstalkers are often obsessed with their targets and have a strong emotional desire to control them. They follow their targets around online, appearing and frequenting places their targets are active, and often leave them intrusive or harassing messages via email, website comments, or social networks. Sometimes they attempt to become friends with a target's inner circle, posing as someone close to the target and trying to gain entry that way. Other times they install spyware on their computers and infiltrate their target's personal files and email accounts, and activate computers' own video cameras to observe their victims in private activities and compromising positions.

Sandra L. Brown, M.A., is the CEO of The Institute for Relational Harm Reduction & Public Pathology Education and the author of *Counseling Victims of Violence: A Handbook for Helping Professionals* (1991, 2006), *How to Spot a Dangerous Man Before You Get Involved Book and Workbook* (2005), and *Women Who Love Psychopaths* (2008). She argues that cyberstalkers fall within "Cluster B Personality Disorders" as defined by the Diagnostic and Statistical Manual of Mental Disorders, which is used by mental health professionals in the United States to classify mental disorders. They usually suffer from low empathy, which is concerning because "without empathy, pathologicals find pleasure in harming others and enjoy seeing the physical or emotional destruction of others."[81]

What to Do If You Are Being Harassed or Stalked

Make sure to check out the Stalking Resource Center at www.victimsofcrime.org, which offers detailed information about what people can do to try to protect themselves against stalkers and what they can do if they're already a target. The site also provides a downloadable "Stalking Incident and Behavior Log."

But once you're being stalked, the action you take against attackers will depend on the severity and frequency of what they've done. Let's say you receive a strange message from someone, for example an email sent to your public email account that says they like the neighborhood where you live, which they say they found when they looked up your home address via online search records. Although it can be disconcerting, without additional action or escalation on their part, there is often no further action to take. Keep a copy of the message, note the circumstances surrounding its receipt (time, place, whether it was in response to something you said or did, who the person is, whether you have a prior connection to the individual, and whether they are known to you), and then file it away. If you feel particularly unsettled, you can go to your local police department and leave a report with them about the incident. In many cases, however, the message will likely be an isolated one, and you won't hear from the person again.

However, if you receive a threatening message or email online, or one that puts you in fear of imminent harm, please immediately seek help from law enforcement and contact an attorney to determine if you have a case that can be pursued legally.

Online and Offline Can Overlap

Although we're taking about what happens in the online environment, you need to understand that the online and offline environments sometimes overlap or blend together. For example, the unwanted behavior may start online and then go offline when the attacker decides to send letters, packages, or other items to the targets' home or office, or publishes their address, phone number, and email online and encourages other people to contact them in those ways. The stalking or harassment may start in people's neighborhood or at their office and then move online. Or it may simply start and remain online.

Endnotes

1. Danny Brown, "Facebook Hacking and the Value of Social Currency," dannybrown. me, July 15, 2012. Link: http://dannybrown.me/2012/07/15/facebook-hacking-social-currency/

2. Danny Brown, "Facebook Hacking and the Value of Social Currency," dannybrown. me, July 15, 2012. Link: http://dannybrown.me/2012/07/15/facebook-hacking-social-currency/

3. Comment left by Danny Brown on July 18, 2012 on Danny Brown, "Facebook Hacking and the Value of Social Currency," dannybrown.me, July 15, 2012. Link: http://dannybrown.me/2012/07/15/facebook-hacking-social-currency/

4. Danny Brown, "Facebook Hacking and the Value of Social Currency," dannybrown. me, July 15, 2012. Link: http://dannybrown.me/2012/07/15/facebook-hacking-social-currency/

5. Comment left by Danny Brown on July 18, 2012 on Danny Brown, "Facebook Hacking and the Value of Social Currency," dannybrown.me, July 15, 2012. Link: http://dannybrown.me/2012/07/15/facebook-hacking-social-currency/

6. Danny Brown, "Facebook Hacking and the Value of Social Currency," dannybrown. me, July 15, 2012. Link: http://dannybrown.me/2012/07/15/facebook-hacking-social-currency/

7. Mary Brandel, "Five ways to defeat blog trolls and cyberstalkers," *Computerworld*, April 27, 2007. Link: http://www.computerworld.com/s/article/9017938/Five_ways_to_defeat_blog_trolls_and_cyberstalkers?taxonomyId=19&pageNumber=1

8. "Trolling The Web," urban75 e-zine. Link: http://www.urban75.com/Mag/troll.html

9. Definition of "lulz." Link: http://ohinternet.com/Lulz

10. Mary Brandel, "Five ways to defeat blog trolls and cyberstalkers," *Computerworld*, April 27, 2007. Link: http://www.computerworld.com/s/article/9017938/Five_ways_to_defeat_blog_trolls_and_cyberstalkers?taxonomyId=19&pageNumber=1

11. Definition of "Troll, a.k.a. trolling," on NetLingo. Link: http://www.netlingo.com/word/troll.php

12. "What Is This" sidebar on dontevenreply.com homepage. Link: http://www.dontevenreply.com/index.php

13. "Comatose Grandma Sitter," DontEvenReply.com, June 9, 2009. Link: http://www.dontevenreply.com/view.php?post=12

14. "Comatose Grandma Sitter," DontEvenReply.com, June 9, 2009. Link: http://www.dontevenreply.com/view.php?post=12

15. Mattathias Schwartz, "The Trolls Among Us," *The New York Times*, August 3, 2008. Link: http://www.nytimes.com/2008/08/03/magazine/03trolls-t.html?pagewanted=all

16. "4Chan: The Rude, Raunchy Underbelly of the Internet," FoxNews.com, April 8, 2009. Link: http://www.foxnews.com/story/0,2933,512957,00.html

17. Mattathias Schwartz, "The Trolls Among Us," *The New York Times*, August 3, 2008. Link: http://www.nytimes.com/2008/08/03/magazine/03trolls-t.html?pagewanted=all

18. Andy Dolan, "'I'm not really dead': Online trolls open fake Facebook account in name of boy, 16, killed in moped crash and then email his mother," Mail Online, April 18, 2012. Link: http://www.dailymail.co.uk/news/article-2131428/Online-trolls-open-fake-Facebook-account-Jordan-Agar-16-email-mother.html

19. Definition of "Wikipedia:Sock puppetry" on Wikipedia.org. Link: http://en.wikipedia.org/wiki/Wikipedia:Sock_puppetry

20. List of sock puppetry forms on Wikipedia. Link: http://en.wikipedia.org/wiki/Wikipedia:Sock_puppetry

21. Kelly Smith, "Bloomington teacher victim of fake Facebook page," *StarTribune*, June 28, 2011. Link: http://www.startribune.com/local/west/124681958.html?refer=y

22. Anne Saunders, "Bass aide resigns for fake website postings: Policy director posed as a liberal blogger," The Associated Press, September 27, 2006. Link: http://www.concord-monitor.com/article/bass-aide-resigns-for-fake-website-postings

23. The Associated Press, "Chick-fil-A president's public stance against gay marriage surprises some advocates," *The Washington Post*, July 19, 2012. Link: http://www.washingtonpost.com/business/chick-fil-a-presidents-public-stance-against-gay-marriage-surprises-some-advocates/2012/07/19/gJQAtC3vvW_story.html

24. "July 20, 2012," The Jim Henson Company's Facebook page. Link: https://www.facebook.com/notes/the-jim-henson-company/july-20-2012/10150928864755563

25. Curtis M. Wong, "Chick-Fil-A Recalling Jim Henson Kids' Meal Toys As Partnership Severed Over Anti-Gay Donations," *The Huffington Post*, July 25, 2012. Link: http://www.huffingtonpost.com/2012/07/24/chick-fil-a-jim-henson-toy-recall-gay_n_1699597.html

26. Rosie Gray, "Chick-Fil-A Denies Making Fake Facebook Account," BuzzFeed, July 25, 2012. Link: http://www.buzzfeed.com/rosiegray/chick-fil-a-denies-making-fake-facebook-account

27. Don Hamel, "Chick-Fil-A Impersonates Young Girl On Facebook To Defend Its 'Biblical Morality,'" Addicting Info, July 25, 2012. Link: http://www.addictinginfo.org/2012/07/25/chick-fil-a-impersonates-young-girl-on-facebook-to-defend-its-biblical-morality/

28. Rosie Gray, "Chick-Fil-A Denies Making Fake Facebook Account," BuzzFeed, July 25, 2012. Link: http://www.buzzfeed.com/rosiegray/chick-fil-a-denies-making-fake-facebook-account

29. Message posted on Chick-Fil-A's Facebook account on July 25, 2012. Link: https://www.facebook.com/ChickfilA/posts/10151241972190101

30. Susana Polo, "Scott Adams Addresses Men's Rights Activism, Backhandedly Insults Everyone Everywhere," The Mary Sue, March 25, 2011. Link: http://www.themarysue.com/scott-adams-mens-rights/

31. "Scott Adams deletes Post (Which You Can Read Here) Where he Calls MRA's Pussies," Pro-Male/Anti-Feminist Technology, March 7, 2011. Link: http://www.antifeministtech.info/2011/03/scott-adams-deletes-post-where-he-calls-mras-pussies/

32. Scott Adams, "How to Get a Real Education," *The Wall Street Journal*, April 9, 2011. Link: http://online.wsj.com/article/SB10001424052748704101604576247143383496656.html

33. Comic strip artist Scott Adam's sockpuppet PlannedChaos's MetaFilter profile. Link: http://www.metafilter.com/user/128528

34. List of all activity by comic strip artist Scott Adam's sockpuppet PlannedChaos on MetaFilter: Link: http://www.metafilter.com/activity/128528/comments/mefi/

35. List of all activity by comic strip artist Scott Adam's sockpuppet PlannedChaos on Reddit. Link: http://www.reddit.com/user/plannedchaos

36. Admission by Scott Adams on MetaFilter that he is the real person behind the sockpuppet PlannetChaos. Comic strip artist Scott Adam's sockpuppet PlannedChaos's MetaFilter profile, MetaFilter, April 15, 2011 at 11:09 a.m. Link: http://www.metafilter.com/activity/128528/comments/mefi/

37. Admission by Scott Adams on MetaFilter that he is the real person behind the sockpuppet PlannetChaos. Comic strip artist Scott Adam's sockpuppet PlannedChaos's MetaFilter profile, MetaFilter, April 15, 2011 at 11:49 a.m. Link: http://www.metafilter.com/activity/128528/comments/mefi/

38. Link to former blog "A Gay Girl in Damascus." Link: http://damascusgaygirl.blogspot.com/2011/06/amina.html

39. Jos, "A Gay Girl in Damascus blogger kidnapped: Take action!" Feministing, June 7, 2011. Link: http://feministing.com/2011/06/07/a-gay-girl-in-damascus-blogger-kidnapped-take-action/

40. Melissa Bell and Elizabeth Flock, "'A Gay Girl in Damascus' comes clean,'" *The Washington Post*, June 12, 2011. Link: http://www.washingtonpost.com/lifestyle/style/a-gay-girl-in-damascus-comes-clean/2011/06/12/AGkyH0RH_story.html

41. Isabella Steger, "Photos of Syrian-American Blogger Called into Question," *The Wall Street Journal*, June 8, 2011. Link: http://blogs.wsj.com/dispatch/2011/06/08/photos-of-syrian-american-blogger-called-into-question/

42. Melissa Bell and Elizabeth Flock, "'A Gay Girl in Damascus' comes clean," *The Washington Post*, June 12, 2011. Link: http://www.washingtonpost.com/lifestyle/style/a-gay-girl-in-damascus-comes-clean/2011/06/12/AGkyH0RH_story.html

43. Esther Addley, "Syrian lesbian blogger is revealed conclusively to be a married man," The Guardian, June 12, 2011. Link: http://www.guardian.co.uk/world/2011/jun/13/syrian-lesbian-blogger-tom-macmaster

44. Esther Addley, "Syrian lesbian blogger is revealed conclusively to be a married man," The Guardian, June 12, 2011. Link: http://www.guardian.co.uk/world/2011/jun/13/syrian-lesbian-blogger-tom-macmaster

45. Melissa Bell and Elizabeth Flock, "'A Gay Girl in Damascus' comes clean," *The Washington Post*, June 12, 2011. Link: http://www.washingtonpost.com/lifestyle/style/a-gay-girl-in-damascus-comes-clean/2011/06/12/AGkyH0RH_story.html

46. Charles McGrath, "Sexted Texts," *The New York Times*, August 10, 2003. Link: http://www.nytimes.com/2003/08/10/magazine/10WWLN.html?ex=1061784000&en=843e4c97d49a9f82&ei=5070

47. Chris Matyszczyk, "Aurora shootings on Twitter: The unforgivable and the serious," CNet, July 21, 2012. Link: http://news.cnet.com/8301-17852_3-57477203-71/aurora-shootings-on-twitter-the-unforgivable-and-the-serious/

48. Statement by CelebBoutique about its Aurora Tweet made on July 20, 2012. Link: http://celebboutique.com/unreserved-apology-for-aurora-tweet-us.html

49. Tweet by Laura R. Charron @ConshoQueen on July 22, 2012 at 6:31 p.m. Link: https://twitter.com/ConchoQueen/status/227184043328950273

50. Tweet by Cutter Mills @CutterMills on July 22, 2012 at 7:19 p.m. Link: https://twitter.com/CutterMills/status/227196173180620800

51. Tweet by SnoopRoc24 @EvilDeedsBaller on July 22, 2012. Link: https://twitter.com/EvilDeedsBaller/status/227172007412912128

52. Tweet by Andy Reed @Revelation137 on July 22, 2012 at 8:47 p.m. Link: https://twitter.com/Revelation137/status/227218223651758082

53. Tweet by Salman Rushdie @SalmanRushdie on July 21, 2012 at 10:10 a.m. Link: https://twitter.com/SalmanRushdie/status/226695658386632704

54. Tweet by Official Wanda Sykes @iamwandasykes on July 22, 2012 at 1:29 a.m. Link: https://twitter.com/iamwandasykes/status/227108000442220544

55. Chuck Raasch, "Theater massacre shatters American's sense of security," *USA Today*, July 22, 2012. Link: http://www.usatoday.com/news/nation/story/2012-07-22/Aurora-shooting-sanctuary-security/56420694/1

56. Tweet by Scott Sigler @scottsigler on July 20, 2012 at 4:45 p.m. Link: https://twitter.com/scottsigler/status/226432760846372864

57. Website of Jack "Jabby" Jablowski. Link: http://www.jabby13.com/page/show/444358-social-media

58. Tweet by Jack Jablonski @Jabs_13 on March 27, 2012 at 6:26 p.m. Link: https://twitter.com/Jabs_13/status/184783369878515712

59. Tweet by Jack Jablonski @Jabs_13 on May 5, 2012 at 1:24 a.m. Link: https://twitter.com/Jabs_13/status/198659494488707072

60. Jana Shortal, "Jabonski becomes target of cyberbullying," NBC KARE11, July 18, 2012. Link: http://www.kare11.com/news/article/983698/391/Jablonski-becomes-target-of-cyberbullying

61. Tweet by BRandoNWiltermuth @ssaint21 on July 20, 2012 at 11:10 a.m. Link: https://twitter.com/ssaintt21/status/226348290311086080

62. Tweet by Number 47 @thenumber47 on July 19, 2012 at 9:56 p.m. Link: https://twitter.com/thenumb47/status/226148464118075393

63. Tweet by Jack Jabonski @Jabs_13 on July 17, 2012 at 3:26 p.m. Link: https://twitter.com/Jabs_13/status/225325690227134464

64. Tweet by Mike Taylor @AdmiralMikey on July 17, 2012 at 5:39 p.m. Link: https://twitter.com/AdmiralMikey/status/225389177829728256

65. Richie Branson, "My Performance in Philadelphia and the Dark side of the Internet," The Official Website of Richie Branson, July 19, 2012. Link: http://richiebranson.com/2012/performance-philadelphia-dark-side-internet/

66. Wickerman316, "So I was kicked out of MC Chris' concert last night, by him over tweet..." Reddit, July 18, 2012. Link: http://www.reddit.com/r/gaming/comments/wrm3v/so_i_was_kicked_out_of_mc_chriss_concert_last/

67. Tweet by Mike Taylor @AdmiralMikey on July 19, 2012 at 9:06 a.m. Link: https://twitter.com/AdmiralMikey/status/225984868457267200

68. mc chris's video "I'm sorry" on his YouTube channel mcvblogs, July 18, 2012. Link: http://www.youtube.com/watch?v=H4sKQBbdPbo&feature=share

69. mc chris's Twitter account. Link: https://twitter.com/_mcchris

70. Richie Branson, "My Performance in Philadelphia and the Dark Side of the Internet," The Official Website of Richie Branson, July 19, 2012. Link: http://richiebranson.com/2012/performance-philadelphia-dark-side-internet/

71. mc chris's Twitter account. Link: https://twitter.com/_mcchris

72. Tweet by Mike Taylor @AdmiralMikey on July 19, 2012 at 7:06 p.m. Link: https://twitter.com/AdmiralMikey/status/226135971303927808

73. Tweet by Mike Taylor @AdmiralMikey on July 22, 2012 at 12:05 a.m. Link: https://twitter.com/AdmiralMikey/status/226905783554678785

74. "IRON MAIDEN Singer To 'Fan': 'You've Been Texting For The Last Three Songs! You're A Wanker!'" Blabbermouth, July 21, 2012. Link: http://blabbermouth.net/ news.aspx?mode=Article&newsitemID=177076

75. "Laws held protect online harassers," SFGate, July 18, 2012. Link: http://www.sfgate. com/technology/dotcommentary/article/Laws-help-protect-online-harassers-3714726. php

76. Jose Martinez, "Brainy ex-model Carla Franklin suing Google to expose cyberbully who called her 'whore' on YouTube," NY Daily News, August 18, 2010. Link: http://www.nydailynews.com/new-york/ brainy-ex-model-carla-franklin-suing-google-expose-cyberbully-called-whore-youtube-article-1.204952

77. "Laws held protect online harassers," SFGate, July 18, 2012. Link: http://www.sfgate. com/technology/dotcommentary/article/Laws-help-protect-online-harassers-3714726. php

78. "Laws held protect online harassers," SFGate, July 18, 2012. Link: http://www.sfgate. com/technology/dotcommentary/article/Laws-help-protect-online-harassers-3714726. php

79. Mark Steyn, "Football and Hockey," National Review Online, July 15, 2012. Link: http://www.nationalreview.com/corner/309442/football-and-hockey-mark-steyn

80. Letter from attorney John B. Williams on behalf of his client Michael Mann to Scott Budd, Executive Editor of The National Review, written on July 20, 2012, available on Michael Mann's Facebook page. Link: https://www.facebook.com/photo.php?fbid=4017 67993212742&set=a.401767799879428.89661.221222081267335&type=3&theater

81. Sandra L. Brown, M.A., "Personality Disorders and Pathology Expert Sandra Brown, M.A. Talks About the Mental Disorders Related to Cyberstalking and Online Attacks," CiviliNation, February 28, 2012. Link: http://www.civilination.org/blog/personality-disorders-and-pathology-expert-sandra-brown-m-a-talks-about-the-mental-disorders-related-to-cyberstalking-and-online-attacks/

5

What's Your Conflict Style?

It's Other People Who Are Making Me Crazy, So Why Are We Talking About Me?

Mack Collier is an American social media strategist and the author of *Think Like a Rockstar: How to Create Social Media and Marketing Strategies That Turn Customers into Fans* (McGraw-Hill 2013). He's earned a strong reputation among his peers in the online space, and one of the reasons is because he's generally considered a nice guy. Recent college graduate Cathryn Sloane experienced that first-hand when Collier took a mentor and older brother-type of approach in responding to her ill-fated article, "Why Every Social Media Manager Should Be Under 25."[1] Many experienced communications professionals responded angrily to Sloane's post and called her ignorant, arrogant, silly, foolish, and entitled. Collier, meanwhile, wrote, "An Open Letter to Cathryn Sloane from Someone over the Age of 25."[2] The first thing he did was show sympathy for the onslaught Sloane found herself under—a nice and human touch. His post wasn't an attempt to defend her, however, but was aimed to show her, in a polite and respectful way, why her article rubbed people the wrong way. He even gave her concrete suggestions for how she could make things right. He counseled her to keep in mind that even though online firestorms can be intense, they tend to pass relatively quickly. And finally, he ended the post with a friendly, "Signed, Someone over the Age of 25 That Works in Social Media and Has Said Stupid Stuff Before Too."

When Collier was singled out in a blog post[3] by Ron Shevlin, author of *Snarketing 2.0: A Humorous Look at the World of Marketing in the Age of Social Media*, Collier responded calmly and politely. That initiated a series of lengthy back-and-forth comments between the two men, an exchange that was substantive and in the end left everyone with greater respect for the other. Shevlin described his approach as "disagreeing with the validity of the IDEA or STATEMENT made, not the validity of the person,"[4] whereas Collier responded, "And THAT is such a welcome relief in this space. The majority of the disagreements in this space are centered on the PEOPLE behind the ideas, not the IDEAS themselves."[5] Likely reflecting the sentiment of other readers, communications veteran and former television journalist Ike Pigott declared, "I love the way they hammered out differences in the comments."[6]

It's easy to point fingers and blame others for behaving badly and causing situations that ultimately get out of control. And unfortunately, as many of us know, there are numerous instances in which someone else is truly to blame. But in other cases, online disputes are the result of a negative dynamic between two or more people created by both. One person may be the instigator, but the other person becomes an active participant, thus leading to a vicious cycle of attack-retaliation-counterattack. Jennifer Hancock, author of the teen-focused, "The Bully Vaccine: How to Inoculate Yourself Against Bullies and Other Petty People," wrote in a blog post that "the lesson I've learned the most from taking responsibility for my side of the conflict isn't that conflicts are avoidable. Often, they are not. It is more that by looking to correct my own behavior first, I do not focus on trying to get the other person to change their behavior at all."[7]

There Is No Single Right or Wrong Conflict Style

As Hancock notes, you have a choice in how you respond. One of the most critical parts of making an informed choice is knowing your personal conflict style. And if you know what it is, you can better anticipate your likely reaction to a problem and thereby make a conscious choice about how to respond, instead of reacting to conflict in a habitual and mechanical way. If your preferred style is to avoid a situation, but you'd be better off defending yourself, being aware of this inclination can help you move outside your comfort zone and respond appropriately. This is the same with situations that bring out a person's competitive streak but that would be better served if a collaborative approach was taken.

Keep in mind that there is no single right or wrong conflict style. Each has its own strengths and weaknesses. Furthermore, your conflict style may vary in different situations. Although you may have a preferred style that you gravitate toward, your chosen conflict styles may vary in different situations. Perhaps you are more competitive at work, but more compromising in your romantic relationship.

That's fine, as long as your chosen style serves you and those around you well. Furthermore, keep in mind that addressing problems and resolving disputes online is often different and more challenging than doing so in person. The relationship you have with someone online may be a preexisting one, or you may not actually know the person except in the most cursory sense. Sometime you know them by name only, and sometimes you can't even identify who they are. All these variations play a role in what online conflict style you adopt.

Adult Personal Conflict Styles

Most people who have heard about the classification of adult personal conflict styles perhaps probably learned about them through the Thomas-Kilmann Conflict Mode Instrument (TKI) created by Kenneth W. Thomas and Ralph H. Kilmann in 1974. The TKI was inspired by the famous Managerial Grid Model developed in 1964 by Robert R. Blake and Jane S. Moulton, which outlined people's different leadership styles based on a grid of "concern for people" and "concern for production." The TKI consists of 30 statement pairs that measure someone's preferred conflict style, which ones they use less frequently, and how they compare against the results of members of the norm group. The TKI breaks personal conflict styles into the following categories:

- Accommodating
- Avoiding
- Collaborating
- Competing
- Compromising

Another well-known conflict measurement tool is Style Matters: The Kraybill Conflict Style Inventory, which was created by Dr. Ronald S. Kraybill and was also inspired by Blake and Moulton's work. It's based on 20 questions arranged in a Likert Scale format that's culturally flexible and differentiates between someone's "calm" responses, or those a person uses when issues or conflicts first arise, and "storm" responses, or those the individual taking the inventory uses when issues or conflicts are unresolved and may have grown in intensity. The Kraybill Conflict Style Inventory, which is the evolution of the earlier Adult Personal Conflict Style Inventory, breaks personal conflict styles into following five categories:

- Directing
- Harmonizing
- Avoiding
- Cooperating
- Compromising

For those who want to measure their conflict style using validated instruments, both the Thomas-Kilmann Conflict Mode Instrument and the Kraybill Conflict Style Inventory are worth purchasing. The self-scoring paper version of the Thomas-Kilmann instrument is available from cpp.com, whereas an automatically scoring and graphing online version is available at kilmanndiagnostics.com. The Kraybill instrument is available as a paper version and as an online version from riverhouseepress.com. Both instruments have been successfully used by individuals and businesses for several decades.

But for our purposes here, focus is on the Online Conflict Style Cluster, which is inspired by the Thomas-Kilmann and the Kraybill models. The Online Conflict Style Cluster is composed of the following styles and their personality namesakes:

1. Competing: The Warrior

2. Coercing: The Bulldozer

3. Circumventing: The Dodger

4. Compliant: The Pacifier

5. Compromising: The Negotiator

6. Covert: The Operative

7. Collaborative: The Resolver

After reading the description of each, you can find out which conflict style and personality you are by taking the quiz at the end of the chapter.

Competing: The Warrior

The competing style is reflected by a black-and-white attitude that there are only two possible outcomes to a conflict, either winning or losing. The Warrior regards winning as representing strength, and his entire focus is therefore on attempting to win through any means possible. The other side's desires or goals are viewed as obstacles and impediments to victory. Unless the other side acquiesces, there is either little or no cooperation between the parties because the Warrior believes that his views and position are the only legitimate and correct ones.

The competitive style can be beneficial when the issues are important or serious and the stakes are high. In situations like that, showing strong assertiveness can put the other party on notice that the Warrior is going to stand up for what he believes in. The downside to this approach is that because the Warrior uses all means at his disposal to win, he may not be regarded as someone who always plays fair. The overall tension between the Warrior and others can therefore rise and the conflict thereby escalate. This can be a negative approach with people that the Warrior cares about or needs to maintain a relationship with.

Revisiting this chapter's opening example of Cathryn Sloane's article, "Why Every Social Media Manager Should Be Under 25," the response by communications professional and professor Mark Story illustrates certain elements of the Warrior's Competing style, and ultimately also serves as a good example of how someone can back away from and reconsider a previously entrenched position.

As shown in Figure 5.1, Story initially responded to Sloane's article by leaving a comment saying, "Catherine, as a 47-year-old director of social media, I thought you might like to know that I wrote a book that it (sic) going to be published on September 1st. It's called *Starting Your Career as a Social Media Manager* (http://www.startingacareerinsocialmedia.com/). You can pre-order it on Amazon. And take my advice on this one: you are going to need it."[8]

Figure 5.1   *Mark Story's comment on "Why Every Social Media Manager Should Be Under 25"*

On the same website on which her article appeared, he also submitted his own piece to counter hers, titled "Dear NextGen: A Rebuttal From the Social Media Old Folks,"[9] which be begins with the sentence "I am the Angry Old Guy representative." In it he credentializes himself by describing his professional background, his experience with communications in general and social media in particular, his university teaching experience, his position at a large government agency, and the publishing of his new book. Story goes on to explain where he thinks Sloane went wrong and where even the follow-up piece by the publication's founder and editor-in-chief was "well intentioned, but still a little tone deaf and came from the wrong person." At the end of his article Story addresses his peers and suggests that, "Turning a negative into a positive and showing Cathryn how it's really done is better than telling her that her career just went up in flames," after acknowledging that he'd first "fir[ed] off angry comments that are the equivalent of telling the young kids to get off your lawn."[10]

Coercing: The Bulldozer

Similar to the competing style, the coercive style represents the world view that conflicts are zero-sum games between two or two parties in which only one can be victorious. If the Bulldozer is in a position of authority, he uses this to get his way and "win" regardless of the other party's needs or wishes. The coercive approach typically includes the use of pressure, whether open and direct or subtle and underhanded. This can involve trying to get the other side to do something or refrain from doing something.

The coercive style can be beneficial when a dispute or conflict needs to be dealt with quickly and there is no time to convince the other parties of the validity of the Bulldozer's position. However, the downside to this approach is that it can create resentment in those being coerced and lead them to want to either get back at the Bulldozer or be obstructionists in the future if they find themselves in conflict with him again. If the Bulldozer needs or wants to maintain either a personal or business relationship with others, this can be a negative approach to take.

Much to the chagrin of its client, 2K Game's public relations agency the Redner Group didn't take kindly to the negative online reviews of its client's Duke Nukem's *Forever* game. It used the Bulldozer's Coercing style in dealing with the problem. According to Ben Kuckera, the former gaming editor for the website Ars Technica, it's not unheard of for professional reviewers to get blacklisted if they publish what's perceived to be an overly critical review.[11] But because of the symbiotic relationship between the press and public relations professionals, he was surprised when he saw a public threat made by the Redner Group against reviewers they felt spoke harshly about the game. The Redner Group apparently tweeted that "too many went too far with their reviews...we are reviewing who gets games next time and who doesn't based on today's venom,"[12] which Kuckera felt basically told reviewers that they should keep quiet or face punishment later. 2K Games subsequently terminated its relationship with the agency, which issued an apologetic statement on Twitter, as shown in Figure 5.2: "I have to apologize to the community. I acted out of pure emotion. I will be sending each of you a private apology."[13]

Figure 5.2   *The Redner Group's Tweet on June 14, 2011*

Circumventing: The Dodger

The circumventing style takes the approach that conflict is negative and something to stay away from, if possible. The Dodger regards disputes as uncomfortable and possibly even dangerous and therefore tries to postpone having to deal with them or even completely avoids them. Because he finds conflicts distressing, he uses a variety of approaches to circumvent them. These can include simply refusing to engage, being unavailable to the other party, deflecting attention onto others, withdrawing from a situation, or shutting down attempts by the other parties to communicate.

Circumventing can be a good approach when the dispute is unimportant and simply not worth dealing with in the grand scheme of things. If there are more pressing issues or disputes to deal with than this one, circumventing it due to the existence of other priorities may be beneficial. It can also be a good temporary approach if the Dodger and the other parties need time to cool down and regain control over their emotions. However, this style doesn't enable people to advocate for their needs and wants. Because they don't speak up, the other parties may believe that the silent Dodger doesn't have any objections with their arguments or position. It can also make Dodgers look evasive. Finally, there is additional risk in using this style because it can inadvertently escalate a conflict that is not being addressed and effectively dealt with.

Discount deal website Groupon ran a controversial commercial created by marketing firm Crispin Porter + Bogusky during the 2011 Super Bowl that some people thought was making fun of the plight of Tibetans. With a voice over by actor Timothy Hutton, the commercial said, "Mountainous Tibet, one of the most beautiful places in the world. This is Timothy Hutton. The people of Tibet are in trouble, their very culture is in jeopardy. But they still whip up an amazing fish curry. And since 200 of us bought at Groupon.com, we're each getting $30 worth of Tibetan food for $15 at Himalayan Restaurant in Chicago."[14] Viewers immediately expressed their displeasure on Twitter. When later asked about his company's screw-up, *The Wall Street Journal* described CEO Andrew Mason's answer as feeling he didn't consider the ad offensive, but rather a spoof on celebrity-endorsed public service announcements.[15] He added to this Circumventing response another one sometimes used by Dodgers, which was lay responsibility on others. Mason is quoted as saying, "We turned off the part of our brain where we should have made our own decisions. We learned that you can't rely on anyone else to control and maintain your own brand."[16]

Compliant: The Pacifier

The compliant style is reflected by the view that conflict is uncomfortable and bad, and that it's therefore sometimes best to "go along to get along" with the other side. The Pacifier accepts the narrative proposed by others, allows them to call the shots, and gives in to maintain the peace. The Pacifier is viewed as nonthreatening because he consistently accommodates the needs and wishes of others and puts his needs and desires in second place behind others. No price is seemingly too high to pay to keep disputes from escalating.

The compliant style is one that's adopted by nearly everyone from time to time, regardless of their overall conflict style. It can be useful when the Pacifier doesn't care about the outcome of a dispute or it's not considered that important because the issue at stake is relatively minor or trivial. Perhaps maintaining harmony or nurturing a positive relationship between the parties is more important to him. This style is also useful if the other side is much more powerful, and it's in your best interest to simply try to deal with the situation with as little discomfort or fall-out as possible. If not used excessively, compliance can also show goodwill. However, if the Pacifier is repeatedly compliant, it can lead to the other side assuming he is weak and easily taken advantage of. This in turn can create a power imbalance, resentment on the part of the Pacifier, and an unhealthy relationship between the parties in the future, which is exactly the opposite of what the Pacifier initially intended.

California Tortilla is a restaurant franchise with locations in several East Coast states. It takes a non-assertive approach to customer service that reflects the Pacifier's Compliant style to problem solving. When customers publicly complain on Twitter, the company doesn't argue with the customer and tell them they're being rude, as seen in Figure 5.3, when one person wrote "Chipotle & Qdoba are way better than California tortilla! California tortilla is nasty, a waste of time & money!"[17] It doesn't try to explain their side of the story, doesn't try to tell the customer why they are wrong, and doesn't try to talk the customer out of their opinion. Instead, as shown in Figures 5.4, 5.5, and 5.6, the company consistently responds quickly and offers to try to fix the problem to avoid the possible escalation and continuation of the problem.

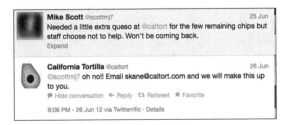

Figure 5.3 *California Tortilla's Tweet on June 26, 2012*

Figure 5.4   *California Tortilla's Tweet on July 13, 2012*

Figure 5.5   *California Tortilla's on July 18, 2012*

Figure 5.6   *California Tortilla's Tweet on July 26, 2012*

The way that California Tortilla responds on Twitter is the way that customer support or online community managers are often trained and expected to respond to complaints—show concern and suggest taking the conversation offline. This can be an effective way of responding to customer issues. Assuming the customer actually emails the company afterwards, the parties can then have a deeper conversation and try to come to a mutually agreeable resolution.

Compromising: The Negotiator

The compromising style reflects a give-and-take approach that takes into consideration the wants and needs of both the Negotiator and the other party. Sometimes the Negotiator's and the other side's wishes are evenly divided, whereas at other times the Negotiator and the other party each agree to give in on some point in exchange for gaining something else. This doesn't necessarily have to be equal in value.

The benefit of the compromising style is that it is perfect for situations in which both sides are willing to give up something without being resentful. It also enables the parties to maintain a positive relationship because the intensity of the exchange isn't as extreme as it is with other approaches, such as the competing style. It can therefore set the stage for positive future interaction. However, a downside is that in their eagerness to move the dispute forward quickly, the parties may compromise on points or issues that they'll later regret having done. Furthermore, because all sides concede in some areas, there's a risk that no one is entirely happy with the outcome.

Just days after the Aurora, Colorado shooting in July 2012, many were incensed and expressed outrage at the parents who had taken their children to the midnight movie showing, feeling that some of the violence committed against the most vulnerable victims could have been avoided if they'd stayed at home. These individuals went on Twitter, left comments on news articles, and blogged about their anger, many in judgmental and vitriolic tones. Child psychologist Heather Wittenberg explained that this was some people's way of coping with the sudden loss of safety they felt about such a violent act taking place in a location where they'd previously felt secure.[18] Jo Ashline, who writes "The Mom Blog" for *The Orange County Register*, opted for another explanation. Ashline wasn't in direct dispute with a particular person, but she did take issue with how some individuals were expressing themselves. Her approach is reflective of the Negotiator's Compromising style. In a blog post, Ashline wrote, "Is a midnight movie (or any movie for that matter) for a 4 month old the wisest parenting decision? We can debate that point ad nauseum. You wanna talk about noise decibel levels and exposure to inappropriate images, and respecting fellow patrons, fine. I get it. But that's not what today's debate has been about and that's what really unnerved me, the hair on my neck standing at attention with each judgmental tweet I read."[19] She pointed out that yes, perhaps there are legitimate reasons why infants and children should not be taken to movie theaters, but that the issue here was actually about something else. She asked people to "turn the focus back on where it should be: that a lunatic opened fire on a room full of fellow human beings—none of whom deserved to die or be attacked that way."[20]

Covert: The Operative

The covert style is similar to the competing style in that the Operative's goal isn't to approach disputes in a positive and constructive manner, but to gain strategic advantage for himself through whatever means necessary. However, unlike the

Warrior, who tends to do so in an open fashion, the Operative goes about this through a secretive, behind-the-scenes, and under-the-radar approach. On the outside he may appear personable and reasonable because this serves his goal to deflect the suspicion of others from himself. Furthermore, his adversary may not even know that she's in his sights because the Operative keeps his feelings masked. Nevertheless, the Operative views the other party as an enemy that must be weakened, overpowered, subdued, and ultimately eliminated. Building alliances with people who view her target as a common enemy is a common tactic used to respond to the perceived conflict, as is using cloaked identities to try to undermine his opponent.

The benefit of the covert style is that it protects the identity of the Operative, making it easy and safe for him to move forward in dealing with the conflict. However, the obvious drawback is that there is no real opportunity for conflict resolution as one side is cloaked and the other does not know who her opponent is. Furthermore, the opportunity to work through potential misunderstandings is impossible for similar reasons.

As mentioned before, conflict can be viewed as an opportunity to peacefully resolve seemingly unbridgeable differences and find common ground and opportunity for mutual growth. But sometimes that's simply not possible. There are examples upon examples online where people act badly toward others, often anonymously so they don't have to suffer the consequences. Those are negative examples of the Covert style. Sometimes, however, the Covert style can be used for good, as this next example shows. Using a fake name, New York City Police Officer Michael Rodrigues friended members of the Brooklyn-based Brower Boys gang on Facebook.[21] He monitored their online discussions, saw when their next burglaries were planned, and had the police set up surveillance videos of break-ins. Gang members even posted pictures of their illegal activities on the social networking site. All this helped law enforcement arrest 14 of the Brower Boys gang and end a year-long crime wave in the area.

Collaborative: The Resolver

The collaborative approach takes a positive view of disputes and conflicts, regarding them as opportunities for growth. Winning versus losing isn't the foundational mindset, whereas finding mutually agreeable solutions that are voluntarily adopted by all sides is. The Resolver is concerned with meeting both his and the other side's needs and wants. All parties are held accountable for the outcome. Collaboration requires emotional maturity, a willingness to openly and actively listen to the other side, and enables creative problem solving.

A benefit of the collaborative style is that the parties have an equal say in the resolution of the dispute. This results in greater satisfaction with and acceptance of the outcome. Furthermore, there is a high likelihood that the relationship between the parties—if that's one of their goals—can be maintained, or at the least that past animosity between them can be reduced. Meanwhile, a drawback is that this approach requires a high degree of trust between the parties, and in situations in which their previous interaction has been painful, trust may prove a difficult hurdle to overcome. In addition, the collaborative approach requires much more time than the other styles and thus may not be suitable for situations in which the dispute must be resolved quickly.

Dell Computers has a strong global reputation as a manufacturer of excellent computers. But what sets Dell apart is its excellence in customer service and addressing customer concerns. It wasn't always that way, however. Back in 2005, the company became the target of an online blogstorm when journalism professor Jeff Jarvis wrote a blog titled "Dell lies. Dell sucks." after a frustrating experience he had with the company.[22] A year later, after ongoing hits against its reputation, Dell realized it needed to change how it went about managing customer problems and decided to do an about-face. It launched a new blog, Direct2Dell in 2006, which specifically tasked technicians with reaching out to bloggers online and addressing the issues they were experiencing. A year later, in 2007, it launched IdeaStorm.com, "as a way to talk directly to our customers" and "to give a direct voice to our customers and an avenue to have online 'brainstorm' sessions to allow you the customer to share ideas and collaborate with one another and Dell."[23] That same year it also launched its @DellOutlet on Twitter, which has more than 1.5 million followers and has earned the company millions of dollars in sales.

Jason Falls, CEO of digital marketing agency Social Media Explorer, visited the Dell campus in Texas in 2011. He notes that the company has more than 24,000 employees who've undergone social media training at Dell's Social Media And Community University, that its customer service and social media teams can engage customers in 11 different languages, and that the company even has an attorney specifically dedicated to social media issues.[24] Dell has come a long way since not knowing how to deal with conflict in a productive and effective way. Today, as Falls says, "The fact of the matter is simply that Dell gets it. [It] understands how chatting with customers online can fuel business.... [It] understands that it's not about controlling the message, but making sure that everyone in the organization—or as many people as possible—can be a part of the message...."[25]

Online Conflict Style Quiz: Which One Are You?

This quiz can help you discover your preferred online conflict style and personality. Read each question carefully and then choose the answer that best matches what your actual response would be.

With some questions, you may be stuck between two equally strong answers. If that happens, choose the response that best reflects the type of choice you've made in the past, or if your response would be different now, choose the answer that matches what you believe you will do going forward. Finally, review the answer against the scoring key to see where you come out.

Question #1: You are the moderator of a Facebook group for small businesses. In violation of group norms, someone repeatedly promotes her own business instead of engaging in a collaborative exchange of information that would benefit all. Your response is

a. Ban the person from the group without warning. The person should have known that her behavior wasn't okay.

b. Message the person privately and tell her that unless she immediately stops self-promoting, she'll be banned from the group.

c. Decide to sit back and see if she continues pushing her own agenda in the group. If she does, you can decide later what you might need to do.

d. Message the person privately; explain to her that she's acting in violation of the group's norm, and ask her to please stop.

e. Post a public comment on the group page telling the person she needs to stop posting self-promotional messages.

f. You know this person's behavior is against group norms, but no one has complained yet, and she isn't otherwise a problem, so you don't see any reason to raise a stink and be confrontational about it.

g. Create a place on the group page where people can talk about their businesses and projects. Then contact the person privately, ask if she'd like to be the first person to introduce her work, and see if you can convince her to limit her self-promotion to this area instead of in the communal part.

Question #2: On your personal blog, you write a blog post about why you're supporting a particular candidate in the upcoming national election. Using their real name, someone leaves a comment whose tone and content you disagree with. Your response is

a. Although you disagree with the writer's comment, you decide to ignore it. After all, why make a big fuss about something someone wrote?

b. You find the commenter's own blog and leave an anonymous negative comment on one of his posts.

c. You engage the commenter directly on your own blog, saying that obviously the two of you have different viewpoints and perhaps the best thing to do is simply agree to disagree on who is right.

d. You directly respond to the person's comment on your own thread, agreeing that perhaps the way you expressed yourself wasn't as carefully done as it should have been.

e. This is your personal blog, and you get to decide what is written on it. You delete his comment and block his IP address.

f. You engage the commenter directly on your own blog, going point by point through what he wrote and countering it.

g. You address the commenter directly on your own blog and thank him for taking the time to read your post. You acknowledge the points he made but respectfully discuss areas you disagree on and why, inviting him to continue the discussion.

Question #3: You see people saying hurtful things on Twitter about a social issue you care deeply about. Your name is included in one of the tweets. Your response is

a. You address them directly and tell them why their remarks are untrue and ugly. People like that need to be told when they're out of line.

b. You internally seethe about their ignorance but decide to remain quiet. People who say things like that aren't interested in hearing alternative viewpoints.

c. You engage them directly and tell them that they better watch out because they'll be in a world of hurt if they keep on saying the things they're saying.

d. You contact your friends and decide to unleash an online lynch mob against the idiots making such statements.

e. You tweet about how people can have different viewpoints on this issue but should first calm down before tweeting when they're highly emotional.

f. You decide to create an online group where people on different sides of this issue can come together to try to find common ground and hammer out their differences.

g. You try to broker a truce between the individuals on your side of the issue and the other side where at least people won't call each other out by name.

Question #4: You belong to an online forum and are one of its earliest members. Most of the group members are genuinely interested in helping others by sharing information sources and personal tips, but a few are actively critical of those members who are asking ignorant "newbie" questions. Your response is

a.   Address the critics directly and suggest that while they may have legitimate points, they'd be more successful getting their points across by softening their tone.

b.   Start a new thread on the forum about how to behave nicely and be supportive of everyone, but don't address the conflict directly.

c.   Leave a private comment for the critics and tell them that you agree with their position but don't want to stir the pot by saying so openly.

d.   Address the critics directly and tell them you don't think their approach is productive or nice and that you expect them to stop or leave the forum.

e.   Address the critics directly and tell them that their approach to the problem isn't helpful and that instead they should be reaching out to forum members who are struggling and offer help, as you're doing.

f.   Start a new thread that asks members to discuss the issue of how to deal with conflict within the group and offer to facilitate the discussion.

g.   Make a mental note that the next time the critics reach out to you for something, you'll make sure to be unavailable.

Question #5: You wrote an off-color but funny comment on one of your personal public social media accounts. HR is concerned that because you are a manager at the company, your comment will reflect poorly on your employer. Even though the company doesn't have a social media policy, the HR manager asks you to delete the comment. Your response is

a.   Tell her that unless she can point to a social media policy that specifically prohibits that sort of thing, you feel it's your legal right to leave it up there as an expression of your personal views.

b.   Tell her you'll take it down immediately, but vow to write something similar as soon as you see the opportunity.

c.   Tell her you would never intentionally do anything to harm the company and then walk away.

d. Tell her that unless she can point to a social media policy that specifically says you can't express your personal views, you feel she's trying to indirectly threaten you and that you plan to speak to your attorney about this.

e. Tell her you are sorry and won't let it happen again.

f. Find out what exactly she found objectionable about the statement to determine if you can leave the statement online in modified form.

g. Tell her you don't want to do anything that could harm the company's reputation, and would like to find out exactly what about your comment was objectionable to her so that you can make sure you understand and can perhaps state things differently in the future.

Scoring Key

Competing, The Warrior: 1e, 2f, 3a, 4e, 5a

Coercing, The Bulldozer: 1b, 2e, 3c, 4d, 5d

Circumventing, The Dodger: 1c, 2a, 3b, 4b, 5c

Compliant, The Pacifier: 1f, 2d, 3e, 4c, 5e

Compromising, The Negotiator: 1g, 2c, 3g, 4a, 5f

Covert, The Operative: 1a, 2b, 3d, 4g, 5b

Collaborative, The Resolver: 1d, 2g, 3f, 4f, 5g

Endnotes

1. Cathryn Sloane, "Why Every Social Media Manager Should Be Under 25," *NextGen Journal*, July 20, 2012. Link: http://nextgenjournal.com/2012/07/why-every-social-media-manager-should-be-under-25/

2. Mack Collier, "An Open Letter to Cathryn Sloane from Someone over the Age of 25," MackCollier.com, July, 2012. Link: http://www.mackcollier.com/an-open-letter-to-cathryn-sloane-from-someone-over-the-age-of-25/

3. Ron Shevlin, "Here's What I Believe (About Marketing And Social Media)," Snarketing 2.0, June 5, 2012. Link: http://snarketing2dot0.com/2012/06/05/heres-what-i-believe/

4. Comment by Ron Shevlin on "Here's What I Believe (About Marketing And Social Media)," Ron Shevlin, Snarketing 2.0, June 5, 2012. Link: http://snarketing2dot0.com/2012/06/05/heres-what-i-believe/#comment-9915

5. Comment by Mack Collier on "Here's What I Believe (About Marketing And Social Media)," Ron Shevlin, Snarketing 2.0, June 5, 2012. Link: http://snarketing2dot0.com/2012/06/05/heres-what-i-believe/#comment-9916

6. Comment by Ike Pigott on "Here's What I Believe (About Marketing And Social Media)," Ron Shevlin, Snarketing 2.0, June 5, 2012. Link: http://snarketing2dot0. com/2012/06/05/heres-what-i-believe/#comment-991

7. Jennifer Hancock, "It takes two to fight," Happiness Through Humanism," July 13, 2012. Link: http://humanisthappiness.blogspot.com/2012/07/it-takes-two-to-fight.html

8. Comment by Mark Story on July 20, 2012 at 4:37 p.m. on Cathryn Sloane's article "Why Every Social Media Manager Should Be Under 25," *NextGen Journal*, July 20, 2012. Link: http://nextgenjournal.com/2012/07/why-every-social-media-manager-should-be-under-25/

9. Mark Story, "Dear NextGen: A Rebuttal from the Social Media Old Folks," *NextGen Journal*, July 22, 2012. Link: http://nextgenjournal.com/2012/07/dear-nextgen-a-rebuttal-from-the-social-media-old-folks-cathryn-sloane/

10. Mark Story, "Dear NextGen: A Rebuttal from the Social Media Old Folks," *NextGen Journal*, July 22, 2012. Link: http://nextgenjournal.com/2012/07/dear-nextgen-a-rebuttal-from-the-social-media-old-folks-cathryn-sloane/

11. Ben Kuchera, "Duke Nukem's PR threatens to punish sites that run negative reviews," Ars Technica, June 15, 2011. Link: http://arstechnica.com/gaming/2011/06/duke-nukems-pr-threatens-to-punish-sites-that-run-negative-reviews/

12. Ben Kuchera, "Duke Nukem's PR threatens to punish sites that run negative reviews," Ars Technica, June 15, 2011. Link: http://arstechnica.com/gaming/2011/06/duke-nukems-pr-threatens-to-punish-sites-that-run-negative-reviews/

13. Tweet by the Redner Group @theRednerGroup on June 14, 2011 at 11:12 p.m. Link: https://twitter.com/TheRednerGroup/status/80850147348709376

14. Emily Steel, "At Super Bowl," Many Ads Fail to Score," The Wall Street Journal, February 7, 2011. Link: http://online.wsj.com/article/ SB10001424052748703989504576128260801960194.html

15. Harry Bradford, "BofA, Goldman And More: 11 Worst CEO Slip-Ups of 2011," *Huffington Post*, December 20, 2011. Link: http://www.huffingtonpost. com/2011/12/19/11-most-embarrassing-ceo-quotes-2011_n_1159119. html#s556673&title=Groupon_We_Turned

16. Brad Stone and Douglas MacMillian, "Are Four Words Worth $25 Billion for Groupon?" Bloomberg BusinessWeek Magazine, March 17, 2011. Link: http://www. businessweek.com/magazine/content/11_13/b4221070014682.htm#p1

17. Tweet by Indya Ade @PoisonMandy on July 18, 2012 at 10:16 a.m. Link: https://twitter.com/PoisonMandy/status/225610003715866624

18. Kevin Fallon, "The Colorado Shooting: Why Mothers Take Babies to Movies," *The Daily Beast*, July 25, 2012. Link: http://www.thedailybeast.com/articles/2012/07/25/ the-colorado-shooting-why-mothers-take-babies-to-movies.html

19. Jo Ashline, "Pointless debate: Do babies belong in movie theaters?" The Mom Blog, The Orange County Register, July 20, 2012. Link: http://themomblog.ocregister. com/2012/07/20/pointless-debate-do-babies-belong-in-movie-theaters/87935/

20. Jo Ashline, "Pointless debate: Do babies belong in movie theaters?" The Mom Blog, The Orange County Register, July 20, 2012. Link: http://themomblog.ocregister. com/2012/07/20/pointless-debate-do-babies-belong-in-movie-theaters/87935/

21. Jose Martinez, "Cop tracked Brooklyn gang Brower Boys by 'friending' them online," *New York Post*, May 31, 2012. Link: http://www.nypost.com/p/news/local/brooklyn/ facebook_em_gang_busted_5ZTTJeeMG2U5BJVztT4CjN#ixzz1wxIPOC9z

22. Jeff Jarvis, "Dell lies. Dell sucks." BuzzMachine, June 21, 2005. Link: http://buzzmachine.com/2005/06/21/

23. About IdeaStorm. Link: http://www.ideastorm.com/idea2AboutIdeaStorm?v= 1343855796359

24. Jason Falls, "Why Dell Is Still a Great Case Study," Social Media Explorer, December 13, 2011. Link: http://www.socialmediaexplorer.com/social-media-marketing/why-dell-is-a-great-case-study/

25. Jason Falls, "Why Dell Is Still a Great Case Study," Social Media Explorer, December 13, 2011. Link: http://www.socialmediaexplorer.com/social-media-marketing/why-dell-is-a-great-case-study/

The 101 of Anger Management

Anger Is a Primal Emotion

In a scene in the movie "Harry Potter and The Order of the Phoenix," Ministry of Magic bureaucrat and professor Dolores Umbridge takes unkindly to Harry's statement that students should learn how to make defensive spells so they can fight Lord Voldemort, who has returned to wreak havoc against all good witches and wizards. As punishment for his outspokenness and insubordination, Umbridge forces Harry to use a blood quill to repeatedly write, "I must not tell lies" on a piece of parchment. A blood quill, for those unfamiliar with this type of torture device, is a writing instrument that uses the writer's blood as ink. The quill also cuts the written words into the nonwriting hand, effectively scarring the person. The process is extremely painful and sadistic, which is what makes it so appealing to Umbridge, who doesn't know how to manage and express her anger other than through destructive means, and certainly doesn't care to learn.

Despite the terrible things that happen in "Harry Potter," at least you know that the books and movies are fiction. However, there are plenty of real-life events that bring a chill to your spine, as you see throughout this book. Sometimes it's the result of a simple misunderstanding that can be rectified; sometimes it's more complicated than that. But more often, anger, or rather uncontrolled anger to be precise, is usually an underlying factor when people act badly online. As you've also seen, the online and offline worlds are inextricably intertwined, making it hard to argue that what happens online doesn't affect what happens in your day-to-day lives and vice versa.

The issue of uncontrolled anger is something that Sue Jacques understands all too well. Today, Jacques is known as The Civility CEO and works as a corporate civility and executive etiquette professional.[1] However, before that she spent more than 18 years as a forensic death investigator, where she performed thousands of medical investigations on the deceased including deaths caused by suicide, negligence, physical mistreatment, and homicide.[2] Looking back at what she learned from all those years staring death in the face, she says: "At the ME's office I was surrounded by irrefutable physical evidence that our actions can have fatal consequences, and I learned that it matters—it really matters—how we treat ourselves and one another. I saw way too many unfinished lives and heard about far too many regrets."[3] On the issue of online civility, Jacques is pensive: "All of us got on that freshly paved electronic highway a few years ago before anyone had a chance to post the road signs. As a result, we started making up rules as we went along.... Of course! We are just now beginning to understand the impact of those behaviors and realizing that electronics, socialization, and focus don't always go hand in hand."[4]

As Jacques realizes better than most people, actions have consequences, and intense emotions such as anger can lead to tragic outcomes, as reflected in a quote taken from her blog post "Life After Death"[5], as shown in Figure 6.1.

> One thing that I know for certain I learned from both death and life. And that is that it matters, it really, truly matters, how we treat ourselves and how we treat one another. *It's simply not worth it to be unkind.*

Figure 6.1 *Sue Jacques, "Life After Death," The Civility CEO, November 30, 2011*

It's negative expressions of anger and their resulting destructiveness that usually come to mind when you think about anger, as shown in Figure 6.2. But the reality is that anger is neither good nor bad; it simply is. In some cases, anger can even be beneficial and serve as a protective device or warning signal. Psychiatrist Neel Burton, author of *Hide and Seek—The Psychology of Self-Deception*,[6] says, "Anger can serve a number of useful, even vital, functions. It can put an end to a bodily, emotional, or social threat, or—failing that—it can [mobilize] mental and physical resources for defensive or corrective action."[7] Carol Tavris, Ph.D., author of the classic work *Anger: The Misunderstood Emotion*,[8] wrote, "Anger, like love, is a moral emotion. I have watched people use anger, in the name of emotional liberation, to erode affection and trust.... And I watch with admiration those who use anger to probe for truth, who challenge and change the complacent injustices of life...."[9]

Figure 6.2   *Are her anger problems and the dent in the wall connected? Zoe Foulks' Tweet on August 18, 2012.*

Because anger is such an important and misunderstood emotion, an entire chapter is spent on it. In this chapter we are going to examine anger and its triggers so you can recognize it in yourself and others whom you deal with online. Understanding anger will help you be more effective at work because it will help you recognize why people get angry, and thus be able to better diffuse anger in others and even yourself. The terms uncontrolled and negative anger are used interchangeably.

An Important Note About This Chapter

This chapter is intended as an overview of the topic of anger and not as a substitute for therapeutic advice. People with anger management problems should seek professional help because their behavior likely has deep-rooted causes. Unfortunately, people with anger management problems often don't voluntarily seek help on their own because they're more focused on pointing to outside "reasons" for why they act the way they do, rather than recognizing that they need to take personal responsibility for their own behavior. This chapter is intended foremost as a resource for those who are exposed to individuals with anger management issues in an online environment. Whether you are a blogger, someone who participates heavily in social media networks like Twitter or Facebook, or if your job is to interface with the public, you should find some helpful advice in this chapter. You will also learn more about your own anger triggers and how to productively deal with them.

What Happens to You When You Become Angry?

According to psychologist Robert Plutchick, Ph.D., author of the book *Emotion: A Psychoevolutionary Synthesis*,[10] there are eight basic human emotion dimensions, namely joy, trust, fear, surprise, sadness, disgust, anger, and anticipation.[11] Meanwhile, Dr. Jaak Pankseep,[12] co-author of *The Archaeology of Mind: Neuroevolutionary Origins of Human Emotions*,[13] defines the fundamental emotions as seeking, rage, fear, lust, care, panic/grief, and play.[14] Although experts may disagree about precisely how many emotions exist, everyone has at one time or another felt angry, even as babies,[15] and it's an emotion we share with many other animals on the planet.

The specific area of your brain that's relevant to feelings of anger is the amygdala, which is a part of your limbic system.[16] Unlike the prefrontal cortex, which is involved in higher reasoning, the amygdala is a relatively primitive area of the brain that's responsible for your protective "fight or flight" response. This section of the brain continues to be an ongoing source of fascination for people. When you feel angry, which is often due to either a perceived or actual threat, either emotional or physical, you tend to try to fight back in some form, which can involve feelings of anger, or you try to flee the situation, which can include feeling fear. In some cases, fear and anger can be intertwined. So what exactly happens to you when you become angry? According to a recent study,[17] when we get angry, levels of the stress hormone cortisol decrease, while our heart rate, arterial tension, and testosterone levels increase.[18] Kevin Fauteux, Ph.D., author of *Defusing Angry People: Practical Tools for Handling Bullying Threats and Violence*,[19] describes some of the typical physical signs we manifest, such as getting a flushed face, feeling warm or hot, having a pounding heart, having tense muscles, and clenching one's jaw or fists.[20] Other signs can include stomach upset or pains and accelerated or shallow breathing. A person's ability to think clearly is also often compromised, with concentration being difficult and short-temperedness fairly common. Fortunately for most people with healthy anger expressions, the emotion goes away after approximately 10–15 minutes.[21]

Are There Differences in Who Becomes Angry and How They Express It?

Socially there are differences between who is allowed to express anger without stigmatization and who isn't. For example, anger is generally considered more acceptable in men than in women. According to anger researcher Raymond DiGiuseppe, Ph.D.,[22] professor and chair of the psychology department at St. John's University, men express their anger more physically than women and are more passive aggressive, whereas women hold on to their anger longer and don't express their anger as openly as men do.[23] Yale University psychologist Victoria Brescoll, co-author with

Eric Uhlmann of the research article "Can an Angry Woman Get Ahead? Status Conferral, Gender, and Expression of Emotion in the Workplace,"[24] noted, "For men, expressing anger may heighten status: Men who expressed anger in a professional context were generally conferred higher status than men who expressed sadness. For women, however, expressing anger had the opposite effect: Professional women who expressed anger were consistently accorded lower status and lower wages, and were seen as less competent, than angry men and unemotional women."[25]

Meanwhile, all other things being equal, researchers have found additional differences in anger expression. People who are under greater financial pressure feel more angry than those who don't have the same hardships (something that Jude in Figure 6.3 understands), whereas people with underage children in the house tend to feel more angry than those who don't have underage children in the house.[26] These and other findings are discussed in detail in the reference work "International Handbook of Anger: Constituent and Concomitant Biological, Psychological, and Social Processes."[27] More educated people are likely to feel fewer bouts of anger compared to their counterparts with less education, whereas younger people feel angry more often than older adults.[28] This last group is perhaps not completely surprising if you consider the fact that humans' prefrontal cortex (the part of our brain that is responsible for analytical thinking and problem solving, weighing of consequences, delaying gratification, and impulse control) isn't fully matured until age 25.[29] Not surprisingly, it appears that sociological and life circumstances have an impact on an individual's degree of anger and anger management.

Figure 6.3 *Jude understands the connection between anger and money problems. Jude's Tweet on August 24, 2012.*

However, people's individual characteristics, combined with how they analyze and react to a given situation, are the most important aspects of why some people seem to easily fly off the handle and others are more even-keeled. Referencing the 1996 work[30] of Jerry L. Deffenbacher, Ph.D.,[31] Ryan C. Martin, Ph.D.,[32] anger researcher and associate professor in the Human Development and Psychology departments at the University of Wisconsin-Green Bay, explains it this way about personal characteristics: "There are actually two things that matter: personality traits and the pre-anger state. Starting with the personality traits, we know that there are certain characteristics that make people more likely to experience anger (e.g., narcissism, competitiveness, low-frustration tolerance).... The second part of this, the pre-anger state, includes how the person was feeling physiologically and psychologically right before the situation. When people are tired, anxious, or already angry, they are more likely to respond with anger."[33] Concerning cognitive appraisal, or how people process and ultimately respond to a given situation, Martin says people become angry when they perceive situations as being unfair, wrong, or otherwise worthy of punishment.[34]

Why do people seem to have different trigger points at which they become angry? What sets them off? According to Matthew McKay, Ph.D.; Peter D. Rogers, Ph.D.; and Judith McKay, R.N.; authors of the book *When Anger Hurts: Quieting the Storm Within*,[35] anger results after a series of precipitating verbal or nonverbal behaviors that bring forth uncomfortable feelings in an individual.[36] Together these behaviors form a link, with "the last link in an anger chain...often called a 'trigger behavior.'"[37] The authors explain that examples of such links can include anything from verbal behaviors that bother the person, such as receiving unwanted advice or complaints, feeling blamed or criticized, or being teased, humiliated or insulted, to physical behaviors such as being scowled at or intimidated.[38] However, you shouldn't make the mistake of abdicating personal responsibility for angry feelings onto outside factors because obviously not everyone reacts to the same trigger equally or equally badly, which suggests that some people deal with anger in more healthy and constructive ways than others.

Mike Fisher is the founder and director of the British Association of Anger Management, an organization that offers support and training for individuals or organizations needing help with anger management issues.[39] In his book *Beating Anger: The eight-point plan for coping with rage*,[40] he describes five different "faces" of anger,[41] namely the various manifestations of people's anger, as follows:

- **The caring face of anger:** Represents anger based on wanting to protect those things we care about most deeply in life, such as our family and friends, our community, the earth or anything else that's near and dear to us.

- **The self-diminishing face of anger:** Represents anger turned self-destructively against oneself in a passive-aggressive way.

- **The numb face of anger:** People hide their actual painful or uncomfortable feelings such as hurt, sadness, fear, or shame.

- **The unrealistic face of anger:** Anger based on people's expectations for others and how the world should operate instead of how it actually does.

- **The addictive face of anger:** The use of a substance or behavior to cover up and avoid having to feel anger. These can include alcohol, drugs, food, sex, gambling, religion, excessive materialism, and hyper intellectualism.

For negative aggressive anger, people in one of two distinct aggressive personality dimensions are more prone to this type of expression:[42] "The first aggressive personality dimension is general aggression, which is characterized by frequent anger and direct retaliation in response to interpersonal provocation in both laboratory experiments and real-world settings....[while] [t]he second aggressive personality dimension is displaced aggression, which is characterized by responding to insults with rumination instead of immediate aggression, and eventually 'taking out' aggressive urges on the innocent."[43] It's the negative expression of anger that this chapter primarily focuses on.

Patricia Evans, author of the bestselling book *The Verbally Abusive Relationship: How to Recognize It and How to Respond*,[44] explains that people who are abusers express anger due to their underlying feeling of powerlessness. "Most verbal abusers are filled with inner tension, which they periodically and unpredictably release with angry outbursts directed at their partners. The tension then builds again until the abuser releases it with another outburst. This build-up of tension and its release become a cyclical pattern of behavior," which reflects what Evans calls the cycle of anger addiction, with the abuser an anger addict.[45]

Why People Become Angry

There are many different reasons why people become angry. Some of these sound reasonable (someone steals your identity online), and others less so (your spouse forgets to wipe the kitchen counter after making dinner). But what are the true underlying reasons people become angry? There are a number of emotional, cognitive, situational, or physical explanations.

Often, anger is a cloak for other emotions we are afraid to admit to others, or even ones we try to personally avoid recognizing. (Anger can even be confused with other emotions, such as annoyance or frustration, which is something talked about in the section, "Don't Confuse Anger With Other, Similar Emotions," later in this chapter.) Anger can be an attempt to mask someone's true feelings of fear, sadness, insecurity, embarrassment, humiliation, vulnerability, disrespect or shame. In other words, people use it to emotionally protect themselves.

For example, rather than express fear and sadness about having lost a job they cherish, some people simply react with anger. Anger can certainly be one feeling they might be carrying with them in that particular situation, but often it's one of several, another perhaps being fear about the future, although anger is the only one that's expressed and consciously felt. Feeling concerned about a loved one can also manifest itself in anger, which appears to have been the situation exemplified in Figure 6.4.

Figure 6.4 *Lars Gotrich expressing anger at his mother's boss. Lars Gotrich's Tweet on August 20, 2012.*

Another example where anger might serve as a cloak for other emotions could involve instances where one feels embarrassed. Imagine a situation, quite common in today's online world, where people post a photo of themselves online. An individual they don't know finds it and uses it as the basis for a hateful meme about ugly people. In that instance, it may be easier to express anger online in response than publicly admit to feeling embarrassed and hurt. A third example might include anger expressed at a partner who wants to get a divorce. In that situation, the person may be feeling hurt, scared, and lonely, but expressing anger seems the emotionally easiest thing to do.

Anger is also triggered by perceived or actual threats against someone's positions, values, or needs, which is discussed in Chapter 1, "Who Gives a Darn About Conflict?" A position is the particular stance that someone takes about an issue or situation. For example, look at the ongoing American hot-button debate about healthcare, in which citizens on both sides of the aisle hold strong and passionate views about the Patient Protection and Affordable Care Act (PPACA). Those in favor of decreasing the number of uninsured Americans with the assistance of the federal government were generally in support of PPACA, whereas those who supported private initiatives to help ease the number of uninsured without government intervention were generally opposed to what they alternatively called "Obamacare,"[46] with some expressing the desire to leave the country if the law was passed.[47]

As previously mentioned, values are personal and moral beliefs that guide individuals' and groups' thoughts and behaviors. Anger and even rage (which in an emotion fundamentally different than anger, and something discussed in the next section) can be triggered when people feel that their values, and by extension themselves, are under threat. For example, the issue of gay marriage in the United States remains a contentious one, with personal values, religious beliefs, and social norms all coming into play. Most of the time anger around these issues stays within the noncriminal realm, but tragically, that's not always the case. In August 2012, a volunteer for The DC Center for the LGBT Community shot and injured a security guard at the conservative Christian and anti-gay Family Research Council,[48] an act formally condemned by 45 lesbian, gay, bisexual, and transgender organizations.[49] And the National Coalition of Anti-Violence Programs stated in its report, "Hate Violence Against Lesbian, Gay, Bisexual, Transgender, Queer, and HIV- affected Communities In the United States in 2011,"[50] that there had been a total of 30 hate violence murders reported to NCAVP in 2011, an 11% increase from 2010.[51]

A perceived violation of someone's needs, which include physical, safety, love, esteem, and self-actualization according to Abraham Maslow's *Hierarchy of Needs*, and which include identity, recognition, security, and personal development, according to conflict analysis and resolution pioneer John Burton, can cause an outburst. Imagine you've received an email or a text that says something like these statements:

> *"Remember the drunk text you sent me where you trash-talked our boss? I'm willing to show it to him if you don't withdraw your name for the promotion you know I'm after."*

> *"You know that topless picture you sent me when we were still dating? Well, I posted it online and its really popular. Guess you shouldn't have trashed me to your friends!"* *"@___ you/militant, right-wing nut/ far-left socialist radical, go crawl under a rock and die."*

How does reading these things make you feel? Probably angry.

Although there are many legitimate reasons why people may become angry, individuals who have an unhealthy predisposition toward feeling that way often exhibit what Dr. Martin and Eric R. Dahlen, Ph.D., co-authors of the article "The Angry Cognitions Scale: A New Inventory for Assessing Cognitions in Anger,"[52] call cognitive errors. There are five different types of these thinking errors, namely misattribution, overgeneralization, inflammatory labeling, demandingness, and catastrophic evaluation.[53]

- **Misattribution:** Involves instances in which people make negative assumptions about something without considering more benign or even positive alternative reasons. ("She sent me a really short, matter-of-fact sounding email, so she must be unhappy with me.")

- **Overgeneralization:** Viewing an event in overly broad and usually negative terms. ("I missed a deadline at work, so I'm sure my boss will now always think of me as a no-good under-performer."
  David D. Burns, M.D., author of *Feeling Good: The New Mood Therapy*, describes it as seeing "a single negative event as a never-ending pattern of defeat."[54]

- **Inflammatory labeling:** Sorting things into negative or instigative categories. ("All those guys working on Wall Street are a bunch of selfish, money-grubbing followers of Ayn Rand.")

- **Demandingness:** The belief and insistence that our own interests, needs, and wishes should come ahead of those of others. ("I know you've got a bunch of other reports you're working on sitting on your desk, but I need you to complete mine before tomorrow, no matter how long it takes.")

- **Catastrophic evaluation:** Where an individual regards events or situation in an unsubstantiated negative and extreme light. ("The car has a flat tire and now we're going to miss our flight, which means we'll miss our class reunion and our entire weekend will be ruined.")

In addition to emotional and cognitive reasons, people can also feel angry due to physical problems. When individuals are sick, they are more mentally and physically taxed than normal and therefore more vulnerable and susceptible to becoming angry because of physical discomfort. Even simply feeling tired can place additional stress on someone, resulting in them being short-tempered. Those suffering from chronic pain also frequently feel angry. Linda Ruehlman, Ph.D., co-founder of Goalistics, which offers computer-based tools for treatment of those with chronic pain and depression,[55] points out that there is a direct connection between anger and chronic pain, with some patients turning their anger inward against themselves, and others turning it outward toward loved-ones, friends, or caretakers.[56]

Meanwhile, according to Gina Simmons, Ph.D., a licensed marriage and family therapist, what we eat and drink can also have profound effects on our mood and anger susceptibility. Simmons says that the chemical effects of anger place considerable stress on our brains and the rest of our body, which over time can deplete them of vital energy. She explains that, "Food is a basic ingredient in the formation of natural mood elevating brain chemicals like serotonin. Serotonin deficiencies cause depression, anxiety, anger problems, and eating disorders. Neurons (brain cells) require food nutrients to make the chemical messengers that influence every system of the body. Your emotions can instantly change depending on what you eat. If you grab fast food, boxed, packaged, or processed food, you get a stimulating high from sugar, salt, and fat. Unfortunately, a crash follows as your brain is starved of serotonin enhancing nutrients. The crash causes food cravings that can lead to...irritability."[57] The 2011 study "Effects of Acute Tryptophan Depletion on Prefrontal-Amygdala Connectivity While Viewing Facial Signals of Aggression,"[58] seems to support this notion. The study found that lowered serotonin levels in the brain, which can be caused by diet, namely not eating or not eating enough, weakened the ability of the brain's amygdala to communicate with the frontal lobes, which in turn could result in a weakened ability to regulate one's emotions.[59]

Perhaps another reason people express anger, especially in the online realm, is because they allow themselves to be easily irritated by things they find bothersome or offensive, even things that have little or even no direct bearing on their lives. Nationally syndicated weekly newspaper columnist, journalist, radio host, and bestselling author David Sirota[60] calls it "the Fake Outrage Machine." Using the admission of Olympian Michael Phelps that he smoked marijuana in 2009 as an example, Sirota argues that the United States has become "a nation now addicted to fake outrage—a nation that feeds on made-up controversies about total non-issues."[61] He argues that unless we rein in this behavior, we won't focus on and solve the legitimately pressing concerns we need to find answer to, such as economic, healthcare, and national security issues.[62] craigslist founder Craig Newmark shares Sirota's view that we are excessively and unnecessarily offended: "The broad context is that there are people always looking to feel offended about something. They feel good when they're outraged about something; maybe they feel good only when they're outraged. I don't know about official psychiatric definitions, but as far as I'm concerned, it's addiction."[63]

What you need to keep in mind when talking about anger is why the anger is expressed in the first place. If the feeling is legitimate given all the circumstances, the only question then remaining is whether the method chosen to express it is appropriate and productive. However, if anger is being used as a defense mechanism, the best thing to do is to determine the real underlying emotion behind it and address it directly. Ask yourself whether anger is being used to try to manipulate, coerce, or even intimidate a target, or to make the target feel so uncomfortable that he or she will give in to the angry person's demands. As noted by Ilona Jerabek, Ph.D., president of PsychTests AIM Inc., "the issue lies in how we release [anger].... Anger needs to be expressed, but it needs to be done calmly [and] assertively, and it needs to incorporate constructive solutions for the problem."[64]

Don't Confuse Anger with Other, Similar Emotions

In 1958, Plutnick created the Wheel of Emotions, a three-dimensional circumplex model that conceptualizes all human emotions.[65] In addition to the eight fundamental emotions listed earlier (joy, trust, fear, surprise, sadness, disgust, anger, and anticipation), this model also features additional ones on each end of the spectrum of every emotion dimension. For example, pensiveness is on the milder side of sadness, whereas grief is on the more intense side. Similarly, serenity is milder than joy, whereas ecstasy is more intense. Furthermore, he also illustrated how the combination of two or more fundamental emotions creates primary dyads, with the combination of joy and acceptance, for example, creating love. According to Plutnick, by mixing emotions from different levels, hundreds of dyads can be created, reflecting the myriad of emotions that humans are capable of feeling.[66]

Plutnick's model underscores the recognition that it's not simply a question of semantics, but that there are important differences between emotions, even those within similar categories.

Yet to accurately label our feelings, we need to understand what the exact definition of each emotion is. As noted on CiviliNation's blog, "The language we use is often imprecise, especially when it comes to describing and naming emotions. We frequently say we are angry when we may actually be feeling a milder emotion such as annoyance or a stronger emotion such as rage, or even a combination of emotions."[67] Figure 6.5 shows that sometimes people even jumble them all together.

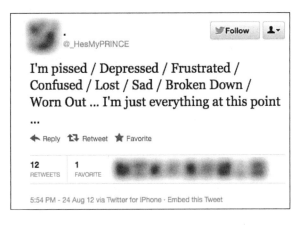

Figure 6.5 *Lots of emotions mixed together. _HesMyPRINCE's Tweet on August 24, 2012.*

Properly labeling feelings can also help you effectively manage them in a given situation. For example, simply being annoyed at something may not warrant taking any corrective action, but feeling aggression, a more intense and jarring emotion, will likely require greater self-restraint, and possibly even outside intervention, to change course.

To start with, let's define anger. According to the American Psychological Association, anger is an emotion represented by antagonism toward someone or something you feel has wronged you.[68] Anger can also be described as "a strong feeling of displeasure or hostility."[69]

Now look at the meanings of some of the words often associated with the term anger.

- Feeling **annoyed** is the state of being bothered, disturbed, or irritated by something.
- Feeling **frustrated** is "a deep chronic sense or state of insecurity and dissatisfaction arising from unresolved problems or unfulfilled needs."[70]
- **Loathing** is "a feeling of intense dislike or disgust."[71]
- **Hostility** is "unfriendly or threatening behavior or feelings toward someone."[72]
- **Aggression** represents "feelings of anger or antipathy resulting in hostile or violent behavior."[73]
- Feeing **furious** is being "extremely angry" or alternatively as "full or anger or energy."[74]
- **Rage** is "violent and uncontrolled anger."[75]

Now see examples of these terms in use. An example of someone feeling annoyed may be this statement: "It bugs me when I see people tweeting all the time about their speaking gigs; it's so obvious they're just showing off and trying to get attention." Someone who feels frustrated may say something like, "I'm tired of the never-ending rudeness I see online; I wish I could just log off for the rest of the week." Loathing may be expressed this way: "I can't stand all the competition about who has more followers online; all the chest-thumping makes me sick." A person who's feeling angry may say, "If I see one more sycophant kiss Dave's butt because he just sold his startup to Google, I'm going to be sick."

An example of expressing hostility may be someone who says, "@___, trust me, you don't want to mess with me because you'd regret it." Aggression might be expressed as "@___, you know that IM chat we had earlier today? Well, after the way you treated me, I posted it on Reddit so everyone can see what a douche you really are." An individual who's furious might say, "I'm so pissed off at Dana right now, I can't even see straight." Finally, someone who is filled with rage may say, "Steve better watch his back. He stole my idea and I'm going to get him if it's the last thing I do, and the best thing is, he'll never know what hit him."

Negative Anger Affects People at Work and at Home

Who can forget actor Charlie Sheen's 2011 public outbursts aimed at Chuck Lorre, co-creator and executive producer of the television show "Two and a Half Men," and TV network CBS? It began on the conservative radio program "The Alex Jones Show" where Sheen launched his attack against Lorre with the statement

> *"Last I checked, [Chuck], I've spent close to the last decade effortlessly and magically converting your tin cans into pure gold, and the gratitude I get is this charlatan chose not to do his job, which is to write. Clearly someone who believes he's above the law."*[76]

After the decision was made to shut down production of the show because of Sheen's behavior,[77] his tirade continued with statements such as "Defeat is not an Option. CBS picked a fight with a warlock" and "Come Wednesday morning, they're going to rename it Charlie Bros. and not Warner Bros. Duh, winning!"[78] Sheen also made fantastical claims about having "tiger blood and Adonis DNA."[79] In an example of art imitating life, Sheen is now starring in FX's show "Anger Management," in which he plays a former athlete whose anger management problems destroyed his career, and who then became a therapist specializing in helping treat people with anger management issues. When asked about his anger issues, Sheen explained in a 2011 interview on *Today*, "I think my passion is misinterpreted as anger sometimes. And I don't think people are ready for the message that I'm delivering, and delivering with a sense of violent love."[80]

Sheen's public display of rage-laced behavior may have been influenced by his admitted use of drugs and alcohol, but out-of-control anger doesn't just happen to disturbed celebrities, it happens everywhere. *Forbes'* Kashmir Hill, who writes about privacy and technology, described the eerie calls she received on her cell phone regarding a "casual encounters" ad on craigslist that listed her phone number and her picture ("casual encounters" is a listing for people interested in no-strings-attached sexual activities).[81] She noted, "Someone was angry at me, and had found a nice, anonymous way to wreak revenge."[82] Meanwhile, in "The screaming boss," S. Colette shares the story of what it was like working for her art dealer boss: "There were several incidents that should have sent me running. Hearing him scream at utility workers, vendors, and the postal service should have been a clue to his emotional imbalance. His tirades would last for hours when a document was misplaced or a package didn't arrive when expected."[83]

Another example involves an incident that ultimately ended in tragedy. For an entire year, one woman was subjected to daily screaming fits from her boss. Not being able to stop his behavior, she and some of her colleagues wrote a 25-page complaint and submitted it to human resources, which did nothing. Eventually she was asked to attend a meeting with senior management, and knew that she would be fired for making the complaint. Instead of letting this happen, she wrote three suicide notes, took a pistol to work, and committed suicide at the office.[84]

Although some experts believe that yelling bosses are becoming workplace relics, that doesn't appear to be reducing the overall amount of anger on the job.[85]

According to Jack Lampl, president of the A.K. Rice Institute for the Study of Social Systems in Rainier, Washington, a more popular method of venting is now the angry email, which "serves as a relief valve, but tends to inflame conflict. It takes a very corrosive role in the workplace, for gossiping and undermining others."[86]

Not surprisingly, it's not just at work that negative expressions of anger erupt; it's common in interpersonal relationships as well. There's the example of Iowa resident Roger Allan Brass, who shot and killed a kitten because he was angry with his parents.[87] Then there's estranged husband Ghulam Kibria, who posed as his wife when he emailed the U.K. Security Service M15 on November 8, 2011, claiming that she'd placed a bomb at a school in Burmingham.[88] At his sentencing the judge said, "You decided to get revenge against your ex-wife and you decided to issue a bomb hoax in her name and the motive simply [is] that you were trying to get her arrested.... It was an [offense] that was inspired by malice and revenge."[89]

If you wonder whether anger moves between the work and the home environments, the answer is yes. What impacts one often spills over into the other, as the 2011 study "The Fallout from Abusive Supervision: An Examination of Subordinates and Their Partners"[90] revealed. The study discusses various abuse employees suffer at the hands of their supervisors, including temper tantrums, and found that abusive bosses can be an important factor in the stress placed not just on the employee but also the employee's spouse and hence the marriage.[91] Dawn Carlson, Ph.D., one of the study's authors, stated, "The evidence highlights the need for organizations to send an unequivocal message to those in supervisory positions that these hostile and harmful behaviors will not be tolerated."[92]

As many people know from their own experiences, children are particularly vulnerable to environments bathed in negative anger, environments perhaps at least partially created by people with the attitude reflected by Shaniqua in Figure 6.6. In his blog post "Anger At Home is Contagious," psychologist Tony Fiory, also known as The Anger Coach, describes how anger was modeled when he was growing up: "In my family of origin, the mood setter was definitely my father. If he was angry, we all had to somehow cope with it, usually by avoiding him and walking around gingerly as if on eggshells. After the explosion, he 'felt better' and was ready to be pleasant with all of us, but unfortunately the emotional damage was done resulting in an attitude that the last thing we wanted at that point was to be with him."[93]

Unfortunately it's not just adults who exhibit behavior that indicates they're not in control of their emotions. A study in the *Archives of General Psychiatry*[94] revealed the disturbing finding that nearly two-thirds of American adolescents have a history of uncontrollable anger. These anger attacks commonly involve destroying property or threatening violence or acting with violence toward others.[95] The study also found that "one in 12 young people—close to six million adolescents—meet criteria for a diagnosis of Intermittent Explosive Disorder (IED), a syndrome characterized by persistent uncontrollable anger attacks not accounted for by other mental disorders."[96]

Figure 6.6   *Tell us how you really feel. Shaniqua's Tweet on August 23, 2012.*

The psychological impact on people exposed to uncontrolled anger can be immense due to the tremendous stress it places on the victims. In situations in which the stress is ongoing and the individual cannot remove themselves from the person or outside cause, it becomes even more of a problem.

A 2012 study in *Nature Medicine*[97] indicated that chronic stress can lead to deterioration of emotional and cognitive functions due to a reduction in overall brain volume.[98] Furthermore, a 2012 study which appeared in *Neuron*[99] revealed that chronic stress can negatively impact memory and decision-making abilities.[100] And in a 2009 study which appeared in *Science,*[101] researchers found that chronic stress affected the decision-making ability of rats. Those areas of their brains responsible for decision-making and goal-directed behaviors atrophied, while those areas responsible for habit formation grew.[102] Of additional concern is a 2012 study that appeared in the *Proceedings of the National Academy of Sciences,*[103] which may have implications for those subjected to prolonged or ongoing anger. This study found that chronic emotional stress had the effect of activating the creation of certain protein aggregates within mice's brain cells, aggregates that are connected to the manifestation of Alzheimer's disease.[104] This effect was particularly pronounced in the hippocampus, an area of the brain linked to memory formation and collection.[105]

The Downside of Expressing Anger Online

As talked about in earlier chapters, there are downsides to venting online. The first is that when something is posted online, it's out of your control forever. Second, it's permanent. Even if the tweet, video, or comment are subsequently removed by the person making them, it is extremely likely that someone has already seen them and possibly has taken screen shots or downloaded the material. Third, even privacy precautions aren't foolproof. As shown, even adjusting one's privacy settings on social networking sites won't prevent someone from copying and publicly sharing the information with others. Fourth, statements and comments can be misconstrued. Context is critically important in communications, and things such as humor translate poorly to an online world that is weighted toward the written medium. Fifth, there is no accounting for the human element. Even private emails shared between colleagues, friends, family members or other confidants are all too often used against them when there is a falling out.

As noted in Chapter 2, your digital footprint—the good, the bad, and the ugly—is used by others in decision making that impacts virtually every aspect of your life. It affects what institution of higher learning you can attend, what health insurance coverage you'll receive, how big your credit line will be, your dating potential and desirability as a mate, and whether you'll be hired for that coveted job. It even affects whether you'll keep your job, which is something that Miami-Dade fire captain Brian Beckmann quickly learned.

Beckman was commenting about the Trayvon Martin shooting on his personal Facebook page when he wrote, "I and my co-workers could rewrite the book on whether our urban youths are victims of racist profiling or products of their failed, sh--bag, ignorant, pathetic, welfare dependent excuses for parents...They're just misunderstood little church-going angels and the ghetto hoodie look doesn't have anything to do with why people wonder if they're about to get jacked by a thug."[106] Nevertheless, after conceding that Beckman was writing as a private citizen, the Miami-Dade Fire Rescue placed him on administrative leave and demanded that he complete a psychological evaluation and diversity training before returning to work in the demoted rank of firefighter.[107]

So if the downside to unrestrained and out-of-control expressions of anger is so great, why do so many people still engage in this risky behavior? In a telephone interview,[108] Dr. Martin said that "impulsiveness is a big part of it" and that the venting "calms them down and serves as a catharsis." Unfortunately, practice makes perfect, as he calls it, and if people repeatedly act this way, it becomes behaviorally ingrained. Martin also believes that the public has been influenced by the entertainment industry, and that for the past decade or so, we've glorified incivility on television. Think about characters such as "House's" Dr. Gregory House, "Scrubs's" Dr. Perry Cox, and "Entourage's" Ari Gold. They're simultaneously mean yet brilliant or funny, with the result that these personas become attractive to people (see Figure 6.7). In terms of anger expression, he believes that "social distancing in an electronic format exacerbates this problem," but readily admits that "online anger is arguably the most underresearched area" in the anger management field.

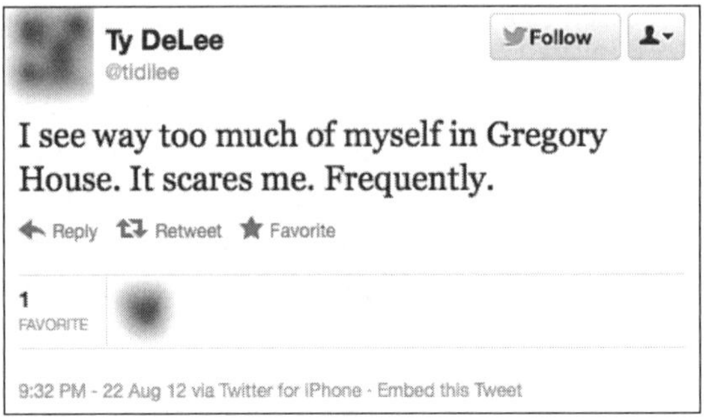

Figure 6.7   *One person who identifies with the nasty yet brilliant and funny television character Gregory House. Ty DeLee's Tweet on August 22, 2012.*

Venting and Self-Control

This book talks a lot about conflict and the negative and damaging expressions of anger created by others. But a lot of what happens online, namely both the content and the tone of everyday interactions, is often up to you. Perhaps to a greater extent than we like to admit, we all play a contributing role in what happens online. You can't control what others do, but you can control your own actions and reactions.

Dillon White, communications director of 5Stone Marketing, suggests that in situations where customers are using social media to vent their anger, a company publicly respond to the individual, preferably via the same channel, so there is a public record that "you are working as hard as possible to change the situation."[109] Tell him or her that you are sorry for the problem, that it is not representative of your company or brand, and offer a way of making things better.[110]

One misconception you need to get out of the way immediately is that "venting" anger is a good thing or perhaps simply benign. As youngsters, some of us were taught to hit items like pillows or punching bags when we were angry to release the intensity of the feeling, a message also propagated by the media. And although it's better than physically lashing out at others, on several occasions the author has even seen someone repeatedly punch himself in the head with both of his fists because he hadn't learned a healthier way of managing his emotions.

But this venting increases aggression, as researchers reported in a 1999 paper:[111] "Our findings suggest that media messages advocating catharsis may be worse than useless. They encourage people to vent their anger through aggressive action, and perhaps even foster the displacement of aggression toward new, innocent third parties. In our research, people who received pro-catharsis messages first chose to vent their anger by hitting a punching bag, but then they went to show elevated aggression toward the person at whom they were angry. They even showed increased aggression toward an innocent third person.... Perhaps media endorsement of cathartic release should come to be regarded as a potential danger to public health, peace, and social harmony."[112]

Because anger management issues involve self-control, you should examine whether you have challenges with self-control. Self-control simply means controlling your own feelings, impulses, and behaviors. With anger, its unhealthy expression can be outward-directed, which is usually what you read about in the news when there's been a violent crime, or inward-directed, which can involve problems like alcohol and drug abuse, eating disorders, self-mutilation, and other psychological and behavioral issues.

The mental health field and the legal field interpret self-control in different ways. Associate professor of law Rebecca Hollander-Blumoff of Washington University School of Law examined these differences in her 2012 research paper "Crime, Punishment, and the Psychology of Self-Control."[113] Stated in somewhat overly simplistic terms, American criminal law takes the general position that in the majority of situations, individuals have free will and that because they have free will, they can exercise the requisite self-control required in life—and that by extension, when they fail to do so, it's a choice for which they will be held accountable if they engage in criminal activity.[114]

However, psychology teaches that people don't think about the short- versus long-term consequences to their behavior in the same way, causing them to occasionally make flawed decisions. Furthermore, self-control "is a finite resource that can be used up by other cognitive demands...[and that] what this means for the individual is that, when she has used her self-control in one setting, she will find it harder to exert self-control in a situation that immediately follows."[115] Nevertheless, the encouraging news is that when an individual consciously practices the art of self-control over a period of time, it will become stronger and last longer.[116]

Weak or diminished self-control is a serious concern, but it's something you can improve. According to Thomas F. Denson, co-author with C. Nathan DeWall and Eli J. Finkel of the 2012 research article "Self-Control and Aggression,"[117] "If you give aggressive people the opportunity to improve their self-control, they're less aggressive."[118]

Anger Management Techniques

Ideally you could prevent all negative anger from occurring, but given the complexity and unpredictability of life, that's unrealistic. The best you can do is learn how to manage anger.

Start by determining where you rank on the anger scale. Although you shouldn't rely solely on the outcomes of these tests to determine what your general anger level is (it's better to consult a licensed clinical mental health provider to assist you with that), here are three free online tests you can take to get you started:

- Online Anger Management Assessment by the AJ Novick Group available at http://www.ajnovickgroup.com/resources/free-online-anger-management-assessment-evaluation.aspx.

- Irritability Quotient test by The Counseling Team International available at http://s.wsj.net/public/resources/documents/anger-quiz-10-03.html.

- Anger Management Test by Queendom available at http://www.queendom.com/tests/access_page/index.htm?idRegTest=3044.

You also need to be aware of your anger triggers. What are the situations that tend to aggravate you? What particular types of people annoy you the most? What are the subjects that bother you? Do you find that you're particularly vulnerable when you haven't had a full night's rest or when you're under stress because of a deadline? Make a written list of these things and keep it nearby. Similar to someone who is on a diet and needs to stay away from the junk food isle at the grocery store, people on an anger diet should avoid intentionally exposing themselves to things that they know they have a hard time dealing with. Using a list as a visual reminder of your hot button issues can help you so that you don't forget the triggers.

Say that you're opposed to hunting, and one of your Facebook friends posts a new series of pictures from his latest hunting safari. You have the option to skip over these quickly, changing your subscription settings to "only important" in the hopes that this sort of thing won't show up anymore in your news feed, or unfriend the person. Perhaps you see one of the people you're following on Twitter linking to a story about antivaccination celebrity Jenny McCarthy making the talk show rounds again, and you're feeling irritated because you believe vaccinating children is important. Don't click the link because doing so would increase your exposure to the information that's getting you hot under the collar. Or maybe you see a news story on Google about a politician making nonsensical statements about women's reproductive systems and rape and you're incensed, like Molly in Figure 6.8. Don't read the story. Move on. Remember that you don't need to intentionally subject yourself to things that make you angry online. Why would you volunteer to do so?

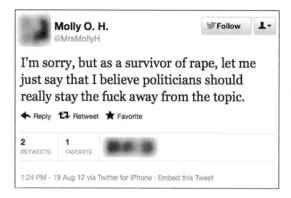

Figure 6.8   *Molly O.H.'s Tweet on August 19, 2012.*

In a similar vein, don't subject yourself or intentionally seek out online environments that push your hot buttons. Do you disagree with particular websites? It's
generally a good idea to be as knowledgeable and educated about important issues
as possible, which includes learning about opposing viewpoints and the reasoning
behind them. But unless you can do so in a rational and calm manner, consider
not exposing yourself directly to them—or doing so in small and manageable
increments.

When you are in a situation that bothers you, figure out what emotion you're
actually feeling. Is it anger or one of the other emotions discussed earlier? Are you
merely feeling annoyed or frustrated, or are you feeling out-of-control rage? If it's a
combination of emotions, for example anger and embarrassment, are you perhaps
using anger as a crutch to avoid having to deal with discomfort, embarrassment, or
the fear of losing face? As mentioned, there are numerous reasons people use anger
as a shield. Sometimes feeling angry can make you feel powerful, and although
negative and out-of-control anger is destructive, for some people facing the underlying emotions and the problems they stem from seems overwhelming. It takes a
courageous person to face reality and admit that they've been misusing anger.

In the online realm, you may have the benefit of time that you don't have in
face-to-face interaction. If you're at the office and involved in a direct conversation
with someone, the expectation is that you'll have a back-and-forth communication
of some sort at that moment. But online, you often have the luxury of more time,
at least compared to in-person interactions. That's not to say you always necessarily have a lot of time, but depending on the situation, it's highly likely that you
have a few minutes or more.

Use the additional time you have online wisely to decide if, when, and how you're
going to respond to a given situation. So far this book uses the words "react" and
"respond" more or less interchangeably, but in reality there's a fundamental and

important difference between the two. When you react, you're doing something because of a stimulus that you are exposed to, for example a statement or an action. Think of the patellar reflex test you probably remember receiving from your pediatrician when you were a child. The patellar test, by the way, is where the term "knee-jerk reaction" comes from, signifying that you do things involuntarily or automatically without thinking. But when you respond, you reply to something and perhaps even engage in a mutual back-and-forth communication with someone. When you respond, you're making a conscious decision to engage, and you're in control, whereas when you're reacting you are not. Also, realize that in many cases, you don't have to respond at all. Doing nothing and getting away from whatever is bothering you may be the smartest thing you can do. If you do decide to respond, mentally go through the various ways you can do so. For example, your word choices and the tone you use online can have an impact on both how you feel emotionally while expressing yourself and how your message is received. Saying "Democrat" versus "liberal" versus "libtard" obviously have different connotations and will be interpreted by others accordingly.

Being aware of your tone and word choices is particularly important if you are hired to represent a brand. Your anger triggers will be the same whether you're working in a professional capacity or just representing yourself online, so keep that in mind when responding online on behalf of a brand.

When you notice yourself feeling angry, one of the first things to do is try to physically relax. As discussed earlier in this chapter, the responses your body has to anger can include shallow or accelerated breathing, tense muscles, and feeling flushed. Your ability to think clearly is often weakened, which makes you vulnerable to reacting badly to your anger triggers. Therefore, as part of the process of gaining control of yourself, take a few minutes (realizing that unlimited time isn't always available) to step back and center yourself. Knowing what your usual physical reactions to becoming angry are can also help you cognitively recognize some of the warning signs before tipping over into unhealthy anger behavior.

Deep breathing exercises are helpful because they cause you to slow down, relax muscles, stop the shallow breathing cycle, and get your mind focused on something besides what initially set you off. Here are instructions for stomach breathing offered by WebMD:[119]

1. Sit in a comfortable position.

2. Put one hand on your belly just below your ribs and the other hand on your chest.

3. Take a deep breath in through your nose, and let your belly push your hand out. Your chest should not move.

4. Breathe out through pursed lips as if you were whistling. Feel the hand on your belly go in, and use it to push all the air out.

5. Do this breathing 3 to 10 times. Take your time with each breath.

One method that researchers have found helps people calm down is called *self-distancing*. In a 2012 article in the *Journal of Experimental Social Psychology*,[120] Dominik Mischkowski, Ethan Kross, and Brad J. Bushman found that taking a detached view about what is happening helps people emotionally remove themselves from the situation and become less angry and aggressive. The distancing even worked for individuals in the heat of the moment. The researchers stated that other things that people sometimes do, such as immersing themselves in their anger as a cathartic coping method, or trying to distract themselves with calming thoughts or by using other diversions, either aren't effective at all, or aren't effective as a long-term approach.[121] Mischkowski explained that the goal is to "not get immersed in your own anger and, instead, have a more detached view.... You have to see yourself in this stressful situation as a fly on the wall would see it."[122]

It's also helpful to know how long it usually takes you to calm down and regain control over yourself. The time may vary depending on the circumstances. Seeing someone spewing forth nonsense on Facebook on an issue that you consider important to your life is likely going to require a longer time to process and move away from than seeing something merely silly but relatively benign.

Another useful trick is to imagine how your intended action or response will look to others online, both now and in the future. Is this something that you won't mind current and future employers seeing? How about potential mates? What if your parents or children saw it? Is this something that you would pass judgment on or cringe about as an objective outsider, if it were done by someone else?

If you're bothered by something and fear that eventually you'd regret your response, try not to participate or engage. If you feel compelled to share your thoughts on an issue, find a more productive way to express your ideas and feelings by chatting with a friend or confidant via private and direct messaging. Although there is no 100% guarantee that this won't be shared or otherwise be made public at some time in the future, this is a better option than blowing off steam in a public setting.

As part of your anger management arsenal, consider using Rational Emotive Behavior Therapy (REBT), which was created in 1955 by Albert Ellis, Ph.D. REBT basically states that what causes us to be upset isn't actually the events that happen to or around us, but the beliefs we hold about them.[123] Ellis described this as the ABC Model: A = something happens; B = we have a belief about the situation; and C = we have an emotional reaction to that belief.[124] A core component of REBT involves reassessment.

In his book *Anger: How To Live With and Without It,*[125] Ellis provides a sample self-help form that contains the following elements:[126]

> **A—Activating Event:** Summarize the situation you are disturbed about, which can be internal or external, real or imagined, and in the past, present or future.
>
> **IBs—Irrational Beliefs:** To identify your irrational beliefs, look for dogmatic demands (musts, absolutes, shoulds), awefulizing (it's awful, terrible), low frustration tolerance (you can't stand it), and self or other rating (I'm/ he/ she is bad or worthless).
>
> **D—Disputing IBs:** Ask yourself whether holding the irrational belief is helpful or self-defeating, where the evidence to support the irrational belief is, whether the belief is logical, and whether it's really not tolerable.
>
> **C—Consequences:** List the major unhealthy negative emotions (e.g. anxiety, depression, rage, low frustration tolerance, shame/embarrassment, hurt, jealousy or guilt) and the self-defeating behaviors.
>
> **RBs—Rational Beliefs:** To think more rationally, aim to make non-dogmatic references, more effectively evaluate badness (e.g. it's unfortunate, it's bad versus it's terrible), develop higher frustration tolerance, and stop globally rating yourself and others.
>
> **E—New Effect:** List the new healthy negative emotions (e.g. disappointment, concern, annoyance, sadness, regret, or frustration) and the new constructive behaviors that come out of the exercise of having identified and disputed the irrational beliefs and having identified the rational beliefs.

You can see an online REBT self-help form based on Ellis's version at http://rebtnetwork.org/library/shf.html.

If you feel that your anger is negatively impacting your personal or professional life or if you've been told that it has, consider getting professional help. Receiving help isn't a sign of weakness; it is a sign that you recognize there is a problem that you want to fix. It's a courageous, mature, and, ultimately, smart thing to do. There are many anger management therapists available around the country, ranging from licensed clinical social workers (LCSW) and marriage and family therapists, to psychologists and psychiatrists. There are court-ordered anger management workshops available in many states, with a list of organizations and professionals that offer such services often available directly from the court (Sacramento Superior Court's Anger Management Services list, for example, is available at www.saccourt.ca.gov/family/docs/fl-dv-anger-management-list.pdf). There are online anger management programs available (search under "online anger management courses"; one popular one is Anger Class Online®, which is available at http://www. angerclassonline.com). There is even the Personal Power Path Anger Management App,[127] available from EDB Media, Inc., which can be completed in 6 weeks.

Endnotes

1. Sue Jacques, The Civility CEO. Link: http://www.thecivilityceo.com/the-civility-ceo.html.

2. Andrea Weckerle, "Former Forensic Death Investigator Speaks Out About the Need for Civility," *CiviliNation*, May 3, 2011. Link: http://www.civilination.org/blog/former-forensic-death-investigator-speaks-out-about-the-need-for-civility/.

3. Andrea Weckerle, "Former Forensic Death Investigator Speaks Out About the Need for Civility," *CiviliNation*, May 3, 2011. Link: http://www.civilination.org/blog/former-forensic-death-investigator-speaks-out-about-the-need-for-civility/.

4. Andrea Weckerle, "Former Forensic Death Investigator Speaks Out About the Need for Civility," *CiviliNation*, May 3, 2011. Link: http://www.civilination.org/blog/former-forensic-death-investigator-speaks-out-about-the-need-for-civility/.

5. Sue Jacques, "Life After Death," Sue Jacques, The Civility CEO, November 30, 2011. Link: http://thecivilityceo.wordpress.com/2011/11/30/life-after-death/.

6. Neel Burton, M.D. *Hide and Seek - The Psychology of Self-Deception* (Acheron Press, 2012).

7. Neel Burton, M.D. "Hide and Seek," *Psychology Today*, August 20, 2012. Link: http://www.psychologytoday.com/blog/hide-and-seek/201208/why-anger-is-pointless.

8. Carol Travis, Ph.D. *Anger: The Misunderstood Emotion* (Revised Touchstone Edition, 1989).

9. Carol Travis, Ph.D. *Anger: The Misunderstood Emotion* (Revised Touchstone Edition, 1989), p. 25.

10. Robert Plutnick, *Emotion: A Psychoevolutionary Synthesis* (Harper & Row, 1980).

11. Robert Plutnick, "The Nature of Emotions," *American Scientist*, 2001; 89 (July–August): 344–350, p. 349.

12. Bio of Jaak Panksepp, Ph.D. Link: http://www.vetmed.wsu.edu/research_vcapp/Panksepp/.

13. Jaak Pankseep and Lucy Biven, *The Archaeology of Mind: Neuroevolutionary Origins of Human Emotions*, W. W. Norton & Company (September 17, 2012). Link: http://www.amazon.com/The-Archaeology-Mind-Neuroevolutionary-Interpersonal/dp/0393705315.

14. Pamela Weintraub, "Jaak Panksepp Pinned Down Humanity's 7 Primal Emotions," Discover Magazine, May 31, 2012. Link: http://discovermagazine.com/2012/may/11-jaak-panksepp-rat-tickler-found-humans-7-primal-emotions.

15. Brenda Scottsdale, "Anger in Babies," Livestrong.com, September 2, 2011. Link: http://www.livestrong.com/article/533875-anger-in-babies/.

16. Limbic System article in Wikipedia. Link: http://en.wikipedia.org/wiki/Limbic_system.

17. Neus Herrero, Marien Gadea, Gabriel Rodríguez-Alarcón, Raúl Espert, Alicia Salvador. "What happens when we get angry? Hormonal, cardiovascular and asymmetrical brain responses." *Hormones and Behavior*, 2010; 57 (3): 276–285. Link: http://www.sciencedirect.com/science/article/pii/S0018506X09002785.

18. "What Happens When We Get Angry?" ScienceDaily.com, June 1, 2010. Link: http://www.sciencedaily.com/releases/2010/05/100531082603.htm.

19. Kevin Fauteaux, Ph.D., MSW, M. Div., *Defusing Angry People: Practical Tools for Handling Bullying Threats and Violence* (New Horizon Press, 2011).

20. Kevin Fauteaux, Ph.D., MSW, M. Div., *Defusing Angry People: Practical Tools for Handling Bullying Threats and Violence* (New Horizon Press, 2011), 29.

21. Thomas F. Denson, William C. Pedersen, Jaclyn Ronquillo, and Anirvan S. Nandy, "The Angry Brain: Neural Correlates of Anger, Angry Rumination, and Aggressive Personality," *Journal of Cognitive Neuroscience*, 2008; 21 (4): 734–744.

22. Professional Profile of Raymond DiGiuseppe, Ph.D., St, John's University. Link: http://www.stjohns.edu/academics/graduate/liberalarts/departments/psychology/faculty/digiusepper/profile.stj.

23. Melissa Dittman, "Anger across the gender divide," American Psychological Association, March 2003. Link: http://www.apa.org/monitor/mar03/angeracross.aspx.

24. Victoria L. Brescoll and Eric Luis Uhlmann, "Can an Angry Woman Get Ahead? Status Conferral, Gender, and Expression of Emotion in the Workplace," *Psychological Science*; 2008: 19 (3): 268–275.

25. Victoria L. Brescoll and Eric Luis Uhlmann, "Can an Angry Woman Get Ahead? Status Conferral, Gender, and Expression of Emotion in the Workplace," Psychological Science; 2008: 19 (3): 268–275, 273.

26. "New Discoveries About the Experience of Anger," ScienceDaily.com, December 1, 2009. Link: http://www.sciencedaily.com/releases/2009/11/091130131326.htm.

27. Michael Potegal, Gerhard Stemmler and Charles Spielberger, eds., "International Handbook of Anger: Constituent and Concomitant Biological, Psychological, and Social Processes," Springer; February 24, 2010. Link: http://www.amazon.com/International-Handbook-Anger-Constituent-Psychological/dp/0387896759.

28. "New Discoveries About the Experience of Anger," ScienceDaily.com, December 1, 2009; Link: http://www.sciencedaily.com/releases/2009/11/091130131326.htm.

29. "Maturation of the Prefrontal Cortex," Office of Population Affairs, U.S. Department of Health & Human Services. Link: http://www.hhs.gov/opa/familylife/tech_assistance/etraining/adolescent_brain/Development/prefrontal_cortex/.

30. Jerry L. Deffenbacher, Rebekah S Lynch, Eugene R. Oetting, Calvin C. Kemper, "Anger reduction in early adolescents," *Journal of Counseling Psychology*, Vol 43(2), Apr 1996, 149–157.

31. Professional Profile of Jerry L. Deffenbacker, Ph.D., Colorado State University. Link: http://psy.psych.colostate.edu/psylist/detail.asp?Num=18.

32. Professional Profile of Ryan C. Martin, Ph.D., University of Wisconsin - Green Bay. Link: https://www.uwgb.edu/martinr/research.htm.

33. Ryan Martin, Ph.D., "All the Rage: Commentary on the scientific study of anger," Psychology Today, October 2011. Link: http://www.psychologytoday.com/blog/all-the-rage/201110/why-we-get-mad.

34. Ryan Martin, Ph.D., "All the Rage: Commentary on the scientific study of anger," Psychology Today, October 2011. Link: http://www.psychologytoday.com/blog/all-the-rage/201110/why-we-get-mad.

35. Matthew McKay, Ph.D. Peter D. Rogers, Ph.D. and Judith McKay, R.N. *When Anger Hurts: Quieting the Storm Within* (New Harbinger Pubns Inc., 1989). Link: http://www.amazon.com/When-Anger-Hurts-Quieting-Within/dp/0934986762.

36. Matthew McKay, Ph.D. Peter D. Rogers, Ph.D. and Judith McKay, R.N. "Anger Trigger Behaviors," *Psych Central.* Link: http://psychcentral.com/lib/2011/anger-trigger-behaviors/.

37. Matthew McKay, Ph.D. Peter D. Rogers, Ph.D. and Judith McKay, R.N. "Anger Trigger Behaviors," *Psych Central.* Link: http://psychcentral.com/lib/2011/anger-trigger-behaviors/.

38. Matthew McKay, Ph.D. Peter D. Rogers, Ph.D. and Judith McKay, R.N. *When Anger Hurts: Quieting the Storm Within* (New Harbinger Pubns Inc., 1989). Link: http://www.amazon.com/When-Anger-Hurts-Quieting-Within/dp/0934986762.

39. Website of the British Association of Anger Management. Link: http://www.angermanage.co.uk/.

40. Mike Fisher, *Beating Anger: The eight-point plan for coping with rage* (Random House UK, 2006). Link: http://www.amazon.com/Beating-Anger-Eight-Point-Plan-Coping/dp/1844135640.

41. Mike Fisher, *Beating Anger: The eight-point plan for coping with rage* (Random House UK, 2006), Chapter 1: Defining Anger, Kindle Edition. Link: http://www.amazon.com/Beating-Anger-Eight-Point-Plan-Coping/dp/1844135640.

42. Thomas F. Denson, William C. Pedersen, Jaclyn Ronquillo, and Anirvan S. Nandy, "The Angry Brain: Neural Correlates of Anger, Angry Rumination, and Aggressive Personality," *Journal of Cognitive Neuroscience*, 2008; 21 (4): 734–744.

43. Thomas F. Denson, William C. Pedersen, Jaclyn Ronquillo, and Anirvan S. Nandy, "The Angry Brain: Neural Correlates of Anger, Angry Rumination, and Aggressive Personality," *Journal of Cognitive Neuroscience*, 2008; 21 (4): 734–744, p. 735–736.

44. Patricia Evans, *The Verbally Abusive Relationship: How to recognize it and how to respond* (Adams Media, 3rd Ed., 2010). Link: http://www.amazon.com/The-Verbally-Abusive-Relationship-recognize/dp/1440504636.

45. Patricia Evans, *The Verbally Abusive Relationship: How to recognize it and how to respond* (Adams Media, 2nd Ed., 2010), p. 102.

46. "Patient Protection and Affordable Care Act," Wikipedia. Link: http://en.wikipedia.org/wiki/Patient_Protection_and_Affordable_Care_Act.

47. Dave Stopera, "People Who Say They're Movng To Canada Because of ObamaCare," BuzzFeed, June 28, 2012. Link: http://www.buzzfeed.com/daves4/people-moving-to-canada-because-of-obamacare.

48. "LGBT volunteer charged in conservative group shooting," CBS News, August 16, 2012. Link: http://www.cbsnews.com/8301-201_162-57494607/lgbt-volunteer-charged-in-conservative-group-shooting/.

49. "Joint statement regarding shooting at Family Research Council (FRC) from lesbian, gay, bisexual and transgender (LGBT) organizations," glaad.org, August 15, 2012. Link: http://www.glaad.org/blog/lgbt-organizations-release-joint-statement-regarding-shooting-family-research-council-frc.

50. "Hate Violence Against Lesbian, Gay, Bisexual, Transgender, Queer, and HIV-affected Communities In the United States in 2011," The National Coalition of Anti-Violence Programs, a program of the New York City Anti-Violence Project, 2011. Report downloadable on website. Link: http://www.avp.org/publications.htm.

51. "Hate Violence Against Lesbian, Gay, Bisexual, Transgender, Queer, and HIV-affected Communities In the United States in 2011," The National Coalition of Anti-Violence Programs, a program of the New York City Anti-Violence Project, 2011, p. 19–20. Report downloadable on website. Link: http://www.avp.org/publications.htm.

52. Ryan C. Martin and Eric R. Dahlen, "The Angry Cognitions Scale: A New Inventory for Assessing Cognitions in Anger," *Journal of Rational-Emotive & Cognitive-Behavior Therapy*, 2007; 25(3): 154-173.

53. Ryan C. Martin and Eric R. Dahlen, "The Angry Cognitions Scale: A New Inventory for Assessing Cognitions in Anger," *Journal of Rational-Emotive & Cognitive-Behavior Therapy*, 2007; 25(3): 154–173, 156–157.

54. David D. Burns, M.D. *Feeling Good: The New Mood Therapy* (HarperColins, 1980), p. 42.

55. About Goalistics, Goalistics.com. Link: http://pain.goalistics.com/about-goalistics.

56. Linda Ruehlman, Ph.D., "Living with Pain: Anger Hurts," Goalistics, March 1, 2012. Link: http://goalistics.com/2012/03/living-pain-angry/.

57. Gina Simmons, Ph.D., "Healing Your Angry Brain: Part 2 of 5," ManageAngerDaily.com, August 10, 2011. Link: http://www.manageangerdaily.com/2011/08/heal-your-angry-brain-part-2-of-5/.

58. Luca Passamonti, Molly J. Crockett, Annemieke M. Apergis-Schoute, Luke Clark, James B. Rowe, Andrew J. Calder, Trevor W. Robbins, "Effects of Acute Tryptophan Depletion on Prefrontal-Amygdala Connectivity While Viewing Facial Signals of Aggression," *Biological Psychiatry*, September 15, 2011. Link: http://www.biologicalpsychiatryjournal.com/article/S0006-3223%2811%2900780-3/abstract.

59. "Serotonin Levels Affect the Brain's Response to Anger," Science Daily, September 15, 2011. Link: http://www.sciencedaily.com/releases/2011/09/110915102917.htm.

60. Biography of David Sirota. Link: http://www.davidsirota.com/biography/.

61. David Sirota, "Our Addiction to Fake Outrage," Huffington Post, February 13, 2009. Link: http://www.huffingtonpost.com/david-sirota/our-addiction-to-fake-out_b_166730.html.

62. David Sirota, "Our Addiction to Fake Outrage," Huffington Post, February 13, 2009. Link: http://www.huffingtonpost.com/david-sirota/our-addiction-to-fake-out_b_166730.html.

63. Craig Newmark, "Trolls, Fake Trolls, and Outrage Addiction," craigconnects., August 2, 2012. Link: http://craigconnects.org/2012/08/trolls-fake-trolls-and-outrage-addiction.html.

64. "Are We Bottling Up Our Anger or Letting It Out? Queendom.com Releases Results of Their Anger Research," Marketwire, October 21, 2011. Link: http://www.queendom.com/about/media/pr_queendom_anger_management_test.html.

65. Robert Plutnick, "The Nature of Emotions," American Scientist, 2001; 89 (July-August): 344–350, p. 349.

66. Robert Plutnick, "The Nature of Emotions," American Scientist, 2001; 89 (July–August): 344-350, p. 350.

67. Andrea Weckerle, "Are You Truly Feeling Anger or Actually Another Emotion Like Annoyance or Frustration?" CiviliNation, March 27, 2012. Link: http://www.civilination.org/blog/are-you-feeling-anger-or-another-emotion-like-annoyance-or-frustration/.

68. Definition of "Anger," American Psychological Association. Link: http://www.apa.org/topics/anger/index.aspx.

69. Definition of "Anger," TheFreeDictionary. Link: http://www.thefreedictionary.com/anger.

70. Definition of "Frustration," MerriamWebster dictionary. Link: http://www.merriam-webster.com/dictionary/frustration.

71. Definition of "Loathing," Oxford Dictionaries. Link: http://oxforddictionaries.com/definition/english/loathing.

72. Definition of "Hostility," Macmillan Dictionary. Link: http://www.macmillandictionary.com/dictionary/british/hostility.

73. Definition of "Aggression," Oxford Dictionaries. Link: http://oxforddictionaries.com/definition/english/aggression?q=aggression.

74. Definition of "Furious," Oxford Dictionaries. Link: "http://oxforddictionaries.com/definition/english/furious?q=furious.

75. Definition of "Rage," Merriam-Webster dictionary. Link: http://www.merriam-webster.com/dictionary/rage.

76. Jennifer Arrow, "Charlie Sheen Rips Two and a Half Men Boss in Shocking Radio Interview," E Online, February 24, 2011. Link: http://www.eonline.com/news/227859/charlie-sheen-rips-two-and-a-half-men-boss-in-shocking-radio-interview.

77. Natalie Finn, *"Two and a Half Men* Shut Down for the Season," E Online, February 24, 2011. Link: http://www.eonline.com/news/227895/two-and-a-half-men-shut-down-for-the-season.

78. Matt Stopera, "14 Charlie Sheen Quotes Presented By Baby Sloths," BuzzFeed. Link: http://www.buzzfeed.com/mjs538/charlie-sheen-quotes-presented-by-baby-sloths

79. Toni Fitzgerald, "Timeline of the Charlie Sheen meltdown," *Media Life Magazine*, March 8, 2011. Link: http://www.medialifemagazine.com:8080/artman2/publish/Television_44/Timeline-of-the-Charlie-Sheen-meltdown.asp.

80. Seamus McGraw, "Sheen demands 50 percent raise for 'Two and a Half Men,'" Today. com, February 28, 2011. Link: http://today.msnbc.msn.com/id/41824830/ns/today-entertainment/#.UDFiiURZBVQ.

81. Kashmir Hill, "Using Craigslist to crowdsource revenge," Forbes, June 1, 2010. Link: http://www.forbes.com/sites/kashmirhill/2010/06/01/using-craigslist-to-crowdsource-revenge/.

82. Kashmir Hill, "Using Craigslist to crowdsource revenge," Forbes, June 1, 2010. Link: http://www.forbes.com/sites/kashmirhill/2010/06/01/using-craigslist-to-crowdsource-revenge/.

83. Jenny Peters, "My Boss Is a Nightmare! Stories of Terrible Management Techniques," AOL, May 17, 2011. Link: http://jobs.aol.com/articles/2011/03/17/my-boss-is-a-nightmare-stories-of-terrible-management-technique/.

84. Stephanie Pappas, "Your bullying boss may be slowly killing you," Today.com, January 1, 2012. Link: http://today.msnbc.msn.com/id/45973010/ns/today-money/t/your-bullying-boss-may-be-slowly-killing-you/#.UDFoEkRZBVQ.

85. Sue Schellenbarger, "When the Boss Is a Screamer," *The Wall Street Journal*, August 15, 2012. Link: http://online.wsj.com/article/SB100008723963904447724045775893021936 82244.html.

86. Sue Schellenbarger, "When the Boss Is a Screamer," *The Wall Street Journal*, August 15, 2012. Link: http://online.wsj.com/article/SB100008723963904447724045775893021936 82244.html.

87. Tom Alex, "Charges filed in Des Moines kitten shooting," DesMoinesRegister.com, April 9, 2012. Link: http://blogs.desmoinesregister.com/dmr/index.php/2012/04/09/charges-filed-in-kitten-shooting/.

88. "Husband jailed after he tried to get estranged wife arrested by emailing MI5 with school bomb threat from her account," Daily Mail, April 4, 2012. Link: http://www.dailymail.co.uk/news/article-2125103/Husband-tried-estranged-wife-arrested-emailing-MI5-school-bomb-plot-account-jailed.html.

89. "Husband jailed after he tried to get estranged wife arrested by emailing MI5 with school bomb threat from her account," Daily Mail, April 4, 2012. Link: http://www.dailymail.co.uk/news/article-2125103/Husband-tried-estranged-wife-arrested-emailing-MI5-school-bomb-plot-account-jailed.html.

90. Dawn S. Carslson, Meredith Ferguson, Pamela L. Perrewe and Dwayne Whitten, "The Fallout from Abusive Supervision: An Examination of Subordinates and Their Partners," *Personal Psychology*, 2011; 64 (4): 937–961.

91. "Your Abusive Boss May Not Be Good for Your Marriage, According to New Study," Science Daily, December 1, 2011. Link: http://www.sciencedaily.com/ releases/2011/11/111128132712.htm.

92. Your Abusive Boss May Not Be Good for Your Marriage, According to New Study," Science Daily, December 1, 2011. Link: http://www.sciencedaily.com/ releases/2011/11/111128132712.htm.

93. Tony Fiore "Anger At Home Is Contagious," The Anger Coach Blog, November 25, 2010. Link: http://angercoach.com/blog/?p=630.

94. Katie A. McLaughlin, Ph.D.; Jennifer Greif Green, Ph.D.; Irving Hwang, MA; Nancy A. Sampson, BA; Alan M. Zaslavsky, Ph.D.; Ronald C. Kessler, Ph.D., "Intermittent Explosive Disorder in the National Comorbidity Survey Replication Adolescent Supplement," *Arch Gen Psychiatry*. Published online July 02, 2012. Link: http://archpsyc.jamanetwork.com/article.aspx?articleid=1206777.

95. "Uncontrollable Anger Prevalent Among Youth," Harvard Medical School, July 2, 2012. Link: http://hms.harvard.edu/content/uncontrollable-anger-prevalent-among-youth-us.

96. "Uncontrollable Anger Prevalent Among Youth," Harvard Medical School, July 2, 2012. Link: http://hms.harvard.edu/content/uncontrollable-anger-prevalent-among-youth-us.

97. Hyo Jung Kang, Bhavya Voleti, Tibor Hajszan, Grazyna Rajkowska, Craig A. Stockmeier, Pawel Licznerski, Ashley Lepack, Mahesh S. Majik, Lak Shin Jeong, Mounira Banasr, Hyeon Son, Ronald S. Duman, "Decreased expression of synapse-related genes and loss of synapses in major depressive disorder," *Nature Medicine*, 2012. Link: http://www.nature.com/nm/journal/vaop/ncurrent/full/nm.2886.html.

98. "How Stress and depression Can Shrink the Brain," Science Daily, August 12, 2012. Link: http://www.sciencedaily.com/releases/2012/08/120812151659.htm.

99. Eunice Y. Yuen, Jing Wei, Wenhua Liu, Ping Zhong, Xiangning Li, Zhen Yan, "Repeated Stress Causes Cognitive Impairment by Suppressing Glutamate Receptor Expression and Function in Prefrontal Cortex," *Neuron*; 2012; 73 (5): 962–977.

100. "How Repeated Stress Impairs Memory," Science Daily, March 7, 2012. Link: http://www.sciencedaily.com/releases/2012/03/120307132202.htm.

101. João C. Sousa, Irene Melo, Pedro Morgado, Ana R. Mesquita, João J. Cerqueira, Rui M. Costa, and Nuno Sousa, "Chronic Stress Causes Frontostriatal Reorganization and Affects Decision-Making," *Science*; 2009 (31 July): 621–625.

102. Natalie Angier, "Brain Is a Co-Conspirator in a Vicious Stress Loop," *The New York Times*, August 17, 2009. Link: http://www.nytimes.com/2009/08/18/science/ 18angier.html.

103. Robert A. Rissman, Michael A. Staup, Allyson Roe Lee, Nicholas J. Justice, Kenner C. Rice, Wylie Vale, and Paul E. Sawchenko, "Corticotropin-releasing factor receptor-dependent effects of repeated stress on tau phosphorylation, solubility, and aggregation," *Proceedings of the National Academy of Sciences*, 2012; 109 (16): 6277–6282.

104. "Chronic Stress Spawns Protein Aggregates Linked to Alzheimer's," ScienceDaily, March 26, 2011. Link: http://www.sciencedaily.com/releases/2012/03/120326160819.htm.

105. "Chronic Stress Spawns Protein Aggregates Linked to Alzheimer's," ScienceDaily, March 26, 2011. Link: http://www.sciencedaily.com/releases/2012/03/120326160819.htm.

106. "Miami-Dade fire captain who posted about Trayvon Martin on Facebook demoted," Miami Herald, May 15, 2012. Link: http://www.miamiherald.com/2012/05/14/2799190/miami-dade-fire-captain-who-posted.html.

107. "Miami-Dade fire captain who posted about Trayvon Martin on Facebook demoted," Miami Herald, May 15, 2012. Link: http://www.miamiherald.com/2012/05/14/2799190/miami-dade-fire-captain-who-posted.html.

108. Personal telephone interview with Ryan C. Martin, Ph.D., on August 16, 2012.

109. Eilene Zimmerman, "Accentuating the Positive to Angry Customers," *The New York Times*, April 7, 2012. Link: www.nytimes.com/2012/04/08/jobs/angry-customers-and-constructive-responses-career-couch.html

110. Eilene Zimmerman, "Accentuating the Positive to Angry Customers," *The New York Times*, April 7, 2012. Link: www.nytimes.com/2012/04/08/jobs/angry-customers-and-constructive-responses-career-couch.html

111. Brad J. Bushman, Roy F. Baumeister, and Angela D. Stack reported in their 1999 paper "Catharsis, Aggression, and Persuasive Influence: Self-Fulfilling or Self-Defeating Prophesies?" American Psychological Association; 1999; 76 (3), 367–376.

112. Brad J. Bushman, Roy F. Baumeister, and Angela D. Stack reported in their 1999 paper "Catharsis, Aggression, and Persuasive Influence: Self-Fulfilling or Self-Defeating Prophesies?" American Psychological Association; 1999; 76 (3), 367–376, 375.

113. Rebecca E. Hollander-Blumoff, "Crime, Punishment, and the Psychology of Self-Control" (May 2012), Emory Law Journal, Vol. 61, No. 501, 2012; Washington University in St. Louis Legal Studies Research Paper No. 12-05-22. Link: http://ssrn.com/abstract=2080858.

114. Rebecca E. Hollander-Blumoff, "Crime, Punishment, and the Psychology of Self-Control" (May 2012), Emory Law Journal, Vol. 61, No. 501, 2012, p. 502–503, 505; Washington University in St. Louis Legal Studies Research Paper No. 12-05-22. Link: http://ssrn.com/abstract=2080858.

115. Rebecca E. Hollander-Blumoff, "Crime, Punishment, and the Psychology of Self-Control" (May 2012), Emory Law Journal, Vol. 61, No. 501, 2012, p. 504; Washington University in St. Louis Legal Studies Research Paper No. 12-05-22. Link: http://ssrn.com/abstract=2080858.

116. Rebecca E. Hollander-Blumoff, "Crime, Punishment, and the Psychology of Self-Control" (May 2012), Emory Law Journal, Vol. 61, No. 501, 2012, p. 504-505; Washington University in St. Louis Legal Studies Research Paper No. 12-05-22. Link: http://ssrn.com/abstract=2080858.

117. Thomas F. Denson, C. Nathan DeWall and Eli J. Finkel's 2012 research article "Self-Control and Aggression" which was published in *Current Directions in Psychological Science*, 2012; 1 (1), 20-25. Link: http://cdp.sagepub.com/content/21/1/20.

118. "Want to Limit Aggression? Practice Self-Control," ScienceDaily, March 28, 2012. Link: http://www.sciencedaily.com/releases/2012/03/120308120028.htm.

119. "Stress Management: Breathing Exercises for Relaxation," WebMD. Link: http://www.webmd.com/balance/stress-management/stress-management-breathing-exercises-for-relaxation.

120. Dominik Mischkowski, Ethan Kross, and Brad J. Bushman, "Flies on the wall are less aggressive: Self-distancing 'in the heat of the moment' reduces aggressive thoughts, angry feelings and aggressive behavior," *Journal of Experimental Social Psychology*, 2012; 48 (5), 1187–1191. Link: http://www.sciencedirect.com/science/article/pii/S0022103112000601.

121. "'Self-Distancing' Can Help People Calm Aggressive Reactions, Study Finds," ScienceDaily, July 2, 2012. Link: http://www.sciencedaily.com/releases/2012/07/120702153216.htm.

122. "'Self-Distancing' Can Help People Calm Aggressive Reactions, Study Finds," ScienceDaily, July 2, 2012. Link: http://www.sciencedaily.com/releases/2012/07/120702153216.htm.

123. "What is REBT?" REBT Network. Link: http://rebtnetwork.org/whatis.html.

124. "What is REBT?" REBT Network. Link: http://rebtnetwork.org/whatis.html.

125. Albert Ellis, Ph.D., *Anger: How to Live With and Without It* (Barnes & Noble, 2003).

126. Albert Ellis, Ph.D., *Anger: How to Live With and Without It* (Barnes & Noble, 2003). p-50–51.

127. Anger Management app by EDB media Inc. Link: http://itunes.apple.com/us/app/anger-management/id339007359?mt=8.

Digital Literacy in a Hyperconnected World

Brett Cohen the Celebrity

New York City is a hotspot for celebrity sightings, and July 27, 2012 was no different. On that hot summer afternoon, Cohen posed with nearly 300 people who wanted to take photographs with him.[1] "What was it like meeting Brett?" the reporter asked the group of young women standing near New York's Times Square. They giddily answered "fantastic" and "I love him," with one swooning, "Let me just say he's beautiful!" One man said, "I think he's excellent, I think he's absolutely awesome, I think he's got a great future and all in the movie business and I just took a picture with him and I feel special." The reporter questioned several people where they knew Cohen from and they replied, "Spider Man." When asked if he'd heard any of Cohen's music, one man replied, "I heard his first single, which is good. I don't know the name of it, but I heard it in the radio."[2] If you're feeling out of the loop because you don't know who Cohen is, that's okay. He's a 21-year-old college student at State University of New York at New Paltz, majoring in media management. With his friend Edward Sturm posing as the reporter, Cohen decided to dress and act like a stereotypical celebrity and see what would happen. He explained, "The idea was, 'I bet if we walked through with bodyguards and photographers, people would go nuts.' And that's exactly what happened."[3] He recruited people through craigslist and instructed everyone not to actually say he was famous, but simply share his name with the crowd to see if people on their own would make the leap to assuming he was a celebrity.[4] And they did. The stunt was later covered by online and television media outlets (so perhaps now Cohen is a star, as suggested by Figure 7.1), which variously mentioned how society is obsessed with celebrity and also how seemingly gullible the public is. One commenter on the website Reddit noted, "That was amusing, but quite pathetic how everyone was so quick to jump on a bandwagon. Complete sheep. Kudos to that guy for having fun with something that is unfortunately rampant in pop icon worship."[5] Another bluntly stated, "It is cringe-worthy stupid. Not the video itself or the people doing it, but all of the brainless mouth-breathers who are diving head-first into the celebrity worship."[6]

Figure 7.1   *Screenshot of Liyana Mohamad's Tweet on September 14, 2012*

The News Media Takes Accuracy Seriously... And Still Sometimes Gets It Wrong

The Brett Cohen incident is amusing and, although a few people ended up looking silly, no one was ultimately hurt in the process. The stunt was benign and served its purpose of poking fun at society's seemingly endless obsession with fame. However, unlike in the online entertainment and gossip arenas, where truth often takes a back seat to page views and advertising revenue, the traditional news media take accuracy, fact checking, and verifiability seriously.

In August 2012, Global news channel RT (Russia Today) first reported that Saudi Arabia planned to build a women-only city, explaining that "The Gulf kingdom is working on the narrow junction between strict Sharia law and the aspirations of active females who wish to pursue their own careers."[7] ABC News' Lara Setrakian commented that "Separate has never meant equal in Saudi Arabia.... What seems like more segregation to outsiders looks like empowerment in Saudis' eyes."[8] Her article was shared close to 300 times on Facebook and tweeted more than 100 times.

The *Guardian's* Homa Khaleeli wrote, "But how can further segregation be expected to solve the problems caused by discrimination? It takes a peculiar leap of logic to think the answer is instead to build whole new cities where women who choose to have careers can be herded.... A culture that does not just segregate women, but enshrines in law that they are second-class citizens, is hardly one worth preserving."[9] Her article was shared more than 500 times on Facebook and tweeted more than 150 times. Meanwhile, the comments left by readers included those like, "They are yet another bizarre manifestation of a culture that cannot function in the modern world. First athletes in bhurkas, now this"[10] and "It seems to me that this is a solution to gathering all the troublesome females in one place to keep an eye on them, control them and prevent them for [sic] infecting the general populace. Very Warsaw 1940."[11]

However, a few days after the initial story by RT, *AL Arabiya* published an article titled "Scratch that! No women-only city in Saudi Arabia" in which it scolded other news outlets with the scathing comment that the female-only city was a fabrication: "Contrary to reports in the *Guardian*, the *Daily Mail*, the *Huffington Post*, ABC News, Russia Today and dozens, if not hundreds, of other sources who published the story apparently without bothering to check facts with the primary source."[12] *AL Arabiya* went on to explain that the international media's error lay in not reading past the title of a press release by the Saudi Industrial Property Authority MODON that stated "MODON' begins Planning and Development for the First Industrial City being readied for Women in the Kingdom."[13]

Perhaps the reason so many people, including members of the media who are by training taught to be skeptical, were willing to believe the existence of a women-only city is because Saudi Arabia prevents women from voting, holding elected office and driving cars. Both Amnesty International[14] and Human Rights Watch[15] criticize Saudia Arabia on multiple fronts. So the idea that the country would create a geographically segregated work environment seems plausible. Nevertheless, it was factually incorrect. Instead, the reality was that, in keeping with Saudi Arabian cultural norms of separating the sexes, particular sections of the factories would be reserved for women.[16]

Unfortunately, the false story was still being disseminated weeks after the first report, as shown in Figure 7.2.

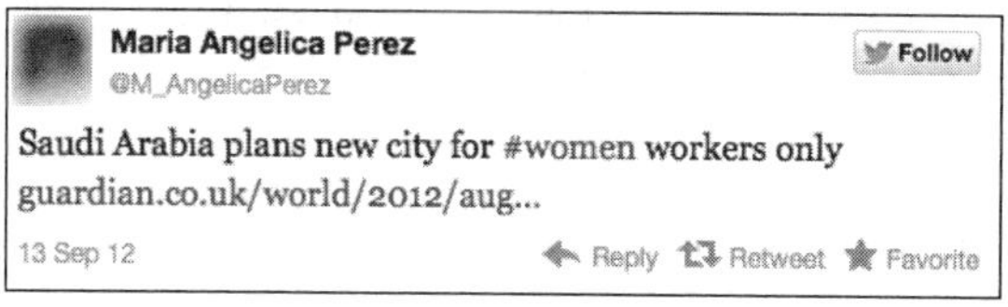

Maria Angelica Perez
@M_AngelicaPerez   Follow

Saudi Arabia plans new city for #women workers only
guardian.co.uk/world/2012/aug...

13 Sep 12   ↩ Reply ⟲ Retweet ★ Favorite

Figure 7.2   *Screenshot of Maria Angelica Perez's Tweet on September 13, 2012*

Digital Literacy and Why It's Important

So what is the lesson you're supposed to take away from all this? Is there a common thread between the Brett Cohen and the Saudi Arabia stories? Most certainly. Although one involves the world of entertainment and one of politics, both examples emphasize the need for the public to learn digital literacy skills.

Digital literacy is a vital component of digital civility and citizenship overall. Digital literacy is the application of traditional media literacy skills to the Internet for purpose of critically analyzing and evaluating online information found on social networking sites, forums, and blogs and in the comment threads of news stories for quality, credibility, accuracy, bias, and manipulation. It also means knowing how to effectively navigate and participate in the global online environment.

Furthermore, digital literacy is important because of the vast amount of information available online. It's difficult to sift through it without having established some sort of system for separating the qualitative from the quantitative, the valuable from the unimportant, the accurate from the inaccurate, and the emotionally manipulative from the rational. In other words, digital literacy requires strong critical-thinking skills.

The number of trained journalists and editors working in media has decreased since the birth of the Web. The availability of professionals who can dig deeply into stories that need to be told and issues that need to be examined, often in the areas of investigative journalism, has been reduced, as have professionals who can help the public understand and dissect important and complex issues. There are upsides to the reduction of "gatekeepers"—empowering the public by giving people a stronger and more influential voice, enabling them to be active and vocal participants in political and social life, and allowing them to play an important role of checks-and-balances to ensure important information isn't withheld from the public. However, in today's polarized environment, many individuals are prone to seek out the information that supports their beliefs, views, and positions (the more extreme, unsupported, and factually outrageous the better), and less likely to challenge their own beliefs by exposing themselves to additional or opposing points of view. Which brings you to a discussion on truth, or rather "truthiness."

Truthiness Is the Word

Stephen Colbert is the host and executive producer of Comedy Central's award-winning show "The Colbert Report." Colbert once explained that the show grew out of the concept of him "trying to ape the 'who is loudest is rightest' idea of... prime time on cable news,"[17] and those who favor "passion and emotion and certainty over information."[18] His character, described by Colbert as "a well-inten-tioned, poorly informed, high-status idiot,"[19] isn't just hilarious in his own right, he's also noteworthy because of the historical role he played in linguistics as the creator of the word "*truthiness.*" With deadpan delivery, Colbert introduced truthi-ness to the world with the following description:

> "*I'm sure some of the word-police, the "wordanistas" over at Websters, are gonna say, 'Hey, that's not a word!' Well, anybody who knows me knows that I am no fan of dictionaries or reference books. They're elit-ist. Constantly telling us what is or isn't true, what did or didn't hap-pen.... I don't trust books. They're all fact, no heart...we are divided by those who think with their head, and those who know with their heart... that's where the truth comes from, ladies and gentlemen...the gut.... The 'truthiness' is, anyone can read the news to you. I promise to feel the news...at you.*"[20]

The concept of truthiness immediately resonated with people, as shown in Figure 7.3, both as a reality in some corners of society and also as frequently expressed behavior in the online world. Perhaps it was this same recognition that led the American Dialect Society to announce that truthiness—"what one wishes to be the truth regardless of the facts"—would be the 2005 Word of the Year.[21]

Figure 7.3   *Screenshot of Sean Jones's Tweet on September 11, 2012*

But the importance of truth and accuracy are no laughing matter, especially online where anyone can be a publisher, when there are few checks for accuracy or reli-ability, and there are endless numbers of gullible individuals who blindly believe what's presented to them. Perhaps this was one of the inspirations for Harvard University's Berkman Center for Internet and Society and the MIT Center for Civic Media to hold a March 2012 symposium that examined propaganda and mis-information in new media."[22]

Wendell Potter, the former head of communications at CIGNA and author of the book *Deadly Spin: An Insurance Company Insider Speaks Out on How Corporate PR Is Killing Health Care and Deceiving Americans*, described what he sees as one of the problems: "Today, because of the digital media, big companies are able to get their propaganda directly to their target audiences.... All this means that the consumer is often, if not most of the time, at a big disadvantage. It's much easier for the dark side to spread misinformation and lies, fear, uncertainty and doubt.... Using the digital media, it has become a much more powerful means for the special interests to manipulate public opinion, to influence public policy, and to get people to vote against their own self-interest."[23]

Examples like those happening within the healthcare industry are the reason why, Potter said, he is glad to see the emergence of fact-checking websites that can point out inaccuracies in political statements and information that's being disseminated.[24] Although Potter points out what he sees as the unfortunate misleading of the public by some companies, the public can help thwart such attempts if it exercises critical thinking.

Critical Thinking Is a Core Component of Digital Literacy

One of the most important skills you need to develop for digital literacy is critical thinking. The concept of critical thinking has been around since the days of Greek philosophers Socrates, Plato, and Aristotle, and yet it's an insufficiently taught and underutilized skill. According to The Foundation and Center for Critical Thinking, "critical thinking is that mode of thinking—about any subject, content, or problem—in which the thinker improves the quality of his or her thinking by skillfully analyzing, assessing, and reconstructing it."[25]

Richard Paul, Ph.D., director of Research and Professional Development at the Center for Critical Thinking, and Linda Elder, Ph.D., president of the Foundation for Critical Thinking and executive director of the Center for Critical Thinking, are co-authors of the book *The Thinker's Guide to Analytical Thinking*. In it they discuss the standards of critical thinking that should be applied to the various elements of thought.[26]

The standards of Critical Thinking follow:[27]

- **Clarity:** Is it understandable and can the meaning be grasped?
- **Accuracy:** Is it true and free from errors or distortion?
- **Precision:** Is it exact to the necessary level of detail?
- **Relevance:** Does it relate to the matter at hand?
- **Depth:** Does it contain complexities and multiple interrelationships?

- **Breadth:** Does it encompass multiple viewpoints?
- **Logic:** Do the parts make sense together and are there no contradictions?
- **Significance:** Does it focus on the important and not trivial?
- **Fairness:** Is it justifiable and not self-serving or one-sided?
- Additional standards that may be necessary depending on the situation, such as completeness, validity, rationality, sufficiency, necessity, feasibility, consistency, authenticity, effectiveness, and efficiency

Meanwhile, the Elements of Thought follow:[28]

- **Purpose:** The goal, objective, or what you're trying to accomplish
- **Question at issue:** The expressed problem or issue
- **Information:** The facts, data, evidence, or experiences used to figure things out
- **Interpretation and Inference:** The interpretations or conclusions you use when trying to understand or determine something
- **Concepts:** The ideas, theories, laws, principles, or hypotheses used to understand and make sense of things
- **Assumptions:** The beliefs that you rely on, which may operate at the subconscious level
- **Implications and Consequences:** The results that flow from ways of thinking and acting
- **Point of View:** The way you look at and regard something

Paul and Elder's Standards and Elements of Thought might initially sound complicated and a bit daunting, but they're simple to follow after you've practiced using them a few times. In fact, you may even realize that you've been applying them all along without even realizing it!

Check Your Biases and Beliefs

American teacher and philosopher Amos Bronson Alcott said, "To be ignorant of one's ignorance is the malady of the ignorant," while international bestselling author and speaker Wayne Dyer, Ph.D. is quoted as saying, "The highest form of ignorance is when you reject something you don't know."

The same statements can be applied to biases. One of the important things to keep in mind with digital literacy is to be aware of biases, both those of others and your own, as well as the beliefs that flow from them, a point humorously made in Figure 7.4. Having biases is natural and even advantageous in certain situations;

for example, having parents positively biased toward their own children can help ensure their offspring are taken care of and protected. But biases can also be harmful, as when one group of people claims superiority over another based on skin color.

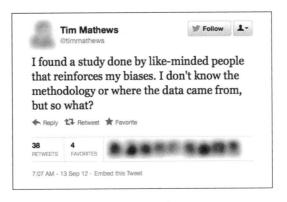

Figure 7.4   *Screenshot of Tim Mathews's Tweet on September 13, 2012*

For those who engage in critical thinking, you're already used to examining and analyzing information. Even then, objectively looking at one's own beliefs and resulting behavior can be challenging and requires practice. But being unwilling to try to determine what they are, why one has them, or where they spring from would be derelict. Instead, it requires discipline and applying the trick you learned in the previous chapter in the section "Anger Management Techniques," namely taking a detached view and examining the situation like "a fly on the wall."

What you should try to avoid is allowing your biases to become so strong that they become twisted caricatures of rational thought. In an article titled "The Wrong Side Absolutely Must Not Win" appearing in the *Richmond Times-Dispatch*, columnist A. Barton Hinkle wrote a brilliant satire about the hyper-partisanship leading up to the 2012 U.S. presidential election. He explained that America would find itself in extreme peril if the "Other Side" wins, and that this threat of disaster should be obvious to anyone who looks at how the "Other Side" has been running a campaign full of distortions and lies.[29] He mentions the "Other Side's" discredited policies and radical failed ideology, while pointing out that "My Side's" supporters are smarter and right about everything.[30] Arguably the best part of the article is where he says, "it's clear that the people on the Other Side are driven by mindless anger—unlike My Side, which is filled with passionate idealism and righteous indignation. That indignation, I hasten to add, is entirely justified. I have read several articles in publications that support My Side that expose what a truly dangerous group the Other Side is, and how thoroughly committed it is to imposing its radical, failed agenda on the rest of us."[31]

Hinkle's piece has meaning beyond politics. It reminds us all to check our beliefs to make sure they're based on accurate facts rather than pure speculation. Can you pinpoint the reasons why you have a particular belief, and does that belief withstand scrutiny? Sometimes the underlying reasons for a belief don't matter in the overall scheme of things, and the specifics supporting it are unimportant. For example, you might prefer red over orange because you think it's a more powerful color, whereas your friend prefers orange because she considers it to be a more energetic color. Unless you're living together and need to decide what color to paint your new living room, who really cares? But if you look at other, more socially relevant issues, your biases and resulting beliefs become more important.

Now use subsidized public transportation as an example. Individual A places a high value on the personal characteristics of independence and self-sufficiency. She also believes that people who rely on government assistance are lazy and in their predicament as a direct result of having made poor financial choices in the past. Individual B believes that protecting the environment and reducing global warming is one of the most pressing issues facing us today. He also believes that the only way individuals and industry will make the necessary changes is if it is either strongly incentivized through financial means, or if it is forced to through legislation. Based on these brief descriptions, it's fairly easy to guess which of the two is likely to be in favor and which likely to be opposed to subsidized public transportation. But are the underlying reasons each of them is pro or con based on fact or based on bias? In the case of Individual A, her belief that those who rely on government assistance are lazy and made poor choices in the past isn't borne out by facts, and Individual B's belief that people make only environmentally friendly choices if they are forced to isn't either.

Now look at another example. How about the fact that attending college makes students more liberal and less religious? Pretty much everyone knows this is true because colleges are largely composed of liberal-leaning academics who impart secular views on their impressionable and malleable charges. The problem is, it's actually not true that students become more liberal as a result of pursuing higher education. In *The New York Times* article "The Indoctrination Myth," Neil Gross, Ph.D., a professor of sociology at the University of British Columbia, explains that although it's correct that college students are slightly more liberal than their non-college attending peers, it's not a direct result of having attended college. Instead, it's based on the reality that liberal students are more inclined to attend college.[32] Furthermore, American undergraduate students are more likely to maintain their faith than those either attending 2-year colleges or not attending college at all.[33] Depending on someone's biases, however, those truths are easily overlooked.

Also be aware that the viewpoints you express and the positions you take are based not just on your own internal preferences, but also external factors and influences of which you may be unaware. In *The New York Times* article "The Mind of a

Flip-Flopper," BoingBoing science editor Maggie Koerth-Baker talked about a 2006 study by researchers from Ohio State University and Colorado State University that revealed how watching television can change the political views of college students.[34] In the study, one group of students viewed a television crime drama that involved a story about the need for the death penalty, while another group watched a different drama without death penalty references. When they were later asked about their views on capital punishment, the students who had watched the crime drama were more likely to speak out in favor of the death penalty, regardless of their political affiliation. The second group of students answered the same question more along traditional political party lines.[35]

Another example of outside factors subconsciously influencing people's beliefs was revealed in the *Scientific American* article,[36] in which author Daisy Grewal, Ph.D., discussed a 2012 paper published in *Psychological Science*.[37] Grewal explained, "Recent research suggests that thinking about our lives in terms [of] choices may reduce our support for public policies that promote greater equality in society. By emphasizing free will over the situational factors that shape people's life experiences, thinking about choice may lead us to view inequality as less bothersome."[38] She went on to say that thinking about choice "led people to feel less empathy toward others who have experienced negative life events. For example, participants who had thought about choices were more likely to blame people who had experienced car accidents, physical abuse, or a loss of their home due to a building collapse."[39] Interestingly, this may be a uniquely Western phenomenon because, according to Grewal, the researchers found that the issue of choice didn't result in the same reaction by Indians, who aren't typically enculturated with the same notion of freedom and choice as those in the United States. So, while the original study deals with views about income and wealth, for our purposes here it's interesting to consider how the findings might be applicable to other areas as well.

Another way that our beliefs may be influenced is through sequentiality and primacy. In other words, we are often swayed by the order in which information is first received. According to Dana R. Carney, Ph.D., and Mahzarin R. Banaji, Ph.D., authors of "First Is Best"[40] published in PLoS ONE, we know through prior research that we tend to better remember those things we experience first, and are more attached to and influenced by them.[41] In the three experiments they conducted, Carney and Banaji "obtained a consistent result that on a deep, automatic level of human cognition, firsts are consistently preferred and chosen."[42] They further noted that "we propose that judgments that are relatively devoid of conscious awareness will consistently reveal an effect in which firsts are considered best because firsts are privileged for several reasons that heuristic processes may rely on."[43] What possible bearing does this have on the online world?

Although the authors don't specifically discuss the Internet, perhaps, for online conflict and especially the frequent disputes that happen on discussion boards, forums and social networking sites, we should consider that the order in which information is shared and disseminated online has an impact on its ability to influence others and be persuasive. This is particularly important when we realize how often information first reported online is incomplete or erroneous, yet persists in the popular consciousness more often and more strongly than the corrected and updated information that is subsequently discovered. Furthermore, maybe it has a bearing on our willingness, even if subconsciously, to absorb or reject new information, and thus affect how arguments play out online.

The bottom line is that although we'll perhaps never be fully aware of what all our biases are based on and where they come from, we should do our absolute best to figure them out. We also need to keep in mind that others are also operating from a position of bias. We therefore need to be on the lookout for both our own and others' biases.

Examining Credibility and Quality

There is no shortage of information available online. So, unlike in centuries past where the challenge lay in trying to obtain access to information, our modern challenge now consists of trying to sift through the mass amount of data at our fingertips and find qualitative and credible information. Here are some things you can do:

- **Examine the source of the information:** What publication is the information published in; what company or organization published or released the information; what is their motivation for sharing the information; and who paid for a quoted study?

- **Examine authorship:** Who is the author; what are the author's social/political/financial affiliations; what is the reason he or she is publishing/broadcasting/otherwise disseminating the information; and is the author someone with expertise in the field he or she is talking about?

- **Examine credibility of the information:** What information does the author mention and what information does he leave out; is the author trying to emotionally manipulate the audience with the use of particular visuals or sounds; are legitimate and trustworthy sources used; and is the communication an opinion piece that solely relies on the author's beliefs?

Inquiring about the sources of information and looking at them with a critical eye is extremely important, especially online. It's too easy for information to be passed along on social networking sites and other online properties without checking whether it's accurate. Failing to do so sometimes leads to unexpected consequences.

In 2011, the Santa Rosa-based California Parenting Institute (CPI) released a disturbing study indicating that regardless of the particular parenting style used to raise children, offspring grow up to be unhappy adults.[44] Lead researcher Daniel Porter stated, "Our research suggests that while overprotective parenting ultimately produces adults unprepared to contend with life's difficulties, highly permissive parenting leads to feelings of bitterness and isolation throughout adulthood."[45] He went on to say, "We found that anything between those two extremes is equally damaging, always resulting in an adult who suffers from some debilitating combination of unpreparedness and isolation."[46] Given the negativity of the findings, it's not surprising that CPI received many concerned calls and emails from educators and parents asking for additional details about the study.[47] However, the study was fabricated, and the source of the original story was The Onion, a satire site which calls itself "America's Finest News Source." Jonah Raskin, Ph.D., chair of communication studies at Sonoma State University, noted, "If you go online, you will find all kinds of things that are false and misleading about products and individuals. If anyone takes The Onion seriously, they are sadly misunderstanding The Onion."[48]

However, this wasn't the only time that The Onion's articles were taken as verbatim truth, as shown in Figure 7.5. In 2011, The Onion published an article with the headline, "Congress Takes Group Of Schoolchildren Hostage" with the lead sentence, "Brandishing shotguns and semiautomatic pistols, members of the 112th U.S. Congress took a class of visiting schoolchildren hostage today, barricading themselves inside the Capitol rotunda and demanding $12 trillion dollars in cash."[49] As many organizations these days do, The Onion promoted its story via Twitter, releasing a series of tweets starting with "BREAKING: Witnesses reporting screams and gunfire heard inside Capitol building" and "BREAKING: Capitol building being evacuated. 12 children held hostage by group of armed congressmen #CongressHostage."[50] The third tweet was linked to the actual article, after which it continued its fake real-time reporting of the hostage situation.[51] The U.S. Capitol Police thereafter issued a written statement to calm the public. Sgt. Kimberly Schneider said, "It has come to our attention that recent twitter feeds are reporting false information concerning current conditions at the U.S. Capitol. Conditions at the U.S. Capitol are currently normal. There is no credibility to these stories or the twitter feeds. The U.S. Capitol Police are currently investigating the reporting."[52] Whether the police were contacted by the public because someone actually believed the story was real, or whether the police wanted to ensure that no one erroneously did so, is unclear. But with more than 4 million followers on The Onion Twitter feed, a strong possibility existed that someone somewhere would misunderstand what was posted, especially because The Onion used the hashtag #CongressHostage and not a hashtag indicating this was in fact a spoof.

These examples aren't the only ones in which people believed The Onion without checking what kind of website actually produced it.[53] Two additional articles stand out in particular. One was the 2010 "Harry Potter Books Spark Rise In Satanism Among Children,"[54] which mirrored the irrational fear by some that J. K. Rowling's work would negatively influence young people to turn to the supernatural. This belief among some segments of society led to actions such as the congregation of a New Mexico church burning Harry Potter books after a sermon by their pastor Jack Brock, who admitted to never having read Rowling's bestsellers but nevertheless felt qualified to state, "Behind that innocent face is the power of satanic darkness. Harry Potter is the devil and he is destroying people."[55] The second example was the 2011 article "Planned Parenthood Opens $8 Billion Abortionplex,"[56], which was taken at face value by Republican Congressman John Flemming, whose Facebook page linked to the original article with the comment "More on Planned Parenthood, abortion by the wholesale.[57]

Figure 7.5   *Screenshot of hello my name is Tweet on September 14, 2012*

In each of the cases mentioned, The Onion cleverly used people's inclinations to believe information that supported their own biases, while also exposing the gullibility of individuals who aren't well versed in digital literacy and critical thinking skills. A site that's capitalized on showcasing such people is Literally Unbelievable (http://literallyunbelievable.org/), which exclusively focuses on examples of people who believe and post The Onion stories on Facebook, or alternatively comment on them, as though they were true. But what you need to take away here isn't that The Onion is good at writing seemingly believable, if occasionally over-the-top, stories—instead, it's that people fall for false stories and incorrect reports from many different sources.

Another thing people need to be on guard about is the strong influence that photographs can have on the believability of accompanying information. A 2012 article appearing in *Psychonomic Bulletin & Review*[58] noted that people believe that claims accompanied by decorative photographs are true, whether or not they actually are.[59] Based on the power of visual images to catch the attention of readers and influence them, is it any wonder that so many online stories feature pictures and not just text?

Part of digital literacy also entails critically examining the background of experts. People often make the mistake of assuming that because people are experts in one field they should be relied upon when they speak about other topics. Of course, experts can acquire knowledge in areas that aren't their originally chosen areas of concentration, but make sure that they've actually done so before relying on what they say or recommend. For example, many people assume that by definition medical doctors are qualified to give nutrition advice. However, most individuals aren't aware that the majority of American medical schools don't even meet the minimum 25 hours of nutrition education recommended by the National Academy of Sciences.[60] According to the study "Nutrition Education in U.S. Medical Schools: Latest Update of a National Survey," published in 2010 in *Academic Medicine*, medical students received only 19.6 contact hours of nutrition instruction during their medical school training, down from a 2004 average of 22.3 hours.[61]

People also often assume that when someone claims to be an expert, they actually are. However, unfortunately, that's not always the case. Ryan Holiday is a savvy media strategist whose clients have included colorful individuals like author Max Tucker and American Apparel CEO Dov Charney. Perhaps most important, Holiday is the author of *Trust Me, I'm Lying: Confessions of a Media Manipulator*, for which he reportedly earned a $500K book deal.[62] In it he recounts, among other things, how he intentionally misused Help A Reporter Out (HARO), a service connecting journalists and sources, by presenting himself as a legitimate source and expert when answering queries for subjects he knew nothing about.[63] A *Forbes* article by David Thier listed some of the media that Holiday appeared in: "On Reuters, he became the poster child for Generation Yikes. On ABC News, he was one of a new breed of long-suffering insomniacs. At CBS, he made up an embarrassing office story; at MSNBC he pretended someone sneezed on him while working at Burger King. At Manitouboats.com, he offered helpful tips for winterizing your boat. The capstone came in the form of *The New York Times* piece on vinyl records—naturally, Holiday doesn't collect vinyl records."[64]

Feelings about Holiday might be mixed, as reflected by Figure 7.6, but Holiday felt that his actions served the noble purpose of exposing media weaknesses that the public should know about. He wrote, "My belief is that today's media cycle—which is driven by blogs—is broken. It is being ruined by several factors including the crushing deadlines, advertising conflicts, page view quotas, poorly trained journalists, greedy publishers, laziness, and countless other practices. These perverse incentives distort everything we read, hear and see...."[65]

Not surprisingly, Peter Shankman, the founder of HARO, wasn't pleased with Holiday. In a post on his own blog, he wrote, "Let's be clear: This idiot (Ryan Holiday, the liar) did this for one reason, and it wasn't anywhere NEAR as altruistic as 'an experiment.' He wrote a book on how to lie and get in the media, and he was promoting it. End of story. Want more proof? You know what this guy did before he wrote this book? HE WORKED FOR TUCKER MAX, the man who's written multiple books on how to lie to get laid. Enough said."[66] He came to his creation's defense by adding, "HARO has grown to include a massive community of 130,000 sources and 30,000 reporters and bloggers. We have a good thing going and we intend to keep it that way. One person should not be entitled to ruin a good thing for the rest of us."[67]

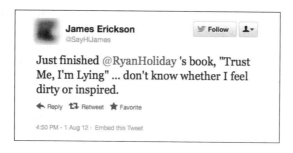

Figure 7.6   *James Erickson's Tweet on August 1, 2012*

Holiday retorted with "Yes, HARO is just a service and as the middleman Peter can't be held totally responsible for lazy reporters who don't fact-check their sources. But then again, it was being aware of such laziness that likely drove him to create the site in the first place, and THAT is precisely what he exploits as a publicist. And today, it's what makes Peter defend the indefensible monster that HARO has become. He makes too much money from it."[68] While not defending his behavior, Thier felt that "A quick Google search would have raised red flags for anyone using [Holiday] as a source."[69]

Examining the credibility of information or sources also involves, as previously noted, knowing about their affiliations. In 2006, a blog called "Wal-Marting Across America" featured Laura and Jim as they drove their recreational vehicle across the United States, stopping at Wal-Mart stores when they needed to rest and parking there for free. Their blog posts shared flattering commentary about the Wal-Mart employees they met, noting that they all seemed to enjoy working at the company.[70] Considering Wal-Mart's generally meager wages and historical opposition to unions, some readers soon became suspicious of the happy employees consistently featured on the blog.[71] Jonathan Reese, Ph.D., a history professor at Colorado State University-Pueblo, wrote, "An Open Letter to 'Jim' and 'Laura,'" asking them to "Please prove to me that you exist,"[72] followed by a second email conceding that while he believed they were in fact traveling cross-country in an RV, he still wanted them to provide "proof that you are not props of the Edelman/Wal-Mart propaganda machine" (Edelman being the public relations firm of record for Wal-Mart).[73]

As pressure mounted to discover the back story to Wal-Marting Across America, the truth was finally revealed. Real couple Laura and Jim decided on their own to RV cross-country, while hoping to park for free at Wal-Mart to save on expenses.[74] To make sure this would be okay, Laura contacted Working Families for Wal-Mart, an organization created by Edelman to counter pro-union groups, with the result that the group decided to sponsor the trip. Unfortunately, the affiliation between the blog, Wal-Mart, and Edelman wasn't revealed until skeptics did some digging,[75] and by then the damage to Edelman's reputation had already taken place. Edelman CEO Richard Edelman wrote a public apology saying, "I want to acknowledge our error in failing to be transparent about the identity of the two bloggers from the outset. This is 100% our responsibility and our error; not the client's."[76] Wal-Marting Across America received the unwelcome recognition of being listed among the "101 Dumbest Moments in Business" by Business 2.0.[77] Although Edelman is one of the premier and most-respected public relations firms in the world, its Wal-Marting blog is still listed as an example in Wikipedia's article "Fake blog."[78]

But it is not just in the media world that companies and individuals dupe people by pretending to be something they're not. Sadly, it can happen in other well-respected industries, such as the sciences, as well. In 2012, it was discovered that Japanese anesthesiologist Yoshitaka Fujii allegedly fabricated an astounding 172 papers during a 19-year timeframe.[79] Before that, there were several other scientists who intentionally wreaked havoc through fabricated research, as noted in Eugenie Samuel Reich's book *Plastic Fantastic: How the Biggest Fraud in Physics Shook the Scientific World*. Twin physicists Igor and Grichka Bogdanov, biologist Hwang Woo-Suk, biology professor Luk Van Parijs, and Jan Hendrik Schön, a researcher at Bell Laboratories, all falsified research.[80] Perhaps that explains why the process of scholarly peer review, in which a professional's work is subjected to review and analysis by experts in the field, is held in such high esteem. It reduces the opportunity for fraudulent or inaccurate work to be released into the public sphere.

Using Fujii and Schön as inspirational springboards, technology and science website Ars Technica wrote a tongue-in-cheek article listing several ways to be a successful fraud in science, which included[81]

- Telling people what they already know
- Doing research nobody cares about
- Not publishing in journals focused on one's respective field
- Spreading responsibility around
- Not outright plagiarizing or using duplicate images because these are easy to spot

Now briefly move from science to politics. As anyone following American politics knows, the 2012 U.S. Presidential race was a contentious one, with both candidates pulling out all stops to try to garner the necessary support to win the election. It naturally was assumed that candidates and their supporters would present themselves and their ideas in the best light possible, while simultaneously trying to point out their opponent's weaknesses and flaws. That's why Barack Obama's Democratic National Convention speech and Mitt Romney's Republican National Convention speech were carefully fact-checked by groups such as PolitiFact.org and FactCheck.org, as well as individuals such as journalist Glenn Kessler, who writes the "Fact Checker" column for *The Washington Post*.

Although pushing the boundaries within politics is par for the course, misleading the public isn't as readily accepted. That's why a Republican National Committee ad called "The Breakup," which aired on television shortly after the Republican National Convention, raised a few eyebrows. It featured a Hispanic women talking to an unseen person sitting across from her: "Listen, this just isn't working. It's been four years. You've changed: Your spending is out of control, you're constantly on the golf course, and you're always out with Hollywood celebrities.... You're just not the person I thought you were. It's not me, it's you. I think we should just be friends."[82] At the end she stands up and leaves behind the cardboard cutout of President Obama.

The way the advertisement was structured suggested that the woman was a previous supporter of Obama who became unhappy with how he governed the country and was therefore turning toward the Republican party.[83] However, the truth is that the woman who played the role was the Republican National Committee's director of Hispanic outreach Bettina Inclan, who, according to online political news organization Talking Points Memo, had not ever been a supporter of Obama, let alone a Democrat.[84] So the question to ask is whether the advertisement should have clearly stated that the person was not actually a former Obama supporter but was simply playing a role? Was there an ethical responsibility to make that fact clear? Or should the public automatically assume that all political ads are semi-truths that range from lies of omission to outright lies?

Regardless of the industry or the situational specifics, as you've seen through the examples discussed in this chapter, the takeaway lesson is the same: Examine sources critically, don't blindly believe what you're told, and verify information when needed.

Don't be Seduced By Gossip and Rumors

Another reason people need to strengthen their digital literacy skills is because it makes them more aware when they're being seduced online. Supermarket tabloids such as the *Globe* and the *National Enquirer* have long enjoyed strong readerships while catering to the lowest common denominator. Replicating the traditional success of print tabloids has become much easier online. With a low barrier to entry and a potential to strike it big, the Internet has become a battleground for website page views and advertising revenue. One of the most popular ways websites try to gain readership is by being gossipy, rumor-friendly, and even inexact when it comes to the truth, as shown in Figure 7.7.

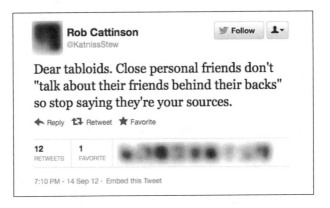

Figure 7.7   *James Erickson's Tweet on August 1, 2012*

In his 2008 book *Against the Machine: Being Human in the Age of the Electronic Mob*, cultural critic Lee Siegel laments, "No one is making a cogent connection between the rise of the Internet and the accelerating blur of truth and falsity in culture."[85] He argues that "Bigness and popularity are all that matter. The reason for popularity is irrelevant. Someone could get big and go 'viral' because he has talent, or because he can eat twenty donuts in sixty seconds."[86] Tyler Cowen, author of *What Price Fame?* points out, "What is scarce on the Internet is not information or material, but context and evaluation."[87]

Meanwhile, on the topic of gossip, Robin Dunbar, author of *Grooming, Gossip and the Evolution of Language*, explains that once upon a time there may have been a social benefit to gossip: "Gossip may have evolved as a mechanism for controlling the activities of free-riders. By exchanging information on their activities, humans are able to use language to both gain advanced warning of social cheats and to shame them [into] conforming to accepted social standards when they do misbehave."[88] Today, however, one is hard pressed to argue that the prevalence and viciousness of online gossip serves a similar purpose.

But what makes online gossip isn't just the content of the information; it's the form of expression as well. Snark, a close friend of gossip, seems to be the expression of choice among tens of thousands of people online. And again, as you often see online, it's not about sharing factually accurate information but about getting readers to pay attention through whatever means possible, even if it's through mean spiritedness, insinuations, or fabrications.

In the book *Snark: It's Mean, It's Personal and It's Ruining Our Conversation,* David Denby offers the following description: "Snark is a teasing, rug-pulling form of insult that attempts to steal someone's mojo, erase her cool, annihilate her effectiveness, and it appeals to a knowing audience that shares the contempt of the snarker and therefore understands whatever reference he makes. It's all jeer and josh, a form of bullying...."[89]

Denby discusses the Eight Principles of Snark, which he covers in great detail in his book: Briefly, these are[90]

1. "The 'Whatever' Principle. Attack without reason.

2. The White Man's Last Stand Principle. Appeal to common, hackneyed prejudices, the more common and hackneyed the better. But disguise the appeal a little, if you can.

3. The Pawnshop Principle. Reach into the rotten head of media references for old jokes, old insults, and give them a twist.

4. The Throw-Some-Mud Principle. Assume anything negative said about someone with power is true—or at least usable.

5. The Reckless Disregard Principle. Ignore the routine responsibilities of journalism. The more flagrantly you disregard them the better.

6. The Hobbyhorse Principle. Reduce all human complexity to caricature. Then repeat the caricature.

7. The You-S**k Principle. Glom on to celebrities in an attitude of adoration and loathing; first adoration, then loathing.

8. The Pacemaker Principle. Attack the old. Your editors and Web publishers want young demographics, so they won't mind."

One company that's perfected the art of snark for commercial gain is Gawker, which was reportedly the most valuable blog in 2011, worth $318 million.[91] Founded in 2002 by Nick Denton, Gawker is the flagship blog of Gawker Media, which now has a total of 17.9 million monthly readers and offers eight branded blogs that "[attract] fans and critics alike for their inimitable delivery of news, scandal, and entertainment." Gawker Media's target market is a 25 to 34-year-old urbanite who is an early adopter of technology.[92] A few years ago Denton revealed the formula behind the site during an interview with a prospective writer. He said that Gawker articles should be 100–200 words maximum and that in terms of content, he was "not interested in think pieces unless they're rants...the ideal gawker [sic] item is something triggered by a quote at a party, or an incident, or a story somewhere else...think of gawker as nyt Sunday Styles, but with much lower threshold for a story."[93] Today Gawker brands itself as a "national news and entertainment site."[94]

Gawker is financially successful because millions of readers find its content entertaining, perhaps specifically because of its mocking tone and acerbic content. Certainly no one can disagree that it represents a winning formula. However, not everyone succumbs to the company's lure. In 2007, Katie Roiphe, assistant professor at New York University and author of the controversial book *The Morning After: Sex, Fear and Feminism,* was mocked by Gawker[95] about a piece she wrote for *New York Magazine* in which she described feeling fine about her impending divorce.[96] The Gawker article, written by Emily Gould, former co-editor of the website, was called "Katie Roiphe Is Big Immature Baby." Fast-forward a few years to 2011, when Roiphe wrote the Slate article "Gawker Is Big Immature Baby" and describes how Gould contacted her to request that she write a blurb for Gould's upcoming book. Roipe dryly noted that, after Gould wrote the mean-spirited article about her on Gawker, "some old-fashioned part of me still found it strange that she would send me her book for a blurb."[97] More interesting, however, was her dissection of Gawker's style: "It's all tone, no content, and the tone itself is monotonously unvaried—namely the sneer.... It's not that one wants one's gossips to be nice, exactly, but one wants them nuanced, substantive. One wants to remember an amazing line, and not have a vague impression of cloudy nastiness."[98]

Even if people invest their personal time reading Gawker, TMZ, and similar online properties, they're hopefully aware that these sites aren't good sources for serious news analysis or investigative content, and instead entertainment sites operating on a sensationalistic, mocking, and voyeuristic platform.

Accuracy and Verifiability of Information

In this chapter and elsewhere in this book, the importance of truth and accuracy is discussed. However, even with the best intentions, you can't fact-check and verify everything you come across online. In situations like that, it's helpful to consult and rely on fact-checking websites.

In "The Fact-Checking Explosion" published in *American Journalism Review*, investigative journalist Cary Spivak explains that American fact-checking operations began in earnest in 2004 when the media was slow to examine the accuracy of claims made by a group called "Swift Boat Veterans for Truth" attacking Democratic presidential candidate Senator John Kerry.[99] Compared to the next presidential election, Spivak wrote, the "2010 election featured fact-checking on steroids. A bitterly divided electorate and a political landscape replete with high-decibel claims and counterclaims on cable television and echoing throughout the blogosphere have made neutral arbiters more crucial than ever."[100] Ari Melber, an attorney and correspondent for *The Nation* magazine, the oldest political weekly in America, noted that "As this year's [2012] presidential campaign enters the homestretch after Labor Day, a new, aggressive model of fact-checking appears to be taking root. It is fast, aggressive and sometimes even outraged about falsehoods on the campaign trail.... This newfound vigor for reporting facts over false equivalency...looks like a mainstay on the campaign trail."[101]

Since then there's been no turning back, with fact-checking and the gleeful publicizing of opponents' or competitors' inaccurate statements an integral part of the political and greater social landscape. Fact-checking is heavily used in the political arena, but it's relevant for many other different industries and fields as well, and particularly in the free-for-all online environment.

The following websites are useful resources that can serve as fact-checking, accountability, and resource tools:

- **NewsTrust.net:** A website owned by the nonprofit journalism training organization the Poynter Institute that features mainstream and independent news stories judged for their accuracy, fairness, sourcing, and context using a variety of web review tools, which is available at http://newstrust.net/.

- **Regret the Error:** A blog written by journalist Craig Silverman and featured on Poynter.org, it monitors and reports on media mistakes and corrections, and is available at http://www.poynter.org/category/latest-news/regret-the-error/.

- **TruthMarket:** A "Marketplace for Truthtelling" that enables the public to fund, organize, and roll out grassroots campaigns that expose false claims and reinforce true claims in commerce and politics, which is available at http://www.truthmarket.com/.

- **Truthy:** An Indiana University research project that analyzes news, major social movement, and political information on Twitter and explains how memes about these subjects spread on the Internet, which is available at http://truthy.indiana.edu/.

- **Snopes.com:** A website founded by Barbara and David Mikkelson that exposes and debunks urban legends, misinformation, rumors, and news stories, which is available at http://snopes.com/.

- **MediaBugs:** An online service for reporting and correcting errors in print, broadcast, or online media for the purposes of improving news quality, which is available at http://mediabugs.org.

- **FactCheck.org:** A project of the Annenberg Public Policy Center of the University of Pennsylvania, which monitors and reports on the accuracy of what U.S. politicians and others involved in the political process state across multiple platforms, which is available at http://www.factcheck.org/.

- **PolitFact.com:** A project of the *Tampa Bay Times*, which fact checks statements by national politicians as well as lobbyists and interest groups, which is available at http://www.politifact.com/.

- **The Fact Checker:** A column written by Glenn Kessler featured in *The Washington Post*, which examines the truth behind political rhetoric and is available at http://www.washingtonpost.com/blogs/fact-checker.

Is a Desire for the Truth Strong Enough to Overcome Bias and Faulty Thinking?

People's desire to obtain the truth is the first step toward developing and strengthening digital literacy skills. However, recent research suggests that this isn't a simple thing to make happen unless we become aware of our personal beliefs and behavioral tendencies, and where they stem from.

Peter K. Hatemi, Ph.D., and Rose McDermott, Ph.D., are co-editors of the book *Man Is by Nature a Political Animal: Evolution, Biology, and Politics*, which examines political preferences through the lens of evolution, genetics, primatology, neuroscience, and physiology. In their 2012 paper published in *Trends in Genetics*,[102] they noted that scientists are increasingly recognizing the connection between genetic influences and political beliefs.[103] They point out, "The foundational elements of political participatory behavior, such as cooperation, trust, and pro-sociality, have a long history in genetics research."[104] Furthermore, "political attitudes in modern human society encompass fundamentally the same issues of reproduction and survival that confronted group life in ancient humans because they involve the same interpersonal traits."[105] And it turns out that many of today's emotionally laden debates, many of which play out online, actually concern age-old questions. The authors explain that modern discussions about immigration actually concern historical questions of how we should best manage out-groups; welfare requires us to examine how we want to share resources; foreign policy involves issues of protecting our in-group against out-groups; and sexual freedom issues ultimately address how we find mates with which to reproduce and raise our offspring.[106]

Meanwhile, behavioral therapist and consultant Andrea Kuszewski, author of the article "Your Brain on Politics: The Cognitive Neuroscience of Liberals and

Conservatives" published in *Discover Magazine*, points out that people embrace issues only when they can find meaning in them, and that how they find meaning differs according to how they are wired.[107] She states, "For liberals to make a case for an idea or cause, they come armed with data, research studies, and experts. They are convinced of an idea if all the data checks out—basically they assign meaning and value to ideas that fit within the scientific method because that's their primary thinking style.... Liberals can get just as emotionally attached to an idea, but it's usually not the primary trigger for acceptance of an idea."[108] In contrast, Kuszewski argues, "Conservatives would be less likely to assign value primarily using the scientific method.... In order for them to find an idea valuable, it has to be meaningful for them personally. It needs to trigger empathy. Meaning, they need some kind of emotional attachment to it, such as family, or a group of individuals they are close to in some way."[109] However, Kuszewski emphasizes that if someone rates high on emotionality, it doesn't mean they are low on rationality, or that someone who rates high on rationality is low on emotionality. She also points out that the findings apply to group differences and not differences between individuals.

You may wonder why you should care about these findings and what importance political beliefs could possibly have on your interactions online. If you think about it carefully, though, they are tied closely together. Whether someone is politically active or not isn't the important point here. Instead, what matters is that political leanings are a reflection of the beliefs, positions, and worldviews that people have, which have a strong bearing on their daily lives and how they communicate and interact online. As shown in previous chapters, the disputes that occur online frequently involve conflicts over particular beliefs, values, and behaviors, many of which can be tied back to interpretations of how the world and society should operate.

So what can you take away from this? In the end, individuals' sincere desire to embrace the truth can help them recognize, deal with, and even overcome any negative biases they may hold and any faulty thinking, which in turn will ultimately improve their critical thinking and digital literacy skills.

Endnotes

1. World Talk LIVE! "Fake Celebrity Pranks New York City," YouTube, August 21, 2012. Link: http://www.youtube.com/watch?v=XYU1a0lTTTw&feature=share.

2. "Fake Celebrity Brett Cohen Discusses Fooling New York City," ABC News, August 24, 2011. Link: http://abcnews.go.com/GMA/video/fake-celebrity-brett-cohen-discusses-fooling-york-city-viral-video-17071691.

3. Philip Caulfield," VIDEO: Man pranks Times Square crowds by posing as a fake celebrity," August 23, 2012. Link: http://www.nydailynews.com/new-york/video-man-pranks-times-square-crowds-posing-a-fake-celebrity-article-1.1142640.

4. Philip Caulfield," VIDEO: Man pranks Times Square crowds by posing as a fake celebrity," August 23, 2012. Link: http://www.nydailynews.com/new-york/video-man-pranks-times-square-crowds-posing-a-fake-celebrity-article-1.1142640.

5. denizenKRIM's comment on "My friend tricked all of Times Square into thinking he was somebody famous and important...here's how it went down," Reddit, August 23, 2012. Link: http://www.reddit.com/r/videos/comments/yo68a/my_friend_tricked_all_of_times_square_into/c5xdom9.

6. azrhei, "My friend tricked all of Times Square into thinking he was somebody famous and important...here's how it went down," reddit, August 23, 2012. Link: http://www.reddit.com/r/videos/comments/yo68a/my_friend_tricked_all_of_times_square_into/c5xexuk.

7. "No man's land: Women-only city planned for Saudi Arabia," RT, August 10, 2012. Link: http://rt.com/news/women-city-saudi-sharia-339/.

8. Lara Setrakian, "Saudi Women to Get Their Own 'City,'" ABC News, August 14, 2012. Link: http://abcnews.go.com/blogs/headlines/2012/08/saudi-women-to-get-their-own-city/.

9. Homa Khaleell, "Saudi Arabia's women-only cities are no blueprint for liberation," *The Guardian*, August 13, 2012. Link: http://www.guardian.co.uk/commentisfree/2012/aug/13/saudi-arabia-women-only-city.

10. Comment by fluffyweebunnykins on August 13, 2012 on Homa Khaleell, "Saudi Arabia's women-only cities are no blueprint for liberation," *The Guardian*, August 13, 2012. Link: http://www.guardian.co.uk/discussion/comment-permalink/17665313.

11. Comment by PatricianInOttowa on August 13, 2012 on Homa Khaleell, "Saudi Arabia's women-only cities are no blueprint for liberation," *The Guardian*, August 13, 2012. Link: http://www.guardian.co.uk/discussion/comment-permalink/17662713.

12. Al Arabiya, "Scratch that! No women-only city in Saudi Arabia," Al Arabiya News English, August 15, 2012. Link: http://english.alarabiya.net/articles/2012/08/15/232445.html.

13. Al Arabiya, "Scratch that! No women-only city in Saudi Arabia," Al Arabiya News English, August 15, 2012. Link: http://english.alarabiya.net/articles/2012/08/15/232445.html.

14. Discussion of Saudi Arabia in "Annual Report 2012: The state of the world's human rights," Amnesty International. Link: http://www.amnesty.org/en/region/saudi-arabia/report-2012.

15. "Human Rights in Saudi Arabia," Human Rights Watch, 2012. Link: http://www.hrw.org/middle-eastn-africa/saudi-arabia.

16. Al Arabiya, "Scratch that! No women-only city in Saudi Arabia," Al Arabiya News English, August 15, 2012. Link: http://english.alarabiya.net/articles/2012/08/15/232445.html.

17. "A conversation with comedian Stephen Colbert," Charlie Rose, December 8, 2006. Link: http://www.charlierose.com/view/interview/93.

18. "A conversation with comedian Stephen Colbert," Charlie Rose, December 8, 2006. Link: http://www.charlierose.com/view/interview/93.

19. Deborah Solomon, "Funny About the News," *The New York Times*, September 25, 205. Link: http://www.nytimes.com/2005/09/25/magazine/25questions.html.

20. "The Word - Truthiness," The Colbert Report, October 17, 2005. Link: http://www.colbertnation.com/the-colbert-report-videos/24039/october-17-2005/the-word---truthiness.

21. 2005 Word of the Year, American Dialect Society. Link: http://www.americandialect.org/woty/all-of-the-words-of-the-year-1990-to-present#2005.

22. About "Truthiness in Digital Media: A symposium that seeks to understand and address propaganda and misinformation in the new media ecosystem," Harvard.edu. Link: http://blogs.law.harvard.edu/truthiness/about/.

23. Wendell Potter on Deadly Spin, Berkman Center's YouTube Channel, April 3, 2012. Link: http://www.youtube.com/watch?v=KnwFv9GbPfk&feature=player_embedded.

24. Wendell Potter on Deadly Spin, Berkman Center's YouTube Channel, April 3, 2012. Link: http://www.youtube.com/watch?v=KnwFv9GbPfk&feature=player_embedded.

25. "Our Concept and Definition of Critical Thinking" Center for Critical Thinking. Link: http://www.criticalthinking.org/pages/our-concept-and-definition-of-critical-thinking/411.

26. "Critical Thinking: Where to Begin," Center for Critical Thinking. Link: http://www.criticalthinking.org/pages/critical-thinking-where-to-begin/796.

27. "Elements and Standards Online Learning Module," Center for Critical Thinking. Link: http://www.criticalthinking.org/ctmodel/logic-model1.htm.

28. "Elements and Standards Online Learning Module," Center for Critical Thinking. Link: http://www.criticalthinking.org/ctmodel/logic-model1.htm.

29. A. Barton Hinkle, "The Wrong Side Absolutely Must Not Win," *Richmond Times-Dispatch*, August 19, 2012. Link: http://www2.timesdispatch.com/news/rtd-opinion/2012/aug/19/tdopin02-the-wrong-side-absolutely-must-not-win-ar-2138869/.

30. A. Barton Hinkle, "The Wrong Side Absolutely Must Not Win," *Richmond Times-Dispatch*, August 19, 2012. Link: http://www2.timesdispatch.com/news/rtd-opinion/2012/aug/19/tdopin02-the-wrong-side-absolutely-must-not-win-ar-2138869/.

31. A. Barton Hinkle, "The Wrong Side Absolutely Must Not Win," *Richmond Times-Dispatch*, August 19, 2012. Link: http://www2.timesdispatch.com/news/rtd-opinion/2012/aug/19/tdopin02-the-wrong-side-absolutely-must-not-win-ar-2138869/.

32. Neil Gross, "The Indoctrination Myth," *The New York Times*, March 3, 2012. Link: http://www.nytimes.com/2012/03/04/opinion/sunday/college-doesnt-make-you-liberal.html.

33. Neil Gross, "The Indoctrination Myth," *The New York Times*, March 3, 2012. Link: http://www.nytimes.com/2012/03/04/opinion/sunday/college-doesnt-make-you-liberal. html.

34. Maggie Koerth-Baker, "The Mind of a Flip-Flopper," *The New York Times*, August 15, 2012. Link: http://www.nytimes.com/2012/08/19/magazine/the-mind-of-a-flip-flopper. html.

35. Maggie Koerth-Baker, "The Mind of a Flip-Flopper," *The New York Times*, August 15, 2012. Link: http://www.nytimes.com/2012/08/19/magazine/the-mind-of-a-flip-flopper. html.

36. Daisy Grewal, "Understanding the Psychology of the American Idea of Choice," *Scientific American*, August 28, 2012. Link: http://www.scientificamerican.com/article. cfm?id=understanding-psychology-of-american-idea-choice.

37. Krishna Savani and Aneeta Rattan, "A Choice Mind-Set Increases the Acceptance and Maintenance of Wealth Inequality," *Psychological Science*, 23 (7), July 2012, 796–804. Link: http://pss.sagepub.com/content/23/7/796.

38. Daisy Grewal, "Understanding the Psychology of the American Idea of Choice," *Scientific American*, August 28, 2012. Link: http://www.scientificamerican.com/article. cfm?id=understanding-psychology-of-american-idea-choice.

39. Daisy Grewal, "Understanding the Psychology of the American Idea of Choice," *Scientific American*, August 28, 2012. Link: http://www.scientificamerican.com/article. cfm?id=understanding-psychology-of-american-idea-choice.

40. Dana R. Carney, Ph.D., and Mahzarin R. Banaji, Ph.D., "First Is Best," PLoS ONE, 7 (6), 2012. Link: http://www.plosone.org/article/info%3Adoi%2F10.1371%2Fjournal. pone.0035088.

41. Dana R. Carney, Ph.D., and Mahzarin R. Banaji, Ph.D., "First Is Best," PLoS ONE, 7 (6), 2012. Link: http://www.plosone.org/article/info%3Adoi%2F10.1371%2Fjournal. pone.0035088.

42. Dana R. Carney, Ph.D., and Mahzarin R. Banaji, Ph.D., "First Is Best," PLoS ONE, 7 (6), 2012. Link: http://www.plosone.org/article/info%3Adoi%2F10.1371%2Fjournal. pone.0035088.

43. Dana R. Carney, Ph.D., and Mahzarin R. Banaji, Ph.D., "First Is Best," PLoS ONE, 7 (6), 2012. Link: http://www.plosone.org/article/info%3Adoi%2F10.1371%2Fjournal. pone.0035088.

44. "Study Finds Every Style Of Parenting Produces Disturbed, Miserable Adults," The Onion, October 26, 2011. Link: http://www.theonion.com/articles/study-finds-every-style-of-parenting-produces-dist,26452/.

45. "Study Finds Every Style Of Parenting Produces Disturbed, Miserable Adults," The Onion, October 26, 2011. Link: http://www.theonion.com/articles/study-finds-every-style-of-parenting-produces-dist,26452/.

46. "Study Finds Every Style Of Parenting Produces Disturbed, Miserable Adults," The Onion, October 26, 2011. Link: http://www.theonion.com/articles/study-finds-every-style-of-parenting-produces-dist,26452/.

47. Kerry Benefield, "The Onion's fake story no laughing matter for Santa Rosa institute," PresDemocrat.com, October 28, 2011. Link: http://www.pressdemocrat.com/article/20111028/ARTICLES/111029463/1350?p=1&tc=pg.

48. Kerry Benefield, "The Onion's fake story no laughing matter for Santa Rosa institute," PresDemocrat.com, October 28, 2011. Link: http://www.pressdemocrat.com/article/20111028/ARTICLES/111029463/1350?p=1&tc=pg.

49. "Congress Takes Group Of Schoolchildren Hostage," The Onion, September 29, 2011. Link: http://www.theonion.com/articles/congress-takes-group-of-schoolchildren-hostage,26207/.

50. Dylan Stableford, "Capitol Police investigating The Onion for fake hostage crisis tweets," Yahoo! News, September 29, 2011. Link: http://news.yahoo.com/blogs/cutline/capitol-police-investigating-onion-fake-hostage-crisis-tweets-185711356.html.

51. Dylan Stableford, "Capitol Police investigating The Onion for fake hostage crisis tweets," Yahoo! News, September 29, 2011. Link: http://news.yahoo.com/blogs/cutline/capitol-police-investigating-onion-fake-hostage-crisis-tweets-185711356.html.

52. Ed O'Keefe, "Onion Twitter joke prompts serious response," *The Washington Post*, September 29, 2011. Link: http://www.washingtonpost.com/blogs/federal-eye/post/onion-twitter-joke-prompts-serious-response/2011/09/29/gIQAqQmL7K_blog.html.

53. Kathy Benjamin, "6 Times The Onion Had People Completely Fooled," Mental Floss, April 1, 2012. Link: http://www.mentalfloss.com/blogs/archives/122056.

54. "*Harry Potter* Books Spark Rise In Satanism Among Children," The Onion, July 26, 2000. Link: http://www.theonion.com/articles/harry-potter-books-spark-rise-in-satanism-among-ch,2413/.

55. "'Satanic' Harry Potter books burned," BBC News, December 2001. Link: http://news.bbc.co.uk/2/hi/entertainment/1735623.stm.

56. "Planned Parenthood Opens $8 Billion Abortionplex," The Onion, May 18, 2011. Link: http://www.theonion.com/articles/planned-parenthood-opens-8-billion-abortionplex,20476/.

57. Dino Grandoni, "Congressman Falls for The Onion's Planned Parenthood 'Abortionplex' Story," The Atlantic Wire, February 6, 2012. Link: http://www.theatlanticwire.com/national/2012/02/congressman-falls-months-old-onion-story-about-planned-parenthood-abortionplex/48344/.

58. Eryn J. Newman, Ph.D., Maryanne Garry, Ph.D., Daniel M. Bernstein, Ph.D., Justin Kantner, Ph.D., and D. Stephen Lindsay. Ph.D., "Nonprobative photographs (or words) inflate truthiness" *Psychonomic Bulletin & Review*, August 8, 2012, online version published August 7, 2012. Link: http://www.springerlink.com/content/98076v3163516k37/?MUD=MP.

59. "Scientists discover the truth behind Colbert's 'truthiness,'" Springer Select, August 8, 2012. Link: http://www.springer.com/about+springer/media/springer+select?SG WID=0-11001-6-1385843-0.

60. Kelly M. Adams, MPH, R.D., Martin Kohlmeier, M.D., and Steven H. Zeisel, M.D., Ph.D., "Nutrition Education in U.S. Medical Schools: Latest Update of a National Survey," Academic Medicine, 85 (9), 1537-1542. Link: http://journals.lww.com/ academicmedicine/Abstract/2010/09000/Nutrition_Education_in_U_S__Medical_ Schools_.30.aspx.

61. Kelly M. Adams, MPH, R.D., Martin Kohlmeier, M.D., and Steven H. Zeisel, M.D., Ph.D., "Nutrition Education in U.S. Medical Schools: Latest Update of a National Survey," Academic Medicine, 85 (9), 1537-1542. Link: http://journals.lww.com/ academicmedicine/Abstract/2010/09000/Nutrition_Education_in_U_S__Medical_ Schools_.30.aspx.

62. Jason Boog, "24-Year-Old Marketing Director Lands Major Book Deal," mediabistro, November 17, 2011. Link: http://www.mediabistro.com/galleycat/24-year-old- marketing-director-lands-major-book-deal_b42516.

63. Ryan Holiday, "Honoring a Reporter's Obligation: Dissecting Peter Shankman's Hypocrisy," Huffington Post, July 23, 2011. Link: http://www.huffingtonpost.com/ ryan-holiday/honoring-a-reporters-obli_b_1693338.html.

64. Dave Thier, "How This Guy Lied His Way Into MSNBC, ABC News, *The New York Times* and More," Forbes, July 18, 2012. Link: http://www.forbes.com/sites/ davidthier/2012/07/18/how-this-guy-lied-his-way-into-msnbc-abc-news-the-new- york-times-and-more/.

65. Ryan Holiday, "Honoring a Reporter's Obligation: Dissecting Peter Shankman's Hypocrisy," Huffington Post, July 23, 2011. Link: http://www.huffingtonpost.com/ryan- holiday/honoring-a-reporters-obli_b_1693338.html.

66. Peter Shankman, "HARO/Forbes: Can One Idiot Ruin it for Everyone? NO." Peter Shankman, July 19, 2012. Link: http://shankman.com/haroforbes-can-one-idiot-ruin-it- for-everyone-no/.

67. Peter Shankman, "HARO/Forbes: Can One Idiot Ruin it for Everyone? NO." Peter Shankman, July 19, 2012. Link: http://shankman.com/haroforbes-can-one-idiot-ruin-it- for-everyone-no/.

68. Ryan Holiday, "Honoring a Reporter's Obligation: Dissecting Peter Shankman's Hypocrisy," Huffington Post, July 23, 2011. Link: http://www.huffingtonpost.com/ ryan-holiday/honoring-a-reporters-obli_b_1693338.html.

69. Dave Thier, "How This Guy Lied His Way Into MSNBC, ABC News, The New York Times and More," Forbes, July 18, 2012. Link: http://www.forbes.com/sites/ davidthier/2012/07/18/how-this-guy-lied-his-way-into-msnbc-abc-news-the-new-york- times-and-more/.

70. Pallavi Gogoi, "Wal-Mart's Jim and Laura: The Real Story," BloombergBusinessweek, October 9, 2006. Link: http://www.businessweek.com/stories/2006-10-09/wal-marts-jim-and-laura-the-real-storybusinessweek-business-news-stock-market-and-financial-advice.

71. Pallavi Gogoi, "Wal-Mart's Jim and Laura: The Real Story," BloombergBusinessweek, October 9, 2006. Link: http://www.businessweek.com/stories/2006-10-09/wal-marts-jim-and-laura-the-real-storybusinessweek-business-news-stock-market-and-financial-advice.

72. Jonathan Reese, "An Open Letter to 'Jim' and 'Laura,'" The Writing On The Wall. Link: http://thewritingonthewal.net/?p=1387.

73. Jonathan Reese, "Another Open Letter to 'Jim' and 'Laura,'" The Writing On The Wall. Link: http://thewritingonthewal.net/?p=1391.

74. Pallavi Gogoi, "Wal-Mart's Jim and Laura: The Real Story," BloombergBusinessweek, October 9, 2006. Link: http://www.businessweek.com/stories/2006-10-09/wal-marts-jim-and-laura-the-real-storybusinessweek-business-news-stock-market-and-financial-advice.

75. http://www.businessweek.com/stories/2006-10-09/wal-marts-jim-and-laura-the-real-storybusinessweek-business-news-stock-market-and-financial-advice.

76. Hamilton Nolan, "Edelman apologizes for Wal-Mart blog disclosure omission," PRWeek, October 18, 2006. Link: http://www.prweekus.com/edelman-apologizes-for-wal-mart-blog-disclosure-omission/article/55835/.

77. Adam Horowitz, David Jacobson, Tom McNichol and Owen Thomas, "101 Dumbest Moments in Business," Business 2.0 on CNNMoney. Link: http://money.cnn.com/galleries/2007/biz2/0701/gallery.101dumbest_2007/54.html.

78. Article about "Fake blog" on Wikipedia. Link: http://en.wikipedia.org/wiki/Fake_blog.

79. Dennis Normile, "A New Record for Retractions? (Part 2)," Science, July 2, 2012. Link: http://news.sciencemag.org/scienceinsider/2012/07/a-new-record-for-retractions-1.html.

80. David Kaiser, "Physics and Pixie Dust," Book Review, American Scientist, November–December, 2009. Link: http://www.americanscientist.org/bookshelf/pub/physics-and-pixie-dust.

81. John Timmer, "Epic fraud: How to succeed in science (without doing any)," Ars Technica, July 18, 2012. Link: http://arstechnica.com/science/2012/07/epic-fraud-how-to-succeed-in-science-without-doing-any/1/.

82. Melinda Henneberger, "'Breaking up' with Barack Obama," The Washington Post, September 6, 2012. Link: http://www.washingtonpost.com/blogs/she-the-people/post/breaking-up-with-barack-obama/2012/09/06/57c0933e-f83a-11e1-8398-0327ab83ab91_blog.html.

83. Brian Montopoli, "GOP ad features woman 'breaking up' with Obama," CBSNews, September 6, 2012. Link: http://www.cbsnews.com/8301-503544_162-57507496-503544/gop-ad-features-woman-breaking-up-with-obama.

84. Pema Levy, "Disillusioned Obama Supporter In Romney Ad Is Actually GOP Staffer," Talking Points Memo, September 6, 2012. Link: http://2012.talkingpointsmemo.com/2012/09/rnc-staffer-plays-obama-supporter-in-gop-ad.php?ref=fpa.

85. Lee Siegel, *Against the Machine: Being Human in the Age of the Electronic Mob*, Random House, New York, 2008, p. 25

86. Lee Siegel, *Against the Machine: Being Human in the Age of the Electronic Mob*, Random House, New York, 2008, p. 105.

87. Tyler Cowen, *What Price Fame?* Harvard University Press, London 2000, p. 180.

88. Robin Dunbar, *Grooming, Gossip and the Evolution of Language*, Faber and Faber Limited, London, 1996, Second Printing 1997, p. 172.

89. David Denby, *Snark: It's Mean, It's Personal and It's Ruining Our Conversation*, Simon & Schuster, New York, 2009, p. 4.

90. David Denby, *Snark: It's Mean, It's Personal and It's Ruining Our Conversation*, Simon & Schuster, New York, 2009, p. 58–89.

91. "The Twenty-Five Most Valuable Blogs In America—2011," 24/7 Wall Street, October 31, 2011. Link: http://247wallst.com/2011/10/31/the-twenty-five-most-valuable-blogs-in-america-2011/2/.

92. PRWeek, "Journalist Q&A: Nick Denton, Gawker Media (Extended)," *PRWeek*, June 1, 2011. Link: http://www.prweekus.com/journalist-qa-nick-denton-gawker-media-extended/article/203316/.

93. "The Gawker Job Interview," *The New York Times*, January 12, 2008. Link: http://www.nytimes.com/2008/01/12/fashion/13gweb.html.

94. PRWeek, "Journalist Q&A: Nick Denton, Gawker Media (Extended)," *PRWeek*, June 1, 2011. Link: http://www.prweekus.com/journalist-qa-nick-denton-gawker-media-extended/article/203316/.

95. Emily Gould, "Katie Roiphe Is Big Immature Baby," Gawker, May 1, 2007. Link: http://gawker.com/256854/katie-roiphe-is-big-immature-baby.

96. Katie Roipe, "The Great Escape," *New York Magazine*, April 22, 2007. Link: http://nymag.com/news/features/2007/sexandlove/30928/.

97. Katie Roipe, "Gawker Is Big Immature Baby," Slate, October 27, 2011. Link: http://www.slate.com/articles/life/roiphe/2011/10/gawker_why_can_t_it_do_nastiness_the_right_way_.html.

98. Katie Roipe, "Gawker Is Big Immature Baby," Slate, October 27, 2011. Link: http://www.slate.com/articles/life/roiphe/2011/10/gawker_why_can_t_it_do_nastiness_the_right_way_.html.

99. Cary Spivak, "The Fact-Checking Explosion," American Journalism Review, December/January 2011. Link: http://www.ajr.org/article.asp?id=4980.

100. Cary Spivak, "The Fact-Checking Explosion," American Journalism Review, December/January 2011. Link: http://www.ajr.org/article.asp?id=4980.

101. Ari Melber, "Why Fact-Checking Has Taken Root in This Year's Election," PBS MediaShift, September 5, 2012. Link: http://www.pbs.org/mediashift/2012/09/why-fact-checking-has-taken-root-in-this-years-election249.html.

102. Peter K. Hatemi and Rose Mcdermott, "The genetics of politics: discovery, challenges, and progress," Trends in Genetics, 28 (10), 28 August 2012, 525–533. Link: http://www.cell.com/trends/genetics/abstract/S0168-9525%2812%2900111-4#Summary.

103. Peter K. Hatemi and Rose Mcdermott, "The genetics of politics: discovery, challenges, and progress," Trends in Genetics, 28 (10), 28 August 2012. Link: http://www.cell.com/trends/genetics/abstract/S0168-9525%2812%2900111-4#MainText.

104. Peter K. Hatemi and Rose Mcdermott, "The genetics of politics: discovery, challenges, and progress," Trends in Genetics, 28 (10), 28 August 2012. Link: http://www.cell.com/trends/genetics/abstract/S0168-9525%2812%2900111-4#MainText.

105. Peter K. Hatemi and Rose Mcdermott, "The genetics of politics: discovery, challenges, and progress," Trends in Genetics, 28 (10), 28 August 2012. Link: http://www.cell.com/trends/genetics/abstract/S0168-9525%2812%2900111-4#MainText.

106. Peter K. Hatemi and Rose Mcdermott, "The genetics of politics: discovery, challenges, and progress," Trends in Genetics, 28 (10), 28 August 2012. Link: http://www.cell.com/trends/genetics/abstract/S0168-9525%2812%2900111-4#MainText.

107. Andrea Kuszewski, "Your Brain on Politics: The Cognitive Neuroscience of Liberals and Conservatives," *Discover Magazine*, September 7, 2011. Link: http://blogs.discovermagazine.com/intersection/2011/09/07/your-brain-on-politics-the-cognitive-neuroscience-of-liberals-and-conservatives/.

108. Andrea Kuszewski, "Your Brain on Politics: The Cognitive Neuroscience of Liberals and Conservatives," *Discover Magazine*, September 7, 2011. Link: http://blogs.discovermagazine.com/intersection/2011/09/07/your-brain-on-politics-the-cognitive-neuroscience-of-liberals-and-conservatives/.

109. Andrea Kuszewski, "Your Brain on Politics: The Cognitive Neuroscience of Liberals and Conservatives," *Discover Magazine*, September 7, 2011. Link: http://blogs.discovermagazine.com/intersection/2011/09/07/your-brain-on-politics-the-cognitive-neuroscience-of-liberals-and-conservatives/.

8

Into the Trenches: Conflict Resolution Skills and Strategies

Could This Dispute Have Been Managed Better and Possibly Even Avoided?

Miami, Florida television station WPLG Local 10 couldn't have imagined what it was getting into when, in late August 2012, its local news website producer posted a slideshow titled "What the Force???: Most bizarre Star Wars Convention sightings" on its site, featuring photos accompanied by ridiculing captions of a Star Wars convention that took place earlier the same month. The images, which showed conference attendees in costume, featured captions such as "Being a Star Wars geek pretty much means you'll get no lovin'...being a Star Wars geek that wears these pajamas guarantees it" and "Dateless men for as far as the eye can see."[1] Some of the images included photos of members of the 501st Legion, an all-volunteer organization of Star Wars costume enthusiasts known and praised for its charity fundraising and volunteer work.[2]

Outrage about the insults led Star Wars fans to express their anger on WPLG Local 10's Facebook page and on Twitter.[3] Members and supporters of the 501st Legion were particularly unhappy with the slideshow. Laura Keeney tweeted, "So apparently @WGLGLocal10 thinks it's OK to mock and bully Star Wars fans with sexist and/or demeaning photo captions. What jerks."[4] A Facebook group called "WPLG Local 10 Owes Star Wars fans a Formal Public Apology" was set up.[5] A Change.org petition titled under the same name was also created, accusing the station of deleting Facebook comments left by angry and disappointed Star Wars fans, as well as banning fans from its Facebook page.[6]

After the public outcry, the slideshow was removed. The station issued an apology on its Facebook page that said, "GOOD NEWS (or BAD NEWS...depending on where you sided). The infamous STA WARS slideshow has been taken down. For those offended (and let us know), sorry. For those who enjoyed it (and let us know), sorry. remember...the force will be with you...always."[7] However, this awkward apology didn't appease the station's critics and was deleted some time later.[8]

The website producer who posted the slide show ultimately issued an online apology but did not offer his name. He explained that he was a Star Wars fan and that the slideshow wasn't posted with any ill intent. However, he said that when he and his colleagues received negative feedback from thousands of Star Wars fans, including some from other countries ("They lit up our phones, filled our Facebook page and inboxes. We were called cyber bullies."[9]), he "realized my mistake, albeit too late for many upset fans. I took the slideshow off the site and my somewhat pithy apology on Facebook regrettably, came across as insincere to many."[10]

Some of the readers of the post didn't accept the apology and expressed the belief that it was made only because of the public backlash. Eric Renderking Fisk said, "I'm just curious, have you ever done a humorless, cruel slideshow on the fat, obnoxious sports fans in your region. I hope you're a genuine equal opportunity offender."[11] Steven Land wrote, "...Who is this apology even from? I do not see a name associated with the post...since there is no specific staff member to place the blame on, we will always associate this very offensive and negative 'look' at Star Wars fandom with the local station in Miami, WPLG Local 10."[12] Other comments criticized the complainers. One called "misinlink" wrote, "...I have been to many conventions of all sorts. You give your consent and likeness away the minute you walk in the doors. The camera does not lie, it captures with no discrimination or judgement (sic) on the subject. So someone has the BALLS to say what is probably on the minds of 80–99% percent of normal functioning society and they are labeled. I sir, will call him/her an 'internet' hero."[13] Meanwhile, a guest commenter noted, "...I am a MASSIVE Sci-Fi/Fantasy/Comic/Anime/Manga/Gaming nerd, and I still found some of those pictures hilarious...I know I'm going to get flamed for this, but I am just tired of everyone acting like children over such petty things. The American people have such an over-inflated sense of entitlement and self-importance, it's become absurd."[14] Many of the comments, however, were more conciliatory and gracious. Kaidlen Shan said, "I thank you for the apology. I was one of the attendees at Celebration VI that happened to be in the background of one of the pictures in the slideshow. I'm the lady in red and black on crutches behind the Darth Vader by the Lego sign. While I have not seen the original comments (nor do I want to see them), I did want to see the pictures. I think that they are great pictures."[15] And Marjon McLain notes, "Apology accepted. As one of the subjects in the slideshow—I was the Jedi in photo #33—I hope this little incident teaches ALL of us how far-reaching our Star Wars family is and how caring it truly can be. The outpouring of support (in the form of outrage) was overwhelming and heart-warming. Yes, apology accepted. Move along, move along...."[16]

In hindsight the situation could have been managed better—if WPLG Local 10's staff had been trained in online dispute resolution skills. For example, the website producer could have realized that his slideshow might come across mockingly and callously to those represented in the images. He might have also considered who else would feel offended by the images, namely not only those directly depicted, but also their family members, friends, and community members. After complaints were made, he also should have ensured that his first apology came across as sincere and contrite. This is an important conflict de-escalation technique. It would have prevented additional backlash against the station and against him as an individual. Finally, although it's not known what actually happened behind the scenes, the website producer and the station could have weighed the pros and cons of going public with the producer's name. This would have given those who felt aggrieved an opportunity to air their concerns at an identified individual instead of a faceless entity, and also perhaps move forward more quickly. (Identifying an individual isn't always a wise thing to do. If there are realistic concerns that someone will become the target of an online lynch mob and his reputation and safety be put in jeopardy, it may be better to protect the individual by keeping his identity private. This needs to be considered on a case-by-case basis.)

Additional takeaway lessons from this situation include

- Realize that the tone of your communication matters and that humor often translates imprecisely in a written medium.
- Know your audience, what they care about and what their sensitivities are.
- When a crisis is brewing, decide if an apology is warranted, and if so, give a sincere apology because it's good for business and because it's also the right thing to do.

Your Conflict Goals and Corresponding Approaches

Previous chapters discussed why your online reputation matters, reviewed the negative professional and personal effects of unresolved conflict, and talked about the different types of conflicts you'll encounter online. After having read the previous chapters, you're also now familiar with the foundational concepts in conflict resolution, namely needs, values, and interests. You know about the different forms of conflict resolution, specifically negotiation, facilitation, mediation, arbitration, and litigation. This chapter delves deeper into conflict analysis and management. And the first thing you need to do is be clear about your ultimate goals related to conflict.

Broadly stated, your goal will fall into one of three general categories, namely prevention, management, and resolution. The feasibility of each, of course, depends on the unique circumstances of your situation. However, it's likely that in almost all cases, *conflict prevention* is your primary goal. This often makes sense from both reputation-protection and financial perspectives, as well as from an emotional perspective since disputes are usually emotionally draining. Many of the things discussed in earlier chapters are conducive to prevention, such as understanding the core concepts of human needs, values, positions, and interests; the implementation of online monitoring programs; and the mastery and application of anger management and digital literacy skills.

But preventing all disputes and conflicts isn't possible. That's where conflict management and conflict resolution come in. *Conflict management*, as discussed in Chapter 1, "Who Gives a Darn About Conflict," is the process of effectively dealing with ongoing or intractable disputes that, for one reason or another, cannot be fully resolved. Meanwhile, *conflict resolution* is the process of addressing the underlying and deep-rooted causes of conflict and finding applicable solutions to these disputes.

You should understand that different conflict approaches can be used for conflict management and conflict resolution. The *power-based approach* relies on power to determine who will prevail in a dispute. Power differences can be identified by who has authority over the other, who has larger financial resources, who has a stronger support network or other backing, who has the greater ability to inflict harm, and so on.

The *rights-based approach* usually involves examining who has legal rights that can be pursued and enforced. It can also be determined by someone's position or job title, which gives them the legal authority to prevail in a dispute. Meanwhile, the *interest-based approach* looks at the interests of the parties to see if they share common, overlapping, or noncompeting interests that might form the basis of reaching a mutually agreeable solution. Think of the example in Chapter 1 where two siblings were fighting over an orange. Recall that instead of becoming entrenched in their respective positions, the children could have shared the reason they each wanted the orange and thereby would have discovered that their reasons weren't mutually exclusive.

The option you choose—whether prevention, management, or resolution— depends on the circumstances and on what short-term and long-term results you hope to gain. Sometimes you can use a combination of approaches to try to achieve your wanted outcome. Now look at one example: Imagine you are an international stock photography company, and a business blogger with a medium-sized readership is guilty of copyright infringement for the unauthorized use of your photograph. You could use a rights-based approach to halt his action. However, suing this blogger could result in a public backlash against you because of the perceived David versus Goliath relationship. So even though you would be within your legal rights to sue the blogger, a better option could be to send the individual a polite but firm letter outlining the violation and requesting he remove the image from his blog to avoid an ongoing problem. Alternatively, there might be reasons why you want to take a heavy-handed approach. If you want to send a strong message to all bloggers who try to make liberal use of your pictures without paying the required fees, perhaps a hard-line, rights-based approach is the way to go—assuming you have also considered any ancillary effects this action could have on your business.

Your Organization's Culture and Conflict Practices

Completing a quick baseline assessment of your organization's conflict culture and resulting conflict practices can help you gage what kinds of approaches the company has tried in the past and the approach with which it is comfortable. This assessment can also enable you to spot any gaps and weaknesses that need to be addressed to ensure improvements in the future.

Although most of these questions address organizations, others are applicable to individuals also, albeit in modified form. For example, knowing what your conflict style is so you know what your general tendencies are in reacting to disputes, or looking at whether you have an articulated conflict management process in mind for when an online dispute occurs is important for both organizations and individuals. Ask yourself the following nonexclusive list of questions:

- How does the organization regard conflict? Is conflict viewed as something to be avoided, as an inevitable part of doing business, or beneficial in certain circumstances to foster growth?
- Does the organization approach conflict proactively or reactively?
- Is there one main conflict management approach that the organization uses or several, depending on the situation and circumstances?
- Realizing that the behavior of executives and leaders within an organization creates the model and sets the tone for others' behavior, what are the conflict styles of members of the management team?
- Do the organizational leaders model constructive conflict management skills?

- Are there formal and articulated processes in place to deal with conflict or is conflict dealt with ad hoc?

- Are there internal-facing and external-facing processes?

- Are these processes uniform across the organization, or are they differences between business units or departments?

- If formal processes exist, are they in writing? Are they easily accessible and reviewable?

- Are employees informed of these processes when they join the organization?

- Are these processes part of a formal conflict resolution system, or are they loosely associated?

- If there is an existing conflict resolution system, what conflict resolution models does the organization use? (Refer to Chapter 1 where negotiation and other forms of conflict management are discussed.)

- Are employees educated and trained in the organization's conflict management processes?

- Does the organization have a formal social media policy that addresses employees' workplace behavior?

- Does the organization have a formal social media policy that addresses employees' personal behavior outside of work?

- Does the organization have specific processes in place for dealing with online disputes and conflicts?

- Who is in charge of managing external-facing online disputes? Is it someone in the public relations department, the online community manager, or an outside contractor? To whom does this person report?

- Who else actively deals with external-facing online disputes? For example, do customer service representatives engage with customers or the public online?

- What power does this person have to resolve online disputes? Does she need to check with a supervisor before making decisions? Are there particular disputes she has authority to resolve on her own and others she needs to receive permission for first, and what are they?

- Is there a public relations professional or team in place that provides guidance on how to manage online conflict?

- Is the public relations professional trained in crisis communication or otherwise have expertise in this area?

- Has this public relations professional received training in how to manage online disputes or otherwise have expertise in this area?

- Does the organization have in-house counsel or a law firm in place that it can reach out to for advice on how to proceed when there is a threat to the organization's online reputation?

- Do the organization's public relations professional and attorney work together to protect and defend the organization's reputation? Do they present a unified approach toward reputation management and protection via blogger and media relations, as well as legal action?

- What types of online conflicts has the organization dealt with in the past? Some possibilities include displeasure with customer service, disagreement over the organization's social stance on particular issues, disagreement with the existence of an organization's products or services, online personality clashes, and so on.

- Are there types of online disputes that have occurred more frequently than others? What are they?

- Have these disputes been successfully managed or resolved?

- What approaches have been used for successful management?

- Could these disputes be prevented with a formalized conflict management approach?

Determining If, When, and How to Respond

If you remember only one thing about how to approach online conflict, it should be this: *Determine ahead of time if, when, and how to respond.*

Ideally, much of the "*if*" will have been decided before a particular issue presents itself online. For example, if you create a spreadsheet identifying the biggest online conflicts and reputational threats your organization faces, along with their possible iterations, you won't be caught off-guard when the inevitable dispute arises. Obviously, not all online issues can or should be addressed (see Figure 8.1), but you must have a good idea of which ones you feel are urgent and require immediate action and which ones can wait. Think through legitimate explanations for why certain situations should take precedence over others. Creating this hierarchy can help you prioritize which disputes will need people and resources, and therefore assist you in allocating the necessary support ahead of time.

"When" to respond to conflict should be largely determined by the type and severity of the dispute. Serious disputes must obviously be dealt with quicker than non-critical ones, but there is also a benefit to quickly dealing with simpler and smaller ones to get them out of the way. You can then decide which ones are next in line but can be dealt with later, and which ones can be simply monitored but don't require any response for the time being.

Figure 8.1   *Ricky Gervais' Tweet of August 8, 2012*

The reaction time for online problems needs to be much quicker than that in the offline environment. For example, social media crisis manager Melissa Agnes notes that with social media, "your first response to the crisis should be made within minutes of you discovering that the crisis exists. Your first response should simply say that you are aware of the situation, that you're looking into it and that you will get back to them (your audience, the victims, the public) as soon as you know more. Your official response should be released/published as soon as you have all answers regarding the crisis—and this should be done as soon as physically possible."[17] Agnes's advice is sound and underscores the importance of speed, but not at the expense of accuracy.

Meanwhile, the "*how*," not surprisingly, must be determined in part by the "if" and "when" previously mentioned. You must look at the disputants, opponents, or critics. If they are influential this is a greater problem than someone who is a bothersome "squeaky wheel" who has limited ability to garner attention and support (keeping in mind, however, that anything can go viral under the right circumstances). Find out whether you're dealing with a normal yet disgruntled and angry individual, or a high conflict individual. According to High-Conflict Institute co-founder Bill Eddy, LCSW, Esq., high conflict individuals "have a pattern of high-conflict behavior that increases conflict rather than reducing or resolving it. This pattern usually happens over and over again in many different situations with many different people."[18] They are people who are exceedingly difficult to deal with because of the intensity of their reaction to problems and their habitual blaming of others for things that go wrong.[19] Deciding how you're going to respond also includes determining which side stands to lose more. Is it you or the other party? This can influence the degree to which someone is willing to negotiate or, alternatively, fight hard if they feel their back is against the wall. Analyzing whether this is a single or repeat-occurrence dispute is also a factor to consider. A repeat occurrence may suggest that you need to approach such disputes differently to minimize their frequency, or that you should consider setting up an entire system to more efficiently deal with these regularly occurring disputes. Furthermore, the resources you have available to you also matter. Included might be a dedicated staff tasked with addressing disputes, in-house public relations professionals or a PR agency with which you have an ongoing relationship, a law firm on retainer in case you need immediate legal assistance, a dispute management budget that enables you to cover unanticipated costs, and supporters that will rally to your defense.

The United States Air Force Public Affairs Agency's "Air Force Web Posting Response Assessment" offers a good example of a response process. It created a chart for how the agency responds to online postings.[20] As you can see in Figure 8.2, the chart, which reflects an updated version of its initial 2008 release, is composed of sections dealing with discovery, evaluation, and response considerations. Although the Air Force's approach is customized to its unique needs, elements of this chart can be used as ideas for the creation of your multi-tiered dispute response system. For example, as previously touched upon, your response to disputes will likely differ depending on the type of person or groups you deal with. In relation to web post creators, the Air Force differentiates between those it calls "trolls," the "rager," the "misguided," and "unhappy customers." Because of the different motivations each problem type is driven by, the recommended approach naturally isn't uniform. For trolls and ragers, the Air Force recommends monitoring and specifically avoiding a direct response (recall from Chapter 4, "Who Are the Troublemakers?" that trolls want nothing more than to get a reaction from you, and preferably an angry or otherwise emotional one), whereas for someone who is misguided and has posted erroneous information, it suggests considering responding with factually accurate information. The Air Force's listed Response Considerations are widely applicable to a variety of companies and online disputes. These include being transparent, providing sources to back up any claims you make, being timely in your response, and writing in an appropriate tone.

The concept of creating an "If, When, and How" plan of action enables you to cognitively and practically prepare for the variety of inevitable disputes you'll encounter online. Nothing beats practice, which was the thinking behind global public relations firm Weber Shandwick's creation of "Firebell," a social crisis simulator application that won Digital Best New Application of the Year 2010 from *PR News*.[21] Firebell creates a live event for clients that enables them to experience, in a safe and private environment, what a simultaneous attack from various social media platforms looks and feels like. David Krejci, senior vice president, Digital Communications at Weber Shandwick, points out that this helps clients because "You can't just speak in abstract terms of how you would respond. It transforms crisis drills from static exercises of imagination to concrete and dynamic dialogue between client and the public."[22] If you don't have the privilege of accessing Firebell, you should consider conducting a cheaper internal exercise where you create a list of potential "anti-company" messages. Assign people on your staff to take the role of various personalities you might find online, such as a competitor, a detractor, an angry customer, and a misguided member of the general public. You can use an instant messaging program such as Skype or GTalk to have a simulated conversation with a simulated angry or misinformed person. To make it more realistic and maintain an element of uncertainty, it works best if the responders don't know who on the staff is playing which role.

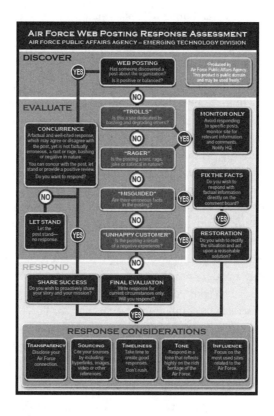

Figure 8.2   *The Air Force Web Posting Response Assessment can be customized for your specific needs*

A Word About the Role of Compassion

Before moving on, briefly think about compassion and whether there is a place for it in the online conflict management process. The story of Dublin-based writer Leo Traynor serves as a good example. In his blog post "Meeting a Troll..." Traynor described how he and eventually also his wife received ugly and hate-filled messages via Twitter and email that included ones like "'Dirty f**king Jewish scumbag'"

and "Your husband is scum. A rotten b*stard and you're a wh*re."[23] One day
he received a package at his home containing a lunchbox with ashes inside. The
accompanying note stated, "Say hello to your relatives from Auschwitz." A few
days later he received a direct message on Twitter that said, "You'll get home some
day & ur b**ches throat will be cut & ur son will be gone." In fear for his life and
not knowing the identity behind the accounts that were harassing him, he decided
to leave Twitter. Shortly thereafter a friend offered to help identify the IP addresses
from which the attacks originated. Shockingly, Traynor discovered that the attacks
came from the 17-year-old son of a friend. The mother said, ""If you want to call
the Garda [the police] we'll support you in that. I'm ashamed of him."[24] The father
of the young man "was horrified at what his son had done. Horrified, but not surprised. He wanted to call the authorities there and then and turn him in. But I said
no."[25] Instead Traynor decided not to press charges that would result in "criminal-
izing a 17-year-old kid and ruining his future," but he insisted that the young man
receive mental health counseling. In other words, Traynor showed compassion for
someone who doesn't seem to be deserving of compassion. Traynor's decision of
how to deal with the boy certainly isn't the best solution for all situations, but in
this case, one hopes that his compassion gave his attacker a fresh start.

Dacher Keltner, Ph.D., co-founder and faculty director of the Greater Good
Science Center at the University of California, Berkeley, and author of the book
Born to Be Good: The Science of a Meaningful Life, recently said that although
"technology is taking us in so many new places," it nevertheless hasn't changed
some fundamental aspects of our nature, namely that our "need for the human
dimension of compassion and kindness is greater than ever."[26] And neurosur-
gery professor James R. Doty, M.D., who serves as the director of The Center for
Compassion and Altruism Research and Education at Stanford University, commented that "while survival of the fittest may lead to short-term gain, research
clearly shows it is survival of the kindest that leads to the long-term survival of a
species."[27]

Certainly not everyone is deserving of compassion. Some of the people who have
been mentioned in this book have done horrific things and have shown, at best, a
severe lack of judgment and, at worst, a callous disregard for their targets. Many of
them, even when confronted with their victims' anguish, have shown no remorse.

However, something to keep in mind is that not all people who act badly online
are undeserving of a second chance. In a post titled "Diary of A Mean Girl," blogger Beth Anne describes how a few years ago she was a lonely newlywed looking
for friends. She joined an online community, but instead of acting nicely, she
"quickly learned the art of 'snark,' otherwise known as a comeback laced with
snap & sarcasm & irony.... I was smart. Biting. Witty. But cruel." Today she regrets
her actions, acknowledging that "I can never take back those words that I flung
so carelessly to strangers. Even if I tried, I could not find every individual that I

spoke to & apologize for my cruelty. In many circles, my online reputation is shattered...."[28] Perhaps she and others like her should receive your sympathy instead of derision and scorn.

Dispute Management Process

After reading the previous chapters, you're in a much better position to deal with online disputes because you have the benefit of understanding why and how problems arise, as well as having mastered many of the skills you need to successfully respond to them. Next is the standard process you can follow to manage disputes.

This process can work only with those people who are willing to "come to the table" and want to resolve the problem. In situations involving trolls, online harassers, hate-obsessed individuals, and similarly questionable people, trying to directly engage with them often fails and possibly even escalates the situation. In cases like that, a crisis management approach is more likely to be effective.

Gather information

Before you respond to a problem, gather and review all the available information about what's going on. Although compiling the following list of things may seem time-consuming and burdensome, it can ultimately help you decide on the right course of action. Think of these steps as similar to a paramedic's function when conducting patient triage at the scene of an accident.

- **What is the problem you're dealing with?** Try to describe it succinctly in one or two sentences. Example: A disgruntled customer is attacking your company online and claiming one of its products harms infants' and young children's skin.

- **Who are the people, groups, or companies involved?** List them by name and affiliation. Example: Susie Smith is a popular "mommy blogger" who recently published a best-selling parenting book.

- **What are the specific facts of the situation?** Example: Smith has a 1-year-old child. Smith purchased your company's new Ultra Dry All Day diapers and claims her son suffered severe rashes and blisters as a result of the chemicals in the product. In addition to writing an angry post on her well-trafficked blog, along with a photograph of her son's reddened bottom, she also left a scathing comment on your branded Facebook page and vented on Twitter. Her post and comments received dozens of sympathetic responses, with other mothers saying they would stay clear of buying Ultra Dry All Day.

- **What is the history and timeline?** Example: Smith wrote her blog post on February 1. It received 30 supportive comments within the first 12 hours and was shared 48 times on social networking sites during that same time period. It was immediately picked up by two other prominent bloggers, and the complaint seems to be gaining traction. That same day, Smith also left comments on your Facebook page and on her personal Twitter account, linking to her blog post. In the 2 days since her initial post, she's kept the criticism alive through comments on her blog post and follow-up commentary with others who have picked up her story.

- **Has the other party expressed her interests?** By carefully looking at what the other party has said and done, you can likely gain useful insight into her interests. Example: As evident from her blog and book, Smith regards herself as a caring mother. Her son's reddened skin is contrary to the image she has of herself as a dedicated parent, and she therefore needs to find someone to blame other than herself for the problem.

- **Has the other party expressed her position and how she wants to see the problem resolved?** Example: Smith hasn't tried to reach out directly to the company to express what she wants in terms of a resolution. However, it's clear she holds your company accountable and wants it to take responsibility.

- **What is the other party's conflict style?** If possible, try to determine, based on how she expresses herself online and what you can see from a quick overview of the online footprint, what kind of conflict style she has. (Refer back Chapter 5, "What's Your Conflict Style?" to compare.) Having an understanding of the usual method of dealing with disputes can help you in crafting a plan of response. Example: Based on a quick assessment of her method and tone of expression, Smith is likely a "Warrior" who prefers the competitive style of conflict management.

- **Is this the first time this problem has arisen? Is this the first time it's arisen with the same person or group?** Example: This is the first time your company has had any problems with Smith, who in the past has mentioned using your company's products and recommended them to other mothers. You haven't received any other complaints about this new product but are concerned that Smith's outspokenness may cause other mothers who use these diapers to falsely believe your product is causing rashes and blisters their babies may be experiencing.

- **Do you have links, screenshots, email copies, and other information about the problem?** Make sure you collect and keep copies of everything you find online that's relevant. Posts and comments sometimes get removed by the person making the particular statement or by a site moderator or administrator, and you can't run the risk of losing critical information that could help you in the dispute resolution process. Monitor to see if any future discussions about this problem take place online, and measure the sentiment.

- **Is there a possible legal issue involved?** Example: There might be if Smith makes unsubstantiated and incorrect claims that your product is defective, which can result in reputation and market share loss, or if she successfully initiates a class action lawsuit. You might decide to let your attorney know what's going on, even though right now there is no need to take either any defensive or offensive legal action.

- **Have you dealt with similar problems in the past and if so, what was your approach, assuming it was successful?** Example: The Ultra Dry All Day diaper is a new product, and there haven't been any problems with it beyond the issue with Smith. However, your company also produces baby wipes, and 2 years ago a handful of parents claimed that the cleansing ingredients in them were causing minor skin irritation. You managed this problem by contacting the parents directly, thanking them for letting you know, and asking them to share the details of their problem so that you could share this with the product development team as feedback to be included in any future product updates.

In applying this list to your specific situation, you also must keep in mind that online, the luxury of having enough time to carefully collect and analyze every bit of necessary information doesn't always exist. In some cases, waiting hours to see if something goes viral is a bad decision, while in others it may be possible. The unique nature and facts of each situation matter. In the Ultra Dry All Day diapers situation, for example, if many other parents join in and also claim that the product harmed their babies, you need to react considerably more quickly.

Consider the longer-term benefit of commenting even when there might only be one vocal critic. As a company representative, your comment may not sway the original critic, and perhaps isn't even directed at her, but instead serves to address the unspoken concerns or questions of those who read about the problem later (the search audience).

Identify the Disputants

Before you start coming up with potential solutions to the problem, you first need to know precisely who all the disputants are. That's simple, you might think: It's my employer and the person who has been writing nasty comments about the company on Twitter. Or, you point out, it's me and the person who just publicly criticized me on the community forum. Not so fast, though. Identifying all the disputants isn't as easy as it initially sounds.

Many people believe that talking about disputants refers exclusively to the parties in dispute because these are the people or entities directly involved. However, disputants can also include stakeholders, namely those for whom the dispute, and the outcome of the dispute, is important for one reason or another. Stakeholders, meanwhile, can be broken down into separate groups, such as allies, active supporters, sympathizers, or those who share a common enemy. An example of an ally might include a business that relies on the success of the company under attack, whereas an active supporter might include the regular volunteer of a nonprofit organization. A sympathizer might be someone who simply doesn't like how a company or individual is treated online, whereas someone who shares a common enemy might include an advocacy group that has the same overarching goals as another group, such as fighting against soft drink manufacturers that they feel contribute to childhood obesity.

Disputants can also include those who aren't immediately recognizable: In other words, hidden disputants who are represented by the visible disputant. These might include someone's spouse or significant other or individuals who can't speak for themselves, such as children or people who is mentally disabled.

For party disputants, in some cases people could be direct disputants, meaning they'd either be directly involved in the dispute or representing people who are, such as your organization or clients. In other situations they could be stakeholders as previously defined. For example, if you work as an online community manager of a company brand and a customer goes on Twitter and starts badmouthing your client via the Twitter account you're managing, you're a party to the dispute because you're the public-facing person the disgruntled individual is engaging with. Alternatively, you may be a disputant because people go after you personally online, not as a representative of your employer but because you represent something they don't like or because you said or did something online that they disagree with.

When identifying all the disputants, it's helpful to determine what their relationship is to each other and to you. Do they have a preexisting relationship, and if so is it personal, professional, or both? Has it been a productive relationship in the past? Is the dispute in question an anomaly or is there a history of conflict? If the relationship is personal, the dispute may be more emotionally intense because of hurt feelings, but if the parties want to maintain or try to save their relationship they may also be more motivated to try to resolve their differences. Meanwhile, if this dispute is an anomaly, and the parties haven't yet gotten into a negative pattern of behavior, it might enable them, all other things being equal, to lean on their past relationship in working through the problem.

In identifying disputants it is also important to consider the bystanders, those who are not a part of the dispute per se but who are likely to see a dispute play out in real time. Bystanders can be swayed to chime in or lend their support to one side if they feel the circumstances call for it. This is especially relevant to remember in the online space where disagreements and disputes are often played out in a dramatic and intense form. Bystanders are a fluid group that can pick up or lose numbers quickly and easily. It can be difficult to determine in every case who and how many they are. However, as long as you keep in mind that bystanders are out there and may become involved in the dispute, you'll take that into consideration when planning how to manage and try to resolve a particular dispute. Because the online arena is a permanent record holder of interactions and communications (recall the Wayback machine from Chapter 1), bystanders might also include those who come across the dispute at a later date—assuming it hasn't yet been resolved but has diminished somewhat in intensity—and decide to bring awareness to it again.

Finally, don't overlook the exploiters and opportunists, those who benefit from the existence of the dispute and either actively try to extend it or try to sway the outcome one way or another. An example of this are the online gossip sites that sensationalize anything they believe will bring them page views and corresponding ad revenue.

Define the Problem from Your Perspective

Clarify in your own mind what is going on and drill down as deeply as possible based on the initial information you have. Is the problem based on a simple misunderstanding that doesn't seriously threaten you or your company's reputation? Then perhaps the misunderstanding is something you can easily rectify to the satisfaction of the person complaining. Or maybe the problem is based on a more serious disagreement that requires considerable investment of time and effort to resolve.

Try to determine if the problem is substantive, procedural, personality-based, or a combination. Here are some examples: A substantive problem might involve the question of whether a customer already paid for an item, which he claims he bought with reward points, but for which the company says it doesn't have a record. A procedural problem might involve a customer disagreeing with a company's exchange or return policy. A personality-based problem might concern conflicting communication styles between a client and a customer service representative. A combination problem might involve a customer trying to get his reward points credited back to his account because he claims he never received the item he ordered, and the customer service representative bluntly refusing to credit the points back to him because her records indicate the item was shipped to him 6 months ago and that he therefore missed the return policy's time frame.

Perhaps at this early point you're not even clear what the underlying issue is and are just aware that you or your company are being attacked online. Maybe someone is tweeting insulting comments about you, or is calling your company nasty names, but it's not clear what triggered the outburst (a point made by comedian Andy Borowitz in Figure 8.3). Or maybe instead someone is tweeting how your company has lousy customer service, but she isn't being specific about what prompted her opinion or to what incident she is directly referring.

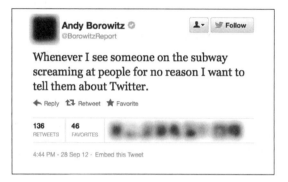

Figure 8.3   *Andy Borowitz's Tweet of September 28, 2012*

Determine What the Other Side Says the Problem Is About

If the other side has clearly stated what he feels the problem is and what he wants to see done to make it right again, consider yourself lucky. Although you may not agree with his framing of the dispute, at least you have an understanding of where he's coming from. This gives you a basis from which to start working.

However, sometimes one of the parties, usually the disgruntled one, is simply unhappy and has gotten to the point where the displeasure is so great and intense that he's not clear how he'd like to see the situation rectified, or alternatively he wants something that's impossible for him to have (for example, getting back the time he lost to the problem). Note, however, that saying what a dispute is about and believing it might be entirely different. Consider an example from the domestic relations front to illustrate this. Imagine that a couple is having a disagreement about a missed garbage day. Despite having promised to do so, the husband forgot to leave the trash container on the curb for the sanitation workers to pick up, and because the homeowner association rules don't permit garbage to be deposited outside except on the night before a scheduled pickup, the trash must stay inside the house until the next pickup date. The wife is livid and tells her husband she's angry that the trash wasn't taken out, and the husband doesn't understand why she is making such a big deal about his innocent mistake, ruining their evening in the process. The wife. however, is actually angry because she feels this is another example of her husband not being responsible and doing his fair share in taking care of the household.

If you believe there might be a discrepancy between what the other side is saying the dispute is about and what they actually believe it involves, you need to dig further. Is the other disputant being intentionally difficult by not telling you what she is specifically upset about? Does she seem legitimately unclear because of her intensified emotions? Or is she afraid to tell you because she's concerned about retaliation on your part? If she seems confused or afraid, in many situations this can serve as a wonderful opportunity to let her know you're interested in resolving the problem as quickly and seamlessly as possible, and providing a safe communication environment to share the concerns with you.

When the Parties Have Different Views About What the Dispute Is About

In the majority of cases, the parties need to agree on what the problem is actually about to try to come to a mutually acceptable resolution. Without a common basis to work from, attempted negotiations run the risk of failing.

In situations where the parties have different notions about the dispute, sometimes reframing is useful. Reframing is a way of looking at facts or a situation in a different, more useful, and often better way. Briefly look at a reframing example within a conflict setting. A private school is reevaluating its school lunch offerings with the goal of offering healthy and nutritionally balanced meals. When discussing fruit, one group suggests the school stick with the canned fruit cocktail that's been on the menu for years because the children enjoy eating it. Another group suggests purchasing the canned fruit variety that doesn't contain the usual sugar syrup. The groups go back-and-forth because there is a considerable difference in price between the fruit cocktail and the fruit without the sugar syrup. One group calls the other fiscally irresponsible, whereas the other claims that its opponents care only about the bottom line. There appears to be an impasse until someone suggests that instead of becoming stuck on the cost of the fruit, the overall concern of the group is actually how to offer nutritious and affordable food to help combat childhood obesity. The reframing toward a joint goal (fighting childhood obesity) eventually helps the parties agree that instead of the canned fruit it'll offer fresh fruit, in season and locally grown, which will be commensurate in price to the fruit cocktail option.

In some cases there may be an actual difference about what the dispute is about, but it may not matter because the solution to the problem is relatively simple.

For example, say a customer goes on Twitter and complains about the taste of the food at your sandwich shop. He claims your lettuce wasn't fresh and your tomatoes were tasteless, and says he is considering going to your competitor across the street for lunch. It so happens that you personally examined the toppings that day and found that they were fresh and tasty. However, instead of getting into an argument about whether the customer is right, your social media manager has been authorized to offer the customer a coupon for 50% off on his next sandwich order, along with a free drink. The customer is happy because he feels his concern has been heard, and the shop is happy because the customer has stopped complaining and may even continue to frequent the restaurant.

However, in other cases, you might want to look at a proposed solution to the immediate problem that enables the parties to move forward despite their seemingly intractable conflict. For example, imagine a situation in which two divorced parents are still involved with frequent and highly intense arguments because of unresolved animosity one of them feels toward the other. Each believes he or she is the better parent to their two school-aged children, and their ongoing in-person and phone conflict is harming the children, who feel caught in the battle and powerless to stop it. After the older child's school counselor calls them into her office to discuss how distraught their son was about having found vicious comments the father made on a popular social networking site about the parents' most recent interaction, they decide to change their form of interaction. Although the father still harbors deep resentment toward the mother, the two adults realize that they need to change their form of interaction. They decide they'll limit their direct and real-time interaction except when absolutely necessary, and from now on use a tool such as Our Family Wizard, Cozi, or other similarly functioning online communication tools.

Regardless of the problem in question, keep in mind that differences in outlook may also be attributable to things such as gender, culture, race, and religion. Be aware of sensitivities surrounding certain issues, try to avoid potential misunderstandings, and immediately clarify if you believe you said or did something in error.

What Does the Other Side Say It Wants?

After identifying what the other party says and believes the dispute is about, the next step is to determine what she says she wants and needs. Before reading further, it would be a good idea to review the definitions of needs and interests provided in Chapter 1 and also review the different conflict issue categories, namely content-based, personality-based, power-based, and identity-based conflicts discussed in Chapter 3, "The Different Types of Conflicts You'll Encounter Online."

Some of the things the disputants want or expect to have happen may be valid and legitimate, whereas others may not be realistic. For example, wanting to receive an apology from someone who's been personally and unjustifiably insulting online is a legitimate wish, whereas wanting to see this individual fired from his job is less realistic, unless the statements were made while the person was representing his employer or the employer independently believes the actions reflect badly on the organization. Decide what you can offer, or what you're willing to negotiate in exchange for getting something you want.

In addition, keep in mind that some of the things the other party wants and needs may be immediately apparent, whereas others may be a bit harder to identify. For example, using the previous example, the person being attacked may make it known that she wants to receive an apology and public retraction of the online insult. However, what she also might need, yet be hesitant to express, is to make sure her attacker refrains from doing the same thing in the future and thereby avoid having to feel that she needs to continuously watch her back online.

Often what the parties focus on are their substantive needs. These are the concrete things that they want to see addressed, corrected, and resolved, namely the problem or problems they're having with the other side. But in addition to their substantive needs, the disputants often also have other needs that must be met to try to resolve the dispute. For example, they need to feel that it is safe to share their thoughts with the other side, that they are being listened to, and that their concerns are being taken seriously. Usually they also need to feel that they are being treated politely, if not because of their views or positions—which may be the things in dispute—but simply as individuals who want to be treated with at least a modicum of respect. This applies even in situations that don't involve interpersonal conflicts. (Think of situations in which you might have had to negotiate with an opponent on behalf of your employer, but felt the other person was being disrespectful and dismissive, and therefore perhaps were unwilling to concede on a particular request he made that in actuality was unimportant to you.) People also need to feel that the process they're following to try to resolve the dispute is fair and contains procedures or rules that are being equally enforced.

Who Are the Decision Makers?

In addition to knowing who the disputants are, you need to know who are the decision makers on your side and the other's side. In many cases, you act on behalf of yourself and don't need to consult with anyone else in deciding if and how to move forward when there is a problem.

There may be situations, however, where you act on behalf of someone else, perhaps your employer or a client. Make sure you understand the exact power you have. In the online realm, problems can occur quickly and being clear on whether you can act without checking with someone else can be a tremendous asset. Understand what types of situations and what kinds of problems you are allowed to address and attempt to resolve on your own. Also make sure this is formally memorialized as policy, so you can refer to it in moments of question (and protect yourself if someone accuses you, after the fact, of having overstepped your position).

Find out whether the problems you're allowed to independently address are limited to a particular type of issue (for example, being allowed to deal with complaints about poor service but not with complaints about poor product design), a specific money amount (for example, being allowed to offer a rebate up to a certain amount but not over that), or a particular type of disputant (for example, dealing with a disgruntled customer but not with a critical journalist), or whether you have broad discretion. In situations that deal with issues that exceed your power, determine ahead of time the specific person or team you need to consult before proceeding, and how to reach them quickly in urgent situations. There may be times when this person is unavailable or unreachable when you need them. Know ahead of time whether there is someone else in the "chain of command" with whom you can get in touch. In addition, find out what the protocol is for taking action if no higher-up is reachable in the necessary amount of time. In that situation, are you expected to wait until someone can be reached that you can consult with, or, if a situation requires immediate or quick action, are you allowed to proceed?

For the decision maker on the other side, know precisely who that person is. Is it the individual you're directly dealing with, or is she just a representative for the actual person or entity calling the shots? In straightforward cases, for example, a complaint about a faulty item someone purchased, you can usually assume that you're dealing directly with the angry customer. In other cases, however, you may need to inquire further to make sure a solution you offer to deal with the problem can be accepted by the individual with whom you're communicating. Knowing who the decision maker is can save you from negotiating with the wrong person.

Agreeing on Process and Ground Rules

In simple situations, for example, the sandwich problem previously discussed, agreeing on a dispute resolution process won't usually be necessary. However, with disputes that are intense, complex, or protracted, agreeing on the process is recommended. In other situations in which an opponent is obnoxious and belligerent, getting her to agree on a process and ground rules may be extremely difficult—and in some cases impossible. She may be hypersensitive to any perceived threat to her power and regard any proposed suggestion of ground rules as an attempt to "suppress" her. In situations like that, directly addressing the creation of formal ground rules may backfire. Instead, simply starting a conversation that's as nonthreatening as possible, and seeing if she reacts favorably, may be a more successful approach to move forward and resolve the problem.

As previously explained for both simple and complex disputes, you'll want a structure in place that enables you to triage disputes as they occur. This, however, is something you'll likely keep confidential within your company as proprietary information.

Agreeing on a process can be done in a simple and indirect manner, for example, publicly tweeting your company email address to a disgruntled customer with the request that he discusses his concerns with you directly and privately. If the customer reaches out to you via that channel, you know he agrees to give that method a try. With disputes that require a more formalized approach such as mediation, a document outlining the process, rules, responsibilities of all the parties, and legal rights is standard.

Sample process and ground rules can include

- Agree on whether you'll communicate in person or via live video, phone, real-time text, or email
- Agree on whether you'll communicate directly or have others represent you or speak on your behalf
- Agree on whether you'll maintain confidentiality concerning the details of the discussions you're having, or whether you and the other side may publicly share what's communicated, and at which point in time
- Avoid generalizations about the problem and instead provide specific and detailed descriptions or examples
- No name calling and intentionally insulting each other during the attempted resolution process
- Participate in the process with a sincere interest in trying to resolve the problem

Always keep in mind that, unless agreed to under a legally-binding agreement, even when the parties promise to keep things private or confidential, there is a chance that if one of the disputing parties isn't happy with the way the situation is going, he may go public with the information.

Know Your BATNA and WATNA

BATNAs and WATNAs are concepts that help the parties figure out what the best and worst outcomes will likely be if they can't agree on a mutual resolution to their problem. BATNA stands for Best Alternative to a Negotiated Agreement and WATNA stands for Worst Alternative to a Negotiated Agreement. In situations in which you can figure out what you and your opponent's BATNA and WATNA are, you can compare what a potential negotiation agreement can offer you against what walking away would bring you.

For example, imagine that there is an online war going on between a gossip website and a San Francisco tech celebrity, the founder of a popular social networking site, who feels he is being treated unfairly online. He and his wife recently filed for divorce, and the gossip site is trying to find any dirt it can about him, including the reason behind the split. The site suggests that perhaps the couple is divorcing because of a too-close relationship between the man and his attractive personal assistant. It published several photos of the man and his assistant having dinner alone in New York City and attending high-profile events together where they're standing close to each other and smiling. The tech titan has threatened to sue the gossip site for making false claims if it doesn't stop hinting at him having been unfaithful. He is concerned that the bad press will hurt his divorce proceedings, in which his wife has already agreed to a reasonable financial settlement and custody arrangement for their teenage son.

The gossip site, on the other hand, hasn't decided whether entering into an agreement with the man will benefit it in the long run. If it agrees to stop writing about the divorce, the man won't sue and the website won't have to incur legal costs. Its WATNA, however, may be that if it agrees to stop publishing stories about the man to avoid the lawsuit from happening, the man may still move forward with the suit, based on the past stories already online. In that case the website will have to incur legal costs defending itself and will also not have had the benefit of having continued to push out a slew of stories about the divorce. However, its BATNA may be the following: The tech founder is an internationally recognized figure whom people both love to love and love to hate. Stories about him always reach the top number of readers. The website isn't actually claiming the man's been unfaithful, just publicly questioning the relationship between him and his employee. The advertising revenue it receives as a result of page views from salacious stories like this exceed what it would have to pay attorneys if it found itself defending a lawsuit—one it's sure it would win in the end. In addition, any publicity as a result of the suit would benefit it even more.

The tech founder's BATNA, meanwhile, might be that although the attempted negotiation between him and the website wasn't successful, the website nevertheless stopped writing stories about him because of a negative backlash by its readers concerning the stressful effect the string of unsubstantiated stories was having on his teenaged son. His WATNA, meanwhile, might be that the website continues to write hurtful and unproven stories, his wife demands a higher settlement amount because she is angry about her name being repeatedly dragged through the mud by the website, and he sues the website and loses.

Creating Possible Solutions

At this point in the dispute resolution process, you and the other party get to be creative.

Both of you should offer suggestions for resolution. Brainstorming can be a useful approach, but be wary of judging ideas too quickly or discounting them as unfeasible without a full analysis. Make sure you have several possible ideas to choose from before you start the evaluation process. As long as they don't work against your interests and aren't harmful to you, the other side, or other stakeholders, and they're not illegal, the ideas can be open for legitimate consideration.

Remember that this part of the dispute resolution process may not occur in a linear fashion. Perhaps you or the other side take offense at a proposed solution, or you experience feelings of anger or hurt because you feel the other side is trying to unfairly take advantage of any actual or perceived weaknesses you have. If that happens, take a moment or two to regain control of yourself, and let the other side do the same, before continuing the discussion.

If an impasse threatens to derail the process, focus on your and the other side's underlying concerns, needs, and interests. Make sure that any behavioral ground rules are followed, and restate your commitment to trying to come to a mutually agreeable resolution.

Despite your best efforts, there may be situations in which jointly coming up with a solution isn't possible. There may not be a feeling of sufficient trust, or the other side may not be interested in expending the time and effort needed to reach a resolution. That doesn't prevent you from trying to come up with resolutions on your own. After you do so, you can reach out to the other side with the suggestion and gauge the response.

Agree on and Implement the Solution

After you brainstorm solutions, the next step is to evaluate them. This is a step you will most likely do on your own, without sharing the strengths or weaknesses of each proposed solution with the other side (think BATNA and WATNA). In a perfect situation, both you and the other side will fully agree on a solution. In other cases, you'll need to tweak a solution to ensure it meets the needs of both sides.

In evaluating the agreement, make sure it satisfies both you and the other side. That doesn't mean everyone will be happy with all aspects of the agreement (although that can happen in some cases), but it means that everyone feels they've come to a solution that's the best under the circumstances and that they can live with. The downside of trying to force the other side into an agreement you like but with which they aren't pleased is that underlying resentment would remain that could cause a future flair-up. You and the other side should agree that all parties are entering into the agreement willingly without duress, that the agreement is fair, that you're not giving up any legal rights without full awareness of the ramifications (unless you've consulted with an attorney who advised you accordingly), and that it can be implemented within the time frame stipulated.

Make sure to include information about what happens if one side breaks the agreement without prior approval of the other party. Be clear about the penalty for noncompliance and the negative repercussions that can result.

After you agree on a resolution, decide whether you want to put your agreement in writing. In many online dispute situations, especially the smaller and more transient ones, it isn't necessary or feasible to come to a written agreement, but with larger, entrenched, or high-stakes disputes where a formal negotiation takes place, having a document that outlines the agreement can serve both as a reminder of the specifics of the agreement and as a legal document the parties can refer to if the dispute recurs after the agreement is reached.

Whether or not you put your solution in writing, make sure that everyone understands and agrees on the specifics that need to take place, which can include both active components (for example, issuing a public apology) and passive ones (for example, refraining from attacking the company online). Pay particular attention to those elements or areas of your agreed-upon solution that put it at risk of failing.

Review Your Progress

After you resolve your dispute, it's time to review and evaluate what happened. Take time to carefully think about and answer the following questions:

- Is there continued interaction with the person or entity you had the dispute with?
- If so, has the interaction with the person or entity permanently improved? Hopefully, the interaction between you and the other side has become neutral or perhaps even positive. There are situations, though, in which the animosity between you hasn't gone away and the other side may be on the lookout for future opportunities to lash out or retaliate for something he feels you've done wrong.
- Was the dispute effectively contained, or did it spread beyond the initial dispute with the original person or entity?
- If it spread, to which channels and outlets did it spread? Were these important or influential communication outlets?

- If it spread, could you have minimized or slowed down the spread of the initial dispute?
- If you or your company's reputation were damaged because of the initial problem, did you mitigate the damage by effectively resolving the dispute?
- How long did it take to stabilize your reputation?
- What factors do you believe led to the successful resolution of the dispute? What people, communication tools, financial resources, and other things helped?
- Of these, what factors can you try to replicate for any future, similar disputes that arise?

Interpersonal Skills for Successful Dispute Management

In addition to the substantive information you've already learned in this book, knowing the core interpersonal skills that are critical to successful management of disputes is also vital. These include focusing on the problem and not the person, avoiding personal attacks and ad hominem fallacies, and using an effective form of expression and active listening.

Focus on the Problem and Not the Person

First among the interpersonal skills you need to master is focusing on the problem and not the person. This may feel like an extremely challenging thing to do when you're in the middle of a dispute, especially if the fight has become personal as fights often do online. But focusing on the *individual* will either distract or derail your efforts to resolve the problem, even if the person is a part of the problem. Perhaps he is truly a pain in the rear and through his behavior exacerbates the negative dynamic. But try to hone in on the actual dispute (for example, a customer leaving damaging comments about your product on a shopping review site) instead of wasting emotional energy thinking about how the person's character irks you (using the same example, thinking about how the individual is sarcastic, obnoxious, self-righteous, and so forth).

Don't Make Personal Attacks or Ad Hominem Fallacies

When you're in an intense situation and are feeling under pressure to fix a dispute as quickly as possible, but are dealing with someone who is being unreasonable, disrespectful, or intentionally pushing your buttons, it's natural to feel frustrated and perhaps even want to get back at the individual by making personal attacks or ad hominem fallacies. (As you may recall, ad hominem fallacies are those where, instead of examining the strength or truth of the statement being made by the other person, the individual himself is being criticized.[29] In other words, the fallacy consists of the focus being on the person instead of the statement.) But don't succumb to the temptation. Control that urge and instead concentrate on staying in problem-solving mode.

Here are some examples of what ad hominem statements look like:

- "Are you really going to buy Steve Jones's new book on personal finance? The guy's a bastard; he cheated on his wife. You can't believe anything someone like that says."

- "Don't lecture me about my quitting smoking, you're the lush who goes through a bottle of whiskey every few days and can't even hold down a job. What do you know about addiction?"

- "Ladies and gentleman of the jury, you can't believe what Mr. Gonzales said. He's an illegal immigrant, someone who's already proven that he doesn't follow the law. What makes you think he's suddenly become an honest man in court?"

There is only one reason why criticism of someone's character or behavior should ever come into play in a dispute. According to Douglas Walton, Ph.D., author of the book *Media Argumentation: Dialectic, Persuasion, and Rhetoric*, that's when the person's character is connected to the issue at hand and the conclusions being made.[30] So, for example, if someone takes a public anti-prostitution stance, as former New York governor Eliot Spitzer did, but is subsequently linked to a prostitution ring,[31] that's fair game.[32]

Form of Expression Matters

If you've read the previous chapters carefully, it's clear that *how* you say something matters nearly as much as *what* you say, and sometimes even more because the message you're trying to communicate won't get though if people are turned off by your approach.

It's wise to keep in mind that purely written communication is devoid of many of the visual cues you use to measure the sender's mood and intention behind a message. Someone who comes across as brusque online may simply have a more direct style of communicating, which may be attributable simply to his personality or perhaps also influenced by his gender (men tend to be more direct and blunt than women), culture (Germans, for example, are more direct than Americans, who, in turn, are more direct than the Japanese) or other sociological reasons.

Because the risk of misinterpretation is great online, it's extremely important to realize that what you say may be misinterpreted by someone online. Even in situations in which you have a positive relationship with someone, sometimes the intent behind your statement is unclear. For example, say you receive a message from a close friend sharing another instance of how his difficult boss is still treating him badly at work. You simply write a quick reply with the word "sigh." Your friend, however, doesn't know whether you mean "sigh" as in "I'm sorry you're still going through this and I wish the situation were different" or you mean, "It's too bad your boss is still being a jerk but stop whining about it and bugging me with constant updates." Conversely, realize that your interpretation of what you see online may not always be accurate either. Keep this in mind before responding to something you see.

Using emoticons can be helpful. Although you don't want to go overboard using them, an occasional "smiley face" or "wink" can let the recipient know that you meant the comment in a friendly or humorous way. However, be aware that emoticons aren't always read the same way across different platforms, which can sometimes cause unfortunate incidences, as described in a recent *New York Times* article: Lisa Bates, Ph.D., sent a work acquaintance an emoticon of a "big hug" from her Blackberry phone, but his iPhone showed the symbols used to make the hug and not the hug image itself. Bates explained that "From his perspective they look like a view of, er, splayed lady parts: ({}). 'He then ran around his lab showing colleagues excitedly what I had just sent him. Half (mostly men) concurred with his interpretation, and the others (mostly women) didn't and probably thought he was kind of a desperate perv'."[33]

Tone also matters online. Think about the different feeling you get from reading "thank you" (polite, neutral, and perhaps perfunctory) and "thank you!" (friendly, enthusiastic, and sincere). Read the following sentences and see how the same words come across differently depending on how they are presented:

- All employees must follow the company's Code of Professional Conduct in every public setting, both online and offline.
- **All employees must follow the company's Code of Professional Conduct in every public setting, both online and offline.**
- <u>All employees</u> must follow the company's Code of Professional Conduct in every public setting, both online and offline.

When communicating online, it's also a good idea to avoid intentionally inflammatory language when addressing someone. Try to use neutral language instead. Using inflammatory words when writing about an issue will serve to rile people up and alienate many who see it. There are, of course, people or entities whose goal is divisiveness, and you'll see that they have a tendency to regularly use hateful and angry words to antagonize people with whom they disagree. (Think of what's regularly seen in online political discussions.) Inflammatory language can consist of derogatory terms, single words that have a negative connotation, entire phrases, or a particular way of saying something. Here are some examples:

- *Libtard* or *Republitards* (derogatory term for someone who is politically liberal or a Republican)
- *F**ktard* (single word)
- *That's so gay* (entire phrase using the word "gay" to imply something is bad)
- Are you deaf? Did you hear what I said?! (particular way of saying something)

Using qualifiers or disclaimers in your online statements can also soften what you're saying and prevent you from coming across dogmatically, abrasively, or arrogantly. Keep in mind, however, that depending on context, even some of these may come across as arrogant. Examples of words to use include:

- Perhaps
- I think that
- In my opinion
- In my view
- All I know is that
- I guess that
- My experience has been that
- Another option may be
- Another way to look at it may be

Active Listening

An important part of your dispute management arsenal includes active listening. It's a skill that's useful in all areas of life, both professionally and personally. *Active listening*, sometimes also called *reflective listening*, is a process by which you give the other person or persons your full attention to completely and accurately hear what they're saying, with the goal of more effectively dealing with their concerns or the conflict between you. Through active listening the other side sees you genuinely interested in what they're saying, and trust between the two of you can thereby be created. Because you are listening to them and making them feel more comfortable to communicate freely and openly about what's bothering them, there is a good chance that the frustration and hostility they feel will also be reduced.

Active listening can be challenging when dealing with someone who rubs you the wrong way or has criticized you online. And it's not something that will be effective with people whose online behavior toward you is extreme, such as someone who has an irrational vendetta against you or someone who's a troll with the goal of simply fanning the flames for laughs. But in situations in which that isn't the case, active listening is a foundational step in resolving the dispute between you. Keep in mind that listening to the other side doesn't mean you agree with what they're saying; it simply means that you're acknowledging their statement and making sure you fully understand it.

Active listening online is slightly different than face-to-face active listening. Although the same overall principles apply, with the latter, the other side can see that you're listening by looking at you and making eye contact, watching your body language and listening to verbal cues. But in a text-only environment, you'll have to give written indications that you're engaged. Short prompts can include statements such as "please go on" or "I understand."

Active listening involves the following basic steps, which can occur in a loop as the conversation proceeds:

1. Invite the other side to share their concern or complaint.

2. Listen to what they have to say without interrupting to make your own points.

3. Ask clarifying questions if you don't understand something they're saying.

4. Provide prompts as needed, such as "please continue," "I see," or "please tell me more."

5. Use open-ended questions to elicit more information from them. (Open-ended questions are those that require an explanation or information from the answerer beyond a simple "yes" or "no.")

6. Stay calm in the face of anger.

7. Paraphrase what they're saying to make sure you understand and to give them the opportunity to correct you or expand upon your reflections. (Paraphrasing is taking the person's statement or main points and using your own words to mirror it back, both in terms of substance and emotion.)

Responses When Someone Bashes You Online

Many online disputes occur when a difference of opinion devolves into name-calling and character assassination. When you find yourself in a situation like that, you need to decide on a case-by-case basis whether it's worth responding to a detractor or whether instead it's best to monitor her for a while to ensure she doesn't escalate or pick up co-detractors along the way. Remember that a frustrated or angry response on your part might be exactly what the other person is looking for. It may also help her decide to keep you on her "target" list.

Bill Eddy, author of "BIFF: Quick Responses to High Conflict People,"[34] says that high-conflict individuals often engage in *blamespeak*, which is "usually emotionally intense and out of proportion to the issues," personal, out of context, and also "often shared with others to emphasize how 'blame-worthy' you are."[35] Eddy, who doesn't specifically address the online realm, recommends thinking carefully about whether to respond to individuals' blamespeak and suggests not doing so in the following situations:[36]

- Only you and the other person are involved in the communication
- It's clear that there is not an issue being discussed, but instead that the person's personality is the proble.
- The issue is the other person's opinion about your actions or personality
- It's clear that the other person's point of view will not change regardless of your response
- When you've previously responded to the issue

In instances in which you've made an informed decision to respond, Eddy recommends writing a BIFF response, namely one that is brief, informative, friendly, and at the same time firm.

Although responding should not be considered the default action, there are legitimate reasons you may want to reply to someone's criticism online. As discussed throughout this book, the online environment reflects a unique culture in which speed, intensity, and global dissemination rule. Accuracy of information and the correction of errors frequently fall by the wayside. Therefore, one reason you may choose to respond to an online detractor is because what the person is saying is factually incorrect, and the error of what he is saying needs to be corrected quickly because it makes you look bad and may affect your reputation if others believe it. Another reason is that a nonresponse, depending on the situation, may make you appear weak and cause an incorrect and negative perception in the public or those who witness the attack. A third reason may be because the statement being made by the other person goes beyond opinion and is actually defamatory. In the last case, it's unlikely that your response will cause the person to retract the defamatory words, but making a firm and unequivocal statement that what was said is false can be an important step in dealing with this type of situation.

If you operate in a professional capacity as a social media manager, public relations professional, customer service representative, or other public-facing employee, check to see if there are any company policies about responding to an online detractor. Although an attack may seem personal, if it's made toward you in connection with your employment, make sure your response is made in accordance with what's expected of you as a representative of your company and not as an individual.

There's a difference between someone trying to engage you on an online platform that you control versus one that's completely open and outside your sphere of control. For example, if someone leaves a comment that you find unacceptable or over the top on your personal Facebook page, you can respond, delete it, or completely block the person if necessary. Meanwhile, if an attack happens on a moderated forum, you can approach the moderator to see if the person's behavior violates the site's or the group's norms. If, however, an attack happens on an open platform such as Twitter, you can either (1) ignore and monitor the person, (2) ask supporters and friends to come to your aid (making sure you let them know you want them to act reasonably and not become attackers themselves, and that they should simply show their support and not explain your side of the story since this is your responsibility and they may get the information wrong), or (3) directly respond.

Based on all the considerations, if you think directly responding to a detractor, or alternatively directly commenting on the statement without addressing the detractor, is a good idea, you have several options, as shown next. The examples refer to a comment you might make on Twitter, where brevity is a technical necessity. Depending on the situation, however, you may give a longer and more involved response on your Facebook page, your blog, your website, or other platform that doesn't have the same space restrictions.

- Acknowledge the statement with a neutral comment. Saying something like "thank you for sharing your thoughts/concerns."

- Acknowledge the statement but also express your dissent, making a comment like "Although it sounds like we see things differently on this issue, thank you for sharing your thoughts/concerns." The other person may try to engage you in more conversation, and perhaps even escalate his statements to hook you, but unless you see a specific and compelling need to respond, you don't need to take the bait.

- If the criticism is the result of a mistake you've made, acknowledge it and apologize. A simple "I'm sorry" or "I regret having said/done that, I'm sorry" gets to the point. Avoid adding a "but" into the sentence because that makes your apology come across as insincere or as laying blame elsewhere.

- Even if you haven't made a mistake, sometimes addressing the other side's feelings is appropriate, as in "I'm sorry for what happened to you" or "I'm sorry that happened and wish things had turned out differently."

- If you believe there's been a misunderstanding or misinterpretation, go ahead and correct it in a factual and constructive way. Don't be defensive or emotional. Try a response along the lines of "It sounds like there's been a misunderstanding, and I want to clarify that what really happened is.../my views on this issue are..." or "Thank you for getting in touch; I'm sorry I didn't explain things properly and would like to do so now."

- Sometimes the detractor simply wants to vent and know that you've heard him. Although his chosen method of communicating may not be appropriate, it's up to you to avoid responding in kind and potentially escalating and prolonging the situation. A response like "thanks for sharing your thoughts/concerns; if you'd like to discuss it further why don't we talk privately? You can reach me at..." might be helpful. Try to avoid a prolonged public discussion of the issue, unless it is to your advantage to let others see the exchange.

- You can directly call out the attacking behavior. "I can see that you're frustrated by the situation, but attacking/insulting me won't solve the problem" or "I can see you disagree with what I said, but attacking/insulting me isn't the solution."

- Respond to the attacking behavior and then detach from further discussion. Here are two suggestions: "We see things differently about this issue and it doesn't sound like we will come to an agreement, so there's no point in talking about it further" or "Sorry you think I am boring, I post things that are interesting to me."

Examples of Effective Online Problem Solving

In this book you've seen many examples of bad online behavior and how not to respond to problematic situations. The good news is that some people and organizations know how to do it right.

University of Wisconsin-Green Bay Professor Ryan C. Martin, Ph.D., whom you met in Chapter 6: "The 101 of Anger Management," is one such person. Martin teaches several psychology courses[37] and frequently communicates with students via email. On his blog "All the Rage: Commentary and Resources on the Science of Anger,"[38] Martin outlined the problem of angry and hostile emails he received from students who disagree with a decision made by the instructor or who receive a bad grade: "Typically, they are full of bolded words, the excessive use of capital letters, and lack any sort of salutation.... It's rude, disrespectful, and makes me feel as though my hard work isn't appreciated. What's worse, though, is that sometimes the student is right in his or her criticism or concern but wrong in how he or she expressed it. In other words, the student is making a very valid point but it's hard to find because it's hidden behind all those exclamation points."[39] He then offers several suggestions, along with the reasons behind them, for how students can communicate more effectively. These include not hitting "send" in the first place, waiting until their anger has dissipated, having someone else read the email before sending it, being professional by using respectful salutations and closings, and asking what the end goal is in sending the message and structure it accordingly.[40] What makes Martin's post so strong is that he describes the problem, acknowledges that the complaints may be legitimate, explains how aggressive emails make instructors feel, and then offers solutions for how emails can be written more effectively— while modeling, through his own behavior, how someone can still react calmly and politely when feeling attacked.

For an example of a company that effectively handled an online mistake that could have hurt its reputation, look to the Red Cross's response of an alcohol-laced mistweet. In early 2012, Red Cross employee Gloria Huang mistakenly sent a tweet from the organization's account instead of her own personal one, and ended up sharing "Ryan found two more 4 bottle packs of Dogfish Head's Midas Touch beer...when we drink we do it right #gettngslizzerd" to @RedCross's 270,000 Twitter followers at the time.[41] (Today the account has more than 842,000 followers.) Realizing the mistake, the nonprofit quickly tweeted, "We've deleted the rogue tweet but rest assured the Red Cross is sober and we've confiscated the keys" and also wrote a follow-up blog post the next day,[42] thus acknowledging the error and also letting supporters know that it was managing the situation. What happened next was fascinating. Dogfish Head Brewery customers created an online fundraising and blood donation drive for the Red Cross with the hashtag #gettngslizzerd, and many of the pubs that distribute the beer offered free beer to patrons who could show they donated blood to the organization.[43] The Red Cross showed its appreciation for an understanding public by saying, "While we're a 130-year-old humanitarian organization, we're also made of up human beings. Thanks for not only getting that but for turning our faux pas into something good."[44]

KitchenAid, meanwhile, is a good example of how to deal with an online social media crisis, even one created from the inside. During a U.S. presidential debate in October 2012, between Barack Obama and Mitt Romney, a tweet was sent from KitchenAid's @KitchenAidUSA's account that said, "Obamas gma even knew it was going 2 b bad! 'She died 3 days b4 he came president'. #nbcpolitics," a statement that was in reference to Obama's grandmother who died shortly before he was elected in 2008. The tweet, which was intended to be sent from a social media team member's personal Twitter account, was instead broadcast to more than 24,000 followers and went viral. The brand, owned by Whirlpool Corp., was accused of engaging in politics, reflecting hyperpartisanship and being tasteless. What did KitchenAid do?[45] First, it deleted the inappropriate message and publicly apologized on Twitter (see Figure 8.4).

KitchenAid @KitchenAidUSA   3 Oct
That said, I take full responsibility for my team. Thank you for hearing me out.
Expand

KitchenAid @KitchenAidUSA   3 Oct
It was carelessly sent in error by a member of our Twitter team who, needless to say, won't be tweeting for us anymore.
Expand

KitchenAid @KitchenAidUSA   3 Oct
I would like to personally apologize to President @BarackObama, his family and everyone on Twitter for the offensive tweet sent earlier.
Expand

KitchenAid @KitchenAidUSA   3 Oct
Hello, everyone. My name is Cynthia Soledad, and I am the head of the KitchenAid brand.
Expand

KitchenAid @KitchenAidUSA   3 Oct
Deepest apologies for an irresponsible tweet that is in no way a representation of the brand's opinion. #nbcpolitics
Expand

Figure 8.4   *KitchenAid's series of Tweets of October 3, 2012*

Next, Cynthia Soledad, senior director of KitchenAid brand strategy and communications development, issued a series of tweets introducing herself, personally apologizing to President Obama for "the offensive tweet sent earlier" and explaining that it was "carelessly sent in error" by someone who "won't be tweeting for us anymore." Most important, Soledad took full responsibility for what happened within her team, even though she hadn't committed the error herself. An added bonus was that instead of hiding from the fallout, she also sent several public tweets to media outlets that were picking up the story and asked to speak with them on the record (see Figure 8.5). Soledad's quick and professional reaction to the problem enabled KitchenAid to minimize and move beyond what could have otherwise been a damaging hit to KitchenAid's reputation.

Using humor to express or respond to complaints can be a tricky thing because there is an inherent risk that the humor might come across as flippant or disrespectful. But one example highlights how humor can be effectively used. It involves Bodyform, a brand of women's sanitary products for use during menstruation. Bodyform received a comment on its Facebook page from Richard Neill (see Figure 8.6) who claimed that the brand's advertisements featuring images of happy women using Bodyform products and engaging in various adventures during their period were a lie. He said that his girlfriend "changed from the loving, gentle, normal skin coloured lady to the little girl from the exorcist with added venom and extra 360 degree head spin. Thanks for setting me up for a fall bodyform, you crafty bugger."[46] His comment received tens of thousands of "likes."

Figure 8.5   *KitchenAid's series of Tweets of October 3, 2012*

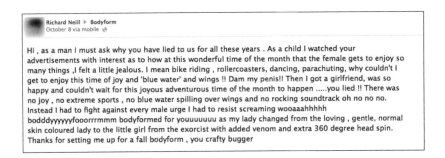

Figure 8.6   *Richard Neil's comment on Bodyform's public Facebook page on October 8, 2012*

Although the comment seems to have been in jest, Bodyform took the criticism in stride and instead of panicking that it was called out for misrepresentation, turned it into an opportunity to show that it knew how to roll with the punches and also how to poke back. First, the brand wrote a Facebook post (see Figure 8.7) thanking Neill for his input, explaining that it had made a video titled "BodyForm Responds: The Truth."[47]

Figure 8.7   *Bodyform's October 16, 2012 reply to Richard Neil's comment left on Bodyform's public Facebook page*

In the video, Bodyform's fictionalized CEO Caroline Williams admits being dishonest. The actress says, "I think it's time we came clean. We lied to you, Richard and I want to say sorry...there is no such thing as a happy period...you Richard, have torn down that veil and exposed this myth, thereby exposing every man to a reality we hoped they'd never have to face...."[48] AdWeek heralded Bodyform's response to the initial criticism, calling it a "brilliant reply to a Facebook rant."[49]

A Special Note About Consumer Review Sites

Sometimes leaving a comment on a consumer review site lets people know you've seen their complaints or criticism and care about what is being said. If necessary, it also enables you to tell your side of the story and give an alternative view of events. When doing so, be sure you don't come across as overly defensive or attacking, because this could backfire and make you look worse than having not stepped into the conversation. When participating in a conversation, the safest approach is to answer in a respectful and approachable manner, and, if applicable, mention how you intend to correct the situation or how the complainer can get in touch with you to receive help. For example, you may say, "Bob, I'm sorry you didn't receive the service you expected from us, and we want to try to make it up to you. Please email us at [direct email address of someone that can provide assistance] or call us at [provide the phone number of the individual or department that handles complaints] and we will work with you to fix this problem.—Sally Jones, Customer Service Representative."

When commenting on a customer review site, you need to be absolutely sure it is a legitimate one. Do some research online to see what others have said, and be sure to read the site's fine print to see what their policy is about information posted by readers and consumers. Does the site have any rules for what kinds of information may be posted? Does it have a policy for removing attacking and vile comments? Does it remove defamatory content upon request? Does it protect the privacy of individuals, within legal parameters, who post on the site? There are unscrupulous websites whose business model consists of encouraging people to post inflammatory reviews or complaints on their sites and then offer a service whereby the person or business being attacked can have this information reviewed and possibly selectively redacted or removed—for a hefty fee.

One site that has come under heavy criticism is RipoffReport.com, of which the court in the case *Giordano and G & G Addiction Treatment, Inc. v. Romeo and Xcentric Ventures, LLC* wrote: "The business practices of Xcentric [the company that operates RipoffReport.com], as presented by the evidence before this Court, are appalling. Xcentric appears to pride itself on having created a forum for defamation. No checks are in place to ensure that only reliable information is publicized. Xcentric retains no general counsel to determine whether its users are availing themselves of its services for the purpose of tortious or illegal conduct. Even when, as here, a user regrets what she has posted and takes every effort to retract it, Xcentric refuses to allow it."[50] If you find that a site has business practices similar to Ripoff Report, stay as far away from it as possible.

Single Versus Repeat Occurrence Disputes

No doubt there will be more than one occasion in which you're unfairly criticized or attacked online. As already discussed, the way you deal with those situations depends on several factors. One of the things to take into consideration is whether the dispute is a single event or repeat occurrence.

A single occurrence dispute can involve one person or group of people, or one problem or incident. A repeat occurrence can involve the same person, the same problem, or both. It suggests that your efforts to effectively resolve the initial dispute failed in one way or another, and that this is the reason it's come back again.

There are situations in which repeat occurrences are unavoidable. Customers will complain about a product they purchased or service they didn't like, and that's an unavoidable part of doing business. But if such everyday problems flair up and become unmanageable or detrimental to your business and reputation, it's time to ask yourself the following questions:

- Is the cause external or internal to you? If it's internal you have greater control over fixing the problem. Examine whether it is a systemic problem that's caused by you in some way. Does your product not fulfill what the customer is promised? In that case, this is something in your control. Is the service or delivery of the product inadequate? Do your social media professionals and online customer service representatives need training in how to deal with angry users? Again, this is something over which you have control.

- Is the dispute caused by the same individual or set of individuals? Perhaps he seems to have it out for you or your business, despite previous attempts by you to resolve the issue. If that's the case, decide whether this is someone to keep your eye on for the time being and monitor to see if the problem escalates, gains traction, or spreads to other people, or someone you need to take stronger action against. The specifics of what this person or group is doing also matters. Is she merely being annoying by leaving bothersome comments on your site, or is she inflicting reputational damage on you? Are they convincing others to take their side or inciting others to gang up against you? And how do others online react to this person? Do they ignore him, criticize him, or take him seriously?

The approaches and skills covered throughout this book will be useful whether you deal with a single occurrence or a repeat occurrence dispute. But a key question to ask yourself is whether the dispute is something you can manage on your own or with which you need outside assistance.

Can You Manage the Dispute on Your Own or Do You Need Outside Help?

In deciding whether a dispute is something you can manage on your own, you need to consider the dispute's intensity and severity. Also consider whether it is spreading and the rate at which it may be doing so, whether social media and mainstream media are taking an interest in the story, and the technology and human and financial resources you have at your disposal.

If the dispute is something that can be resolved with a simple apology, consider doing so. If you need to post a longer explanation on your company's website or Facebook page, by all means do so as well. The public is generally forgiving with individuals and organizations that take responsibility for a mistake, say they are sorry, and implement processes that help avoid future recurrences. However, take into consideration whether the apology would put you at a legal disadvantage or make it appear you are taking responsibility for something that could put you at legal risk. Check with your attorney if there are any questions.

Consider asking your supporters and friends for assistance as well. If the problem you're encountering involves detractors unjustifiably using you for a punching bag, presenting a show of force can sometimes cause them to back off and drop the attack. However, there is a risk in asking for outside help, namely that in trying to do the right thing, other's actions may take on mob-like behavior where the initial bad actor suddenly becomes the victim. The words you use to ask for help, and the parameters you place around the request, can go far in striking the right balance between representing strength in numbers and inadvertently having unleashed an online lynch mob, as represented by Figure 8.8.

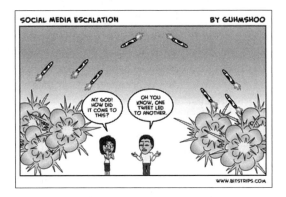

Figure 8.8 *"Social Media Escalation" by Andrew Fowler, creator of Guhmshoo Cartoons*

In terms of dispute resolution processes, negotiating with the other side, which was first mentioned in Chapter 1, is something you can initiate on your own. Even facilitation is a process you can independently initiate. Finding someone to serve as a facilitator doesn't require her to have undergone specialized training, but instead she just needs to be willing to help guide the communication between you and the other party.

If, however, you believe that either mediation or arbitration is the right approach to take, you'll need outside assistance to do so. Unless it is court-ordered or otherwise agreed upon by contract, all parties must voluntarily agree to mediation. Without court intervention, arbitration similarly requires either the consent of the parties or prior contractual agreement. For a list of experienced mediators, you can check out Mediate.com, available at http://www.mediate.com/mediator/search.cfm. A good starting place to find expert arbitrators, many of them attorneys, is the American Arbitration Association, available at www.adr.org/.

However, if you have a customer dispute you'd like to settle, consider looking at Modria. It was founded by Colin Rule, the first director of online dispute resolution for eBay and PayPal and one of the world's leading online business dispute resolution experts. Modria, calling itself "the Internet's justice system," is a resolution platform that consists of four modules: Diagnosis, Negotiation, Mediation, and Arbitration, each building on the previous one. Its pricing schedule ranges from a modest fixed-cost amount for consumer cases to a set cost for business cases depending on the valuation amount.

There are situations in which outside legal help will be necessary. In situations in which there is public disclosure of private facts, in which there has been intentional infliction of emotional distress, or in which, for example, you have been defamed, you should determine your legal options with the assistance of an experienced attorney. An experienced attorney can listen to the facts of your case, discuss with you the strengths and weaknesses, give you an honest opinion of whether legal action is recommended, provide an estimate for how much the effort will likely cost you, and determine your chances of success.

But perhaps what you or your company need isn't a resolution of a particular dispute, but rather help cleaning up your online reputation. To improve the search results of your personal name on Google, you can use the free BrandYourself service, available at https://brandyourself.com/. (It can't be used for businesses.) It helps people create relevant content that rises high in the search engines, thus pushing unfavorable or negative content down where it's less likely to be found. For a service that offers assistance to both individuals and businesses, Reputation. com is recommended. Available at http://www.reputation.com/, Reputation.com helps push negative information down beyond the first two pages of search engines and also helps keep private information from being made public. Founded by Michael Fertik, J.D., it won the 2011 World Economic Forum Technology Pioneer award.

Crisis Management Approach

There may be times where you'll be faced with an online crisis. A crisis is generally an event that's unexpected (although sometimes you receive a brief advance notice that something bad is going to happen), may not be in your control (otherwise hopefully you will have taken all possible precautionary measures to avoid it), requires an immediate response ("immediacy" will be dictated by the circumstances of the crisis, ranging from a few minutes to 1-2 hours hour response time), and risks harming your or your organization's reputation and bottom line.

Although this book isn't intended as a substitute for receiving expert crisis management advice, there are basic things you need to consider or know about effective crisis management so that you're prepared for the inevitable online attack.

1. Having a crisis plan already in place will prevent you and your company from scrambling if a crisis occurs. This plan should be reviewed frequently and regularly updated. In creating it, research and learn from similar crises experienced by other companies to see what worked for them and what they might have done differently.

2. The faster you respond to a crisis, the better. You want to get ahead of the rumors and the false information that's likely to get passed around online.

3. Understand that you need to be concerned with both the public relations and reputational issues surrounding the crisis as well as any potential legal issues.

4. Have a prebuilt "dark site" that can be activated if a crisis occurs. This dark site should be a part of your regular website that can be activated within minutes if needed. It should contain all critically important information about your company that you need to share in a crisis and that people will want to know about. Items to include are details about the problem or incident (what happened, when, and who was involved); contact names and information for the key person in charge of communicating with the public; a section providing background information about the company that the media can use when covering the story; and updates on the problem or incident as they arise.

5. Release an official statement on the front page of your website and on the crisis management portion of your site, and link to it from your social media channels. Keep the message simple, clear, and specific. Make sure any important updates are widely communicated and easy to understand.

6. Designate one person as the contact person for media and other related inquiries. This should be as high-ranking a person as possible, given the situation. Identifying who the point of contact is will avoid having many people speak about the issue and provide incomplete or conflicting information.

7. Refer your social media channels back to the activated crisis management portion of your website, but remember to provide information on your social media sites as well because not everyone will visit your website.

8. Create a set of key messages you can repeatedly use with the media for the duration of the crisis. These might include stating what you're doing to fix the situation, letting the public know that you're investigating how and why things went wrong, and admitting when you don't yet have all the answers and are committed to finding them.

9. Provide regular updates on the situation, even when you have no new information to share. Letting people know you're on top of the situation is critical, even if it means saying you are still working on the issue and will keep them informed of additional progress.

10. Express sadness or remorse for anyone harmed or inconvenienced. Your customers', users', and the public's priorities and what they consider important will likely be different from your own. They and the media want to know that although you have a business and bottom line to look out for, you understand there is a human element to the crisis and are placing that before profit. This point alone can make or break you.

11. Unless advised against it by your crisis management team or attorney, offer to speak directly to the media and influential bloggers.

12. Monitor social media for any fallout from the crisis. Depending on the severity of the crisis, do this around the clock for the first several days.

Endnotes

1. Pink Sith, "UPDATE WPLG Channel 10 in Miami Engages in Cyber Bullying towards Star Wars Fans," September 5, 2012, PinkSith.com. Link: http://www.pinksith.com/2012/09/wplg-abc-news-affiliate-engages-in.html.

2. Mission of the 501st Legion. Link: http://www.501st.com/mission.php.

3. Kyle Munzenrieder, "Local 10 Apologizes for Cyber-Bullying Star Wars Fans," *Miami New Times*, September 6, 2012. Link: http://blogs.miaminewtimes.com/riptide/2012/09/local_10_apologizes_for_cyber.php.

4. Laura Keeney @onnabugeisha's tweet of September 12, 2012 at 5:23 p.m. Link: https://twitter.com/onnabugeisha/status/243474473376940033.

5. Facebook group "WPLG Local 10 Owes Star Wars fans a Formal Public Apology." Link: https://www.facebook.com/groups/142539569221352/.

6. Change.org petition "WPLG Local 10 owes Star Wars Fans a formal apology," Change.org. Link: http://www.change.org/petitions/wplg-local-10-owes-star-wars-fans-a-formal-apology.

7. Pink Sith, "UPDATE WPLG Channel 10 in Miami Engages in Cyber Bullying towards Star Wars Fans," September 5, 2012, PinkSith.com. Link: http://www.pinksith.com/2012/09/wplg-abc-news-affiliate-engages-in.html.

8. Pink Sith, "UPDATE WPLG Channel 10 in Miami Engages in Cyber Bullying towards Star Wars Fans," September 5, 2012, PinkSith.com. Link: http://www.pinksith.com/2012/09/wplg-abc-news-affiliate-engages-in.html.

9. "The Force failed this one: A Star Wars fan says I'm sorry," September 6, 2012, Local10.com. Link:http://www.local10.com/news/The-Force-failed-this-one-A-Star-Wars-fan-says-I-m-sorry/-/1717324/16511424/-/2f9l7oz/-/index.html.

10. "The Force failed this one: A Star Wars fan says I'm sorry," September 6, 2012, Local10.com. Link: http://www.local10.com/news/The-Force-failed-this-one-A-Star-Wars-fan-says-I-m-sorry/-/1717324/16511424/-/2f9l7oz/-/index.html.

11. The Force failed this one: A Star Wars fan says I'm sorry," September 6, 2012, Local10. com. Link: http://www.local10.com/news/The-Force-failed-this-one-A-Star-Wars-fan-says-I-m-sorry/-/1717324/16511424/-/2f9l7oz/-/index.html#comment-644330194.

12. The Force failed this one: A Star Wars fan says I'm sorry," September 6, 2012, Local10. com. Link: http://www.local10.com/news/The-Force-failed-this-one-A-Star-Wars-fan-says-I-m-sorry/-/1717324/16511424/-/2f9l7oz/-/index.html#comment-642505208.

13. The Force failed this one: A Star Wars fan says I'm sorry," September 6, 2012, Local10. com. Link: http://www.local10.com/news/The-Force-failed-this-one-A-Star-Wars-fan-says-I-m-sorry/-/1717324/16511424/-/2f9l7oz/-/index.html#comment-642548459.

14. The Force failed this one: A Star Wars fan says I'm sorry," September 6, 2012, Local10. com. Link: http://www.local10.com/news/The-Force-failed-this-one-A-Star-Wars-fan-says-I-m-sorry/-/1717324/16511424/-/2f9l7oz/-/index.html#comment-643697857.

15. The Force failed this one: A Star Wars fan says I'm sorry," September 6, 2012, Local10. com. Link: http://www.local10.com/news/The-Force-failed-this-one-A-Star-Wars-fan-says-I-m-sorry/-/1717324/16511424/-/2f9l7oz/-/index.html#comment-642666881.

16. The Force failed this one: A Star Wars fan says I'm sorry," September 6, 2012, Local10. com. Link: http://www.local10.com/news/The-Force-failed-this-one-A-Star-Wars-fan-says-I-m-sorry/-/1717324/16511424/-/2f9l7oz/-/index.html#comment-642535826.

17. Melissa Agnes, "Your Social Media Crisis FAQ," Melissa Agnes, July 12, 2012. Link: http://www.melissaagnes.com/your-social-media-crisis-faq/.

18. Bill Eddy, LCSW, Esq., "Who Are High Conflict People," High Conflict Institute, 2012. Link: http://www.highconflictinstitute.com/about-hci/who-are-high-conflict-people.

19. Bill Eddy, LCSW, Esq., "Who Are High Conflict People," High Conflict Institute, 2012. Link: http://www.highconflictinstitute.com/about-hci/who-are-high-conflict-people.

20. David Meerman Scott, "The US Air Force: Armed with social media," WebInkNow, December 15, 2008. Link: http://www.webinknow.com/2008/12/the-us-air-force-armed-with-social-media.html.

21. 2010 Digital PR News: New Digital Service/ Product/App, PR News. Link: http://www. prnewsonline.com/pr_awards/prdigital/14252.html.

22. "Weber Shandwick Launches Social Crisis Simulator, FireBell," Press Release, Weber Shandwick, November 18, 2010. Link: http://www.webershandwick.com/Default.aspx/ AboutUs/PressReleases/2010/WeberShandwickLaunchesSocialCrisisSimulatorFireBell.

23. Leo Traynor, "Meeting a Troll," Traynor's Eye, September 24, 2012. Link: http://www. traynorseye.com/2012/09/meeting-troll.html.

24. Leo Traynor, "Meeting a Troll," Traynor's Eye, September 24, 2012. Link: http://www. traynorseye.com/2012/09/meeting-troll.html.

25. Leo Traynor, "Meeting a Troll," Traynor's Eye, September 24, 2012. Link: http://www. traynorseye.com/2012/09/meeting-troll.html.

26. Angela Hill, "If you can't say anything nice, come log on to the Internet," *Mercury News*, September 4, 2012. Link: http://www.mercurynews.com/bay-area-living/ ci_21427144/if-you-cant-say-anything-nice-come-log.

27. James R. Doty, M.D., "The Science of Compassion," *Huffington Post*, June 7, 2012. Link: http://www.huffingtonpost.com/james-r-doty-md/science-of-compassion_b_1578284.html.

28. Beth Anne, "Diary of Mean Girl," Ok, BA!, Februaray 11, 2011. Link: http://theheirtoblair.com/2011/02/11/diary-of-a-mean-girl/.

29. Argumentum ad Hominem, Philosophy 103: Introduction to Logic, Lander University. Link: http://philosophy.lander.edu/logic/person.html.

30. Yvonne Raley, "Character Attacks: How to Properly Apply the Ad Hominem," May 29, 2008, *Scientific American*. Link: http://www.scientificamerican.com/article.cfm?id=character-attack.

31. Danny Hakim and William K. Rashbaum, "Spitzer Is Linked to Prostitution Ring," *The New York Times*, March 10, 2008. Link: http://www.nytimes.com/2008/03/10/nyregion/10cnd-spitzer.html.

32. Yvonne Raley, "Character Attacks: How to Properly Apply the Ad Hominem," May 29, 2008, *Scientific American*. Link: http://www.scientificamerican.com/article.cfm?id=character-attack.

33. Judith Newman, "If You're Happy and You Know It, Must I Know, Too?," The New York Times, October 21, 2011. Link: http://www.nytimes.com/2011/10/23/fashion/emoticons-move-to-the-business-world-cultural-studies.html.

34. Bill Eddy, *BIFF: Quick Responses to High Conflict People*, HCI Press, 2012 (Kindle edition).

35. Bill Eddy, Section titled "Blamespeak" in Chapter One, "High-Conflict People and Blamespeak" in *BIFF: Quick Responses to High Conflict People*, HCI Press, 2012 (Kindle edition).

36. Bill Eddy, Section titled "Do You Need To Respond?" in Chapter Two, "Writing a BIFF Response" in *BIFF: Quick Responses to High Conflict People*, HCI Press, 2012 (Kindle edition).

37. List of courses taught by Ryan C. Martin, Ph.D. at the University of Wisconsin. Link: http://www.uwgb.edu/martinr/Courses.htm.

38. Ryan C. Martin, Ph.D. and Eric Dahlen, Ph.D., *All the Rage: Commentary and Resources on the Science of Anger*, University of Wisconsin-Green Bay. Link: http://blog.uwgb.edu/alltherage/.

39. Ryan C. Martin, Ph.D., and Eric Dahlen, Ph.D., *All the Rage: Commentary and Resources on the Science of Anger*, University of Wisconsin-Green Bay. Link: http://blog.uwgb.edu/alltherage/.

40. Ryan C. Martin, "Avoiding the Angry Email," All the Rage: Commentary and Resources on the Science of Anger," University of Wisconsin-Green Bay, June 21, 2011. Link: http://blog.uwgb.edu/alltherage/avoiding-the-angry-email/.

41. Laurie Segall, "Boozy Red Cross tweet turns into marketing bonanza for Dogfish Brewery," CNNMoney, February 15, 2011. Link: http://money.cnn.com/2011/02/17/smallbusiness/dogfish_redcross/index.htm.

42. Wendy Herman, "Twitter Faux Pas," American Red Cross Blog, February 16, 2011. Link: http://redcrosschat.org/2011/02/16/twitter-faux-pas/.

43. Laurie Segall, "Boozy Red Cross tweet turns into marketing bonanza for Dogfish Brewery," CNNMoney, February 15, 2011. Link: http://money.cnn.com/2011/02/17/smallbusiness/dogfish_redcross/index.htm.

44. Wendy Herman, "Twitter Faux Pas," American Red Cross Blog, February 16, 2011. Link: http://redcrosschat.org/2011/02/16/twitter-faux-pas/.

45. Jonathan Rick, "How KitchenAid Spun A Twitter Crisis Into A PR Coup," Fast Company, October 4, 2012. Link: http://www.fastcompany.com/3001908/how-kitchenaid-spun-twitter-crisis-pr-coup.

46. Comment by Richard Neill on Bodyform's Facebook page left on October 8, 2012 at 1:30 p.m. Link: https://www.facebook.com/Bodyform/posts/10151186887359324.

47. "Bodyform Responds: The Truth," YouTube, October 16, 2012. Link: http://www.youtube.com/watch?v=Bpy75q2DDow.

48. "Bodyform Responds: The Truth," YouTube, October 16, 2012. Link: http://www.youtube.com/watch?v=Bpy75q2DDow.

49. Tim Nudd, "Maxipad Brand Goes for Blood in Brilliant Reply to Facebook Rant Blunt apology for years of false advertising," *AdWeek*, October 16, 2012. Link: http://www.adweek.com/adfreak/maxipad-brand-goes-blood-brilliant-reply-facebook-rant-144500.

50. John Giordano, individually, and G & G Addiction Treatment, Inc. a Florida corporation, Appellants, vs. Donna L. Romeo, and Xcentric Ventures, LLC, an Arizona Limited Liability Corporation, Appellees. Third District Court of Appeal, State of Florida, July Term, A.D. 2011. No. 3D11-707, Lower Tribunal No. 09-68539

9

Legal Aspects of Online Disputes and Conflicts

Is Questionable Behavior Illegal? It Depends on the Facts and Circumstances

Nicknamed Superstorm by some because of its ferocity and Frankenstorm by others because its timing coincided with Halloween week 2012, Hurricane Sandy was the largest Atlantic hurricane on record, covering an unbelievable 1.8 million square miles.[1] It unleashed devastation on Haiti and Cuba and also affected other Caribbean countries.[2] In the United States it bore down most heavily on the Mid-Atlantic and Northeast regions, hitting New Jersey and New York State particularly hard, resulting in floods, fires, and millions of people without power. In New York City the dead included 2 year-old Brandon and 4 year-old Connor, swept away from their mother Glenda Moore,[3] and off-duty police officer Artur Kasprzak, who rescued seven members of his family before succumbing to the storm.[4] In terms of the financial cost of Sandy, in the United States costs were estimated to be $60 billion dollars in property damage and additional billions of dollars in lost business, according to forecasting firm IHS Global Insight.[5]

In anticipation of the magnitude and severity of the storm, social media sprang into overdrive to provide information both to those affected by the storm and to their loved ones, who were desperate for updates on family members' and friends' well-being. Information sources such as the "Hurricane Sandy Relief Resources" Facebook group[6], started by Allyson Kapin, founder of Women Who Tech, were independently created. Meanwhile, federal and local agencies provided both pre-event and interevent communication.[7] Through its national public service advertising campaign Ready, which educates and prepares the public for emergencies, the federal government made information available on the Ready website (http://www.ready.gov/). And the Federal Emergency Management Agency (FEMA) provided regularly updated information on its website (http://www.fema.gov/) and on its blog, Twitter feed, Facebook page, and YouTube channel.

Unfortunately, not everyone used social media for good. *PR News* reported that on October 29, 2012, as Hurricane Sandy bore down on New Jersey and New York, retailer the Gap Store tweeted "All impacted by #Sandy, stay safe! We'll be doing lots of Gap.com shopping today. How about you?"[8] The company suffered an angry backlash from the public (see Figure 9.1), causing it to give a defensive explanation (see Figure 9.2) and deleting the offensive statement, but not before screenshots of the original Tweet were taken.[9]

Figure 9.1 *This statement, written 2 days after the Gap posted its offending Tweet, is representative of other criticism the Gap immediately received from the public*

Figure 9.2 *The Gap's apology tweeted on October 29, 2012*

Other companies that were accused of acting in bad taste during Sandy were American Apparel, which sent out an email about a 20% discount for buyers of states affected by the storm; Urban Outfitters, which offered a special 1-day-only, free shipping deal and hashtagged it #ALLSOGGY on Twitter; and Sears, which was promoting generators, air mattresses, and more to those affected by the hurricane.[10]

Certainly some of the marketing efforts were in bad taste. However, it is important to note that in disasters, it can be a slippery slope when deciding what is the "right" or the "wrong" course of action. Companies often need to take calculated risks in deciding whether to piggy-back off a disaster or simply express support for victims.

Unfortunately, it wasn't only overly exuberant companies that served as examples of off-base actions during Sandy. Fake images were passed along on social networking sites, sometimes intentionally and sometimes perhaps ignorantly.[11] But no one could reasonably argue that they were illegal. However, there wasn't consensus on how the behavior of Shashank Tripathi should be classified.

At the time of Hurricane Sandy, Tripathi was a Wall Street analyst who also served as campaign manager for Republican Christopher Wight who was running for U.S. Congress.[12]

In a series of Tweets about what was happening in New York City, Tripathi, who hid his real identity behind the Twitter handle @ComfortablySmug, made some fabricated statements introduced with the word, in all capital letters, "BREAKING,"[13] suggesting that the information he was passing along was both important and assumed to be accurate. Among others, these Tweets stated that Con Edison, the city's electricity provider, was shutting down power in all Manhattan; that the NYSE was flooded under 3 feet of water; and that the Metropolitan Transportation Authority announced all New York City subways would be closed for the entire week,[14] thus effectively stranding millions of people. One of his tweets allegedly received more than 500 retweets.[15]

Errors in reporting a live event can and do occur—such is the nature of breaking stories. But as *The New York Times* reporter Jenna Wortham noted, "While people are learning to accept information posted to the social Web with a large grain of salt, they may not be able to distinguish between useful updates and fake ones during a crisis or disaster, which can become dangerous."[16] Intentionally false reports made during disasters or other emergencies are therefore particularly troublesome. It was Tripathi's seeming intentionality that rubbed people the wrong way. Perhaps this was in part the motivation behind some people digging into his past and revealing such salacious facts as the sex diary he wrote for *New York Magazine*[17] and his 2009 interview with the same magazine where he admitted, "I'm not as blatantly an a**hole in person, but I still have a**hole tendencies."[18]

Shortly after @ComfortablySmug's identity was revealed, Wight released a statement on his campaign website that read in part, "I also remain shocked and disgusted by the actions of my former campaign manager, Shashank Tripathi. His actions were all the more distressing, occurring as they did, in the midst of

Monday's disastrous weather—during a time when no one was truly safe. I learned from online reports yesterday, just as others did, that Shashank had been spreading false information from a personal and anonymous Twitter account.[19] An announcement the next day stated that Wight had accepted Tripathi's resignation.[20] Perhaps chagrinned by the totality of the fallout from his actions, which didn't just include criticism on social networking sites but also included media coverage by NBC News, ABC News, CBS News, *Christian Science Monitor*, *Forbes*, *The Guardian*, *New York Magazine*, Daily Beast, and others, Tripathi released an apology on Twitter expressing his regret, as shown in Figure 9.3.

Figure 9.3   *Comfortably Smug's apology tweeted on October 30, 2012*

Not everyone agreed that Tripathi should be held responsible for the fallout from his Tweets. Heidi Moore, an editor with *The Guardian*, argued that anyone who would have looked at the entirety of his @ComfortablySmug feed would have noticed that he was someone who enjoyed joking and creating mischief online.[21] She was appalled at the hostility leveled at him afterward, noting that "a Twitter search for 'Shashank Tripathi' reveals the kind of invective usually reserved for criminals and murderers, not stupid pranksters."[22] Instead, she felt that the irresponsible retweeting by the media and government outlets such as the National Weather Service enabled what was meant as a joke to be taken seriously by so many.[23] In sharply worded criticism, she argued that "Tripathi, as an Internet troll, was completely in character, and he had no responsibility to the public. But journalists do have that responsibility—and so, if Tripathi's silly tweets made it into the national press, it is the national press that is, at heart, to blame for not protecting journalistic standards as well as they should. It is a matter of a few minutes to call a spokesperson or check a live camera, and that is what journalists get paid to do."[24]

Nevertheless, there were those who weren't feeling as magnanimous as Moore. New York City Councilman Peter F. Vallone Jr., a former assistant district attorney, wanted Tripathi to face prosecution on the basis that Tripathi sent the tweets with the purpose of misleading the public.[25] "Everyone knows the example of yelling fire in a crowded movie theater," he said.[26] Presumably, Tripathi's actions would fall within the specific New York law addressing the filing of false incident reports.[27] Attorney Jeff John Roberts, a reporter for *GigaOM*, noted that Tripathi's behavior stood out because "1) he's regularly retweeted by other media outlets (and knows this); 2) he knew exactly what he was doing; 3) it was a genuine emergency."[28] The real question, according to some legal experts, would therefore be whether the New York law (and, by extension, Tripathi's false Tweets) would withstand the U.S. Supreme Court's 2012 ruling in *U.S. v. Alvarez*.[29] In *Alvarez*,[30] the Court found that lying may, under particular circumstances, have free speech protection. An exception would be making a false statement to government officials in communications concerning official matters.[31] Duke University School of Law Professor Stuart Benjamin explained that "a challenge to the New York law likely would turn on whether sending an alarming tweet had the same or similar effect as sending a false report or warning to the government."[32] As the examples in previous chapters have shown, it's indisputable that people are harmed, reputations are damaged, and lives are destroyed due to the unrestrained behavior of wrongdoers online. However, where such offending behavior should fall on the legal spectrum is a hotly debated issue, as illustrated by the differing viewpoints regarding Tripathi's culpability for the resulting confusion and dissemination of his fabricated statements.

The Imperfect Nature of Legal Rights and Responsibilities Online

Attorney Jessica Alan aptly explains people's view of the relationship between the Internet and the law this way: The Internet "has become a part of civil society, and thus users quickly sought to apply their own values and legal framework to it from day one. This should not be surprising, as it is similar to the attitudes taken on by early settlers, colonizers, and pioneers who arrive in new territories. Some bring their own values and seek to implement them in new communities, while others may claim that a new territory needs new laws, and yet some others may clamor for lawlessness."[33] What Alan describes is the crux of what we see online. A comprehensive and in-depth discussion of existing legal rights and responsibilities as they pertain to online activities is impossible to cover in one chapter. Entire books have been written about these issues, for example, *The Future of Reputation: Gossip,*

Rumor, and Privacy on the Internet by Daniel J. Solove; *I Know Who You Are and I Saw What You Did: Social Networks and the Death of Privacy* by Lori Anderson; and the *International Libel Law and Privacy Handbook: A Global Reference for Journalists, Publishers, Webmasters, and Lawyers* by Charles J. Glasser, Jr. The next several pages can therefore serve merely as a brief introduction to some of the areas of the law that affect you online every day; the author encourages readers to pursue additional information and research about these issues.

Freedom of Speech

Freedom of speech is one of the most revered rights. It is guaranteed under the First Amendment to the United States Constitution, which reads, "Congress shall make no law...abridging the freedom of speech, or of the press..."[34] But there are two misconceptions people frequently have about freedom of speech.

The first is that it protects individuals from interference by private entities, when the First Amendment protects individuals from *government* interference. Thus private employers are not prevented from taking action against employees for expressing views they disagree with or for saying things that the company believes places the organization in a bad light (assuming the statements aren't otherwise legally protected). Throughout this book, you've seen several examples where employees were terminated for things they said that their employer found questionable or inappropriate.

The second misconception people often have is that freedom of speech enables them to say or do whatever they want, wherever they want. However, that too is false. In his Congressional Research Service report "Freedom of Speech and Press: Exceptions to the First Amendment,"[35] attorney Henry Cohen outlines the areas upon which First Amendment prohibitions or restrictions are placed. For example, obscene speech[36] and child pornography are disallowed. (Although individuals are not prohibited from having pornography in the privacy of their own homes, that right doesn't extend to pornography involving minors.) Speech harmful to children may similarly be restricted.[37]

In interpreting the First Amendment, the U.S. Supreme Court also recognizes content-based and non-content-based restrictions on free speech. The former includes speech that represents true threats, immediate harm, or advocates action that is likely to incite or result in imminent lawless action.[38] As Cohen notes, in situations in which content-based restrictions do not involve threats or unlawful advocacy, the Supreme Court applies *strict scrutiny*, allowing a restriction on content only when it is necessary to promote a "compelling" state interest and is the least restrictive way of doing so.[39] With regard to non-content-based restrictions, the Supreme Court applies *intermediate* scrutiny that concerns situations in which the government's interest is significant, substantial, or important.[40] This scrutiny applies both to time, place, and manner restrictions, as well as to restrictions focused on conduct that ends up inadvertently restricting speech.[41] For example, although a few people walking on a public sidewalk wearing costumes would be permissible, a Halloween parade that blocks street traffic would require prior receipt of a permit that specifies the date, location, and other rules for the event to take place. Similarly, placing zoning restrictions on adult entertainment establishments is allowed as long as the government can show that regulating the club's location isn't intended to suppress the entertainment, but instead serves a substantial public interest such as preventing the exposure of children to adult sexual behavior or damaging neighborhood property values. Furthermore, laws that attempt to restrict freedom of speech are unconstitutional if they are vague (drafted in such a way that ordinary people are unclear about what they mean and how they are applied), overly broad (prohibit protected speech as well as unprotected speech), or represent an attempt to exercise prior restraint, namely prohibiting speech prior to expression or publication. (Although the publication of information related to national security is prohibited.)[42]

Although the U.S. Constitution grants us strong freedom of speech rights, these are not limitless. As law professors Saul Levmore and Martha C. Nussbaum state in their book *The Offensive Internet*, "We often hear any proposal to limit or regulate speech described, without further argument, as censorship or as 'a violation of the First Amendment.' But the absolutist view of the First Amendment is implausible, and it has never prevailed. Regulation of speech is uncontroversially constitutional with respect to threats, bribery, defamatory statements, fighting words, fraud, copyright, plagiarism, and more."[43] You can't threaten imminent harm against people, incite others to inflict physical harm against individuals or groups, intentionally inflict extreme emotional distress on someone,[44] invade an individual's privacy, or defame others. However, much of what you see online that people find objectionable *is* protected speech. Don't like the way someone looks? Don't like their gender, sexual orientation, or any number of other possible things? You can state that in crass, insulting, and offensive ways, as it appears that the person in Figure 9.4 does: Your opinion and viewpoints are legally protected.

Danielle Citron, professor at the University of Maryland Francis King Carey School of Law, points out that in terms of free speech rights and other legal issues, the Internet creates a new set of challenges that previously didn't exist. "Online, bigots can aggregate their efforts even when they have insufficient numbers in any one location to form a conventional hate group. They can disaggregate their offline identity from their online presence, escaping social opprobrium and legal liability for destructive acts," she says.[45] She argues that the injuries inflicted by bad actors on their victims "also ought to be understood as civil rights violations"[46] because the harm inflicted on traditionally repressed groups such as women and people of color isn't limited to these groups, but affects society as a whole: "When mobs succeed on their professed goal of driving bloggers offline, or of using online attacks to silence their victims' offline speech, they impoverish the dialogue society depends on for purposes great and small."[47]

Figure 9.4   *Sarah Williams's tweet on November 21, 2012*

Although this chapter largely focuses on American law, briefly glimpse how some other countries address certain freedom of speech issues. Article 19 of the United Nations Universal Declaration of Human Rights, which was adopted by the UN General Assembly on December 10, 1948, holds that "Everyone has the right to freedom of opinion and expression; this right includes freedom to hold opinions without interference and to seek, receive and impart information and ideas through any media and regardless of frontiers."[48] Meanwhile, Article 10, Section 1 of the European Convention of Human Rights (ECHR), which governs freedom of expression, was signed on November 4, 1950, and entered into force on September 3, 1953.[49] The convention states in part that "Everyone has the right to freedom of expression. This right shall include freedom to hold opinions and to receive and impart information and ideas without interference by public authority and regardless of frontiers." However, although freedom of speech is widely regarded as a basic human right, this shouldn't be taken as meaning that all countries interpret freedom of speech the same way as the United States does. In France, public insults based on national origin, race, ethnicity, or religion are prohibited,[50] as well as anti-Semitic and xenophobic activities, including Holocaust denial.[51] Similarly, Holocaust denial is illegal in Germany, and the country constitutionally prohibits the use of Nazi symbols, such as the swastika or the Hitler salute.[52] (It was in compliance with German law that Twitter, in a precedent-setting move, prevented Germany-based Twitter users from accessing the account of a neo-Nazi group banned in the country.[53]) Furthermore, in Britain it is impermissible to send a message that is "grossly offensive or of an indecent, obscene or menacing character" through a public electronic network.[54] In Australia, public acts that are likely to offend, insult, humiliate, or intimidate and address race, color, national, or ethnic, origin of a person or group of people are illegal.[55] In Mexico, meanwhile, civil insult laws are in existence and although the federal criminal defamation statute was abolished in 2007, criminal defamation statutes still remain in nearly one-half of the country's states.[56] And in the Philippines, one provision of a new and heavily criticized law addressing cybercrime makes libel criminally punishable by up to 12 years in prison.[57]

Reasonable people can certainly disagree where the boundaries between permissible and impermissible speech should lie. There will be differences of opinion about what types of speech should be limited or prohibited, under what circumstances they should be restricted, and whether the penalties for violation should be civil or criminal. And although this book makes a strong argument that words can irrevocably harm and destroy individuals' lives and companies' reputations, these serious harms should not be paid for with death. However, in some parts of the world, people's pursuit of freedom of speech and the press results in the ultimate sacrifice. Although the exact number of private individuals who have been imprisoned, tortured, and executed around the world for peacefully expressing themselves both online and offline is hard to determine, according to the International Press Institute, know that more than 100 journalists and media professionals were killed globally between 2009 and 2012 because of their jobs.[58]

Defamation

Defamation is another important exception to the First Amendment. It is particularly relevant to the online environment where damaging insinuations, insults, and attacks are released fast and furiously. As noted in Chapter 4, "Who Are the Troublemakers?," defamation is a term that encompasses both libel, which is defamation that's broadcast, published, or otherwise put in writing, and slander, which is defamation that's spoken. To be guilty of defamation, someone must have made a false and unprivileged statement of fact about an individual that's harmful to that person's reputation. The statement must have been published, meaning that someone besides the person making it and the person whom it is about must have heard or seen it. Furthermore, the statement must have been made due to negligence or with actual malice, and must be more than simply an opinion. Someone commenting on a social networking site that "my married boss sucks" without providing more detail is expressing an opinion, whereas writing that their married boss "sucks because he doesn't take the time to train new employees, except for the new girls he hopes to sleep with" might be defamatory if the statements are false. A defense against defamation is that the statement is true. In other words, even if a statement is harmful to someone's reputation, the fact that it is true means that a defamation action will likely fail. Libel per se, meanwhile, refers to a false statement recognized as being so damaging to the person it's about that it's automatically assumed to be defamatory (for example, a false statement that the town's Catholic priest is engaging in sexual relationships with underage parishioners).

An important point in defamation cases is how the plaintiff is classified. If the plaintiff is a public official, a public figure, or a limited purpose public figure, he must prove that the statement was made with actual malice. A limited purpose public figure might include someone who is an active member of a large company-branded online community who publicly and regularly participates in the community and received recognition for their contributions, but not someone who is otherwise considered a public figure, such as the CEO of that company.

Meanwhile, if the plaintiff is a private figure, she is required only to prove that the defendant negligently made the statement, which is an easier standard to meet. However, in today's rapidly moving online environment, the lines between public and private figures are blurring. Linton Weeks, NPR's national correspondent for Digital News, wrote, "Celebrities and politicians make their livelihoods by eschewing privacy and seeking full-frontal public attention. They are public figures by choice.... But what about the rest of us? In today's Facebooking Twitterverse—with the proliferation of cell phone cameras, community-building websites, photo-sharing apps and ever-expanding companies dedicated to exposing as much of our lives and predilections as possible—we are all becoming public figures whether we want to be or not."[59] And that will eventually have a bearing on how the law views us.

Suing someone for online defamation can be a difficult and draining process. First, there is the issue of trying to identify the defendant, which can be problematic in situations in which attacks and defamatory statements are made anonymously. Attorney Colette Vogele explains that it can cost a minimum of $10,000 in legal fees to issue a subpoena to an online company to get it to reveal an individual's IP address.[60] For private individuals, this amount can be cost-prohibitive, never mind the additional legal fees that moving forward with a case would cost. Second, there is the risk that a lawsuit would bring further unwanted attention to a situation and the defamatory claim. If the goal is to bury unfavorable information online, initiating a lawsuit often has the opposite effect. Third, suing someone, whether an individual or a publisher, only provides potential recourse for past defamatory actions. For example, suing and winning against an online gossip site for a defamatory statement it made about you claiming you'd accepted a bribe doesn't preclude the website from attacking you in the future with a different defamatory statement, such as stating that you are stalking the CEO of a technology company.

Carefully weigh the pros and cons before moving forward with a defamation claim. There will be situations in which the financial and emotional cost are not worth it, and others in which taking a stand for justice seems to be the only viable option, regardless of the outcome. As litigator Mark J. MacDougal and risk management expert Tommy Helsby explain in their article "The real price of reputation,"[61] "whether a false story is a planned attack by a competitor, a misguided government inquiry, or the work of a sloppy or unscrupulous journalist, the damage from a reputational attack can be devastating." They recommend a hardline approach to dealing with such matters, arguing that "Fighting an attack on corporate reputation is not a subtle matter, and lawyers are the professional masters of the aggressive response."

Some, such as Geoffrey R. Stone, professor at the University of Chicago Law School, believe that speech on the Internet should be accorded the same legal protection as speech in other venues, not more.[62] Nevertheless, even Stone admits that speech on the Internet can result in greater and more serious harm. "It is sometimes said that the harm from speech on the Internet is potentially greater than the harm from speech in other media, because the potential audience is much larger, the speech remains indefinitely discoverable, and information can be easily located through search engines like Google. All of this is true. A false and defamatory statement can cause more harm to its victims if it is conveyed on the Internet than if it is communicated over a backyard fence or in a local newspaper...."[63] Others, like Brian Leitner, law professor and director of the Center for Law, Philosophy, and Human Values at the University of Chicago Law School, feel that when it comes to helping individuals who are harmed online, the law leaves a lot to be desired. "The Internet is currently full of cyber-cesspools," he says, and unfortunately "for private individuals without substantial resources, the law provides almost no effective remedies for tortious harms, and none at all for dignitary harms."[64]

Privacy

Privacy has always been an important issue in American society, and with the creation of the Internet and proliferation of online communications and social networking sites, it's become a more complex legal issue as well. Online privacy covers a broad range of issues often revolving around who has actual access to information about you, who has the legal right to information about you online, and under what circumstances, and for what that information can be used. Organizations as varied as Electronic Privacy Information Center, Electronic Frontier Foundation, Privacy Rights Clearinghouse, and the American Civil Liberties Union work to educate the public about privacy issues and advocate for individuals' and consumers' privacy rights.

Government involvement in surveillance activities is an increasingly contentious issue, with the National Security Agency's surveillance program representing one particularly hot area. After the September 11, 2001, attacks on the United States, amendments to the Foreign Intelligence Surveillance Act allowed warrantless wiretapping of Americans suspected of communicating with someone outside the country. As it currently stands, citizens are left without the ability to object to the surveillance because the government, citing national security reasons, does not confirm whether someone is being monitored.[65] Other federal privacy laws, such as the Electronic Communications Privacy Act, are considered woefully antiquated.

When the law was passed in 1986, email older than 180 days received little privacy protection because it was largely regarded as discarded.[66] However, with the proliferation of email, it is now common practice to save email communications in different folders or one's in-box for future reference. Under the current law, it's possible to access these materials without a judge's permission and simply with an administrative subpoena.[67] Many privacy experts find this disturbing.

However, it's not just the government and federal laws that create privacy concerns. Privacy Rights Clearinghouse notes that even without knowing it, individuals reveal a vast amount of personal data: "When you are online, you provide information to others at almost every step of the way."[68] In its fact sheet about online privacy,[69] it lists some of the different activities that inadvertently reveal someone's personal information online. These include signing up with an Internet Service Provider, using email, surfing the Internet, using instant messaging, using social networks, and creating personal blogs. As a result, an individual's Internet Protocol address can be revealed, personal email addresses may be shared without express permission, email may be monitored by employers, instant message conversations can be stored by the other party, and cookies can be placed on someone's computer. Julie E. Cohen, a professor at Georgetown Law Center, argues that privacy "is an indispensable structural feature of liberal democratic political systems,"[70] yet points out that "The recent additions of social media, mobile platforms, cloud computing and artificial intelligence-driven data mining now threaten to tip the scales entirely, placing privacy in permanent opposition to the progress of knowledge."[71]

Law professor Daniel J. Solove, a leading expert on privacy law and author of the book *Nothing to Hide: The False Tradeoff between Privacy and Security*, says that historically, in both the United States and countries within the European Union, the law has reflected a privacy self-management model. People are provided a set of legal rights that include making decisions about notice, access, and consent concerning the collection, disclosure, and overall management of their personal data.[72] This model, however, doesn't address whether the collection and use of information is good, but rather whether consent to its use has been given.[73] Solove says that the weakness inherent in such a model is that, "It is impossible at the time of data collection for a person to make a sensible judgment about the future privacy implications."[74] He feels that for privacy concerns, "Knowledge is particularly absent and difficult to obtain at the time the decision is made.... Privacy is speculation in the dark."[75] Solove further takes issue with the commonly heard statement that if-you-don't-have-anything-to-hide-you-don't-need-to-worry. He argues, "There are good reasons why law-abiding citizens want to maintain privacy about certain things even when they are not embarrassing or disgraceful. They want privacy because they don't want to have to justify their actions or explain their behavior to government officials."[76]

Section 230 of the Communications Decency Act

Section 230 of the Communications Decency Act of 1996[77] provides legal protections for Internet service providers and other online distributors of content.
Specifically, §230(c)(1) states, "No provider or user of an interactive computer
service shall be treated as the publisher or speaker of any information provided by
another information content provider."[78] The original intent behind the CDA was
to promote the development of the Internet and to preserve its competitive free
market environment.[79] In practice, it means that "interactive computer services,"
which includes internet service providers, websites, blogs, forums, and social networking sites, are not held legally accountable for the content that third parties
post on these sites because the providers are considered distributors and not actual
publishers of the content. Section 230 thus protects these entities from a variety of
tort claims such as defamation, negligent misrepresentation, emotional distress,
intentional nuisance, interference with business expectancy, breach of contract,
and violations of federal civil rights.[80]

Harvard University-based Berkman Center for Internet & Society's Citizen Media
Law Project explains what type of activities fall within §230 protection:[81] passively
hosting third-party content; exercising regular editorial functions (although alter-
ing the meaning of content must be avoided); correcting, editing, or removing
objectionable content; and inviting or compensating third parties for content they
create and submit.[82] Meanwhile, the Citizen Media Law Project points out that
§230 protection has been limited in the following instances:[83] editing content that
materially alters its meaning, such as turning a non-defamatory statement into a
defamatory one; engaging with website users through drop-down forms that create discriminatory content;[84] and failing to follow through on a promise to remove
material from a website, which the individual making the request relied on, even if
there were no legal requirement for removal.[85]

Nancy S. Kim, professor at California Western School of Law, points out an important discrepancy in the way that interactive computer service providers present
themselves. On the one hand, she says, "They exercise property-like control over
certain aspects of the site," and on the other hand, "They claim powerlessness
when it comes to harassing content."[86] In other words, "borrow[ing] the rhetoric
of free speech as though they were public forums while taking full advantage of
their sites as private businesses."[87] She believes that it is incorrect to view online
harassment "th[r]ough the prism of free speech" because online and offline communication are fundamentally different.[88] She explains, "Although harassment
and bullying have always existed, when such behavior is conducted online, the
consequences have different dimensions. The anonymity of harassers, section 230
immunity, the ease of widespread digital dissemination, and the inability to contain and eliminate online information change the nature of harassment when it
is conducted on the Internet."[89] She therefore proposes, "a more responsible role

for Web site sponsors"[90] that includes contractual and architectural constraints they can impose on their users or visitors (such as users having to register with a website before being allowed to post comments or instituting "report abuse" buttons),[91] as well as increasing accountability through a variety of options such as self-regulation and placing proprietorship liability on them.[92]

Not all countries follow the same liberal approach the United States does for protecting Internet service providers, underscoring the importance of recognizing that actions that may be legal in one jurisdiction are not so in another. One recent Australian case that received a lot of media attention involved a man named Milorad Trkulja. In 2004, Trkulja was shot in the back by an unidentified gunman. At some point thereafter, Google search results for his name brought up images of gangster Tony Mokbel[93] and the link to a crime website (now defunct) that listed gang-related activity.[94] Trkulja contacted Google in 2009, requesting that the material be removed on the grounds that it suggested that he had ties to the underworld and had been the target of a professional assassination attempt.[95] When his request was denied, he decided to sue Google for defamation. Google argued that it wasn't the publisher of the information and that, under the "innocent defamation" defense, it wasn't liable because it posted a link to the material, which it didn't know was defamatory.[96] The jury nevertheless found Google liable based on the fact that the company failed to remove the defamatory content after it was contacted by Trkulja's lawyers.[97] Judge David Beach awarded Trkulja $200,000 AUD ($208,000 US), explaining that "Google, Inc., is like the newsagent that sells a newspaper containing a defamatory article.... While there might be no specific intention to publish defamatory material, there is a relevant intention by the newsagent to publish the newspaper for the purposes of the law of defamation."[98]

Drafting Robust and Legal Social Media Policies

If you're a business or other organization, you must have a strong social media policy in place that can help guide the behavior of those working for and representing you. You also need to create social media policies that address the behavior you expect from users or visitors to your sites. The policies must be flexible enough to enable your organization to freely engage with its customers while also safeguarding its reputation, and simultaneously ensure that employees' and visitors' legal rights are protected.

You must create a customized social media policy that meets the needs of your company or organization. But don't simply adopt a generic one you find online.[99] Also, make sure you don't just list the rules you want to see followed, but also provide specific examples for each point you are making. This can assist your employees in understanding what you are trying to convey and also help your social media policy better withstand legal scrutiny.[100] In addition, think carefully about the tone you use in writing your company's social media policy. Including the things that employees, users, and visitors to your site may do, rather than just mentioning what they are precluded from doing, can come appear as less dogmatic than a document that is a strict list of prohibitions.

Consider incorporating the following points into your social media policy:

- An explanation for why a policy is created in the first place (for example, to encourage the interaction between employees and customers, to enable community members to engage with each other about topics they're interested in, and to provide a safe place where people can support each other).

- An explanation for portions of a policy that may be controversial (for example, a real-names requirement for private community sites to build trust between members and to emphasize the importance of being accountable for one's statements).

- What platforms the policy covers (for example, the company's website, its social media channels, and employees' own social media channels when they are acting on behalf of their employer).

- What employees the policy covers (for example, full-time, part-time, nonunionized, and so on).

- Expressly state that the social media policy is not intended to interfere with employees' right to engage in protected speech.[101]

- The importance for employees to avoid conflicts of interest and the appearance of conflicts of interest (for example, journalists endorsing particular political candidates).

- The importance of revealing any relevant professional associations when commenting on social media or other websites, or otherwise participating in online communications (for example, working for a green energy company and sharing public opinions about the benefits of green energy over other energy sources).

- The importance for employees to adhere to existing laws and to consider bringing legal questions or concerns to their supervisor and/or the company's attorney.

- The importance for employees to try to correct any potentially damaging factual errors about the company that they make online (for example, posting the incorrect release date of a new product line).

- The importance for employees not to misuse their professional position for personal gain (for example, a restaurant employee offering to give a restaurant critic a free meal in exchange for keeping quiet about him propositioning the critic).

- What employee actions will be frowned upon (for example, making intentionally defamatory statements, expressing threatening behavior, revealing confidential corporate information except as otherwise protected by law, and stating intentional lies that can harm the company).

- What the consequences of an employee's violation of the organization's social media policy may be (for example, an official reprimand).

- What the consequences of a user's or visitor's violation of the organization's social media policy may be (for example, reprimand, and temporary or permanent loss of user privileges).

- A requirement that employees should make it apparent that the views expressed on their personal social media sites are their own and not those of their employer, unless clearly stated otherwise (see Figure 9.5).

Figure 9.5   *Ike Pigott clearly states that his Tweets represent his own views and not those of his employer*

- Any special expectations or requirements that the company or organization may have based on its respective industry (for example, certain categories of professionals such as lawyers, certified public accountants, and mental health professionals are required to adhere to codes of professional conduct).

Make sure you have an attorney review your social media policy before asking employees or online community members to adhere to it. The law is still evolving for social media usage, and you must have a knowledgeable attorney ensure your business is in compliance with all existing laws.

The National Labor Relations Board's Acting General Counsel Lafe Solomon released a report in May 2012[102] providing examples from actual corporate social media policies that are unlawful under the National Labor Relations Act.[103] Attorney Brian Heidelberger, chair of the Advertising, Marketing and Entertainment Law Practice at law firm Winston & Strawn LLP, explains that Solomon's report discusses the following impermissible actions: Prohibiting or restricting the "friending" of other employees, prohibiting employees from talking to their colleagues, prohibiting employees from writing about their company, prohibiting employees from talking to their colleagues, prohibiting employees from talking to their media, and prohibiting talking about inflammatory topics.[104]

Solomon also notes that simply adding a "savings" type clause[105] to a social media policy is insufficient.[106]

Meanwhile, Solomon held up Wal-Mart's Social Media Policy, dated May 4, 2012, as a positive example[107] and stated that its "entire revised social media policy—with examples of prohibited conduct—is lawful."[108] Wal-Mart's policy is posted in full in Solomon's May 2012 memo and includes, among others, sections titled, "Know and follow the rules, Be respectful, Be honest and accurate, Post only appropriate and respectful content and Retaliation is prohibited." [109] It also includes sections on using social media at work and employee parameters for talking to the media.[110] Solomon noted that Wal-Mart's "revised social media policy is not ambiguous because it provides sufficient examples of prohibited conduct so that, in context, employees would not reasonably read the rules to prohibit Section 7 activity.[111] Based on Solomon's analysis of Wal-Mart's policy, presumably the company's social media policy can be safely used as a framework for crafting your own policy (but make sure you customize it for your own company's needs).

Endnotes

1. "NASA Satellites Captire Hurricane Sandy's Massive Size," *ScienceDaily*, October 30, 2012. Link: http://www.sciencedaily.com/releases/2012/10/121030143216.htm.

2. Jonathan Watts, "Caribbean nations count cost of hurricane Sandy," *The Guardian*, October 29, 2012. Link: http://www.guardian.co.uk/world/2012/oct/29/caribbean-nations-hurricane-sandy.

3. Tim Hume, "Young brothers 'denied refuge,' swept to death by Sandy," CNN.com, November 3, 2012. Link: http://www.cnn.com/2012/11/02/world/americas/sandy-staten-island-brothers/index.html.

4. "Off-duty NYPD officer dies saving his family from Sandy," NBC News, October 31, 2012. Link: http://usnews.nbcnews.com/_news/2012/10/31/14835765-off-duty-nypd-officer-dies-saving-his-family-from-sandy?lite.

5. Associated Press, "Hurricane Sandy Estimated to Cost $60 Billion," Time, October 31, 1012. Link: http://business.time.com/2012/10/31/hurricane-sandy-estimated-to-cost-60-billion/.

6. "Hurricane Sandy Relief Resources" Facebook group. Link: https://www.facebook.com/HurricaneSandyReliefResources.

7. Gabi Ben-Yehuda, "Hurricane Sandy: How Government Uses Social Media for Disaster Response," Government Executive, October 26, 2012. Link: http://www.govexec.com/excellence/promising-practices/2012/10/hurricane-sandy-four-ways-government-uses-social-media-disaster-response/59052/.

8. Scott Van Camp, PR News, "During Sandy, Retailers Forget 'Audience First' PR Rule," PR News, October 31, 2012. Link:http://www.prnewsonline.com/free/During-Sandy-Retailers-Forget-Audience-First-PR-Rule_17320.html.

9. Screenshot of the Gap's October 29, 2012 Tweet of 14:32 taken by The Media Blog. Link: https://twitter.com/TheMediaTweets/status/263041834660532225/photo/1.

10. Connor Simpson and Rececca Greenfield, "The Worst Social Media Fails of Hurricane Sandy," *The Atlantic Wire*, October 30, 2012. Link: http://www.theatlanticwire.com/national/2012/10/worst-social-media-fails-hurricane-sandy/58515/.

11. Jenna Wortham, "On Twitter, Sifting Through Falsehoods in Critical Times," October 31, 2012. Link: http://www.nytimes.com/2012/11/01/technology/on-twitter-sifting-through-falsehoods-in-critical-times.html.

12. Doug Gross, "Man faces fallout for spreading false Sandy reports on Twitter," CNN, October 31, 2012. Link: http://www.cnn.com/2012/10/31/tech/social-media/sandy-twitter-hoax/index.html.

13. Jack Stuef, "The Man Behind @ComfortablySmug, Hurricane Sandy's Worst Twitter Villain," BuzzFeed, October 30, 2012. Link: http://www.buzzfeed.com/jackstuef/the-man-behind-comfortablysmug-hurricane-sandys.

14. Andrew Kaczynski, "How One Well-Connected Pseudonymous Twitter Spread Fake News About Hurricane Sandy," BuzzFeed Politics, October 30, 2012. Link: http://buzzfeedpolitics.tumblr.com/post/34623254677/how-one-well-connected-pseudonymous-twitter-spread.

15. Andrew Kaczynski, "How One Well-Connected Pseudonymous Twitter Spread Fake News About Hurricane Sandy," BuzzFeed Politics, October 30, 2012. Link: http://buzzfeedpolitics.tumblr.com/post/34623254677/how-one-well-connected-pseudonymous-twitter-spread.

16. Jenna Wortham, "On Twitter, Sifting Through Falsehoods in Critical Times," October 31, 2012. Link: http://www.nytimes.com/2012/11/01/technology/on-twitter-sifting-through-falsehoods-in-critical-times.html.

17. Arianne Cohen, "The Self-Obsessed, Emotionally Detached Hedge-Funder," New York Magazine, October 6, 2008. Link: http://nymag.com/daily/intel/2008/10/the_self-_obsessed_emotionally.html.

18. "The Curious Case of 'Comfortably Smug,'" New York Magazine, October 25, 2009. Link: http://nymag.com/daily/intel/2008/10/the_self-_obsessed_emotionally.html.

19. "Wight Condemns Actions of Former Campaign Manager," Wight 2012, October 31, 2012. Link: http://wight2012.com/wight-condemns-actions-of-former-campaign-manager/.

20. "Wight Announces New Campaign Manager," Wight 2012, October 30, 2012. Link: http://wight2012.com/wight-announces-new-campaign-manager/.

21. Heidi Moore, "Even a superstorm is no excuse for journalists not to check Twitter trolling," *The Guardian*, October 31, 2012. Link: http://www.guardian.co.uk/commentisfree/2012/oct/31/superstorm-journalists-check-twitter-troll.

22. Heidi Moore, "Even a superstorm is no excuse for journalists not to check Twitter trolling," *The Guardian*, October 31, 2012. Link: http://www.guardian.co.uk/commentisfree/2012/oct/31/superstorm-journalists-check-twitter-troll.

23. Heidi Moore, "Even a superstorm is no excuse for journalists not to check Twitter trolling," *The Guardian*, October 31, 2012. Link: http://www.guardian.co.uk/commentisfree/2012/oct/31/superstorm-journalists-check-twitter-troll.

24. Heidi Moore, "Even a superstorm is no excuse for journalists not to check Twitter trolling," *The Guardian*, October 31, 2012. Link: http://www.guardian.co.uk/commentisfree/2012/oct/31/superstorm-journalists-check-twitter-troll.

25. Andrew Kaczynski, "Councilman Pushes For Charges Against Twitter User Who Spread Falsehoods," BuzzFeed, October 30, 2012. Link: http://www.buzzfeed.com/andrewkaczynski/councilman-pushes-for-charges-against-twitter-user.

26. Andrew Kaczynski, "Councilman Pushes For Charges Against Twitter User Who Spread Falsehoods," BuzzFeed, October 30, 2012. Link: http://www.buzzfeed.com/andrewkaczynski/councilman-pushes-for-charges-against-twitter-user.

27. N.Y. PEN. LAW § 240.50 available at http://codes.lp.findlaw.com/nycode/PEN/THREE/N/240/240.50.

28. Comment left by Jeff John Robert on Jeff John Robert's article "Tweeting fake news in a crisis - illegal or just immoral?" Gigaom, October 30, 2012. Link: http://gigaom.com/2012/10/30/tweeting-fake-news-in-a-crisis-illegal-or-just-immoral/#comment-1131327.

29. Joe Palazzola, "Is Lying on Twitter a Crime?" *The Wall Street Journal*, November 5, 2012. Link: http://blogs.wsj.com/law/2012/11/05/is-lying-on-twitter-a-crime/.

30. United States V. Alvarez, 567 U.S. (2012).

31. United States V. Alvarez, 567 U.S. (2012).

32. Joe Palazzola, "Is Lying on Twitter a Crime?" *The Wall Street Journal*, November 5, 2012. Link: http://blogs.wsj.com/law/2012/11/05/is-lying-on-twitter-a-crime/.

33. Jessica Alan, "How Has The Internet Changed The Way We View Legal Ethics?" YouBlawg, April 27, 2012. Link: http://www.youblawg.com/law-blog-2/how-has-the-internet-changed-the-way-we-view-legal-ethics-2.

34. U.S. CONST. amend. I.

35. Henry Cohen, Legislative Attorney, "Freedom of Speech and Press: Exceptions to the First Amendment," Congressional Research Service, October 16, 2009.

36. *Miller v. California*, 413 U.S. 15, 27 (1973). *Miller* applies a three-pronged test that questions (a) whether the "average person applying contemporary community standards" would find that the work, taken as a whole, appeals to the prurient interest; (b) whether the work depicts or describes, in a patently offensive way, sexual conduct specifically defined by the applicable state law; and (c) whether the work, taken as a whole, lacks serious literary, artistic, political, or scientific value.

37. Henry Cohen, Legislative Attorney, "Freedom of Speech and Press: Exceptions to the First Amendment," Congressional Research Service, October 16, 2009, p. 13.

38. Henry Cohen, Legislative Attorney, "Freedom of Speech and Press: Exceptions to the First Amendment," Congressional Research Service, October 16, 2009, p. 3.

39. Henry Cohen, Legislative Attorney, "Freedom of Speech and Press: Exceptions to the First Amendment," Congressional Research Service, October 16, 2009, p. 3–4.

40. Henry Cohen, Legislative Attorney, "Freedom of Speech and Press: Exceptions to the First Amendment," Congressional Research Service, October 16, 2009, p. 4–5.

41. Henry Cohen, Legislative Attorney, "Freedom of Speech and Press: Exceptions to the First Amendment," Congressional Research Service, October 16, 2009, p. 4.

42. "Free Speech," Electronic Privacy Information Center. Link: http://epic.org/free_speech/.

43. Saul Levmore and Martha C. Nussbaum, eds., The Offensive Internet (Harvard University Press, 2010), p. 6.

44. Intentional Infliction of Emotional Distress is a civil wrong that contains the following elements: (1) the defendant must act intentionally or recklessly; (2) the defendant's conduct must be extreme and outrageous; and (3) the conduct must be the cause (4) of severe emotional distress. Link: http://www.law.cornell.edu/wex/intentional_infliction_of_emotional_distress.

45. Danielle Keats Citron, Cyber Civil Rights, 89 Boston University Law Review 61 (2009), p. 63. Link: http://digitalcommons.law.umaryland.edu/fac_pubs/613/.

46. Danielle Keats Citron, Cyber Civil Rights, 89 Boston University Law Review 61 (2009), p. 62. Link: http://digitalcommons.law.umaryland.edu/fac_pubs/613/.

47. Danielle Keats Citron, Cyber Civil Rights, 89 Boston University Law Review 61 (2009), p. 85. Link: http://digitalcommons.law.umaryland.edu/fac_pubs/613/.

48. Article 19 of the United Nations Universal Declaration of Human Rights. Link: http://www.un.org/en/documents/udhr/index.shtml.

49. "Freedom of Expression in Europe: Case-law concerning Article 10 of the European Convention on Human Rights," Council of Europe Publishing, March 2007, p. 6. Link: www.echr.coe.int/NR/rdonlyres/.../DG2ENHRFILES182007.pdf.

50. Owen, Bowcott, "Muhammad cartoons: how freedom of expression is curtailed across the globe," The Guardian, September 19, 2012. Link: http://www.guardian.co.uk/world/2012/sep/19/muhammad-cartoons-freedom-expression.

51. "Analysts See Double Standard in European Free Speech Laws," Voice of America, September 21, 2012. Link: http://www.voanews.com/content/analysts_double_standarts_in_european_free-speech_law/1512559.html.

52. Cameron Abadi, "Despite banning Nazi symbols, Germany's constitution and legal tradition complicate cases against neo-Nazis," MinnPost, February 16, 2010. Link: http://www.minnpost.com/global-post/2010/02/despite-banning-nazi-symbols-germanys-constitution-and-legal-tradition-complicat.

53. Nicholas Kulish, "Twitter Blocks Germans' Access to Neo-Nazi Group," October 18, 2012. Link: www.nytimes.com/2012/10/19/world/europe/twitter-blocks-access-to-neo-nazi-group-in-germany.html.

54. Henry Chu, "Britain's crackdown on Web comments sparks free-speech debate," November 8, 2012, *Los Angeles Times*. Link: http://articles.latimes.com/2012/nov/08/world/la-fg-britain-free-speech-20121109.

55. "What is the racial hatred act?" Australian Human Rights Commission. Link: http://www.humanrights.gov.au/racial_discrimination/media_guide/whatis.html.

56. "Mexico," *Freedom in the World 2012*, Freedom House. Link: http://www.freedomhouse.org/sites/default/files/Mexico%20draft.pdf.

57. "Philippine cybercrime law takes effect amid protests," BBC, October 3, 2012. Link: http://www.bbc.co.uk/news/technology-19810474.

58. "IPI Death Watch," International Press Institute. Link: http://www.freemedia.at/our-activities/death-watch.html.

59. Linton Weeks, "Privacy 2.0: We Are All Celebrities Now," NPR, April 26, 2011. Link: http://www.npr.org/2011/04/27/135538176/privacy-inc-we-are-all-celebrities-now.

60. "Laws held protect online harassers," SFGate, July 18, 2012. Link: http://www.sfgate.com/technology/dotcommentary/article/Laws-help-protect-online-harassers-3714726.php.

61. Mark J. MacDougal and Tommy Helsby, "The real price of reputation," *Gulf Magazine*, November 30, 2008, Vol. 13, Issue 9, p. 107. Link: www.akingump.com/files/Publication/.../106-107_Mark.pdf.

62. Geoffrey R. Nussbaum, "Privacy, the First Amendment, and the Internet," in Saul Levmore and Martha C. Nussbaum, eds., *The Offensive Internet* (Harvard University Press, 2010), p. 175.

63. Geoffrey R. Nussbaum, "Privacy, the First Amendment, and the Internet," in Saul Levmore and Martha C. Nussbaum, eds., *The Offensive Internet* (Harvard University Press, 2010), p. 175.

64. Brian Leiter, "Cleaning Cyber-Cesspools: Google and Free Speech," in Saul Levmore and Martha C. Nussbaum, eds., *The Offensive Internet* (Harvard University Press, 2010), p. 155.

65. "NSA's secretive surveillance program goes to the Supreme Court," RT, October 26, 2012. Link: http://rt.com/usa/news/surveillance-fisa-supreme-wiretap-324/.

66. Gerry Smith, "Why David Petraeus' Email Troubles Should Make You Nervous," *Huffington Post*, November 14, 2012. Link: http://www.huffingtonpost.com/2012/11/14/petraeus-scandal-protecting-private-emails_n_2129905.html?utm_hp_ref=technology.

67. Gerry Smith, "Why David Petraeus' Email Troubles Should Make You Nervous," *Huffington Post*, November 14, 2012. Link: http://www.huffingtonpost.com/2012/11/14/petraeus-scandal-protecting-private-emails_n_2129905.html?utm_hp_ref=technology.

68. "Fact Sheet 18: Online Privacy: Using the Internet Safely," Privacy Rights Clearinghouse. Link: https://www.privacyrights.org/fs/fs18-cyb.htm#Nonprofit.

69. "Fact Sheet 18: Online Privacy: Using the Internet Safely," Privacy Rights Clearinghouse. Link: https://www.privacyrights.org/fs/fs18-cyb.htm#Nonprofit.

70. Julie E. Cohen, draft, "What Privacy is For," November 5, 2012, p. 2, forthcoming in 126 HARV. L. REV. _ (2013). Link: www.harvardlawreview.org/symposium/papers2012/cohen.pdf.

71. Julie E. Cohen, draft, "What Privacy is For," November 5, 2012, p. 1, forthcoming in 126 HARV. L. REV. _ (2013). Link: www.harvardlawreview.org/symposium/papers2012/cohen.pdf.

72. Daniel J. Solove, draft essay "Privacy Self-Management and the Consent Paradox," p. 2, available at Social Science Research Network, November 4, 2012, forthcoming in 126 HARV. L. REV. _ (2013). Link: http://ssrn.com/abstract=2171018.

73. Daniel J. Solove, draft essay "Privacy Self-Management and the Consent Paradox," p. 2, available at Social Science Research Network, November 4, 2012, forthcoming in 126 HARV. L. REV. _ (2013). Link: http://ssrn.com/abstract=2171018.

74. Comment by Daniel Solove on November 6, 2012 at 5:53 p.m. left on Daniel Solove, "Harvard Law review Symposium on Privacy & Technology," Concurring Opinions, November 5, 2012. Link: http://www.concurringopinions.com/archives/2012/11/harvard-law-review-symposium-on-privacy-technology.html.

75. Comment by Daniel Solove on November 7, 2012 at 12:48 a.m. left on Daniel Solove, "Harvard Law review Symposium on Privacy & Technology," Concurring Opinions, November 5, 2012. Link: http://www.concurringopinions.com/archives/2012/11/harvard-law-review-symposium-on-privacy-technology.html.

76. Jay Stanley, "Q&A with Daniel Solove on How Bad Security Arguments Are Undermining Our Privacy Rights," Blog of Rights, ACLU, July 14, 2011. Link: http://www.aclu.org/blog/technology-and-liberty/qa-daniel-solove-how-bad-security-arguments-are-undermining-our-privacy.

77. Text of the Communications Decency Act of 1996. Link: http://thomas.loc.gov/cgi-bin/query/F?c104:1:./temp/~c104pJaZJq:e253753:.

78. "47 USC § 230 - Protection for private blocking and screening of offensive material," Legal Information Institute, Cornell University Law School. Link: http://www.law.cornell.edu/uscode/text/47/230.

79. "47 USC § 230 - Protection for private blocking and screening of offensive material," Legal Information Institute, Cornell University Law School. Link: http://www.law.cornell.edu/uscode/text/47/230.

80. "Section 230 Protections," Legal Guide for Bloggers, Electronic Frontier Foundation. Link: https://www.eff.org/issues/bloggers/legal/liability/230.

81. "Immunity for Online Publishers Under the Communications Decency Act," Citizen Media Law Project, Berkman Center for Internet & Society. Link: http://www.citmedialaw.org/legal-guide/immunity-online-publishers-under-communications-decency-act.

82. "Immunity for Online Publishers Under the Communications Decency Act," Citizen Media Law Project, Berkman Center for Internet & Society. Link: http://www.citmedialaw.org/legal-guide/immunity-online-publishers-under-communications-decency-act.

83. "Online Activities Not Covered by Section 230," Citizen Media Law Project, Berkman Center for Internet & Society. Link: http://www.citmedialaw.org/legal-guide/online-activities-not-covered-section-230.

84. This activity refers to the case Fair Housing Council of San Fernando Valley v. Roommates.com, CV-04-56916 (9th Cir. 2008) where users of the website Rommates.com had to indicate whether they were willing to live with male or female roommates who were straight or gay. See discussion in "Online Activities Not Covered by Section 230," Citizen Media Law Project, Berkman Center for Internet & Society. Link: http://www.citmedialaw.org/legal-guide/online-activities-not-covered-section-230.

85. "Online Activities Not Covered by Section 230," Citizen Media Law Project, Berkman Center for Internet & Society. Link: http://www.citmedialaw.org/legal-guide/online-activities-not-covered-section-230.

86. Nancy S. Kim, "Website Proprietorship and Online Harassment," 2009 UTAH L. REV. 993, p. 997. Link: http://papers.ssrn.com/sol3/papers.cfm?abstract_id=1354466.

87. Nancy S. Kim, "Website Proprietorship and Online Harassment," 2009 UTAH L. REV. 993, p. 1014. Link: http://papers.ssrn.com/sol3/papers.cfm?abstract_id=1354466.

88. Nancy S. Kim, "Website Proprietorship and Online Harassment," 2009 UTAH L. REV. 993, p. 997. Link: http://papers.ssrn.com/sol3/papers.cfm?abstract_id=1354466.

89. Nancy S. Kim, "Website Proprietorship and Online Harassment," 2009 UTAH L. REV. 993, p. 997–998. Link: http://papers.ssrn.com/sol3/papers.cfm?abstract_id=1354466.

90. Nancy S. Kim, "Website Proprietorship and Online Harassment," 2009 UTAH L. REV. 993, p. 1013. Link: http://papers.ssrn.com/sol3/papers.cfm?abstract_id=1354466.

91. Nancy S. Kim, "Website Proprietorship and Online Harassment," 2009 UTAH L. REV. 993, p. 1015–1016. Link: http://papers.ssrn.com/sol3/papers.cfm?abstract_id=1354466.

92. Nancy S. Kim, "Website Proprietorship and Online Harassment," 2009 UTAH L. REV. 993, p. 1027, 1034. Link: http://papers.ssrn.com/sol3/papers.cfm?abstract_id=1354466.

93. Dan Oakes, "Google hit with $200,000 damages bill over Mokbel shots," *The Sydney Morning Herald*, November 12, 2012. Link: http://www.smh.com.au/technology/technology-news/google-hit-with-200000-damages-bill-over-mokbel-shots-20121112-297gk.html.

94. "Australian wins $208k from Google for defamation," PhysOrg, November 12, 2012. Link: http://phys.org/news/2012-11-australian-208k-google-defamation.html.

95. "Australian wins $208k from Google for defamation," PhysOrg, November 12, 2012. Link: http://phys.org/news/2012-11-australian-208k-google-defamation.html.

96. Dan Oakes, Google hit with $200,000 damages bill over Mokbel shots," *The Sydney Morning Herald*, November 12, 2012. Link: http://www.smh.com.au/technology/technology-news/google-hit-with-200000-damages-bill-over-mokbel-shots-20121112-297gk.html.

97. Dan Oakes, Google hit with $200,000 damages bill over Mokbel shots," *The Sydney Morning Herald*, November 12, 2012. Link: http://www.smh.com.au/technology/technology-news/google-hit-with-200000-damages-bill-over-mokbel-shots-20121112-297gk.html.

98. "Australian wins $208k from Google for defamation," PhysOrg, November 12, 2012. Link: http://phys.org/news/2012-11-australian-208k-google-defamation.html.

99. Lance Goddard, "Does Your Social Media Policy Pass Muster With the NLRB? Take the Test...," Social Media today, October 2, 2012. Link: http://socialmediatoday.com/index.php?q=lggodard/866571/does-your-social-media-policy-pass-muster-nlrb-take-test.

100. Lance Goddard, "Does Your Social Media Policy Pass Muster With the NLRB? Take the Test...," Social Media today, October 2, 2012. Link: http://socialmediatoday.com/index.php?q=lggodard/866571/does-your-social-media-policy-pass-muster-nlrb-take-test.

101. Lance Goddard, "Does Your Social Media Policy Pass Muster With the NLRB? Take the Test...," Social Media today, October 2, 2012. Link: http://socialmediatoday.com/index.php?q=lggodard/866571/does-your-social-media-policy-pass-muster-nlrb-take-test.

102. Memorandum OM 12-59, Report of the Acting General Counsel on the National Labor Relations Board Concerning Social Media Cases, May 30, 2012. Link: http://www.scribd.com/doc/95479772/NLRB-on-social-media.

103. Mary Swanton, "NLRB memo offers social media policy guidance," Inside Counsel, July 31, 2012. Link: http://www.insidecounsel.com/2012/07/31/nlrb-memo-offers-social-media-policy-guidance?t=technology.

104. Brian Heidelberger, "Eight Ways Your Employee Social-Media Policy May Violate Federal Law," Ad Age, June 12, 2012. Link: http://adage.com/article/digitalnext/employee-social-media-policy-violate-federal-law/235313/.

105. Definition of "Savings Clause," *The Law Dictionary*. Link: http://thelawdictionary.org/saving-clause/.

106. The text reads: "we looked at the Employer's 'savings clause': National Labor Relations Act. This policy will not be construed or applied in a manner that improperly interferes with employees' rights under the National Labor Relations Act. We found that this clause does not cure the otherwise unlawful provisions of the Employer's social media policy because employees would not understand from this disclaimer that protected activities are in fact permitted." Memorandum OM 12-59, Report of the Acting General Counsel on the National Labor Relations Board Concerning Social Media Cases, May 30, 2012, p. 12. Link: http://www.scribd.com/doc/95479772/NLRB-on-social-media.

107. Sec. 7. [§ 157.] RIGHTS OF EMPLOYEES of the National Labor Relations Act states: "Employees shall have the right to self-organization, to form, join, or assist labor organizations, to bargain collectively through representatives of their own choosing, and to engage in other concerted activities for the purpose of collective bargaining or other mutual aid or protection, and shall also have the right to refrain from any or all such activities except to the extent that such right may be affected by an agreement

requiring membership in a labor organization as a condition of employment as authorized in section 8(a)(3) [section 158(a)(3) of this title]." Link: http://www.nlrb. gov/national-labor-relations-act.

108. Memorandum OM 12-59, Report of the Acting General Counsel on the National Labor Relations Board Concerning Social Media Cases, May 30, 2012, p. 19. Link: http://www. scribd.com/doc/95479772/NLRB-on-social-media.

109. Memorandum OM 12-59, Report of the Acting General Counsel on the National Labor Relations Board Concerning Social Media Cases, May 30, 2012, p. 22-24. Link: http://www.scribd.com/doc/95479772/NLRB-on-social-media.

110. Memorandum OM 12-59, Report of the Acting General Counsel on the National Labor Relations Board Concerning Social Media Cases, May 30, 2012, p. 22-24. Link: http://www.scribd.com/doc/95479772/NLRB-on-social-media.

111. Sec. 7. [§ 157.] RIGHTS OF EMPLOYEES of the National Labor Relations Act states: "Employees shall have the right to self-organization, to form, join, or assist labor organizations, to bargain collectively through representatives of their own choosing, and to engage in other concerted activities for the purpose of collective bargaining or other mutual aid or protection, and shall also have the right to refrain from any or all such activities except to the extent that such right may be affected by an agreement requiring membership in a labor organization as a condition of employment as authorized in section 8(a)(3) [section 158(a)(3) of this title]." Link: http://www.nlrb. gov/national-labor-relations-act.

10

30-Day Plan for Better Conflict Management Online

Putting Knowledge into Action

Serial entrepreneur and environmentalist Paul Hawken said, "If we see only the worst, it destroys our capacity to do something. If we remember those times and places—and there are so many—where people have behaved magnificently, this gives us the energy to act, and at least the possibility of sending this spinning top of a world in a different direction."[1]

Hawken's words are relevant to the online world, where you see both the best and the worst of humanity expressed. But if you've read this book, it's clear you're not willing to turn a blind eye to the egregious behavior found online—you want to make things better! And after reading the previous nine chapters, you're no doubt eager to roll up your sleeves and get to work applying what you've learned. But how exactly do you do that? This chapter provides the answers. It lays out a 30-day plan for better conflict management online that includes everything you need to do. Keep in mind that if you're part of a larger or more complex business, it may take a bit longer to complete all the steps, but regardless, at the end of 30 days, you'll be well on your way! Ready to start?

Day 1: Start Your Conflict Inventory and Assessment

This is the first step and one of the most important ones you'll take because it sets the foundation for everything that comes later. Get it right and you'll have invaluable information to work with. The goal is to take a careful look at your existing conflict culture, collect your past and current online conflict history, review the data, analyze it to identify where your greatest risk factors are, and determine your areas for improvement and growth. Go through the following items and answer them to the best of your ability. Some of them you'll recognize from Chapter 8: "Into the Trenches: Conflict Resolution Skills and Strategies." Perhaps not all the items are applicable to your business, and perhaps there are other items you think are important that you'd like to add. Although the following list is comprehensive, use it as a guideline only in completing your organization's conflict inventory and assessment.

- ☐ Examine your organization's culture and its view toward conflict. Ask the following questions:
  - Is the organization's approach proactive or reactive? If it is a combination, what affects whether the approach is proactive or reactive?
  - Is conflict viewed as something to be avoided, as an inevitable part of doing business, or beneficial in certain circumstances to foster growth?
  - What is the overall approach toward conflict taken by the company's executives and leaders?
  - How is the view toward conflict reflected? Is it memorialized in written policies, or is it just communicated via behavioral examples?

- ☐ Is there one main conflict management approach that the organization uses or several, depending on the situation and circumstances?
  - What is it/are they?
  - How is it/are they applied?
  - Who decides how it is/they are applied?
  - Has the conflict management approach been successful in the past and if so, to what do you attribute this?

- ☐ Are there already formal and articulated processes in place to deal with conflict, or is conflict dealt with ad hoc?
  - What is it/are they?
  - Are they in writing?
  - Are they easily accessible and reviewable by all employees?
  - Are employees informed of these processes when they join the organization?

- Are these processes part of a formal conflict resolution system, or are they loosely associated?
- How is the conflict management process(es) applied?
- Who decides how it should be applied?

☐ Does the organization already have specific processes in place for dealing with online disputes and conflicts?

- What are they?
- Are they in writing?
- Are they easily accessible and reviewable by all employees?
- Are employees informed of these processes when they join the organization?
- Are these processes part of a formal conflict resolution system, or are they loosely associated?

☐ Is there already a formal conflict management training program for online disputes in place at the organization?

- Is the program comprehensive?
- How long has it been running?
- Who designed the program? Was it someone knowledgeable in conflict management and online communications?
- Is participation mandatory or voluntary?
- Who is required to/allowed to take the training?
- Who leads the training? Is it someone knowledgeable in conflict management and online communications?
- Has the program been successful? In what way has this success been determined (for example, reduced number of disputes between employees or better conflict resolution skills in dealing with the public)?

☐ What types of online disputes have you been involved in online? If there were only a few disputes, list them all, and if there were many, list the most frequent, severe, and important ones.

- Interpersonal conflict
- Intellectual property disputes
- Disputes about differing values
- Disputes about differing interests
- Disputes about process or procedures
- Legal issues

- ☐ How frequent have the disputes been?
  - Daily
  - Weekly
  - Monthly
  - Variable depending on disputes

- ☐ Who was involved in the disputes?
  - Individuals
  - Were these prominent or influential individuals?
  - Groups
  - Were these important or influential groups?
  - Were there any repeat occurrences with particular individuals or groups?

- ☐ Who initiated the disputes?
  - Mostly you
  - Mostly your organization
  - Mostly the other side
  - It varied

- ☐ Were the disputes resolved?
  - What percentage?
  - Were the most serious disputes resolved?
  - The disputes are ongoing.

- ☐ How were the disputes resolved?
  - Yes, through apology
  - Yes, through financial incentive (for example, exchange or coupon)
  - Yes, by initiating legal communication from an attorney
  - Yes, by filing a lawsuit and settling before trial
  - Yes, by filing a lawsuit and winning in court
  - The disputes went away on their own after a while

- ☐ How long did it take before the disputes were resolved?
  - Hours
  - Days
  - Weeks
  - Ongoing
  - Variable (Describe what this was based on.)

☐   Were there any negative outcomes for you as a result of the disputes?

- Negative publicity
- Reputation loss
- Defamation
- Intellectual property infringement
- Lost opportunity costs
- Lost customers/clients
- Staff/employee loss
- Market share loss
- Legal repercussions
- Lost time and money
- Other

☐   Were you able to recover from the negative effects of the disputes?

- Yes
- No (Provide details)
- There were no long-term negative effects
- There were no negative effects

☐   How long did recovery from the negative effects of the disputes take?

- A few days
- A few weeks
- A few months
- Several years
- Don't know yet, still ongoing

Day 2: Identify Your Greatest Online Conflict Concerns

The assessment you started on Day 1 can help you identify your top conflict concerns. In some cases your concerns may overlap—damage to reputation, for example, often leads to financial harm. Be as clear and detailed as possible when itemizing your concerns because this can help you clarify your conflict management goals, which you'll work on during Day 4.

☐   Negative publicity

☐   Reputation loss

- ☐ Defamation
- ☐ Intellectual property infringement
- ☐ Lost opportunity costs
- ☐ Lost customers/clients
- ☐ Staff/employee loss
- ☐ Market share loss
- ☐ Legal repercussions
- ☐ Lost time and money
- ☐ Other

Day 3: Measure Your Existing Digital Footprint

To take inventory of your existing online presence, you need to examine the sites and the profiles you've created about your company and yourself, the ones created about you and your company by others, and the sentiment of the various sites or discussions taking place about your company and you, as well as their accuracy, weight, and importance.

- ☐ List all the websites you've created and any other sites that carry your name.
- ☐ Make a list of all the social media sites you use.
- ☐ Make a list of all the discussion boards and forums you participate in. (If you are a business, you may be using your business name, but more likely a designated person will be posting and commenting on your business's behalf, identifying themselves as speaking on behalf of the organization.)
- ☐ Make a comprehensive list of all the places you're possibly mentioned online. (Start by putting your or your business's name into all the major search engines to see what comes up, checking up to the first 10 pages, and making sure to do so both while logged into and out of any Google products such as Gmail, Google calendar, or YouTube.)
- ☐ Check the images and videos featured on search engines to see if you or your company are mentioned (search engines Google, Yahoo, Bing; image search engine Imagery at http://elzr.com/imagery; the photo sharing sites Flickr and Photobucket, and websites such as Ask.com;[2] and the video sharing sites YouTube, Metacafe, Vimeo, Dailymotion, Viddler, Revver and blip.tv).
- ☐ Check the discussion boards and forums that cover your particular industry to see if you or your company are mentioned, starting with Bog Boards and Boardtracker.

☐ Check the consumer review sites to see if you or your company are mentioned, including Angie's List, Epinions, Shopping.com, Amazon.com, the Better Business Bureau, Yelp, TripAdvisor, and any industry-specific consumer sites that are relevant to you.

☐ Check online complaint sites to see if you or your company are mentioned (Complaints Board, Pissed Consumer, iRipoff.com, and Ripoff Report, and specialized ones such as Unhappy Franchisee or Bitterwaitress.com).

☐ Check people search directories and data aggregation sites for your name and those of your company's key executives or public-facing employees (Spokeo, PeopleFinders, Intelius, US Search, iSearch, Pipl, and GovRecordsAccess).

☐ Check the comments sections of your hometown or regional newspaper for your name to see if someone may have written about you, as well as "hyper local" sites that focus on particular areas, communities, or neighborhoods.

☐ After you collect all the information found about you or your business online, determine if the information is positive, neutral, or negative. Ideally, it will be mostly neutral and positive; although, if you are a business or a prominent individual, it's likely that someone has made negative comments or otherwise posted negative information about you somewhere online.

Day 4: Start Identifying Your Online Conflict Management Goals

It's safe to assume that your overall goal is to reduce the number and intensity of your online conflicts, but you need to be more specific than that. The more concrete you can be about your goals, the better. This can help you identify and earmark the necessary resources, get the required support, and start planning how you'll go about things. Use the acronym S.M.A.R.T. to help you, which stands for specific, measurable, attainable, relevant, and time-bound. Your goals should be specific, namely clear and detailed, and provide answers to the questions of who, what, where, when, and so on. They should be measurable, which will help you evaluate whether you've been successful in your efforts. The goals should be attainable and realistic, which means they can be ambitious but shouldn't be out of reach. They should also be relevant and fit into your company's larger mission. Finally, your goals should be time-bound with clear schedules and deadlines. Look over the following items to help you start. Because circumstances may change in the future, you should periodically review your goals to make sure they're still applicable to your situation.

☐ Is your goal to prevent online conflicts? Which types of online disputes do you believe can be prevented?

- [ ] Is your goal to manage online conflicts? Which types of online disputes do you believe can be better managed?

- [ ] Is your goal to help your business become more proactive instead of reactive about online conflict?

- [ ] Is your goal to get your organization to view conflict management as a business process?

- [ ] Is your goal to reduce the company's cost associated with online conflict?

- [ ] Is your goal to have your staff, especially those like customer service representatives or social media professionals, well trained in online conflict management processes?

- [ ] Is your goal to reduce employee turnover due to online conflict? By how much within what time frame?

- [ ] Is your goal to reduce the risk of reputational harm?

- [ ] Is your goal to reduce your company's risk of legal exposure?

- [ ] Is your goal to improve your relationship with clients/customers?

- [ ] Is your goal to create a better working environment between your employees?

- [ ] Is your goal to improve your reputation within the community or industry?

- [ ] Is your goal to make simple changes within the organization to see how they work and then introduce additional processes, or is your goal to institute a complete top-to-bottom approach to improved online conflict management?

Day 5: Identify Your Internal Champions

If you're a key decision maker within your organization and are interested in proactively managing online conflict, that's wonderful. You can eliminate some of the hurdles right away. But in many situations, other people lead the business, and you must convince them that your ideas about conflict management are beneficial to the organization and worth the time and financial investment. As with any new initiative or change, there is likely to be resistance on the part of some individuals who either want to maintain the status quo or who raise ongoing objections about why change is a bad idea, isn't feasible, and so forth. To prepare yourself for this possibility, it's critical that you identify an internal champion, someone besides yourself, who wants to help create and get behind a robust online conflict management system. Ideally, this individual has enough influence within the organization to get the attention of key decision makers or is already in a position in which her work involves policy creation. This might be someone within the human resources department, a risk manager, a public relations professional, a customer service manager or an in-house attorney. However, anyone who is committed to the idea and who is willing to advocate for it within the company will be a strong asset.

Day 6: Get Buy-in from Leadership

After you identify your online conflict management goals and find an internal champion, the next step is to get buy-in from the organization's leadership. These are the people who ultimately have to sign off on any resources needed to create or implement your ideas about training, policies, technical support, staff allocation, hiring, and other items. Explaining the long-term benefits to the organization, along with a timeline and cost estimates for rolling out your suggestions, can increase your chances of getting the necessary approval.

Day 7: Get Human Resources's Buy-In

To hope for any level of success, the conflict management processes and training you want to implement must be aligned with the values of the human resources department. HR's role covers a broad range of responsibilities, which include hiring and associated personnel functions, ensuring cost and quality controls, legal compliance management, and employee training. In other words, HR is tasked with ensuring that the execution of administrative functions goes smoothly. But HR can also be a strategic partner in the creation of a civil work environment. Because one of its traditional roles is employee training, the human resources department can spearhead the implementation of staff training programs about online conflict management and help measure and track their success.

Day 8: Identify the Stakeholders and Key Personnel You'll Need

As previously mentioned, introducing any new idea, even a good one such as more effectively managing online conflict, sometimes meets with skepticism or even resistance. Having an internal champion on your side, as well as buy-in from the company's leadership and human resources, is vital. But there are others whose support and assistance you also need. Depending on the size of your organization and its industry focus, these may include some of the individuals listed here.

- ☐ Social media manager/team
- ☐ Public relations manager/team
- ☐ Online community manager
- ☐ Risk management team

- ☐ Legal team
- ☐ Department heads
- ☐ Supervisors
- ☐ Customer service manager

Day 9: Identify the Financial Resources You Need

Regardless of the benefits that reduced online conflict bring, there are initial costs associated with getting there. You must accurately identify what these are so you can make sure you have the necessary resources or can create a plan for getting them. Many of the costs associated with online conflict management involve service costs—in other words the time for either an internal expert or an outside consultant to design and implement the necessary components. However, the cost investment can pay for itself many times over in reduced online conflict and associated costs, a better working environment, lowered employee turnover, and so forth.

- ☐ Buying domain names.
- ☐ Cost for yearly use of certain social media services.
- ☐ Signing up with an online monitoring service.
- ☐ Signing up with a sentiment analysis service.
- ☐ Hiring an administrator for your social media properties, or allocating time for an internal employee to do so. (Calculate the number of hours a week this will take and multiply by 52 weeks to determine the yearly cost.)
- ☐ Having an attorney on retainer.
- ☐ Time cost for creating robust internal social media policies or reviewing existing ones.
- ☐ Time cost for creating robust social media policies or reviewing existing ones for your external-facing social media properties.
- ☐ Time cost for creating your company website's "dark site."
- ☐ Cost for developing your company's conflict management training program. (This can include time cost for internal professionals and costs for hiring external consultants and specialists.)
- ☐ Time costs for training your staff.
- ☐ Time costs for training your public-facing staff in front-line conflict management skills.

☐ Cost for developing your company's crisis management plan. (This can include time cost for internal professionals and costs for hiring external consultants and specialists.)

☐ Time costs for training your crisis management team.

Day 10: Claim Your Online Identity

As mentioned in Chapter 2: "Why Your Online Reputation and Privacy Matter," it is vital to claim your online identity. If you don't, you run the risk that someone else will do it. Review the list of items here and add any others you feel are applicable to your business.

☐ Buy the domain names for your business, including .com, .net, .org, .biz, and others.

☐ Buy the major negative domain names for your business, including .com, .net, .org, .biz. and others (for example, YourBusinessNameSucks.com)

☐ Consider registering your domain names, particularly the ones that you are purchasing to protect yourself from reputational smears, under a private domain registration. (See GoDaddy's information at http://www.godaddy.com/domainaddon/private-registration.aspx.)

☐ When you buy your domain names, set them to auto renew, so your names don't lapse and someone hijacks them.

☐ If you are an individual, register your username on the major email providers, social networking sites, message boards, and forums that are personally or professionally relevant to you.

☐ Sign up with Facebook.

☐ Sign up with Twitter—main Twitter handle and "smear" iterations.

☐ Sign up with LinkedIn.

☐ Sign up with Google+.

☐ Sign up with YouTube.

☐ Sign up with Pinterest. (This is becoming an increasingly popular social networking site.)

☐ Sign up with Flickr—main Twitter handle and "smear" iterations.

☐ Consider signing up with other sites such as Bebo, Quora, Reddit, and Diigo.

☐ Consider other social networking sites relevant to your business or industry.

☐ As a business, get listed in online search directories (for example, Ask.com, Yellowpages.com, Whitepages, Switchboard, CitySearch, Local.com, ThinkLocal, Mapquest, and BizJournals.com).

Day 11: Choose an Online Monitoring Tool

After you measure your existing digital footprint and claim your online identity, you need to continue monitoring your online reputation. The best way to do this is by choosing an online monitoring tool that meets your specific needs. There are several available, both free and payment-based, with different levels of functionality. Research each one and decide which is best for you.

- ☐ Google Alerts
- ☐ Mention (https://en.mention.net)
- ☐ CustomScoop
- ☐ Trackur
- ☐ Radian6
- ☐ Attensity
- ☐ Simplify360
- ☐ Visible Technologies
- ☐ Bandwatch
- ☐ Sysomos

Day 12: Set Up an Online Conflict Tracking System

Set up an online conflict tracking system that regularly collects background information and generates a monthly report on your online conflict status. This report can help you determine your specific problem areas, and whether you're making progress in meeting your online conflict management goals. If you use an online monitoring tool, some of the supporting data may already be compiled for you. You can research commercial conflict tracking products or set up a simple spreadsheet-style system on your own. The minimum data points that should be entered into the spreadsheet include the following.

- ☐ Date
- ☐ Type of dispute
- ☐ Online location of the dispute
- ☐ Length of the dispute
- ☐ Parties involved
- ☐ Who initiated the dispute (you or the other side)
- ☐ Status of the dispute
- ☐ Disposition of the dispute

☐ Who managed the dispute on your side

☐ Whether the dispute required legal intervention

☐ Whether law enforcement became involved

☐ Public relations effect of the dispute

☐ Your reputational cost of the dispute

☐ Financial (both direct and indirect) cost of the dispute

☐ Time cost of the dispute

Day 13: Set Up Your Social Media Sites

On Day 10, you signed up for the major social networking sites. Now it's time to set up your profile. It is fine to show personality, but be careful with posting profanity, questionable images, or pornography. Remember that your social media sites are your online calling cards.

☐ Brief description or tagline about you.

☐ A link to your company website or, if applicable, your personal website.

☐ A way to get in touch with you.

☐ Your social media or commenting policy.

☐ Your privacy policies for social networking sites, forums, and other online properties

☐ Decide how often you'll post content.

☐ Decide what criteria you'll use in responding to those that negatively comment about you on your social media sites or website.

☐ Decide what criteria you'll use in responding to those who negatively comment about others on your social media sites or website.

Day 14: Create Your Company's Social Media Policy or Review Your Existing One

As discussed in Chapter 9, "Legal Aspects of Online Disputes and Conflicts," in the section "Drafting Robust and Legal Social Media Policies," it's vital that you have a strong social media policy in place that addresses how your employees and also how you'll deal with users or visitors to your website and social media properties. Given the importance of social media policies and the unsettled law around their enforceability, it's vital that you ask an attorney to either help you draft a policy or review your existing one.

Day 15: Hire Someone to Manage Your Social Media Properties

Hire someone who can devote the necessary time to managing and monitoring your social media properties and online community. You probably don't want a volunteer in charge of managing your brand online, and similarly, you probably shouldn't ask an intern to manage your social media properties (although they can assist a designated professional in managing the sites). The person you hire should be a seasoned professional with strong communication and social media skills, be someone who has the bandwidth to oversee the sites even in the evening or during nontraditional hours (after all, the Internet doesn't sleep), and someone who is comfortable in crisis situations. Before you hire someone to manage your sites—in effect managing an important part of your online presence and therefore reputation—make sure you've checked out his own online presence to see if any warning signs crop up.

Day 16: Hire an Attorney

If you already have an existing relationship with an attorney, or have an in-house attorney, that's great. If not, sign a retainer agreement with an attorney so you have immediate access to her if a legal question or problem crops up. You don't want to find yourself already in a jam and suddenly also having to scramble to find someone who can help you. Your attorney needs to be knowledgeable about social media and how the online communications culture operates. She may have to deal with First Amendment issues as they pertain to online communications, civil rights issues, employment law, privacy law, intellectual property issues, tort law, and a host of other areas.

Day 17: Determine Whether You Need to Bury or Remove Negative Information

Depending on the type or amount of negative information about you online, it may not be worth the effort of trying to bury or get it removed from websites and major search engines. However, in other situations, if negative information about you online is having a damaging effect on you personally or professionally, taking action is critical.

- ☐ What is the negative information?
- ☐ Where is the negative information posted? Is it posted on a legitimate news site, on a consumer review or complaint site, or a gossip site? Your chances of successfully asking a website to remove the negative information is greater

when the website isn't a gossip or consumer complaint site, which makes advertising money from high readership and therefore has an incentive to provide a forum for negative, outrageous, or salacious content.

- [ ] Is the negative information showing up on the first two pages of the major search engines?
- [ ] Did the information contain images that were posted against your will or without your consent?
- [ ] Does the posted information violate your privacy? (Check with an attorney.)
- [ ] Is the information posted in any way a copyright violation? (Check with an attorney.)
- [ ] What is the size of the readership of the negative information? In other words, is the website where it is posted heavily trafficked?
- [ ] Is the negative information believable, or is it clear that it's satire, fabricated, or conjecture?
- [ ] Is the negative information protected by the First Amendment? (Check with an attorney.)
- [ ] If the negative information is defamatory, consult with an attorney.
- [ ] Have you suffered any negative repercussions, such as being fired, losing clients, or losing business opportunities?
- [ ] Does the information contain threats to your safety and well-being or that of your family? Have you contacted law enforcement about it?
- [ ] Have you already contacted the website and search engines and politely asked them to remove the content?
- [ ] Is the negative information posted on a website registered in the United States, or is it registered in another jurisdiction not subject to U.S. laws?
- [ ] If you are an individual, see if you can bury the negative content. (Try the free online tool BrandYourself.com.)
- [ ] If you need more serious help or are a business, consider hiring a professional company to bury negative content (for example, Reputation.com, Reputation Changer, and Reputation Hawk).
- [ ] If the negative information is defamatory, violates your privacy rights, is a threat to your identity, or represents an intentional infliction of emotional distress (the conduct must go beyond merely offensive or hurtful), consult with an attorney who can advise you on your legal options.

Day 18: Start Developing Your Company's Online Conflict Management Training

Nearly everyone is online, and in those rare cases where they're not, their colleagues, employees, friends, and others who know and talk about them are. Online conflict is an unavoidable part of your daily life, but how effectively you manage it is up to you. In today's business environment, it's therefore imperative that a company's employees be trained in basic online communication and conflict management skills. Although some of the training is the same as it would be in a traditional conflict management program, you must remember that in the online world, communication is faster, more intense, often has a shorter timeframe between initial action and reaction, is not retractable, and is global in its dissemination. The person who designs the training should be aware of all the differences between online and offline conflict and how these play out in an amplified medium. When designing and developing your training program, consider the following points.

- ☐ Be clear about what you hope to achieve with the training, whether it is an improved working environment or a reduced number of online disputes that negatively affect your reputation.

- ☐ Decide who will receive the training, whether it will be all employees (which is recommended) or only public-facing ones.

- ☐ Decide what particular elements to include in the training, such as

  - Helping people understand the amplified nature of online versus offline communication

  - Teaching basic elements of conflict resolution, such as the difference between positions, needs, and values

  - Helping people identify their own conflict style

  - Helping people learn how to deal with those who have a different conflict style

  - Teaching active listening skills in a largely text-based environment

  - Teaching people how to keep their cool when dealing with angry clients or customers

  - Helping people understand what their responsibilities toward the organization are online

  - Helping people understand what their individual legal rights are online

  - Helping people understand the risks to their reputation when they act badly online

  - Teaching people the privacy implications of certain online actions

  - Discussing case studies

- Using role play
- Using simulations

☐ Decide if the training should be customized for certain job functions or standardized across the organization.

☐ Decide how long the training will be
- One half day
- One full day
- Several days

☐ Decide what format the training will be offered in
- In-person
- Live online
- Online only and on-demand
- A combination of in-person and online

☐ Decide how frequently it will be offered
- Monthly
- Bi-monthly
- Quarterly
- Online and on demand

☐ Decide whether the training will be elective or mandatory.

☐ Decide who will design the training:
- An experienced outside consultant with social media and online communications skills
- An experienced outside consultant with conflict management skills
- An experienced outside consultant with legal skills
- Human resources
- Public relations
- Risk management

☐ Decide who will conduct the training:
- An experienced public relations professional
- An experienced social media professional
- A human resources professional
- An attorney knowledgeable in social media law
- An outside consultant with a social media and conflict management background

Day 19: Establish Criteria for Measuring Success of Conflict Management Training Program

Consider both qualitative and quantitative elements when measuring success.

- ☐ Increased knowledge on part of employees
- ☐ Increased level of dispute-management skills
- ☐ Improved relationships with colleagues
- ☐ Improved relationships with customers and users
- ☐ Reduction in conflict cycle time
- ☐ Reduction in the cost of conflict, both direct cost outlays and investment of personnel
- ☐ Reduction in total number of disputes
- ☐ Reduction in the number of volatile disputes
- ☐ Improved online reputation
- ☐ Improved customer support costs

Day 20: Create a Social Media Conflict Response Flow Chart

As a shorthand process for dealing with online conflict, create a visual social media conflict response flowchart, similar to the Air Force Web Posting Response Assessment posted in Chapter 8. Incorporate the following elements, and then expand on or customize to your company's needs.

- ☐ Notice the situation:
  - Notice whether someone has mentioned you or your company online.
  - Identify whether it is a single post, comment, or communication or part of a series.
  - Determine whether the post, comment, or communication is localized on one particular site or has been placed on several sites.
- ☐ Evaluate the situation:
  - Determine if the posting is positive, neutral, or negative.
  - If it is positive or neutral, no action is needed, although you have the option of thanking the commenter or providing additional information.
  - If the comment is negative, consider the content and the source.

- If the negative content is someone's opinion based on factually inaccurate information, consider correcting the information in a friendly, non-confrontational way.

☐ Respond to the situation:

- If the negative content is based on someone's displeasure about a purchase or service, see if the individual is open to your offer of help in making the situation better.

- If the negative content is by a known and repeat attacker, consider not responding and simply monitoring the situation to see if it escalates and gains traction.

Day 21: Start Offering In-Depth Conflict Management Training to Your Social Media Professionals, Public Relations Professionals, and Online Community Managers

Your social media professionals, public relations professionals, and online community managers are your external-facing employees and thus deal with the public and key stakeholders on a constant basis. More than nearly anyone else in your company, with the exception of C-suite executives, your company's reputation lies in their hands. Because they deal with online conflict on a more frequent and intense basis than other employees, they should receive supplemental training beyond the standard level of information covered in your basic Online Conflict Management Training. Specifically, they should receive additional and more in-depth training focused on the following areas:

☐ Role playing

☐ Simulations

☐ Deeper training in managing the anger of others

☐ Deeper training in maintaining emotional equilibrium when dealing with angry people

☐ Learning conflict-mapping skills

☐ Learning how to properly triage online disputes, so they know which ones need immediate attention and which ones can wait

☐ Learning best practices in online dispute management

Day 22: Start Drafting Your Crisis Management Plan

Because reputations can be easily damaged and even destroyed online, you must not only train your staff in basic online conflict management skills, but also have an online crisis management plan in place in case the unexpected happens. The overarching goal of a crisis management plan is damage control. Effective crisis management requires skills that include staying cool under fire, making decisions when not all the relevant information is available, responding quickly, dealing with many moving elements, and being flexible enough to change course at a moment's notice if the situation requires. Build on these elements:

- ☐ Define what your organization considers an online crisis:
  - Imagine your worst case scenario(s).
  - Be as specific as possible in differentiating between an online dispute and a full-blown crisis.
  - Provide examples.

- ☐ Place the victim's or the public's welfare above corporate interests:
  - It's the right thing to do.
  - It will damage your reputation if it's later discovered that you placed your own interests first.

- ☐ Agree to tell the truth about a situation:
  - If you don't have all the information, it is all right to say so.
  - As needed, ensure that all public statements are approved by your attorney to ensure you are not making a legally incriminating statement.

- ☐ Determine the response strategies your company may take during different types of crises, which will depend on a variety of factors:
  - Express regret that the incident or behavior happened.
  - Apologize for the incident or behavior.
  - Explain factual inaccuracies.
  - Justify the incident or behavior. (Be careful if you choose this option.)
  - Show concern and sympathy for victims, even if you are not at fault for their hurt.

- ☐ Identify the different response strategies your company should never take because they will create ill-will and ultimately backfire:
  - Lie or bend the truth.
  - Withhold critical information (except on the advice of an attorney).

- Deny the incident happened if it actually did.
- Counter-attack.
- Be unsympathetic to the victims.

☐ If applicable, be forthcoming with information.

☐ If applicable, express a sincere commitment to improving the situation and ensuring it doesn't happen again.

☐ If applicable, offer to make things right and then do so as quickly as possible.

☐ Determine in which situations you will communicate with your critic or attacker and in which you will consider a non-response, coupled with ongoing monitoring, a better option, even if only a temporary one.

☐ Identify the online communication tools and social media channels you will use to communicate with your critic, attacker, or the victim.

☐ Identify the online communication tools and social media channels you will use to communicate with the public and the media.

☐ Have an online crisis management team in place and ready to go if a crisis occurs.

☐ Have online monitoring tools in place so you can gage the intensity, growth, and spread of the crisis.

☐ Establish response time protocols.

- Determine how quickly you will publicly respond to the situation.
- Determine how quickly you will respond to media inquiries.

☐ Establish post-mortem reporting protocols so you can learn from the crisis.

Day 23: Identify Your Online Crisis Management Team

Selecting the right people for your crisis management team is important. Not only should they represent certain job functions, but also they should be individuals who work well under pressure. In most cases, choose someone from the public relations team, social media team, corporate communications, legal department, and the executive suite.

☐ Assign each member of the team specific roles and responsibilities, and put these in writing:

- Who is responsible for communicating with the critic or attacker, if applicable
- Who is responsible for addressing the public

- Who will draft the public statement
- Who will manage the social media channel
- Who will monitor online communications during the crisis

☐ Establish what the communication processes and protocols will be, and put these in writing.

☐ Get everyone's contact information, which includes email, cell phone, instant messaging handle, Twitter handle, and Facebook account, so they are accessible anywhere at any hour of the day if a crisis occurs.

Day 24: Decide Who Your Public Face Will Be in an Online Crisis

Designate one person who will serve as the public face during an online crisis. Have all communications originate from this person. Ideally, this will be as high-ranking a person as possible because this will make a statement that your company takes the crisis seriously. Your crisis plan can designate different people as the public face for different types of problem situations, but be clear what those are so no confusion occurs within the team in the midst of a crisis.

Day 25: Train Your Public Relations Team and Social Media Team in Crisis Management Skills

Even though you will have an online crisis management plan in place, provide additional crisis management skills training for your public relations and social media team members. There may be situations that don't qualify as full-blown crises but would still benefit from the application of the skills. Also, because these individuals are the ones generally tasked with interacting with the public, customers, or site users, in the rare instance when the officially designated crisis management team is unavailable or certain team members are missing, they can step in and take over some of the roles and responsibilities.

Day 26: Develop Your Company Website's "Dark Site"

In preparation for a possible online crisis, you should have your company website's "dark site" ready to go. As mentioned in Chapter 8. this is a part of your website that can be activated when necessary and to which you can point the public, stakeholders, media, and other interested parties. The dark site can contain all the information you believe would be relevant in the event of a crisis, but should, at a minimum, contain the elements listed next. In case your IT department is unavailable, make sure that members of your crisis management team know how to activate the site. Shortly before activating it, make sure it contains all the necessary information relevant to the crisis; if it doesn't, add it as soon as possible.

- ☐ Key background information about the company
- ☐ Relevant FAQs about the company
- ☐ The contact information of your crisis team member designated to communicate on behalf of the organization
- ☐ A description of the crisis
- ☐ An explanation of what the company is doing in response or to rectify the situation
- ☐ A copy of any public statement the company makes
- ☐ Updates on the status of the crisis, if applicable

Day 27: Start Developing Your Anger Management Training Course

As mentioned repeatedly throughout this book, conflict is an unavoidable part in life and especially so online. The real question, however, is how much is unnecessary and avoidable if people were to have better control over their own anger. There are countless examples of even successful or highly educated people having weak control over their emotions and erupting online. Your employees are spending more and more time on the Internet, certainly in their personal lives and often in their professional ones as well, yet often lack some of the most basic skills in effectively managing their frustrations. Introducing a basic anger management course may reduce the incidences of less-than-ideal behavior you've seen expressed in the examples of some employees described in this book.

Day 28: Start Developing Your Digital Literacy Training Course

As discussed in Chapter 7, "Digital Literacy in a Hyperconnected World," digital literacy skills are more important today than ever before. As previously noted, we get so much of our information from online sources and yet often cannot differentiate between the qualitative and the quantitative, the valuable and the unimportant, the accurate and the inaccurate, and the emotionally manipulative and the rational. Digital literacy skills are critical for online conflict management because they enable people to better identify their own biases and beliefs, as well as those of others, and thus recognize tendencies that may make them vulnerable to certain types of online disputes. Digital literacy also sharpens people's critical thinking skills, an important element in effective conflict management.

Day 29: Simulate an Online Conflict Crisis

Nothing prepares people better for a real crisis than prior experience, and simulating an online crisis is the closest and safest way of doing that. Set aside one-half a day to run through a challenging and difficult scenario from start to finish, perhaps one culled from your list of greatest online conflict concerns, and make the simulation as realistic as possible. In real life, an actual conflict will often last longer than just a few hours, but even that abbreviated time frame can help the crisis management team get a feel for what the real deal will be like. Throw in a few unexpected elements, such as having someone posing as a reporter calling one of the team members who is not authorized to speak on behalf of the company and demanding answers, or having employees comment about the conflict on their personal social networking sites, contradicting the information being officially released by the company.

Day 30: Conduct the Online Crisis Simulation's Post Mortem

After the simulated crisis has ended, conduct a post mortem. Analyze what went well, what didn't, what took the team by surprise, and what it needs to work on to be better prepared for the next time. Incorporate these lessons into the procedures and documents you've prepared for the crisis management team.

If you follow these steps, you will be prepared for any online crisis. The keys are being proactive and giving yourself, and your team if you have one, all the tools to be successful in those inevitable online crises.

Endnotes

1. "Last Call," Utne reader, July/August 2002. Link: http://www.utne.com/2002-07-01/last-call.aspx.

2. Ask.com. Link: http://www.ask.com/pictureslanding.

Index

N

O